TITANIC

Titanic

A Night Remembered

Stephanie Barczewski

**hambledon
continuum**

Hambledon Continuum

The Tower Building,
11 York Road,
London SE1 7NX

80 Maiden Lane,
Suite 704,
New York, NY 10038

First Published 2004 in hardback

This edition published 2006

ISBN 1 85285 500 2

A description of this book is available from the
British Library and from the Library of Congress.

Typeset by Carnegie Publishing, Lancaster.
And printed in Great Britain by MPG Books.

Contents

Illustrations

Illustration Acknowledgements

The author and publishers are grateful to the following for permission to reproduce illustrations: Harland & Wolff, nos 2–5, 9, 12–13; Mayfair Cards of London, nos 1, 10; Southampton City Collections, nos 6–8, 21. Illustrations 11, 14–20 are by the author.

Acknowledgements

In the course of writing this book, I have incurred a long list of debts, both professional and personal. First, I owe tremendous gratitude to the numerous people in the United Kingdom and the Republic of Ireland who assisted my research. In Southampton, I would like to thank Lindsay Ford of the Southampton Maritime Museum; T. P. Henry of the Totton and Eling Historical Society; Kevin White, Conservation Manager for Southampton City Council; and Nigel Wood and Derek Amey of the West End Local History Society. My special appreciation goes to Brian Ticehurst, President of the British *Titanic* Society, who generously provided time, insight and a warm welcome to his home (complete with tea and biscuits); he even allowed me to hold a steward's locker key that was actually on the *Titanic*. In Belfast, I am extremely grateful to Michael McCaughan of the Ulster Folk and Transport Museum; John Parkinson, Jim Carlisle and Stephen Cameron of the Ulster *Titanic* Society; and Patrick Toms of the Shannon Ulster *Titanic* Society. I must single out for special gratitude Una Reilly of the Ulster *Titanic* Society, who welcomed me to the *Titanic: Made in Belfast* celebration in the spring of 2002 with tremendous warmth and grace. During the same event, John Wilson Foster of the University of British Columbia helped me to understand the Ulster dimension of the *Titanic* story.

In Godalming, John Young of the Godalming Museum was very helpful in my research on Jack Phillips; Leslie Clarke of the Town Clerk's office allowed me to see the postcard in Phillips's handwriting that still hangs on the wall there. In Colne, Christine Bradley of the Colne Public Library supplied me with essential material about Wallace Hartley; and, although we never managed to meet, Alan Sutherland was also of great assistance in providing information about the *Titanic*'s bandmaster. In Dalbeattie, Tommy Henderson of the Dalbeattie Museum contributed invaluable material on William Murdoch. I would

also like to thank Gillian Hutchinson and Arthur Janes of the National
Maritime Museum; Jo Wisdom of St Paul's Cathedral; Alan Scarth of
the Merseyside Maritime Museum; Stephen Deuchar, Director of Tate
Britain; and Roger Knight of the Greenwich Maritime Institute.

This book is a product of my seven years at Clemson University, where
I have enjoyed the benefits of wonderful colleagues and a supportive
environment for research. I am particularly grateful to Paul Anderson,
Susanna Ashton, James Burns, Elizabeth Carney, Roger Grant, Alan
Grubb, Steve Marks and Don McKale for their friendship, insight and
willingness to listen whenever I had a particular problem to iron out.
My department chair, Tom Kuehn, successfully fought for a sabbatical
leave against the wielders of the budgetary axe so that I could complete
the preparation of the manuscript.

To my students, as well, I owe a debt. Many of the ideas this book
contains emerged from a seminar I taught under the auspices of the
Calhoun Honours College, in which the participants could always be
relied upon for stimulating discussions. The Calhoun Honours College
also granted me the funding to purchase many of the materials on which
I have relied in both teaching and researching the *Titanic* story. The
research I carried out in the United Kingdom and Republic of Ireland
would not have been possible without Clemson's support, and in particular without the Lightsey Fellowship that I received in 2001. Special
thanks goes to William Lasser and the Clemson National Scholars
Program for giving me the opportunity to take some of Clemson's best
and brightest students to Britain in the summers of 2002 and 2003.

Beyond Clemson in the wider academic community, I will be forever
indebted to the two people most responsible for my scholarly accomplishments, David Cannadine and Linda Colley. I would also like to
thank Miles Taylor for inviting me to present an early version of my
research at the University of Southampton, and David Bell of Johns
Hopkins University for providing various forms of support over the
years. Tony Morris of Hambledon and London has long been a friendly
voice in the publishing wilderness, and Martin Sheppard took a chance
on this project and gave me a book contract before I had written a
single word. Much of the writing took place in the British Library; it is
remarkable how productive and efficient a scholar can be in such an
ideal environment.

Every book is the product of one's personal as well as professional life, and an author incurs personal as well as professional debts in the course of writing. Ed Moisson has made and continues to make my research trips to London much more fun. My mother and father, Patsy and Steven Barczewski, have been, as always, my best supporters. My husband, Michael Silvestri, is the source of my greatest assistance, advice and joy; there is simply no way to express in words what he has contributed to this book and to my life. And without my dogs, Boomer and Whopper, the petty grievances of life would be far slower to dissipate; it is remarkable how soothing it can be to watch them chase each other around the backyard, wrestle over a toy or trot jauntily around the block on their daily walk. For that reason, I dedicate this book to them.

For Boomer and Whopper

Introduction

Like millions of other people around the world, I saw the epic film *Titanic*, directed by James Cameron, shortly after its release in late 1997. Although I agreed with those critics who faulted the film for its clumsy dialogue and hackneyed, melodramatic plotline, I also readily grasped the key to its overwhelming popularity. The tragedy that befell the *Titanic* on the night of 14 and 15 April 1912 is one of the most fascinating single events in human history. It is a story of how much human ingenuity can achieve and how easily that same ingenuity can fail in a brief, random encounter with the forces of nature. It is a story of how different human beings react differently to dire peril, some by calmly accepting death and stepping aside so that others may have a chance to live, others by fighting to their last breath and doing anything necessary to ensure their own survival. It is a story in which the closest bonds that human beings can form were put to the test as people were forced to make impossible choices. Many women, in particular, had to choose between relationships, as they weighed whether it was better to remain on board with their husbands or to get into a lifeboat with their sons and daughters. And all of this took place in the pitch blackness of a North Atlantic night, on the sloping decks of a sinking ship, amidst scenes of increasing chaos and panic as the *Titanic*'s end drew near.

Above all, what continues to compel our interest in the *Titanic* story is that it is at its heart a story that reminds us of our limitations. Whenever human beings, in their moments of hubris, start to feel themselves masters of their universe, the memory of the *Titanic*'s fate serves to jolt them from their complacency. The *Titanic* represented any number of superlatives – it was the biggest and most luxurious ship ever built – but it still sank less than three hours after brushing against an iceberg, a collision so slight that most of its passengers did not feel it. God, nature or fate, with a gesture that was almost disdainful, swept aside something in which humanity had vested immense pride. After the sinking, it became common to claim that one of the workers who had built the *Titanic* had asserted that 'God Himself could not sink this ship', and although this sentiment had almost certainly not been actually expressed by a shipyard worker or anyone else, it had been felt in the hearts of many, hearts that were now stricken with guilt at their willingness to blaspheme so readily.

These components of the *Titanic* story are universal. They are what made Cameron's film a hit all over the world. They also continue to generate a deluge of *Titanic*-related books, songs, television documentaries and other cultural effusions in a variety of languages for a variety of audiences around the globe. In certain places, however, the *Titanic* story possesses a special meaning. The particular meaning of the story in these places has never been explored by a professional historian, an omission that this study will attempt to correct. Many of those local contexts are in Britain, because that is where the ship was built and registered and where most of its officers and crew were from. But the tragedy resonated in the United States as well, for the wealthiest and most socially prominent passengers were American. The two nations, as we shall see, responded to the tragedy in very different ways.

When the 1997 film *Titanic* was released in Britain, many critics responded with hostility to what they perceived as its anti-British tone. Director James Cameron structured the film as a clash between an older, more hierarchical world of strict adherence to class distinctions (represented by Caledon Hockley, Rose Bukater's snobbish and ultimately dastardly fiancé) and a newer, more democratic world of reliance on one own's resources (represented by Jack Dawson, the creative, free-spirited artist with whom Rose falls in love). To be part of the Old World was to sip brandies in the smoking room after dinner and 'congratulate each other on being masters of the universe', while to be part of the new was to spit, sweat, drink beer and dance Irish jigs in steerage.[1] And it just so happened, British critics hastened to point out, that the characters who fell into the former camp were either British or wealthy, East Coast Anglophile Americans with clipped mid-Atlantic accents, whereas those in the latter camp were wholesome, Midwestern Americans or Irish and Italian immigrants on their way to America.

Titanic, complained Christopher Tookey of the *Daily Mail*, was full of 'brainless Brit-bashing'. 'In common with virtually every Hollywood movie of the Nineties, *Titanic* bashes the British – as usual, we're cold, cowardly, conceited and cruel.'[2]

There is some truth to such assertions. Certainly, the film creates an alliance between Jack Dawson, the heroic but sensitive rebel, and a romanticized vision of Irish culture represented by Jack's friend Tommy Ryan, by the band that provides the focal point of the party in steerage that Jack and Rose attend and by James Horner's mournful, Celtic-influenced score. That alliance is set against the oppressive, stifling world of first class with its archaic sense of social relations, a world rife with British aristocrats and American plutocrats seeking to emulate them. A few characters, to be sure, are permitted to transcend the boundaries separating the two groups, but they are the exceptions that prove the rule. The brash millionairess Molly Brown is depicted as a welcome breath of fresh air, and the ship's builder, Thomas Andrews, is portrayed with great sympathy. But Brown is a thoroughly American – as opposed to Anglophile – American, and Andrews, despite his Ulster origins, is portrayed by actor Victor Garber as if he were a southern Irishman from County Cork, fitting him neatly, if inaccurately, into Cameron's 'British bad, Irish good' paradigm.

Cameron is also something less than charitable towards the *Titanic*'s British crew. Captain Smith is a genial but hapless figure who fails to resist the exhortations of J. Bruce Ismay, the managing director of the White Star Line, for greater speed. As the *Titanic* heads into the open sea for the first time, Smith contentedly sips a cup of tea, linking his complacency to his enjoyment of that most quintessentially British beverage. Once the ship is sinking, he stands on the deck in a befuddled state; Second Officer Charles Lightoller has to shake him from his lethargy in order to extract a mumbled order to begin loading the lifeboats. First Officer William Murdoch gets even harsher treatment: he is shown accepting a bribe from Cal for a place in a lifeboat and later shoots Jack's friend Tommy Ryan and then himself. 'Give us a chance to live, you limey bastards!' Ryan screams at Murdoch shortly before he is shot, a further indication of Cameron's desire to make clear the contrasting nationalities of *Titanic*'s heroes and villains.[3] (And an inaccurate one, given that Murdoch was Scottish, not English.)

The objections of British critics, however, went beyond the anglophobic content of Cameron's film, which after all contains no overtly
anti-British statements. They reacted equally as strongly, if not more so,
to the way in which, as they saw it, *Titanic* as a pop cultural phenomenon
represented the Americanization of British – and global – culture. The
film, they claimed, was a romanticized and simplistic depiction of history
that prioritized action and glitzy special effects over intelligent dialogue,
character development and factual accuracy. In the film magazine *Sight
and Sound*, Laura Miller commented, that 'everything about *Titanic* –
from its stereotyped characters to its bright, even lighting – feels ersatz
and obvious may only trouble the kind of people who dislike the
immaculate, synthetic recreations of real places in Disney theme parks'.
Paul Goodman complained in the *Daily Telegraph*, 'If emotional restraint
can drive a life on to the rocks, cannot emotional indulgence, too? "They
don't make them like that any more", we sigh, as we watch those pre-war
films in which real people grapple with the complexities of life. Indeed
they don't. They make them like this'. Other British critics pointed to
the film's exorbitant cost as yet another example of American vulgarity.
'With this kind of budget', Geoff Andrews wrote in *Time Out*, 'you'd
think we could expect something less hackneyed and manipulative, more
complex and genuinely moving; sadly, such hopes seem to be quite
forlorn.'[4]

The virulence of these attacks on the film went beyond any attempt
to assess its cinematic virtues and deficiencies. Instead, they represented
a spirited defence mounted by a nation that felt its claim of proprietorship over the *Titanic* story was being challenged by a Hollywood
juggernaut. Cameron had taken a quintessentially British story featuring
'British virtues', such as chivalry, self-sacrifice and an ability to maintain
a stiff upper lip in the direst of circumstances, and transformed it into
a quintessentially American story of individual self-discovery. The point
of the film is not to celebrate the heroic stoicism of the passengers and
crew, as British versions of the story tend to do, but to celebrate Rose's
liberation from the shackles of snobbery and social elitism, characteristics which, as we have already seen, Cameron associates with Britain.

The negative reactions of the British press to the film demonstrate
that the *Titanic* story is regarded in Britain with a sense of ownership.
The real *Titanic*, the film's critics implicitly argued, was a British

ship, and the fictional *Titanic* should therefore be a British cultural possession. How dare Cameron attempt to wrest it away from them? This proprietary interest of British critics in the *Titanic* story stems in part from the fact that there are many places in the United Kingdom with a direct connection to the tragedy. The ship was built in Belfast, at what at the time was the world's largest shipyard, Harland & Wolff. It left British shores for the first and last time from Southampton on the southern coast of England, carrying over nine hundred local residents who served as crewmen and women. Other places were connected to the ship, and to the tragedy that befell it, on a more personal level. All of the *Titanic*'s senior officers were British, including the two whose conduct was most questionable: Captain Edward J. Smith, who was from Hanley (now part of Stoke-on-Trent) in the Midlands, and First Officer William Murdoch, from Dalbeattie in south-western Scotland. Also of British birth were several of the heroes who emerged from the tragedy, in particular Jack Phillips, the senior wireless operator, from Godalming, Surrey, and Wallace Hartley, the bandmaster, from Colne, Lancashire. Thomas Andrews, the ship's builder, hailed from the northern Irish province of Ulster, but would almost certainly have identified himself as British.

All of these local connections give the *Titanic* story roots in British soil, roots that give British claims to ownership of the story legitimacy. The ship was built in the British Isles and sailed by an almost exclusively British crew. At the same time, however, it must be remembered that the *Titanic* was not in point of fact a British ship, as its operators the White Star Line had been purchased by the American billionaire J. P. Morgan's International Mercantile Marine consortium. Nor were the majority of its passengers British: while third-class was filled with polyglot emigrants from around the world, first-class was dominated by wealthy Americans. Thus the sinking had tremendous impact in the United States as well. There, however, it was not perceived as a *national* tragedy the way it was in Britain, for reasons which this book will explore.

On both sides of the Atlantic, the tragedy continues to resonate as it approaches its centenary. In conducting the research for this book, I constantly encountered a strong emotional connection to the disaster that lingers almost a full century afterwards. Numerous random conversations with people who enquired after the subject of my research yielded frequent claims of ancestors who had died on the *Titanic* or of other *Titanic* links. In many cases, these were patently untrue. I remember one conversation on a train in which a man attempted to convince me that his relatives had owned a boarding house in Liverpool where many of the *Titanic*'s passengers stayed the night before the ship sailed. My gentle protestations that the *Titanic* did not sail from Liverpool and in fact never visited that city at all were to no avail. Everyone, it sometimes seemed, wants to claim a connection to the *Titanic*.

1

What Have We Struck?

Precisely at noon on 10 April 1912 a sonorous blast on the ship's whistles signalled the departure of the first – and, as the world well knows, last – voyage of the White Star Line's RMS *Titanic*. The *Titanic* was, as is also well known, the largest ship in the world, stretching a sixth of a mile from bow to stern, standing ten stories high from its keel to the top of its four funnels and displacing over 45,000 tons. Everything about the *Titanic* was on a grand scale: a locomotive could pass through each funnel, and a double-decker tramcar through each of its twenty-nine boilers. Its rudder was longer than a cricket pitch, and its anchors weighed fifteen tons each.

The *Titanic* was, however, more than a behemoth. Unlike the deliberately ponderous ships being built by White Star's German competitors Hamburg-Amerika and Norddeutscher Lloyd, the *Titanic* was a graceful vessel, with clean lines and balanced proportions. To be sure, once its massive engines – each four stories high – began to crank and its three immense propellers started to churn, there could be no disguising the ship's 55,000 horsepower. But as the *Titanic* lay in its berth at Southampton Docks, gangways buzzing as the final passengers and crew members hurried on board, the impression the ship gave was one of quiet strength, not tremendous bulk. 'So perfect are her proportions', declared the maritime engineering journal the *Shipbuilder*, 'that it is well-nigh impossible for the inexperienced to grasp her magnitude except when seen alongside another vessel.' [1]

Beneath the *Titanic*'s hull that appearance of strength was given reality by a system of safety features designed to eliminate the risks posed by ocean travel. In contemplating those risks, the *Titanic*'s builders, Harland & Wolff of Belfast, had determined that there were three reasons why a ship might sink. First, it could run aground. Secondly, it could run into an object, either another ship or a natural hazard. Thirdly, another ship could run into it. Provide safety measures that could cope with those circumstances, the builders reasoned, and much of the risk would be eliminated. To deal with the first threat, Harland & Wolff gave the *Titanic* a double bottom, which meant that its keel carried a second set of steel plates seven feet above the first. If the keel scraped the seabed, the ship would thus not be opened to the sea. To deal with the second and third threats, the builders fitted the *Titanic* with a system of fifteen bulkheads that divided the hull into sixteen watertight compartments. If the *Titanic* ran into something that crushed its bow, it could float with the first four of these compartments flooded. And if something ran into it, then the *Titanic* could float with any two of the central compartments flooded, so that even if another ship hit precisely at the junction of two compartments, and breached them both, the hull would remain seaworthy. It was necessary to have some openings in the bulkheads to allow the passengers and crew to get from one part of the ship to another, but these openings were equipped with watertight doors that could be closed with the flip of a switch from the bridge. Each door was also fitted with a float mechanism that automatically closed it if a compartment became flooded with more than six inches of water.

No wonder the builders felt proud of their new creation. Most ships, after all, had only one or two 'collision bulkheads' in the bow, not sixteen watertight compartments. Certainly the naval engineering world was impressed: 'practically unsinkable', declared the *Shipbuilder*.[2] The system seemed foolproof. So confident were Harland & Wolff that the *Titanic*'s plans did not call for a double hull, as White Star's rival Cunard had given its flagships, the *Lusitania* and *Mauretania*. This certainly pleased White Star, because it saved considerably on construction expense. And when White Star also suggested cutting the number of lifeboats from the forty-eight called for by the original plans to twenty, Harland & Wolff put up little resistance. It would cut down further on costs, after all, as well as reduce the amount of clutter on the *Titanic*'s decks. This meant that the *Titanic* would carry sufficient lifeboat space for only about a third of its 3300-person capacity, but what harm would that do? Its extensive safety features made the ship its own lifeboat, and twenty boats were still four more than the law required.[3] White Star's money, both owners and builders agreed, was better spent on ensuring the ship's reputation as the most luxurious vessel afloat. About the meeting in which the plans for the *Titanic* and its sister ship the *Olympic* were finalized, Harland & Wolff's managing director Alexander Carlisle recalled, 'We spent two hours discussing the carpets for the first-class cabins and fifteen minutes discussing lifeboats'.[4]

The *Titanic*'s design, however, contained a flaw, or at least it was based on assumptions that proved erroneous. The watertight bulkheads that enhanced safety also created problems, for passage through them had to be limited, therefore inhibiting the movement of passengers and crew around the ship. They also added expense. For those reasons, White Star wanted the bulkheads to go no higher than was absolutely necessary. Accordingly Harland & Wolff's designers calculated that the bulkheads needed to go only up to D Deck fore and aft and only up to E Deck amidships. This meant that in places their tops would be a mere fifteen feet above the waterline; but Harland & Wolff determined that that was sufficient. Even if two of the compartments were breached in a collision with another ship, the weight of the incoming water would not be enough to sink the ship. And even if the first four compartments were breached in a head-on collision, the bow would not dip so low as to pull it under and take the rest of the ship down. Now if, hypothetically, an accident were to occur in which the first *six* compartments were breached, then the bow would plunge so low that water would spill over the top of the bulkhead separating the sixth compartment from the seventh, and then the seventh from the eighth, and back and back until the ship sank. But what sort of accident could cause that kind of damage? There was no precedent in maritime history.

The *Titanic*'s builders and owners could have been excused a sense of pride as they gazed at their new creation as it lay in its berth at Southampton. The ship was an unparalleled technological marvel even in an age of technological marvels, representing everything that human ingenuity could accomplish.

As the *Titanic*'s giant engines throbbed into life and the massive triple screws at the stern began to turn, however, an incident occurred that provided a warning that even the most carefully thought out plans cannot take into account every eventuality. On that April day, Southampton's docks were overflowing with ships that had been left idle by a coal strike.[5] The ships had to be tied up side by side, for there were not sufficient berths to hold them all. Directly across from the *Titanic*'s berth lay the *Oceanic* and, on the outboard side, the *New York*, two smaller passenger steamers. As the tugboats helped the *Titanic* make its way slowly out into the harbour, the huge ship displaced a tremendous volume of water and pushed it under the *New York*, lifting it upwards and causing the mooring lines which secured it to the pier to slacken. Then, as the *Titanic* moved past the *New York*, the volume of water in the vicinity dramatically decreased, causing those same lines to suddenly go taut. The ropes could not take the strain and snapped one by one, sounding like gunshots. The *New York*'s stern started to swing out towards the *Titanic* and a collision appeared inevitable. At the last moment, however, the tug *Vulcan* was able to get a line onto the *New York* and, straining with all its might, managed to hold the ship just long enough for the *Titanic* to slip by, with only three or four feet to spare. The *Titanic*'s captain, Edward J. Smith, then demonstrated his seafaring experience and expertise by ordering a quick 'full astern' on the ship's engines, which washed the *New York* back towards its berth.[6]

It was a narrow escape, and some of the *Titanic*'s passengers were a little unnerved. Renee Harris, whose husband Henry was a noted theatrical producer in New York, was watching from the rail when a stranger asked her, 'Do you love life?'

'Yes, I love it', she replied, surprised by the question.

'That was a bad omen. Get off this ship at Cherbourg, if we get that far. That's what I'm going to do.'[7]

Others were more amused than alarmed by the incident. Steward Seaton Blake mailed a humorous postcard to the Mayor of New York City:

> Guess you had better chain up the Statue of Liberty to a skyscraper in Fifth Avenue or to the ramparts of Fort Pitt, as I 'reckon and calculate' that the foundations are liable to be swallowed up by the wash of this 'octopus' from the other side, which sucked up from its moorings like a barnacle the Yankee Doodle liner *New York* yesterday in Southampton docks. Better instruct the United States fleet to tow her in, or I guess New York will be wiped off the map.[8]

The excitement of the near-accident soon faded, and the *Titanic*'s passengers and crew began settling into a shipboard routine. Stewards set out deck chairs and prepared the dining rooms for lunch, while far below in the boiler rooms stokers were busy shovelling the 650 tons of coal the *Titanic*'s engines devoured each day. The passengers, meanwhile, tried to find their way around the huge ship. As they boarded, stewards had greeted them and shown them to their cabins, but without their help the ship was a maze of corridors and stairwells. The crew was in many cases equally befuddled. The *Titanic*'s Second Officer, Charles Lightoller, was an extremely experienced seaman, but he later wrote that 'it took me fourteen days before I could find my way with confidence from one part of the ship to the other'. The other members of the crew, many of whom did not come on board until the morning of the sailing, did not have that much time to become thoroughly acquainted with the gigantic ship. Most of them had transferred from White Star's smaller vessels, and they found the *Titanic*'s vastness utterly bewildering. 'I never knew my way', complained Steward William Lucas.[9]

On the evening of 10 April the *Titanic* reached Cherbourg, where it took on 142 first-class, thirty second-class and 102 third-class passengers. Among the first group were some of the *Titanic*'s most socially prominent passengers, including the richest man on the ship, forty-seven-year-old John Jacob Astor, owner of vast holdings of New York real estate. As he boarded the *Titanic*, Astor's wealth was undeniable, but his reputation was less secure. Three years earlier, he had divorced his wife of eighteen years to marry Madeleine Force, who at eighteen was younger than Astor's son Vincent. In the early twentieth century, divorce still carried a considerable stigma, particularly under such tawdry circumstances. Astor had assumed that his wealth and name would protect him, but he was wrong. The couple was viciously 'cut' by New York society, who boycotted the reception that Astor gave at his Fifth Avenue mansion to celebrate his nuptials. On the opening night of the season at the Metropolitan Opera his box was ignored by former friends. In an effort to weather the storm, the Astors had fled abroad in late 1911, spending the winter in France and then travelling to Egypt. Now, however, Madeleine was four months pregnant, and they were returning home, hoping that the scandal had dissipated and that the gossipmongers had moved on to other pursuits.

While in Egypt, the Astors had been travelling with Margaret Tobin Brown, whose husband J.J. had struck it rich mining in Colorado. When Brown received news that her grandson Lawrence was ill, she decided to return home on the first available ship, which turned out to be the *Titanic*, on which the Astors had already booked their passage. Also boarding at Cherbourg was Benjamin Guggenheim, whose family's business interests had expanded from their roots in mining and smelting to a variety of financial and manufacturing pursuits. In contrast to Astor, Guggenheim had adhered to social convention in his personal affairs: for the last several months, he had been in Paris with his mistress, Madame Aubart, while his wife remained at home in New York. Guggenheim's demeanour was quiet, but his fellow first-class passengers would have been well aware of his immense wealth and power.

Astor, Brown and Guggenheim joined a glittering array of first-class passengers who collectively earned the *Titanic* the nickname the 'Millionaire's Special'; the net worth of the entire first-class complement of 337 (46 per cent of the ship's capacity) was estimated at well over $500 million. Also included among it were Isidor Straus, part-owner of Macy's department store; George Widener, the Philadelphia tramway magnate; John B. Thayer, president of the Pennsylvania Railroad; Arthur Ryerson, the Philadelphia steel baron; Washington Augustus Roebling, director of the engineering firm that had designed and built the Brooklyn Bridge; and Charles Hays, president of the Grand Trunk Railroad. The *Titanic*'s first-class passenger list included, however, more than just wealthy men of business and industry. There were also political figures such as Major Archibald Butt, military aide to the American President William Howard Taft, who was returning from a diplomatic mission to the Vatican. Amongst the American plutocrats were sprinkled a few members of the British elite, such as Sir Cosmo and Lady Duff Gordon and the Countess of Rothes, on her way to join her husband on his fruit farm in British Columbia. Finally, the *Titanic* carried several prominent representatives of cultural accomplishment, including the theatrical producer Henry B. Harris, the painter Frank Millet, the author Jacques Futrelle, the actress Dorothy Gibson and the journalist W. T. Stead. In the 1880s, Stead had been the editor of the Liberal *Pall Mall Gazette*. Its spirited crusades had attracted a wide-ranging readership as Stead railed against Bulgarian atrocities in the Balkan Wars, conditions in Siberian labour camps and slavery in the Belgian Congo. He also tackled causes closer to home, such as adoption and housing for the poor. His infamous article 'The Maiden Tribute of Modern Babylon', in which he had detailed how for £5 he had been able to secure the services of a thirteen-year-old prostitute, had landed him in jail on charges of abduction. The ensuing public outcry had, however, secured his quick release, as well as the passage of parliamentary legislation that raised the age of consent from thirteen to sixteen. In 1890 Stead founded the *Review of Reviews*, which quickly became one of the most influential publications of the day. Its mission, as Stead saw it, was to champion all 'oppressed races, ill-treated animals, underpaid typists, misunderstood women, persecuted parsons, vilified public men, would-be suicides, hot-gospellers of every sort and childless parents'.[10] By 1912, Stead's credibility had been somewhat eroded due to his fascination with spiritualism, but he still was a sufficiently powerful voice to merit a personal invitation from President Taft to speak at an international peace conference scheduled to begin in Washington on 21 April.[11]

Stead and his fellow first-class passengers must have been impressed with the quality of their accommodation on the *Titanic*. From their globetrotting lifestyles, they would have been well accustomed to the level of luxury offered by the world's finest hotels. Even so, the particular splendours of the *Titanic* must have been novel. There were, for example, uncommon amenities such as a swimming pool (the first ever installed on board a ship), a gymnasium, a Turkish bath and a squash court. The traditional shipboard sickbay had been transformed into a mini-hospital, complete with a modern operating theatre, and passengers who fancied themselves as amateur photographers could develop their photos in a fully-equipped darkroom. In addition to the regular first-class dining saloon, which at 114 feet was the longest room afloat, there was an *à la carte* restaurant where passengers could dine at whatever time they preferred and order from a menu as if they were in a fine restaurant in Paris or London. Some of the first-class passengers had already crossed the Atlantic on the *Olympic*, but the *Titanic* offered them even greater luxury with unique features such as Café Parisien, a replica of a Paris sidewalk café staffed by real French waiters. The *Titanic* had also benefited from the *Olympic*'s experience: the *Olympic*'s Promenade Deck had been left open to allow first-class passengers to take the sea air, but they had complained of getting splashed by spray. On the *Titanic*, therefore, the Promenade Deck had been enclosed by a glass screen.

Every room in first class was decorated to the highest standard. The

centrepiece was the Grand Staircase, which began under a domed skylight on A Deck and descended four stories to D Deck, where it led
to the first-class dining saloon. Back up on A Deck, the smoking
room was a masculine preserve with its carved mahogany panelling and
overstuffed leather chairs; the atmosphere was that of an exclusive
gentlemen's club. The first-class staterooms were equally resplendent.
Instead of the usual bunk or berth, there was an individual bedstead,
as well as a washstand with hot-and-cold running water and a telephone
for shipboard communication. The wealthiest passengers occupied
suites, the two most expensive of which featured private fifty-foot-long
promenade decks. These suites cost nearly £1000, the equivalent of more
than £20,000 today; at close to £10 per square foot, they were the most
expensive floating real estate in the world.[12]

The luxuries of first class were unparalleled, but White Star did not
neglect the *Titanic*'s other areas. Second class was the equivalent of first
on most ships, with its own electric elevator (first class had three), its
own impressive staircase and its own smoking room and library. As
an added attraction, second and first class shared the main galley, and
thus the quality of the food in second class was extremely high. The
271 second-class passengers (40 per cent of full capacity) were delighted
with their accommodation, as well as with their cultured and well-
educated shipboard companions, many of whom would have travelled
first class on a less expensive ship.[13]

In third class, or steerage, White Star had gone to considerable lengths
to ensure that the 712 passengers (70 per cent of full capacity) were
comfortable, even if they enjoyed far fewer luxuries than their counterparts in first and second class. Frank Goldsmith, a thirty-three-year-old
machinist from Strood in Kent who was immigrating to Detroit along
with his wife and young son, was delighted to discover that his accommodation was as fine as first class had been twenty years earlier. The
dining room featured individual chairs instead of the customary benches,
and the food served was hearty and plentiful, although considerably
simpler than what the rest of the ship ate. There were two bars as well as
a general room with pine-panelled walls and teak benches. Cabins were
small and spartan but pleasant; single men and married couples were
berthed forward, while single women and families were aft. Many of the
third-class passengers would have never experienced the prospect of five

days with nothing to do but enjoy themselves, and they were determined to do so. Every night of the voyage, there was a spontaneous party in the general room, when those travelling with musical instruments would form an impromptu band. They had come from all over the world – Asia and Africa as well as a bevy of European countries – but language barriers were overcome by the spirit of anticipation that prevailed. Almost all of them had purchased one-way tickets as they headed towards a new – and, they hoped, better – life in the United States.

Departing from Cherbourg on the night of 10 April, the *Titanic* steamed towards her final port of call at Queenstown, Ireland, which it reached the following morning. At Queenstown, 123 more passengers boarded, all but ten of them third class. Now carrying 1320 passengers and 915 crew members, the ship headed out into the North Atlantic. For three days, the *Titanic* made steady progress, covering 386 miles on the 11th, 519 on the 12th and 546 on the 13th, when the ship averaged over twenty-two knots per hour. The *Titanic*'s performance so far was as close to flawless as possible; even a perfectionist like Thomas Andrews, the managing director of Harland & Wolff, found only the most minor of problems. Andrews was on board as part of an eight-member 'guarantee party' from the builders that would assess the ship's construction and correct any unforeseen defects, but to date there had been little to do. The hot press in the first-class galley was not working properly, and Andrews thought that the pebble-dashing on the private promenade decks was too dark and that there were too many screws in the coathooks in the staterooms. But the *Titanic* was clearly a splendid ship. 'I believe her to be as nearly perfect as human brains can make her', he said to passenger Albert A. Dick in the first-class smoking room.[14]

The weather was also cooperating: it was clear and exceedingly calm, if a little cold for the time of year. Only the worst sailors among the passengers were suffering from seasickness. And everyone marvelled at the lack of vibration from the *Titanic*'s engines and the steadiness of the ship. 'The weather was fine and the sea calm', recalled Dr Washington Dodge. 'At all times one might walk the decks with the same security as if walking down Market Street, so little motion was there to the vessel. It was hard to realize, when dining in the large spacious dining saloon, that one was not in some large and sumptuous hotel.'[15]

Sundays at sea usually began with a time-honoured ritual, the boat drill, in which a picked crew would uncover and swing out one of the ship's lifeboats. (The passengers were not required to participate, nor were boat assignments customarily posted in their cabins.) On 14 April, however, Captain Smith decided to forgo the drill. Instead, he led a religious service in the first-class dining saloon at 10.30 a.m. This was the only occasion on which second- and third-class passengers were permitted in first class, and they must have been amazed by their lavish surroundings.

Also that morning, the *Titanic*'s wireless operator Jack Phillips received an ice warning from the *Caronia* at 9 a.m.: 'West-bound steamers report bergs, growlers and field ice in 42 N, from 49 to 51 W'.[16] This was the first of eight warnings regarding ice that the *Titanic* would receive that day; all along the North Atlantic shipping lanes, vessels were encountering a large belt of ice.[17] This was not surprising news, for it had been a bad season for ice in the North Atlantic. A warm winter had caused numerous bergs to break off from the coast of Greenland and drift into the Labrador current, which carried them south into the shipping lanes off the Grand Banks. Only a few days earlier, a collision with ice had knocked two holes in the hull of the steamer *Niagara*, but the ship had managed to limp into New York. As the *Titanic* travelled west along the same course, the airwaves crackled with information regarding the location and extent of the ice field. The response to this news varied. In 1912, when ships had only been equipped with wireless sets for a little over a decade, many captains distrusted the new technology, preferring to rely on their experience and navigational skills. Smith was not among the sceptics, however, and he immediately posted the *Caronia*'s warning on the bridge when Phillips delivered it.

At lunch, Smith dined with J. Bruce Ismay, the managing director of the White Star Line, on board in honour of the *Titanic*'s maiden voyage. During this lunch, one passenger later reported overhearing a conversation that remains one of the most controversial episodes of the *Titanic* story. According to this passenger, Ismay said to Smith, 'Today we did better than yesterday, and tomorrow we shall do better still. We shall beat the *Olympic*'s time to New York and arrive Tuesday night!'[18] The assumption is that Ismay, eager for the good publicity that an early arrival would generate, pushed Smith to drive the ship faster. There are, however, problems with this theory. Docking a huge vessel like the *Titanic* at night would have been virtually impossible, and it is unlikely that Smith or Ismay would have attempted such a risky manoeuvre. Moreover, a lavish welcome ceremony had been prepared for Wednesday morning, at which many reporters would be in attendance.[19] Ismay was well aware that the *Titanic*'s arrival would be big news, no matter what time it occurred. In any event, he had never been an advocate of speed, always believing that passengers were more interested in a comfortable journey on a ship that could be relied upon to meet its scheduled time of arrival.

At 1.42 p.m. the *Titanic* received another ice warning, this one from the *Baltic*, followed three minutes later by one from the *Amerika*. The *Baltic*'s message was delivered to Smith as he stood on the deck talking to Ismay. Smith, for reasons that are unclear, handed the message to Ismay, who stuck it in his pocket. Later, Ismay showed it to two female passengers, Emily Ryerson and Marion Thayer. It was not until that night at dinner that Smith asked for the message back and had it posted on the bridge. The *Amerika*'s message, meanwhile, seems never to have reached the captain at all, or if it did it was never acknowledged. This may have been because the *Titanic*'s wireless operators were struggling with a mountain of messages from passengers fascinated by the new technology. These messages were mostly of the banal 'wish you were here' variety, but Phillips and his assistant Harold Bride were well aware that sending them was their first priority. They were not employed by the White Star Line but by the British Marconi Company, whose profits were earned not from navigational messages, sent from one ship to another, but from the fees that passengers paid to send messages to their friends, family and business associates ashore. And since the speed of the transmission was the main source of wireless's appeal, these messages had to be sent promptly. On the *Titanic*, the situation was aggravated because the wireless set had broken down on Friday night, necessitating repairs that took until Saturday morning. The seven hours of downtime had created a backlog of messages, and Phillips and Bride were still struggling to catch up. The novelty of being on the world's largest ship was enticing more than the usual number of passengers to use their services; a typical message was 'Arrive Wednesday. *Titanic* maiden voyage. Meet me vessel. Worth seeing.'[20] By Sunday, the two operators were exhausted. Ice warnings would be delivered to the bridge when they had a spare moment, not before.[21] In any event, they had already passed along the previous warnings; the captain and officers should have been well aware that there was ice in the ship's path.

On Sunday evening the temperature dropped precipitously, driving all but the hardiest passengers indoors. Between 5.30 and 7.30 it fell ten degrees, until it hovered at just above freezing. This was a further indication of ice in the area, but the *Titanic* continued to steam full-speed ahead. The failure to reduce speed has led over the years to an assumption that the *Titanic*'s officers behaved with a cavalier complacency that ultimately doomed the ship. There is some truth to this, but at the same time it cannot be said that they took no precautions to deal with the threat of encountering ice. At 5.50 p.m. Captain Smith ordered the *Titanic*'s course to be altered to the south west, from S 62 W to S 85 W; the bridge officers assumed that this was done to avoid the ice. At 7.15 First Officer William Murdoch ordered the forward fo'c'sle hatch and skylight over the crew's galley to be closed so that the glow from the lights would not impede the ability of the lookouts in the crow's nest to see hazards in the distance. Later that evening, Captain Smith departed early from a party in the first-class restaurant so that he could return to the bridge, knowing that the ship was nearing the vicinity of the ice. On the bridge, he discussed the conditions with the officer on watch, Second Officer Lightoller:

> We commenced speaking about the weather. He said, 'There is not much wind'. I said, 'No, it is a flat calm'. I said that it was a pity the wind had not kept up with us whilst we were going through the ice region. Of course he knew I meant the water ripples breaking on the base of the bergs [would make them easier to see] ... I remember saying, 'Of course there will be a certain amount of reflected light from the bergs', with which the Captain agreed.

Lightoller and Smith also concurred that even in the case of a 'blue berg', one that had recently turned over in the water, there would still be a white outline. Smith then retired to his cabin, telling Lightoller, 'If it becomes at all doubtful let me know at once'. Although he like Smith was confident that any icebergs in the ship's path would be spotted in time, Lightoller warned the lookouts to be especially vigilant, telling them to 'keep a sharp lookout for ice, particularly small ice and growlers'.[22]

It would never, however, have occurred to Smith, Lightoller or any other of the *Titanic*'s officers to slow down. In the North Atlantic passenger shipping trade, adhering to a schedule took precedence over everything else. Passengers expected to be whisked from breakfast in London on Monday to dinner in New York on Saturday, and the ship's officers were responsible for making sure that these expectations were met. Regardless of weather conditions, they drove the liners at full speed, knowing the importance of arriving on time. Warnings about hazards received by wireless or from other sources were treated as calls to greater vigilance, but not to action.[23] No officer would alter the ship's speed without the explicit permission of the captain. 'I have never known speed to be reduced in any ship I have ever been in, in fair weather', Lightoller later testified at the British inquiry into the disaster.[24] As a result, the officers on merchant ships became accustomed to near-misses, and came to believe that nerves of steel and a cool head in a crisis would always get them through. They also figured that the risk was relatively minimal, for ships had experienced severe collisions with icebergs in the past and survived. In 1907 the German liner *Kron-Prinz Wilhelm* had rammed headlong into an iceberg in the North Atlantic; its bow had crumpled but the forward bulkheads held and the ship was able to make it safely into port. There was no clear case, in fact, in which a sizeable vessel was known to have sunk as a result of an encounter with an iceberg.[25] And if other ships had managed to escape relatively unscathed, then how could ice pose any real danger to a modern technological marvel like the *Titanic*? Most officers put great faith in the innovations in marine architecture that had been achieved over the preceding decades, believing their ships to be all but invincible. 'I cannot imagine any condition which would cause a ship to founder', Captain Smith declared in an interview in 1907. 'Modern shipbuilding has gone beyond that.'[26]

As Sunday evening turned into night, the *Titanic* received two more ice warnings. At 7.30, Phillips overheard a transmission from the *Californian* to the *Antillian* reporting 'three large bergs five miles to southward of us'. Bride later remembered delivering this message to the bridge, though he did not recall to whom he gave it. At 9.40 a message came in from the *Mesaba*: 'In latitude 42 N to 41 25, longitude 49 W to longitude 50 30 W, saw much heavy pack ice and great number large

icebergs, also field ice, weather good, clear'.[27] Had the coordinates
provided by the *Mesaba* been plotted on a chart, they would have shown
that the *Titanic* was already well within the rectangle of ice they denoted.
But the message never made it to the bridge: Bride was trying to get
some sleep, and Phillips was still extremely busy sending passenger
messages to the relay station at Cape Race, Newfoundland. Waiting for
a spare moment, Phillips stuck the message under a paperweight on his
desk; he had no way of knowing how close the coordinates of the ice
seen by the *Mesaba* were to the *Titanic*'s current position.

At 10 p.m., Lightoller was relieved as officer of the watch by Murdoch.
Murdoch remarked on the cold, and Lightoller informed him that the
ship would be up on the area of ice at any time. A half hour later, the
eastbound freighter *Rappahannock* passed by close enough to contact
the *Titanic* by Morse lamp, passing along the message, 'Have just passed
through heavy field ice and several icebergs'. The ice had been so severe,
in fact, that it had significantly damaged the *Rappahannock*'s rudder.
The *Titanic* flashed back, 'Message received. Thank you. Good
night'.[28] Shortly before eleven, the *Titanic* received one last ice warning.
Phillips was still busy with Cape Race traffic when suddenly a transmission from the *Californian* crashed through: 'We are stopped and
surrounded by ice'. The message was so loud that it nearly deafened
Phillips, suggesting that the *Californian* was extremely close to the
Titanic's position. By breaking in so abruptly, the *Californian*'s wireless
operator, Cyril Evans, had not followed proper professional etiquette;
he should have sent a preliminary call informing Phillips that he had
a message for him and then waited for a response from the *Titanic*
telling him to go ahead. Phillips, exhausted from sixteen straight hours
on duty, had every reason to be annoyed, and he snapped, 'Shut up,
shut up, I am busy; I am working Cape Race, you are jamming me'.
His tone sounds rude, but such messages were common among wireless operators at the time. There was no regulation of the airwaves, and
rival companies frequently tried to jam each other's transmissions. It
was common for one operator to tell another 'QRT' ('Keep quiet, I'm
busy') or, more bluntly, GTH OM QRT ('Go to hell, old man, keep
quiet, I'm busy').[29] The rebuffed Evans made no further attempt at
communication, and at around 11.30 he switched off his set and went
to bed.[30]

Ten minutes later, lookouts Frederick Fleet and Reginald Lee were in the *Titanic*'s crow's nest, well aware that the ship was in an area of ice. A slight haze had appeared on the horizon, and they strained their eyes to see what might lie beyond it. (They were supposed to have binoculars, but these had been misplaced in Southampton.) Suddenly, Fleet saw an object in the distance, small at first and then looming larger and larger. Identifying it as a huge iceberg directly in the ship's path, he rang the bell above his head three times, the signal for 'object dead ahead'. He then picked up the telephone that provided a direct line to the bridge.

'Are you there?'

'Yes', answered Sixth Officer James Moody. 'What do you see?'

'Iceberg right ahead.'

'Thank you.' [31]

Moody relayed the message to Murdoch, who ordered Quartermaster Robert Hitchens to 'hard-a-starboard', or put the ship's wheel hard over in a left turn.[32] He also telegraphed the engine room to stop and then reverse the engines.

Hitchens spun the wheel as quickly as he could until it was hard over. At first, the *Titanic* continued to head straight towards the iceberg, and Fleet and Lee braced for a collision. At the last moment, however, the bow swung left, and it appeared as if the ship would clear. The *Titanic* scraped by, dislodging a substantial amount of ice from the iceberg, which fell on the forward decks. A major collision seemed to have been avoided, and Fleet and Lee breathed a sigh of relief, believing it to have been nothing more than a close shave. But from far below there was a faint grinding sound, and a slight tremor passed through the ship. Unsure if the *Titanic* had sustained any damage, Murdoch flipped the switch that closed the watertight doors separating its sixteen compartments.

Seconds after the impact, Captain Smith appeared on the bridge. 'What have we struck?' he demanded of Murdoch.

'An iceberg, sir. I hard-a-starboarded and reversed the engines and I was going to hard-a-port around it, but she was too close. I could not do any more. I have closed the watertight doors'.

'The watertight doors are closed? And you have rung the warning bell?'

'Yes, sir.' [33]

Smith went out to the starboard bridge wing, looking aft to see if he could spot the berg. He ordered the engines to be stopped and sent Fourth Officer Joseph Boxhall to conduct an inspection of the forward part of the ship and to report on any damage. Boxhall returned fifteen minutes later, having seen no damage above F Deck. He told the captain, however, that postal clerk John Smith had informed him that the lower mail room was awash.[34] Boxhall was still giving his report when ship's carpenter Jim Hutchinson burst onto the bridge and blurted, 'She's making water fast!'[35]

At this point Chief Officer Henry Wilde appeared and asked Smith if the damage was serious. Smith replied, 'Certainly. It is more than serious'. He asked for Thomas Andrews to be summoned to the bridge, and then turned and examined the commutator, which measured if the ship was listing. Already, it showed a list of five degrees to starboard and two degrees down by the head. Smith stared at it for a few seconds and then murmured, 'Oh, my God!', so quietly that only Boxhall heard him.

Next to arrive on the bridge was J. Bruce Ismay, wearing carpet slippers and a suit over his pyjamas. Smith informed him that the ship had collided with an iceberg.

'Do you think the ship is seriously damaged?' Ismay inquired.

'I'm afraid she is', Smith responded.[36]

Once Andrews had reached the bridge, Smith asked him to accompany him on an inspection of the ship. Using crew passageways to avoid attracting attention, they examined the forward area more thoroughly than Boxhall had done. What they saw was horrifying. The *Titanic* had struck the iceberg with enough force, the United States Hydrographic Office later calculated, to lift fourteen Washington Monuments for one second each.[37] The ship's first six compartments – the forepeak, number one cargo hold, number two cargo hold, number three cargo hold, number six boiler room and number five boiler room – had been opened to the sea by a spar projecting from the iceberg below the waterline.[38] The water was already fourteen feet above the keel; there was no possibility of shoring up the damage. With the six compartments flooding independently, the bow would be pulled down by the weight until the water spilled over the top of the bulkhead that separated the sixth compartment from the seventh, back and back as if the *Titanic* were an ice-cube tray being tilted at a steeper and steeper angle. The ship, both Andrews and Smith now knew, was doomed. Both men were also well aware that there was only lifeboat capacity for about half of the passengers and crew. Smith asked Andrews how long the *Titanic* had left, and Andrews did some quick calculations: 'An hour and a half. Possibly two. Not much longer'.[39]

At this point, only they were aware of the extent of the damage. For the *Titanic*'s occupants, the experience of the collision depended greatly on their location in the ship. The higher up and further aft they were, the less they had felt the impact. Andrews, who knew the ship better than anyone, had been in his cabin on A Deck and had felt nothing. Others had felt a curious sensation, but certainly nothing that seemed to be of any great significance. Ella White felt as if the ship had run over 'a thousand marbles', and Charlotte Appleton heard a ripping sound, as if someone was tearing a long piece of cloth. Major Arthur Peuchen, an experienced yachtsman, thought that a heavy wave had struck the ship, while the young Swiss girl Marguerite Frolicher recalled the notoriously bumpy landings of the ferries in Zurich. Hugh Woolner was playing cards in the first-class smoking room when he felt

> a sort of stopping, a sort of – not exactly shock, but a sort of slowing down. And then we sort of felt a rip that gave a sort of twist to the whole room. Everybody, so far as I could see, stood up and a number of men walked out rapidly through the swinging doors on the port side, and ran along the rail that was behind the mast ... I stood hearing what the conjectures were. People were guessing what it might be, and one man called out, 'An iceberg has passed astern'.[40]

Even crew members more accustomed to the feel of a ship thought that nothing of note had occurred. Steward James Johnson was sitting around a table in the first-class dining room with three of his comrades when they heard the table settings rattle. Johnson assumed that the *Titanic* had dropped a propeller blade, an event he had experienced on the *Olympic* a year earlier, and the other stewards began joking about returning to Belfast for repairs. Chief Night Baker Walter Belford felt a shudder that caused a pan of freshly baked rolls to tumble onto the floor, to his great annoyance.[41] On C Deck, Seamen Frank Osman, Edward Buley, Walter Brice and Frank Evans were in the forward mess hall on the port side, smoking cigarettes and swapping yarns, when they heard Fleet ring three bells in the crow's nest above. A few moments later, they felt what Buley described as a 'slight jar. It seemed as though something were rubbing alongside of her'. Osman ran out on to the forward well deck and saw the iceberg passing the ship.[42]

There were those who suspected that the impact was of greater significance. It was most obvious in boiler room six, where there was a screech of tearing metal and then a tremendous bang as the starboard side of the ship caved in. The sea thundered in as the men leapt through the rapidly closing watertight door into the next compartment or scrambled up the escape ladders towards the higher decks. They were ordered to return, however, and shut the dampers on the boilers to prevent them from exploding on contact with the cold seawater. Working in a rising cloud of steam, they managed to put out the fires. By the time they finished, the water was up to their waists.

In their cabins up near the forepeak on D Deck, a group of firemen had just woken up and were preparing to go on watch at midnight. The crash sent them sprawling from their bunks. 'It was a harsh, grinding sound', reported Fireman John Thompson. 'I ran on the deck and found the forward well deck covered with masses of ice torn from the berg.'[43] One level further down on E Deck, Trimmer Samuel Hemming felt the impact and stuck his head through a porthole to see what the ship had hit. From the fo'c'sle head, he could hear a hissing sound, which he soon identified as air escaping from the forepeak tank as seawater poured in. Hemming returned to his bunk, but a few minutes later a bosun entered and announced, 'Turn out, you fellows ... you haven't half an hour to live. That is from Mr Andrews. Keep it to yourselves, and let no one know'.[44]

With their cabins forward on the lower decks, the single men in third class were some of the first passengers to know that something was seriously wrong. Carl Johnson was awakened by a loud noise and jumped out of bed. Almost immediately, water began seeping under his door, and as he dressed it rose high enough to cover his shoetops. Nearby, Daniel Buckley also heard the collision but remained in his bunk until he heard voices in the corridor outside his cabin. When he finally got up, he landed in water up to his ankles.[45] Elsewhere on the ship, a few of the more enterprising passengers tried to find out what had occurred. First-class passenger Norman Chambers was in his stateroom when he heard what sounded like 'jangling chains whipping along the sides of the ship':

> At the request of my wife I prepared to investigate . . . I looked at the starboard end of our passageway, where there was the companionway leading to the quarters of the mail clerks and farther on to the mail room and, I believe, the mail sorting room. And at the top of the stairs I found a couple of mail clerks, wet to their knees, who had just come up from below, bringing their registered mailbags. As the door in the bulkhead in the next deck was open, I was able to look directly into the trunk room, which was then filled with water, and within eighteen inches or two feet of the deck above.

Chambers, however, was not particularly alarmed; he joked with the mail clerks about 'our baggage being completely soaked and about the correspondence which was seen floating about on top of the water'.[46]

Most of the *Titanic*'s passengers, meanwhile, remained in their cabins. If anything alerted them that something unusual had occurred, it was not the collision itself but the cessation of the vibrations from the *Titanic*'s engines. Second-class passenger Lawrence Beesley was lying on his bunk reading when he felt the gentle motion of his mattress stop. On B Deck in first class seventeen-year-old Jack Thayer had just bade his parents good night when the breeze ceased blowing through his half-open porthole. Renee Harris saw her dresses stop swaying on their hangers in her wardrobe. Bells began to jangle for stewards; Emily Ryerson flagged down one, who told her, 'There's talk of an iceberg, ma'am, and we've stopped so as not to run over it'. She debated about whether to wake her husband but decided not to. Beesley's steward informed him that he did not know why the ship had stopped but 'I don't suppose it's much'. George Harder was told, 'Oh, it'll be a few hours, then we'll be on our way again'.[47]

A few passengers were curious enough to go up on deck and see what they could find out. They milled about in the frigid air, unsure of what to do. Rumours that the ship had grazed an iceberg were confirmed by the chunks of ice littering the *Titanic*'s decks. This ice was treated as a novel curiosity: third-class passengers played football with it on the forward well deck, while Greaser Walter Hurst had a piece tossed into his bunk by his father-in-law, who was also a crewman. First-class passenger Clinch Smith asked his friend Archibald Gracie if he would like a souvenir to take to New York and handed him a small fragment

about the size of a pocket watch. In the stewards' quarters someone
brought in a fist-sized fragment with the comment, 'There are tons of
it forward!'

Unimpressed, Steward F. Dent Ray rolled over in his bunk, saying,
'Well, that will not hurt anything'.[48]

At 12.05 a.m., twenty-five minutes after the collision, Captain Smith
ordered the lifeboats to be uncovered and a distress call to be sent.
Boxhall went to rouse the rest of the officers, while Murdoch began
mustering the passengers. The *Titanic* had no public address system,
and so the stewards had to pass through the ship, knocking on the door
of every cabin individually. In first class, passengers were politely told
to bring their lifejackets and come up on deck; in third class, doors
were banged open and light switches flipped on. Still, many refused to
believe that anything significant had occurred. When an officer came
through the first-class smoking room, shouting, 'Men get on your
lifebelts, there's trouble ahead!', hardly anyone looked up.[49] Jokes were
still the order of the day. Vera Dick remembered a stranger telling her
as he helped her into her lifejacket, 'Here, try this on – it's the latest
thing. Everybody's wearing them'. Clinch Smith saw a young girl
carrying a Pomeranian puppy and remarked, 'Well, I suppose we ought
to put a life preserver on the little doggie, too'.[50]

Only slowly did the passengers begin to comprehend that something
was truly wrong. Arthur Peuchen was standing by the rail watching the
third-class passengers play with the ice when he suddenly observed to
Charles Hays, 'Why she is listing! She should not do that! The water is
perfectly calm and the ship has stopped!' In second class Lawrence
Beesley had trouble putting his feet where he wanted to on the stairs,
as if the ship was tilted forward. And William Sloper was walking on
the Promenade Deck when he commented to his companion that he
felt as if he were going downhill.[51] Still, only a handful of people knew
that the ship was mortally wounded. Everyone else anticipated nothing
worse than a delay in getting into New York.

By 12.20 a.m., the loading of the lifeboats had commenced. There were
sixteen regular boats, numbered from fore to aft, with odd numbers on
the starboard side and even on the port side. Underneath Boats 1 and 2
were two collapsible lifeboats made of canvas, and two more collapsibles

were lashed to the roof of the officers' quarters. (The extreme inaccessibility of their location indicated just how unlikely Harland & Wolff thought that their use would be.) Murdoch was in charge of the boats on the starboard side and Lightoller of those on the port. Smith ordered them to 'put the women and children in and lower away', which Murdoch took to mean women and children *first* but Lightoller interpreted as women and children *only*. This meant that Lightoller put all the women and children that he could find in his boats and lowered them even if there were still empty seats, but Murdoch allowed a limited number of men to get in if there were no more women and children nearby. Both officers, however, launched a number of boats at considerably under their full capacity. Possibly, neither man was aware that there were not nearly enough places in the boats for all of the *Titanic*'s passengers and crew, or perhaps they had calculated that there was no time to lose trying to round up reluctant passengers and that once in the water the boats could pick up more people. They also may have been afraid that a boat fully loaded to its capacity of sixty-five might buckle as it hung from the davits, though Thomas Andrews could have told them that the boats had been thoroughly tested by Harland & Wolff.

Not surprisingly, the response of the passengers to the order to enter the boats was unenthusiastic. The *Titanic* might have a slight list, but it still seemed far safer than an open boat in the middle of an icy ocean. And what about the watertight compartments? Weren't they supposed to keep the ship afloat in just such an emergency as this? Nothing made of ice could sink the mighty *Titanic*. Adding to the difficulty of loading the boats was the roar coming from the *Titanic*'s funnels as the steam was let off from the boilers, 'kicking up a row that would have dwarfed the row of a thousand railway engines thundering through a culvert', according to Lightoller.[52] It took twenty minutes for the first lifeboats to be loaded, and even then they had to be lowered with numerous empty seats. Boat 7, the first to reach the water, held only twenty-five occupants. Boat 1, a special cutter with a capacity of forty, was lowered with only twelve people on board. Walter Hurst had been released from his duties as a greaser and stood watching the boats being lowered from the forward well deck. Seeing Boat 1 hit the water, he commented to a shipmate, 'If they are sending the boats away they might as well put some people in them'.[53]

In the wireless shack, Phillips was getting increasingly worried: no ship that had responded to his distress call was anywhere near the *Titanic*. Moreover, other ships were having trouble believing that the unsinkable *Titanic* was really in such grave peril. The *Olympic*, eastbound on the return journey from New York, asked if *Titanic* was steaming south to meet it, while the German liner *Frankfort* kept inquiring what was the matter. Phillips tried to be patient, but as the *Frankfort's* operator continued to behave obtusely, he finally tapped back, 'You fool, stand by and keep out!' 54 In any event, both the *Olympic* and the *Frankfort* were hundreds of miles away, much too far to be of any assistance. At 12.25 Philips did hear from a closer ship, the Cunard liner *Carpathia*, fifty-eight miles away and coming hard, but even so it would take nearly four hours to reach *Titanic's* position, four hours that Phillips knew the *Titanic* did not have. Where, he must have wondered, was the *Californian*, whose signal had nearly blown out his eardrums only an hour or so earlier? Unbeknownst to him, the *Titanic's* officers had spotted another ship off the port bow, its green running lights showing clearly when Boxhall looked at it through his binoculars. The ship appeared to be no more than ten to twelve miles away, and Smith told Boxhall to try contacting it by Morse lamp, but there was no response.

Around 12.45, Quartermaster George Rowe was at his post standing watch on the *Titanic's* after bridge. Earlier, he had noticed a slight change in the motion of the ship, and then had been startled to see what looked a full-rigged sailing ship pass perilously close by on the *Titanic's* starboard side. He quickly realized that he was looking at an iceberg, so high it towered over him even in his elevated position nearly sixty feet above the water. Shortly afterwards, the ship had stopped and begun to vent steam. But no one had contacted him to tell him what was going on, so he had stayed where he was, awaiting further instructions. Now, over an hour later, he was surprised to see a lifeboat, only about a third full, floating in the water. He immediately telephoned the main bridge, and, when Boxhall answered, asked him if he knew that there was a boat adrift. Incredulous, Boxhall ordered him to get to the main bridge immediately and bring some distress rockets with him. Rowe grabbed a box of twelve rockets from a locker and headed forward.

When he got there, Smith told him to start launching the rockets. The first one went up shortly before 1 a.m. with a hiss and a loud bang, followed by an explosion of white stars. This, finally, alerted the passengers that the situation was truly serious. 'Everyone knows what rockets at sea mean', Lawrence Beesley later wrote. The crewmen loading the boats began to have no shortage of eager volunteers, and the first signs of panic appeared. Revolvers had earlier been distributed amongst the officers, and the need for them now became apparent. Fifth Officer Harold Lowe was loading Boat 14 when an adolescent boy jumped in and tried to hide amongst the women already on board. Lowe drew his gun and ordered the boy to get out, but he pleaded to be allowed to stay. Lowe thrust his gun in the boy's face, telling him, 'I'll give you just ten seconds to get back onto that ship before I blow your brains out!', but the boy only pleaded harder. It was only when Lowe told him, 'For God's sake, be a man. We've got women and children to save' that the boy finally relinquished his seat. While Lowe was distracted, another man, possibly Daniel Buckley, managed to sneak into the boat by putting a woman's shawl over his head. A male passenger who tried to follow him, however, was spotted and thrown back. He landed among a group of second-class men, who beat him senseless. The situation was deteriorating rapidly, and Seaman Joseph Scarrott, who was manning the boat, was able to hold back a group of male passengers only by using the tiller bar as a club. Lowe had had enough: he pointed his gun down the side of the ship, fired it three times, and shouted, 'If anyone else tries that this is what he'll get!' The crowd fell back, and Boat 14 was quickly lowered.[55]

Over on the port side, Murdoch was having similar problems. Half a dozen men rushed Boat 15, and Murdoch screamed at them to get back. Forward, at Boat 2, Lightoller was trying to evict a group of male passengers and crew. He drew his gun and levelled it at them, shouting, 'Get out of there you damned cowards!' The men quickly jumped out of the lifeboat, unaware that Lightoller's gun was not loaded.

At the same time as these scenes of panic were taking place, there were other, quieter, more poignant moments. Husbands urged their wives to get into the boats, and fathers bade goodbye to their children. At Boat 8, Ida Straus was about to climb in, but she suddenly changed her mind and stepped back. 'We have been living together for many years', she said to her husband Isidor. 'Where you, I go.' The couple retreated to a pair of deck chairs and calmly watched the proceedings.

Ben Guggenheim appeared on the boat deck at around 1.30 wearing white tie and tails. He gave a message to his steward, Henry Etches:

> I think there is grave doubt that the men will get off. I am willing to remain and play the man's game if there are not enough boats for more than the women and children. I won't die here like a beast. Tell my wife ... I played the game out straight and to the end. No woman shall be left aboard this ship because Ben Guggenheim was a coward.[56]

A large number of the *Titanic*'s passengers never got the chance to make such a noble sacrifice. Third class had been held below decks until 12.30, when the word had come down for the women and children to proceed up to the Boat Deck. But this was easier said than done. On their own, third-class passengers had almost no chance of negotiating the maze-like passageways that separated them from the boats. In addition, American immigration laws required that there be physical barriers between third class and other areas, and so most of the access points were blocked by locked gateways. Steward John Hart recognized that there was a problem and began to organize an effort to lead third-class women and children up to the boats, but it was slow going. He could take no more than twenty at a time, and each trip took over ten minutes: up the stairs to the third-class lounge on C Deck, across the after well deck, past the second-class library, along a stretch of corridor that led past the surgeon's office, into the private dining saloon for the servants of the first-class passengers, and finally out onto the Grand Staircase and up to the Boat Deck. By 1.15 Hart had managed to bring up only two groups, totalling about fifty passengers, when he was ordered by Murdoch to man Boat 15. Hart's was the last organized effort to lead third class to the boats; after that they were left to shift for themselves. Many of them continued to wait patiently below decks, believing that their turn would come once first and second class were loaded. Others were unable to comprehend what was happening due to language barriers, and some refused to leave their luggage, which contained everything they owned. Those who tried on their own to get to the boats often found their way blocked by locked gates, or else they simply got lost in the *Titanic*'s corridors. A few, by luck or by sheer resourcefulness, were able to make it up. An Irish passenger convinced a crewman to open one of the gates, while another gate on E Deck was battered down. A few of the more physically agile third-class passengers crawled up the cargo crane on the after well deck to a railing on B Deck, from which it was an easy journey to the boat deck. They were the lucky ones, however. The vast majority of the *Titanic*'s third-class passengers never got anywhere near a lifeboat that night.

By 1.45 a.m., the *Titanic*'s bow was underwater and the ship had developed a severe list to starboard. Chief Officer Wilde ordered everyone to the port side to help straighten the ship up, but the end was drawing near. The sea was now pouring into the forward hatchways, hastening the *Titanic*'s demise. Around this time Phillips briefly left the wireless room to see what was happening; when he returned he told Bride, 'Things look very queer outside, very queer indeed'.[57] Only a few lifeboats remained, with enough people still on board to fill them many times over. Collapsible C, which had been fitted into Boat 1's davits, was the source of a fierce struggle. Purser McElroy was forced to draw his revolver and fire it twice into the air, but two stewards ran past him and jumped into the boat anyway. Two passengers, Hugh Woolner and Bjorn Steffanson, dragged them back out again. Assisted by Murdoch, McElroy got as many women and children as he could into the boat and began lowering. As the boat's gunwale reached the level of the deck, J. Bruce Ismay, who had also been assisting with the loading, jumped into an empty place near the bow.

At Boat 4, John Jacob Astor helped his pregnant wife negotiate the rail. He asked Lightoller if he could join her, explaining that she was in a 'delicate condition'. Lightoller told him no, and Astor made no further argument.[58] After Boat 4 was lowered, Lightoller turned to Collapsible D, which was put into Boat 2's davits. Taking no chances with the desperate crowd still left on board, he had a group of crewmen and reliable passengers form a ring around the boat, arms locked together. Only women and children were allowed through, and those who were still reluctant to go were picked up and thrown in; there was no time to waste trying to convince them. As the boat filled, Wilde suggested that Lightoller get into the boat and take command. 'Not damn likely', Lightoller replied.[59]

Other crew members were equally attentive to their duty. In the wireless shack, Phillips and Bride continued to transmit distress calls, even after Captain Smith returned and told them, 'You can do no more. Abandon your cabin. Now it's every man for himself ... That's the way of it at this kind of time'.[60] At 2.10 the *Virginian* picked up two faint 'V's, the *Titanic's* final transmission. Far below in the *Titanic's* engine rooms, the ship's thirty-five engineers tried to keep power supplied to the wireless set and to the lights for as long as possible, even though they knew their chances of escape were slim. (Not a single one of them survived.) And out on the boat deck, the *Titanic's* eight-member orchestra, led by bandmaster Wallace Hartley, continued to play until the waves washed them overboard; most accounts name their final tune as the hymn 'Nearer My God to Thee', though some witnesses heard another hymn, 'Autumn'.[61]

There were now only two boats remaining, Collapsibles A and B, still lashed atop the officer's quarters. Glancing down a nearby stairwell, Lightoller saw that the water was up to C Deck. There was clearly not a second to lose, but how to get the boats, each of which weighed over two tons, down to the davits? Lightoller had the remaining crewmen and a few helpful passengers build makeshift ramps using oars and planking. They managed to slide Collapsible A down, but Collapsible B broke its ramp and crashed to the deck in an inverted position. As he worked frantically, Lightoller noticed Trimmer Samuel Hemming, whom he had earlier ordered to go with Boat 6, the first boat he had launched. 'Why haven't you gone yet, Hemming?' he asked. 'Oh, plenty of time yet, sir', Hemming replied.[62]

Hemming's optimism was misplaced. The *Titanic* took a sudden plunge forward, and an enormous wave rolled over the boat deck. Collapsible A had been fitted into Boat 1's davits, but before it could be launched the onrushing water washed it off the deck. Steward Edward Brown cut the stern falls, and the boat floated away. At the same time, Collapsible B was also washed off, still upside-down, with Harold Bride, clinging to one of the rowlocks, trapped underneath. With no more boats available, people began jumping from the *Titanic's* decks into the freezing water. As he straddled the starboard rail abreast the second funnel, Jack Thayer turned to his friend Milton Long, shook his hand and wished him luck. As Thayer was removing his overcoat, Long asked him, 'You are coming, boy?' 'Go ahead', Thayer replied. 'I'll be right with you'.[63] Long slid down the side of the ship but was swallowed up by the torrent that was being sucked into A Deck. Thayer never saw him again. Ten seconds later, Thayer leaped off the rail, thrusting himself as far from the ship as possible in order to avoid his friend's fate. The shock of the icy water knocked his breath out of him, but he quickly recovered and began swimming away. Forty yards from the ship, he paused and looked back: 'The ship seemed to be surrounded with a glare, and stood out of the night as though she were on fire. I watched her. I don't know why I didn't keep swimming away. Fascinated, I seemed tied to the spot'.[64]

From the roof of the wheelhouse, Lightoller also decided that he would be better off taking his chances in the water than amongst the crowd that remained on board. He dived in and swam towards the crow's nest, but suddenly realized the danger of hanging onto anything attached to the sinking ship. He began swimming away when he was suddenly sucked into an airshaft directly in front of the first funnel. The sea was pouring into the shaft. If the grating covering it gave way, Lightoller knew that he would be swept down into the bowels of the ship. 'Now we'll see if Christian Science really works', he thought. At that moment, a blast of hot air blew out through the shaft, probably from an exploding boiler far below, and threw him back up to the surface. Another ventilation shaft briefly sucked him down a second time, but he again fought his way free. As he surfaced, overturned Collapsible B was floating nearby, and he was able to grab a rope trailing from it and scramble aboard.[65]

Amidst all the chaos, some passengers continued to carry on as if everything were normal. In the first-class lounge, where liquor was now on the house, a foursome that included Archibald Butt, Arthur Ryerson and Frank Millet continued to play bridge, ignoring the increasingly steep slant of the table. Others took these final moments to try and comprehend what had happened. In the smoking room, Thomas Andrews, who had done all he could to save as many passengers as possible by helping to load the boats and then throwing everything he could find that would float overboard to serve as rafts, stood staring at the painting of Plymouth Harbour that hung over the fireplace. His life-jacket, which he had worn all night in order to set a good example, lay on a nearby table. Steward John Stewart asked him, 'Aren't you even going to try for it, Mr Andrews?', but received no reply.

At 2.15 the *Titanic*'s bridge dipped under. Almost simultaneously, the forward funnel collapsed, its guy wires unable to support its weight as the decks tilted at a steeper and steeper angle. Ripping out planking from the deck as it fell, it crashed into the water with an enormous splash, crushing several swimmers. To Charlotte Collyer in Boat 14, it was as if 'something in the very bowels of the *Titanic* exploded, and millions of sparks shot up in the sky, like rockets in a park on the night of a summer holiday'. Those still on board rushed towards the stern, but the slant of the decks was now so steep that it was extremely difficult to walk on them, and many people slid down into the water. Others clung to the rails and deck houses, desperate to stay on the ship for as long as possible. There was an enormous burst of noise as everything moveable in the ship broke loose, from plates to grand pianos to boilers, and crashed towards the bow. Lawrence Beesley recalled the sound as 'partly a roar, partly a groan, partly a rattle and partly a smash, and it was not a sudden roar as an explosion would be; it went on successively for some seconds ... But it was a noise no one had heard before, and no one wishes to hear again; it was stupefying, stupendous, as it came to us along the water'. Adding to the cacophony was a series of muffled booms from below the water as the *Titanic*'s bulkheads crumpled, unable to withstand the enormous strain. The cork lining the bulkheads spewed up and spread out over the surface of the ocean. The lights dimmed a dull red, flashed brightly one final time and then went out for good, plunging the scene into the pitch black of a moonless night. Steerage passenger Carl Jansen recalled:

> We were suddenly plunged into darkness ... I could not accustom myself to the change for several minutes. I think I was in a sort of daze and have no clear recollection of what happened afterward or how long a time had elapsed. Suddenly I heard shrieks and cries amidships ... People began to run by me toward the stern of the ship, and as I started to run I realized that the boat was beginning to go down very rapidly ... her nose was being buried.[66]

From his position in the water, Jack Thayer could see 'groups of the fifteen hundred people still aboard, clinging in clusters or bunches, like swarming bees; only to fall in masses, pairs or singly as the great afterpart of the ship, two hundred fifty feet of it, rose into the sky'.[67] As the stern continued to rise, the ship's steel hull could no longer support such a massive weight, and it split between the third and fourth funnels. As the bow, now completely filled with water, disappeared under the surface, the stern settled back almost level for a brief moment, causing some people in the boats to think that a miraculous safety mechanism had clicked into place. But in a short time the stern, too, filled with water, its descent accelerated by the force of the still partially attached bow pulling on it. At 2.20 a.m., the blue ensign on the flagpole at the *Titanic*'s stern slipped under the water with barely a ripple, and the world's largest ship was gone. 'At the last', first-class survivor Helen Candee wrote later, 'the end of the world.'[68]

Of the 1500 people who had not managed to get a seat in a lifeboat, the vast majority were still alive for some time after the *Titanic* sank beneath them.* Almost all of them had lifejackets, so that they were in no danger of drowning. They were in grave danger, however, from the 28°F water in which they were floating, which was cold enough to kill even the hardiest soul within half an hour. Lightoller likened the sensation of entering that frigid water to being stabbed with 'a thousand knives'. Except for Collapsibles A and B, the lifeboats had rowed as far away as possible, fearing that suction would take them down when the ship sank or that they would be swamped by the hundreds of desperate people flailing in the water. About two dozen people managed to make it to Collapsible A; two of the last to reach it were August Wennerstrom and his friend Edvard Lindell. After Wennerstrom climbed in, he looked back for Lindell's wife Elin, whom he saw still struggling in the water. He managed to grab her hand, but he did not have the strength to haul her aboard. He hung on for a time, but eventually was forced to let go. He was unsure if Elin was alive or dead when she slid into the water. He turned to Edvard to tell him about his wife, but he realized that he, too, was dead.[69]

Other swimmers converged on Collapsible B, still floating upside down near the wreck site. Lightoller was among the first to arrive, followed by Jack Thayer, Archibald Gracie, Harold Bride (who was finally able to get out from underneath and scramble aboard) and around two dozen others. Soon thirty men were perched precariously

---

* For a full account of who survived in which lifeboat, see Appendix 1, pp. 291–319.

on the boat's keel, and with each new arrival the boat, which had not been designed to float in an inverted position, sank a little lower in the water as the air pocket underneath diminished. Some of the men used oars to beat back others who tried to climb up. Lightoller realized that he had to take charge of the situation. He had the men form two parallel rows on each side of the centreline, and, as the swell pitched the boat from side to side, he would call out to them to lean left or right. This kept the boat afloat, but the water continued to rise first to the men's ankles and then to their knees, and several men, exhausted and freezing, slid off into the sea. The others on board were powerless to help them.

In the other lifeboats the struggle for survival was less desperate, and their occupants could hear the frantic cries for help coming from the 1500 people rapidly freezing to death in the water. To Helen Candee in Boat 6 it sounded like 'a heavy moan as of one being from whom final agony forces a single sound'. Nine-year-old Franky Goldsmith later moved to Detroit, where he lived near Tiger Stadium. Every time a home run was hit in a baseball game there, the roar of the crowd reminded him of that terrible night.[70] At least a few people argued in favour of going back to pick up survivors. In Boat 5, Third Officer Herbert Pitman ordered the men at the oars to pull for the wreck site, but the women in the boat protested, fearing that they would be swamped. 'Why should we lose all our lives in a useless attempt to save others from the ship?' one woman asked. Pitman gave in, but he felt guilty for the rest of his life. In Boat 2, Fourth Officer Boxhall also wanted to search for survivors, but his passengers, like Pitman's, objected. In Boat 8, Seaman Thomas Jones tried to go back and was supported by the Countess of Rothes, but everyone else, including the three oarsmen, refused. 'Ladies, if any of us are saved', Jones told them, 'remember *I* wanted to go back. I would rather drown with them than leave them.'

Later, Margaret Brown would come to be regarded as a heroine for her efforts to get Boat 6 to go back. After the *Titanic* went down, she and several other women in the boat began demanding that Quartermaster Robert Hitchens return for some of those in the water. Hitchens refused, saying that 'there's no use going back, because there's only a lot of stiffs there'. Brown then requested that the women be allowed to row in order to keep warm, but Hitchens only wanted to drift with the current. Fed up, Brown pushed her way to the stern and took over the tiller from him. When he protested, she told him that if he made a move toward her, she would throw him overboard. Defeated, he sank into a sulky silence, announcing that they were doomed, without food, water or a compass. Brown told him to shut up, backed up by Leila Meyer, who called him a coward. Hitchens swore at them, but made no further attempt to reclaim the leadership of the boat.

By the time the power struggle in Boat 6 was resolved, there was no point in returning to the wreck site. In the end, only one lifeboat tried to save those struggling in the water, Boat 14, commanded by Fifth Officer Lowe. Once his boat was safely away from the *Titanic*, Lowe began rounding up all the others he could find and tying them together, gradually assembling a little flotilla of five. He then began transferring the passengers in his boat to the others. After it was emptied of all but its oarsmen, Lowe waited for the cries in the water to 'thin out' and then headed back to the wreck. He had overestimated how long people could survive in the frigid water, however, and when he reached the site he found only three people still alive amidst hundreds of frozen corpses.[71]

In the other boats, the reality of what had occurred slowly sank in as their occupants recovered from the initial shock. All they could do was wait for a ship to rescue them, and hope against hope that somehow their loved ones had survived. A few people sobbed or cried out, but most retreated into a sombre silence. Everyone shivered violently in the cold. Ruth Dodge had not buttoned her shoes before leaving her cabin, and now her feet were almost numb. A seaman offered her his stockings, assuring her that they were 'perfectly clean. I just put them on this morning'. Clara Hays called out to every passing boat, 'Charles Hays, are you there?' but never received an answer. Madeleine Astor leant her shawl to a crying child.[72] The hours passed slowly, and only the occupants of overturned Collapsible B, where Harold Bride had ended up, had any idea about what ships were coming and when they were likely to arrive.

Help was indeed on its way. Just before midnight on 14 April, the Cunard liner *Carpathia* was eastbound on a voyage from New York to the Mediterranean, carrying 743 passengers. After a long day transmitting a steady stream of passenger messages, wireless operator Harold Cottam was getting ready for bed. He was waiting, however, for a confirmation of an earlier message to the *Parisian*, and so he kept his headphones on as he undressed. The last thing he did before retiring was to switch over to the Cape Cod land station to pick up any news items or information of general interest. He heard Cape Cod transmitting a few commercial messages to the *Titanic* and jotted them down, planning to transmit them in the morning. But for some reason Cottam changed his mind and decided to call the *Titanic* immediately: 'I say, old man, do you know there is a batch of messages coming through for you from MCC [Cape Cod]?' The reply from Phillips must have stunned him.

'Come at once. We have struck an iceberg. It's CQD, old man.'[73]

Cottam did not hesitate. 'Shall I tell my captain? Do you require assistance?'

'Yes. Come quick.'[74]

Cottam ran to the bridge, bursting in and blurting the news to the *Carpathia*'s First Officer, H. V. Dean. Dean and Cottam then ran to the captain's cabin, where Captain Arthur Rostron had just gone to bed. The two men barged in without knocking, and Rostron was initially irritated by the intrusion. But when Cottam informed him of the *Titanic*'s distress call, he immediately got up and threw on his clothes. He could not, however, suppress a feeling of disbelief. 'Are you certain?' he asked Cottam.

'Yes, sir.'

'Absolutely certain?'

'Yes, sir.'[75]

Once on the bridge, Rostron quickly calculated a new course that would bring the *Carpathia* to the *Titanic*'s position. He summoned the bosun's mate and told him to get the ship's lifeboats ready for lowering, informing him only that they were going to the rescue of another vessel. Next, Rostron ordered the chief engineer to put on every available stoker and make all possible speed. The chief steward and chief purser were instructed to have their men at the gangway ready to rescue passengers from a sinking passenger liner. To their astonishment, they were informed that the stricken vessel was the *Titanic*. The *Carpathia*'s crew could hardly believe the news, but they set about their preparations with great diligence. Tea, coffee and hot soup were prepared for the survivors.

Blankets were laid out. All public rooms and officer's cabins – even the captain's – were made ready for the *Titanic*'s passengers. Powerful lights were strung at the gangways, as well as chairs to help the weaker survivors aboard. Canvas bags were made ready to haul children up. Chains were laid out in case any of the *Titanic*'s survivors had gone insane and needed to be restrained.

Within a few minutes of receiving the distress call, the *Carpathia* was heading towards the *Titanic*'s position at over seventeen knots, though its maximum speed was supposed to be only fourteen. Every ounce of available steam was diverted, and the ship's decks shook as the engines strained to produce more power than they had ever been called upon to do before. As they felt the vibrations and heard the stewards moving around the corridors, the *Carpathia*'s passengers wondered what was happening, but all requests for information were met with a polite but firm order to remain in their cabins. Rostron was well aware of the likelihood of encountering the same icefield that had already done grievous harm to the mighty *Titanic*. He posted extra lookouts, but he kept the ship steaming forward at full speed. Rostron later recalled:

> More and more now we were all keyed up. Icebergs loomed up and fell astern; we never slackened, though sometimes we altered course suddenly to avoid them. It was an anxious time with the *Titanic*'s fateful experience very close in our minds. There were seven hundred souls on *Carpathia*; these lives, as well as all the survivors of *Titanic* herself, depended on a sudden turn of the wheel.[76]

As the *Carpathia* approached the *Titanic*'s position, Rostron saw only a black, empty sea. At 4 a.m., a green light appeared about three hundred yards ahead, so low in the water that it could only come from a very small boat. Rostron sounded the liner's whistle to tell those in the boat that they had been seen, and then ordered 'dead slow ahead' so that he could take it alongside. As they neared the boat, a female voice called out, 'We have only one seaman in the boat and can't work very well'. It was Boat 2, and within ten minutes its occupants were climbing aboard the *Carpathia* through an open gangway. The boat contained twenty-five women and Fourth Officer Boxhall, whom Rostron immediately summoned to the bridge. Without preliminaries, Rostron asked, 'Where is the *Titanic*?'

'Gone!' Boxhall replied. 'She sank at 2.20 a.m.'

'Were there many people left on board when she sank?'

'Hundreds and hundreds! Perhaps a thousand! Perhaps more! My God, sir, they've gone down with her. They couldn't live in this cold water.' [77]

Despite the order to stay below, the *Carpathia*'s passengers, their curiosity aroused, had begun to trickle up on deck, and an increasing number lined the railings to see what was going on. As dawn broke, the light revealed a string of lifeboats, each bearing the White Star insignia and the name '*Titanic*'. There was ice all around; when Rostron sent one of his officers up to the crow's nest to count the large icebergs, he saw more than two dozen higher than two hundred feet. One by one, the boats crept towards the *Carpathia* and unloaded their chilled and devastated occupants. The last survivor to board was Charles Lightoller, who along with the others from overturned Collapsible B had been picked up by another lifeboat. When Lightoller reached the *Carpathia*'s deck, he was greeted with surprise by his old friend H. V. Dean, who exclaimed, 'Hullo, Lights! Whatever are you doing here?' [78]

Such cheery greetings were rare. Rostron later recalled that what was most striking about the scene was the almost total silence in which the *Titanic*'s survivors boarded the *Carpathia*. There was no celebration of rescue or outpourings of grief; many women still hoped that their husbands had been rescued by other ships. Most survivors went directly to the berths that had been prepared for them, in cabins or in some cases in the ship's public rooms. J. Bruce Ismay was taken immediately to the doctor's cabin and given a sedative; he did not emerge until the *Carpathia* reached New York.

The *Carpathia* was extremely crowded, but the only other ship available to transport the *Titanic*'s passengers was the *Olympic*, and it was decided that the shock of seeing the *Titanic*'s twin sister might be too much for the survivors. Rostron therefore decided to turn back and take them to New York himself. After searching the area for additional survivors and holding a brief religious service over the *Titanic*'s last reported position, Rostron headed west at around 9 a.m. Just as he was about to depart, the *Californian* arrived on the scene. Rostron had not heard from this ship previously, despite all the frantic radio traffic that had been going back and forth during the night and early morning hours, and he must have wondered where it had been all this time.

Indeed, that would become one of the most controversial questions of the *Titanic* story.

At 10 p.m. on Sunday 14 April, the Leyland Line freighter *Californian* was steaming east towards Boston when its captain, Stanley Lord, saw a huge field of ice ahead and decided to stop for the night. He was about to go and get some sleep on the chartroom couch when he saw a light to the east that he thought was an approaching vessel. He pointed it out to Third Officer Charles Groves and then headed below, but before retiring he stopped by the wireless room and asked operator Cyril Evans what other vessels were in the vicinity. Evans told him that there was only the *Titanic,* but Lord replied that the ship he could see was not big enough to be the White Star liner. He told Evans, however, to contact *Titanic* and tell them that the *Californian* was stopped and surrounded by ice. This was the message that came crashing through on Phillips's headphones at around 11 p.m. Lord could have opted to send a Master Service Message, which would have required Phillips to deliver it to the *Titanic's* bridge and Captain Smith to acknowledge it, but he did not.

At 11.15 Groves saw a ship steaming up from the east about ten to twelve miles away. He could see that it was a large passenger liner, its decks brightly lit and piled one on top of the other. He estimated it to be about five miles away. He went down to the chartroom and informed Lord, who suggested that Groves try to contact the ship by Morse lamp. He did so, but received no reply. At 11.40 Groves saw the big liner suddenly appear to stop and put out most of its lights, which he assumed had been done to encourage the passengers to go to bed. (In reality, he was almost certainly seeing the sharp turn that the *Titanic* made in the futile effort to avoid the iceberg.) Lord, who had been watching from below, reappeared on the bridge and looked through his binoculars at the mystery ship. 'That doesn't look like a passenger steamer', he commented to Groves. 'It is, sir. When she stopped she put out most of her lights – I suppose they have been put out for the night.' Lord grunted noncommittally in reply and then returned to the chartroom, telling Groves to inform him if the ship's bearing changed.[79]

A few minutes before midnight, Second Officer Herbert Stone was heading for the bridge to take the 12 to 4 watch. He encountered Lord at the wheelhouse door and was told about the steamer that had come up from the east about an hour earlier. Lord repeated his instruction to inform him if the ship altered its bearing. To Stone the vessel appeared to be dead abeam of the *Californian*'s starboard side; like Lord, he thought it to be a small tramp steamer, not a large passenger liner. At 12.10 he made another attempt to contact it with the Morse lamp but was again unsuccessful; the ship appeared to be out of range.

Groves, meanwhile, did not go straight to bed after being relieved, but instead stopped by the wireless room. He asked Evans, 'What ships have you got, Sparks?' 'Only the *Titanic*', the drowsy operator replied. Groves put on the headphones, hoping to catch some traffic. Evans had been teaching him Morse code, and he could now make out some signals. He did not know, however, that after the set had been turned off the magnetic signal detector had to be wound up again, so he heard nothing. Evans was tired and wanted to go to sleep, so he did not tell Groves how to turn the set back on. Bored, Groves departed. It was around 12.15, and Jack Phillips had just sent out the *Titanic*'s first distress call.[80]

At almost the same time, Fireman Ernest Gill had come off duty and was out on deck smoking a cigarette before heading to his bunk. Off the starboard side he saw 'a very large steamer, about ten miles away'. Shortly afterwards he went below to bed, but was unable to sleep and went back up on deck. At around 12.40, he saw a white flash in the sky about ten miles off on the starboard side. At first he thought it was a shooting star, but seven or eight minutes later he observed a second flash in the same place and realized that it was a rocket. Gill, however, decided that 'it was not my business to notify the bridge or the lookouts'. Besides, he reasoned, 'They could not help but see them [the rockets]'. He returned to bed shortly thereafter, 'supposing that the ship would pay attention to the rockets'. He knew nothing further until he awoke the next morning and was shocked to hear that the *Titanic* had sunk.[81]

On the bridge, Stone also saw the rockets. He counted five in all before he called down the voice tube to Lord in the chartroom. 'Are they company signals?' Lord asked. 'I don't know, sir, but they appear to me to be all white.' Stone knew that shipping lines generally used coloured rockets to send signals between their ships, whereas white was traditionally reserved for distress signals. Lord told him to continue

trying to contact the ship by Morse lamp and to let him know if anything
changed. Stone was now joined on the bridge by James Gibson, an
apprentice officer. Looking through his binoculars, Gibson saw another
white rocket go up; the lenses were powerful enough that he could see
the rocket streaking up into the sky and then bursting in a shower of
stars. As he continued to watch he saw a seventh rocket flash white
above the mystery ship. Stone borrowed Gibson's binoculars and took
a look, commenting, 'She looks very queer out of the water – her lights
look queer'.[82]

Taking the glasses back, Gibson observed that the ship seemed to be
listing, with 'a big side out of the water'. At around 1.40 a.m. they saw
an eighth rocket.[83] 'A ship is not going to fire rockets at sea for nothing.
There must be something wrong with her', Stone remarked, and Gibson
concurred. As they watched, the ship seemed to steam away and disappear; its red port light became invisible and only its stern light could
still be seen. Shortly after 2 a.m., Stone sent Gibson to inform the
captain. Gibson later testified that he roused the sleeping Lord and told
him about the other ship's departure and about the rockets. He stated
that the captain acknowledged his report and then asked, 'Are you sure
there were no colours [in the rockets]?' He also asked what the time
was. Lord, however, later claimed that he did not recall the conversation
with Gibson. In a sworn affidavit, he stated that 'I have recollection
between 1.30 and 4.30 of Gibson opening the chartroom door and closing
it immediately. I said: "What is it?" but he did not reply'.[84]

For the next hour all was quiet. Then at 3.30 Stone and Gibson saw
another rocket, followed quickly by two more. The ship that was firing
them was below the horizon and thus invisible. Half an hour later, Chief
Officer George Stewart came on watch, and Stone told him of the night's
events. Stewart looked through his binoculars and saw a single-funnelled
steamer. He asked Stone if this was the ship that had fired the rockets;
Stone replied that he was certain it was not. Stone then went off duty,
leaving Stewart on the bridge with an uneasy feeling that 'something had
happened'. At 4.30 he awakened Lord and began recounting what Stone
had told him, but Lord stopped him halfway through and said that he
already knew all about it. Lord went up to the bridge and began working
out a course to get the *Californian* out of the ice, but Stewart suggested
that they should first try to learn why the mystery ship had been firing

rockets. Lord looked through his glasses at the single-funnelled steamer and said, 'She looks all right. She's not making any signals now'. Stewart said nothing further, but at 5.30 he went down to the wireless room and asked Evans to turn on his set: 'Sparks, there's a ship been firing rockets in the night. Will you see if you can find out what is wrong?' It was only then that the *Californian* learned of the accident to the *Titanic*.[85]

Lord calculated that the *Californian* was nineteen and a half miles from the wreck site, and he proceeded there with all possible speed. He sent a lookout up to the crow's nest to watch for survivors or boats. Along the way, he saw two other vessels, the *Mount Temple* and the *Almerian*, before he met the *Carpathia* at around 8.30 a.m. In an exchange of flag signals, it was decided that the *Carpathia* should depart immediately for New York while the *Californian* continued to search for survivors. For the next few hours they searched the area, seeing some scattered debris but no bodies. There was little else they could do, so the *Californian* resumed its voyage to Boston, unaware that its arrival would occur amidst a storm of controversy.[86]

During the journey to New York, the atmosphere on the *Carpathia* was sombre. Rostron had his crew collect a list of survivors' names and came up with a total of 705. This meant that 1523 people had perished. The *Carpathia*'s passengers and crew did all they could, giving up their berths, donating clothing or stitching it out of blankets, serving hot food and drinks. Nothing they did, however, could dissipate the pall that hung over the ship. 'This ship is in gloom', *Carpathia* passenger Daniel H. Burnham recorded in his diary. 'Everybody has lost friends, and some of them near relations.'[87]

As the *Carpathia* made its way to New York, it crossed paths with another ship which was heading for the *Titanic* wreck site. Once it had been confirmed that the *Titanic* had sunk, the White Star Line had contacted its agents in Halifax, A. G. Jones and Company, and chartered a cable-laying vessel called the *Mackay-Bennett*, under the command of Captain F. H. Lardner, to search the vicinity of the wreck and recover as many bodies as it could find. Nova Scotia's largest undertaker, John Snow and Company, was also hired to oversee the collection and preservation of the bodies. The task was so formidable that Snow asked for help from virtually every embalmer in the maritime provinces of

Canada. One of them, Annie F. O'Neill of St John, New Brunswick, was specially designated to embalm the women and children.

As the *Mackay-Bennett* prepared to set sail, tons of ice were poured into its holds, and more than one hundred wooden coffins were stowed on board. The crew consisted entirely of volunteers, who were paid double the normal wage due to the grim nature of the voyage. The ship sailed on Wednesday, 17 April. As it neared the wreck site, the wireless operator sent out a message requesting all ships which had seen wreckage or bodies to relay the appropriate coordinates. Most passenger ships had been giving the area a wide berth, due not only to the fact that the shipping lanes had been shifted sixty miles south the day after the disaster to avoid ice, but also because no company wanted to present its passengers with the grisly spectacle of hundreds of floating corpses. There had been a number of sightings, however, all of which indicated an area near latitude 42° 01′ N and longitude 49° 20′ W. Johanna Stunke, a passenger on the westbound liner *Bremen*, reported seeing

> the body of one woman dressed only in her night dress, clasping a baby to her breast. Close by was the body of another woman with her arms clasped tightly round a shaggy dog ... We saw the bodies of three men in a group, all clinging to a chair. Floating by just beyond them were the bodies of half a dozen men, all wearing lifebelts and clinging desperately together as though in their last struggle for life.[88]

The *Mackay-Bennett* arrived on the scene on the evening of Saturday, 20 April. The embalmer John Snow Jr reported that bodies were strewn over the surface of the water 'like a flock of white sea gulls at rest on the sea'. Closer inspection revealed that all of the watches worn by the men had stopped at ten minutes past two, 'there was not the very slightest deviation'.[89]

The recovery effort began the following morning and continued throughout the day; the men worked in chilly winds and heavy seas. 'Hauling the soaked remains in saturated clothing over the side of the cutter', reported cable engineer Frederic Hamilton, 'is no light task.'[90] As each body was brought on board, a canvas tag with a number stencilled on it was attached. This number corresponded to an entry in a ledger that contained a detailed description of the corpse, including height, weight, hair and eye colour, and any other obvious physical

characteristics. Establishing the age of the victims was particularly
difficult, for days of continuous exposure to water and salt air made
many of them appear older than they were, and persons in their twenties
were regularly guessed to be forty or more. A full inventory of the
contents of the deceased's pockets and clothing was also made. Information such as addresses on letters, names on passports and numbers
on passage tickets was carefully recorded in order to assist in the
identification of the body. All personal property was placed in canvas
bags, each bearing a number that matched the one on the canvas tag.

By 5 p.m., the crew of the *Mackay-Bennett* had collected fifty-one
bodies. One crewman observed that

> everybody had on a lifebelt and bodies floated very high in the water in spite
> of sodden clothes and things in pockets. Apparently people had lots of time
> and discipline must have been splendid, for some had on their pyjamas, two
> or three shirts, two pairs of pants, two vests, two jackets and an overcoat. In
> some pockets a quantity of meat and biscuits was found, while in the pockets
> of most of the crew quite a lot of tobacco and matches, besides keys to the
> various lockers and stateroom doors were found.[91]

Twenty-seven bodies were embalmed, while the remaining twenty-four,
which were so badly disfigured that there was no hope of identification,
were buried at sea. It was, Hamilton recorded, a 'weird scene':

> The crescent moon is shedding a faint light on us, as the ship lies wallowing
> in the great rollers. The funeral service is conducted by the Reverend Canon
> Hind, for nearly an hour the words 'For as much as it hath pleased the
> Lord ... we therefore commit this body to the deep' are repeated, and at each
> interval comes, splash! As the weighted body plunges into the sea, there to
> sink to a depth of about two miles. Splash, splash, splash![92]

The next day, Sunday, was a day of rest and remembrance. The
recovery operation resumed on Monday, when another twenty-seven
bodies were retrieved, fifteen of which were buried at sea, 'some of them
very badly smashed and bruised', according to a crewman.[93] One of the
most battered was John Jacob Astor, though he could still be identified
by the initials 'J.J.A.' on his shirt collar. The *Mackay-Bennett* continued
to receive a steady stream of wireless messages from other ships reporting
sightings of wreckage and bodies, and for the next few days Captain
Lardner combed the area. By now, the *Mackay-Bennett*'s facilities and

manpower were under severe strain: there was no proper refrigeration equipment on board, and many of the bodies, exposed to the elements for a week, were in an advanced state of decomposition. Lardner sent a wireless message to White Star's New York office requesting assistance. A second cable-laying vessel, the *Minia*, was chartered, but its departure was delayed because it had to wait for a local factory to produce more coffins. The ship finally set sail at midnight on 22 April, carrying 150 coffins and twenty tons of ice. The ice was dumped on top of a hundred miles of cable in the *Minia*'s hold because there had not been time to remove it. Steaming east at full speed, the ship arrived at the disaster site at 12.45 a.m. on Friday, 26 April.

Meanwhile, the *Mackay-Bennett* continued the recovery effort. The busiest day was Thursday, 25 April, when eighty-seven bodies were recovered, all of which were tagged and kept on board. The following day, the ship headed for Halifax. It had recovered a total of 306 bodies, 116 of whom were buried at sea because they were deemed too badly damaged to be identified. Only first-class passengers were placed in coffins, while second- and third-class passengers were sewn up in canvas bags. The bodies of crew members were placed on the foredeck, packed in ice and covered by a tarpaulin.

At Halifax, relatives and friends of the victims anxiously awaited the *Mackay-Bennett*'s arrival, which occurred at 9.30 a.m. on 30 April. Every flag in the city was at half-mast, and many local business displayed photographs of the *Titanic* draped with black bunting in their windows. The ship docked not at its normal berth but at a coaling wharf belonging to the Royal Canadian Navy, which allowed better crowd control and privacy for the bereaved. Twenty sailors from the naval cruiser *Niobe*, which was in port for repairs, served as an impromptu guard of honour as the bodies were unloaded. The *Halifax Herald* described the scene:

> The sun shone brightly but there was nonetheless a species of darkness that could be felt from the time that the church and the fire bells began their solemn tolling, as the *Mackay-Bennett*, her afterdeck piled high with coffins and on her forward a hundred unshrouded bodies. Not more than a score of people saw the bodies carried off the ship by the pier by the bareheaded sailors who rapidly and silently transferred them to the big squad of undertakers. In less than five minutes after the first body was landed the initial

hearse in a string of twenty started off for the extemporised morgue, the
sentries at the gate for three long hours saluting with dreary monotony as
the death carriages passed ... Never before was the dockyard so carefully
guarded, soldiers on the roofs of the departmental buildings within the walls
and on every eminence patrolling with special instructions to stop every
attempt at photography. In these efforts they were successful, so it is doubtful
a single picture was taken.[94]

One member of the press did manage to breach security: Jim Hickey,
the news editor of the *Halifax Chronicle*, made arrangements with Canon
Hind for an exclusive story. As the *Mackay-Bennett* entered the harbour,
Hind tossed a bottle containing a list of the names of the dead to Hickey,
who stood on a tugboat he had hired. Hickey had the story in print
before the coroner's office had full information regarding the identity
of the bodies.

A week later, the *Minia* returned to Halifax; it had found seventeen
more bodies, including that of Charles Hays, president of the Grand
Trunk Railroad, which was subsequently returned to Montreal on his
private railway car. The *Minia*'s wireless assistant, Francis Dyke, wrote
to his mother:

> I honestly hope I shall never to come on another expedition like this as it
> is far from pleasant. The Doctor and I are sleeping in the middle of fourteen
> coffins (for the time being) they are all stacked round our quarters aft. The
> *Titanic* must have blown up when she sank, as we have picked up pieces of
> the grand staircase and most of the wreckage is from *below* deck, it must
> have been an awful explosion, too, as some of the main deck planking four
> feet thick was all split and broken off short.[95]

A third attempt to recover the bodies of the *Titanic*'s victims was
made by the Canadian Ministry of Marine and Fisheries ship *Montmagny*, which was dispatched on 3 May from Sorel, Quebec. It found
four more bodies, one of which was buried at sea and the others brought
ashore on 13 May. The *Montmagny* then put to sea again, but found
only wreckage on its second attempt. On 15 May, White Star chartered
one last vessel, the *Algerine*, to search the vicinity of the wreck; it found
only a single body, that of saloon steward James McGrady. In total, 328
bodies were recovered by the four ships, 209 of which were brought
back to Halifax.

After they were unloaded, the bodies were taken to a nearby curling rink which had been set up as a temporary morgue. The coroner worked furiously to produce the documentation necessary for issuing death certificates. In each case, the cause of death was listed as 'accidental drowning, SS *Titanic*, at sea'. After the embalmers had finished their work, the bodies were placed in canvas-enclosed cubicles where they could be viewed by relatives and friends for positive identification. One undertaker, Frank Newell, received a nasty surprise: one of the victims was his uncle, Arthur W. Newell, who had been a first-class passenger on the *Titanic*. The biggest shock, however, was reserved for Catherine Harbeck of Toledo, Ohio, who arrived to claim her husband's body but was told that she could not be Harbeck's wife because Mrs Harbeck had perished in the sinking. It was subsequently discovered that a woman named Henriette Yrois had registered as Mrs Harbeck, and that Mr Harbeck had died clutching her purse, which contained his wedding ring. Catherine took her husband's body back to Toledo, but she did not pay for a headstone to be placed on his grave.

There was also a potential for fraudulent claims to a victim's body, and the deputy registrar of deaths imposed a rigorous system of identification for all claimants in an effort to prevent any errors. Even so, the remains of travelling salesman Stanley Fox were nearly erroneously turned over to a woman who claimed to be his wife Cora. The woman turned out to be Cora's sister Lydia; her plans were foiled at the last minute by a telegram from the real Cora ordering the Halifax authorities not to release Stanley's body. It had already been placed on a train, but it was removed in Truro, Nova Scotia, and shipped directly to Cora in Rochester, New York. The reasons for Lydia's actions remain obscure, though she may have been interested in the $2100 in personal effects found on Fox's body.

Such cases were highly unusual, for most people came to Halifax simply to retrieve the remains of their loved ones. As the bodies were brought out one by one, the bereaved waited at the eastern end of the rink, where spectators normally watched the curlers. They were then escorted to the cubicles to make a positive identification. A makeshift hospital, staffed by a nurse and stocked with smelling salts and other restoratives, was set up in case the procedure proved too overwhelming. Upon payment of a first-class fare (double for express shipment), a conclusively identified body was placed in a casket and transported via

rail to wherever the victims family or friends desired; the normal re-
strictions governing transfer of bodies across the Canadian-American
border were suspended by the American consulate. The first body to be
released was John Jacob Astor's, which was claimed by his son Vincent.

The bodies were kept at the curling rink for two weeks; in that
period fifty-nine were claimed and taken away for burial elsewhere. In
the cases of the 150 that were unclaimed, a more detailed physical
description was recorded and photographs were taken. The bodies
were then prepared for burial in one of three local cemeteries: the
non-sectarian Fairview, the Roman Catholic Mount Olivet, and the
Jewish Baron de Hirsch. The first group of victims was scheduled for
interment in Fairview Cemetery on 3 May, but the night before Rabbi
Jacob Walter visited the curling rink, opened all of the coffins and
claimed that forty-four of the occupants had been of the Jewish faith.[96]
(Presumably he examined the victims to see if they had been circum-
cised.) This seemed an unusually high percentage, and the authorities
were suspicious. Upon closer examination, one of Walter's 'Jewish'
bodies was found to be that of an Irishman from Galway; several of
the others had been claimed by family members and were awaiting
collection. The authorities eventually permitted only nine of the coffins
to be assigned to the Baron de Hirsch Cemetery. Not satisfied, Walter
examined the coffins again as they sat on the ground at Fairview,
decided that ten more of the bodies were Jewish and commandeered
them. When five Protestant ministers arrived at 3 p.m. to conduct the
graveside service they were alarmed to find that ten coffins were missing.
After two days of wrangling, Walter was ordered to return the coffins
to Fairview, though by then they had been damaged in all of the
commotion, and new ones had to be purchased.

Once the religious issue had been cleared up, the interments could
proceed. A number of memorial services were conducted at St Mary's
Cathedral, which overflowed with mourners. The first service, at 9.30 a.m.,
was for four unidentified female victims, who were buried at Mount
Olivet Cemetery. (They had been identified as Catholics by the rosaries
and scapulars found on their bodies.) That afternoon, fifty-nine victims
were interred at Fairview, on a grass-covered slope overlooking the
sea. At the conclusion of the graveside service, the Royal Canadian
Regiment band played 'Nearer My God to Thee'. The following day, a

single victim was buried, a male child who had remained unidentified despite diligent efforts on the part of the local authorities and the White Star Line. Numerous local individuals and institutions had offered to pay for his burial, but the honour went to Captain Lardner and the crew of the *Mackay-Bennett*. At the memorial service, St George's Anglican Church was filled with flowers, for all of Halifax had been touched by the sad story. Six sailors from the *Mackay-Bennett* carried the tiny coffin to the hearse. The ship's crew also paid for a headstone which read, 'Erected to the Memory of an Unknown Child Whose Remains Were Recovered after the Disaster to the *Titanic*, April 15th, 1912'. For decades, the child was believed to Gösta Leonard Pålsson of Sweden, whose mother and three siblings, all of whom perished, had been on their way to Chicago to join his father. In 2002, however, the 'unknown child' was at long last identified accurately: DNA testing established that he was thirteen-month-old Eino Panula from Finland. Eino's mother Maria and four siblings also perished in the disaster.

The burials continued until 12 June 1912, when the last body, that of James McGrady, was interred at Fairview. In total, 121 of the *Titanic*'s victims were buried in Fairview, nineteen in Mount Olivet and ten in Baron de Hirsch. Each grave was marked with a simple black granite headstone, except in the few cases where family or friends paid for something more elaborate. The most impressive headstone was provided by J. Bruce Ismay for Ernest Freeman, the *Titanic*'s chief steward; the inscription read: 'He Remained at his Post of Duty, Seeking to Save Others, Regardless of his Own Life, and Went Down with the Ship'. The White Star Line donated $7500 to provide for the perpetual care of the graves. (Today, this obligation is continued by the Cunard Line, which merged with White Star in 1934.) Unless the family had specified – and paid for – an additional inscription, each headstone recorded only the victim's name, if it was known, or number, if they were unidentified, along with the date of their death, 15 April 1912. There was no mention of the *Titanic*.

A full month after the sinking, the White Star liner *Oceanic* encountered the *Titanic*'s Collapsible Lifeboat A at a position two hundred miles south east of the wreck site. It contained the bodies of three men – first-class passenger Thomson Beattie, a steward and a fireman – who had frozen to death the night of the sinking and had been set adrift after the surviving occupants of the boat had been rescued by the *Carpathia.* One of the *Oceanic's* passengers, Sir Shane Leslie, recounted the scene:

> Orders from the bridge dispatched a lifeboat with an officer and a medical officer. What followed was ghastly. Two sailors could be seen, their hair bleached by exposure to sun and salt, and a third figure wearing full evening dress flat on the benches. All three were dead and their bodies had been tossing on the Atlantic swell under the open sky ever since it had seen the greatest of ocean liners sink. The boat was full of ghastly souvenirs, such as rings and watches and even children's shoes from those who had been unrescued and had been consigned to the ocean one by one.[97]

The three bodies were sewn up in canvas bags which were weighted with steel bars. They were then buried at sea, splashing into the ocean one after another, the last of the *Titanic's* victims to be laid to rest.

2

The Best Traditions of the Sea

In the early hours of Monday 15 April 1912, a young wireless operator named David Sarnoff was listening to maritime traffic from his station at the top of the Wannamaker's building in Philadelphia when he caught bits and pieces of information regarding an accident to the White Star liner *Titanic*, the world's largest ship, which was on its way from Southampton to New York on its maiden voyage.[1] Sarnoff quickly realized that an event of major significance was unfolding and began relaying the signals to other stations. Gradually, the news spread, as additional bulletins began to come in from the Marconi Company's land station at Cape Race, Newfoundland, and from other wireless stations up and down the east coast of the United States.

These early wireless transmissions were at best fragmentary and at worst utterly garbled, as they had to be relayed multiple times to reach shore. Not surprisingly, the first press accounts of the *Titanic* disaster were speculative and often completely erroneous. Most newspapers reported on Monday 15 April that the *Titanic* had struck an iceberg but was still afloat and being towed to Halifax, Nova Scotia, by the Allen Line steamer *Virginian*, with all passengers safely transferred to other ships. The confusion seems to have resulted from the conflation by amateur radio operators of two wireless transmissions, one about the *Virginian* going to the *Titanic*'s rescue and another about a disabled oil tanker being towed ashore by another ship, the *Asian*. The *New York Journal*'s approach was typical: a headline proclaimed 'All Safe on *Titanic*', topping a story stating that the liner was under tow and that all its passengers had been transshipped to other vessels with no casualties.[2] The *Wall Street Journal* confidently editorialized that 'the gravity of the damage to the *Titanic* is apparent, but the important point is that she did not sink'.[3] Only the *New York Times* got it right; its headline summed up all of the known facts with no speculative embellishments:

'New Liner *Titanic* Hits Iceberg; Sinking by the Bow at Midnight;
Women Put Off in Life Boats; Last Wireless at 12.27 a.m. Blurred'. The
story beneath noted that the *Titanic*'s wireless transmissions ended
abruptly; although it did not explicitly state that the *Titanic* had sunk,
its ominous tone made it clear that this was the most likely scenario.[4]
But the *Times* was a rare voice of pessimism, as most of the other New
York papers took a more hopeful line.

The time difference meant that the New York press stole a march on
its London counterparts: the first stories about an accident to the *Titanic*
appeared in New York on Monday morning, but in London they had
to wait for the evening editions. '*Titanic* Sinking', reported the *Evening
Standard*: 'Wireless messages state that the leviathan is sinking by the
head, but the passengers have been taken off in lifeboats'. Similarly, the
Evening News's headline read 'The Largest Shipwreck in the World',
while the story underneath claimed that 'all passengers' had been 'safely
taken off by lifeboats' and that the 'crippled vessel' was 'steaming to
Halifax'.[5]

On both sides of the Atlantic, much of the media's confusion stemmed
from a lack of information coming from the White Star Line or from
any of the ships that had been in direct contact with the *Titanic*. In
his New York office, Phillip Franklin, vice-president of International
Mercantile Marine, the American conglomerate that owned White Star,
clung to his faith in the *Titanic*'s invincibility for as long as possible.
'We place absolute confidence in the *Titanic*. We believe that the boat
is unsinkable', he declared on Monday morning, in spite of the worrying
wireless messages that were coming in. Throughout the day, Franklin
continued to offer repeated reassurances: the ship was unsinkable; everyone was safe; there was no need for concern. When a message reporting
that the *Virginian* was towing the damaged *Titanic* into Halifax came
into the White Star offices at noon on Monday, Franklin chartered a
fast train to bring the *Titanic*'s passengers to New York. The rumours,
he assured anxious relatives, that the *Titanic* had sunk with serious loss
of life were just that, rumours; the truth would not be known until
ships that had been in direct contact with the *Titanic* came within
wireless range.

Of those ships, only the Cunard liner *Carpathia* knew the full story
of what had occurred, for it was on its way back to New York with all

of the *Titanic*'s 705 survivors. Those survivors included a devastated
J. Bruce Ismay, White Star's managing director. A few hours after Ismay
had come on board, *Carpathia*'s captain, Arthur Rostron, paid him a
visit and suggested that he send a message to White Star informing the
line of the magnitude of the disaster that had befallen the *Titanic*. On
a slip of paper, Ismay scribbled, 'Deeply regret advise you *Titanic* sunk
this morning after collision with iceberg, resulting in serious loss of life.
Full particulars later'.[6] Rostron later testified that the message was
delivered to the *Carpathia*'s wireless room on Monday morning, but it
was not received in New York until two days later.[7]

For the time being, then, the *Carpathia* was silent, and it was not
until Monday evening that the extent of the disaster became known on
shore. At 6.15 p.m., White Star received a transmission from Captain
Herbert Haddock of the *Olympic*, the *Titanic*'s sister ship, stating: '*Carpathia* reached *Titanic*'s position at daybreak. Found only boats and
wreckage. *Titanic* had foundered at about 2.20 a.m. in 41.16 north,
50.14 west. All her boats accounted for. About 675 souls saved, crew
and passengers, latterly nearly all women and children'.[8] It took three-
quarters of an hour for Franklin to regain his composure sufficiently so
that he was able to inform the press. 'Gentlemen', he announced, 'I
regret to say that the *Titanic* sank at 2.20 this morning.' In a further
briefing three hours later, he broke down and openly wept, telling
reporters that there had been a 'horrible loss of life'.[9]

When the morning editions of Tuesday 16 April confirmed that the
Titanic had indeed sunk, the news was so shocking that a Member of
Parliament, J. P. Alexander, dropped dead after reading the headlines.[10]
But even though the truth about the ship's fate was now known, con-
fusion continued to reign. Most papers had been preparing their front
pages to follow up on stories of all passengers being rescued and the
stricken liner being towed ashore when they suddenly had to shift gear.
The information they contained therefore often contradicted itself,
with new headlines affixed to stories that they did not fit. The *Daily
Chronicle*'s headlines read 'Appalling Disaster at Sea' and '1683 Not
Accounted For', but the story beneath reported that the *Titanic* was 'still
afloat, and is being towed by the *Virginian*, while the *Olympic* and the
Baltic are nearing her rapidly to take passengers from the overloaded
Parisian and *Carpathia*'.[11] The *Daily Mirror* was equally confused: one

story claimed that the ship had sunk only 'after her passengers had been saved', while another stated that 'many lives were lost'.[12] The *Daily Express* contained stories declaring that the ship was still afloat and that all passengers had been 'transferred in mid-ocean', but also on the front page was a box with the 'stop-press news' that the ship had sunk with a substantial loss of life.[13]

Confirmation of the disaster only intensified the chaos at White Star's offices in the United States and Britain, now besieged by anxious friends and relatives of the *Titanic*'s passengers and crew. In New York, the police had to be summoned to hold the increasingly hysterical crowd in check. Some people were eager to reproach White Star for its earlier confidence: whenever an employee of the line appeared in the doorway, they would shout 'You lied to us!'[14] Slowly, a list of survivors began to trickle in, transmitted by the *Carpathia*'s exhausted wireless operator Harold Cottam, with the assistance of the *Titanic*'s junior operator Harold Bride, who was suffering from frostbitten feet as a result of spending the night of 14 April atop overturned Collapsible Lifeboat B. Obeying Rostron's orders, Cottam and Bride ignored all requests from the press or from private individuals for further information; even the American President William Howard Taft's inquiry regarding his friend Major Archibald Butt (who had not survived) went unanswered. This meant that the earliest press accounts regarding the sinking of the *Titanic* were based on extremely limited information and could offer little but speculation in response to the pressing questions about the disaster. How could an iceberg sink a ship? Why had so many people died if the ship had complied with all safety regulations? Why could the iceberg not be avoided, especially given that ice was commonly found in that vicinity at that time of year? And, above all, how could a supposedly unsinkable ship sink?

Until the *Carpathia* docked in New York on 18 April, the *Titanic*'s survivors were unable to begin providing answers to these questions. In the meantime, the press did the best they could, printing survivors' names as they became known and adjusting the casualty figures with each passing day. The accurate total of around 1500 finally appeared on 18 April; by that point it was clear that some of the *Titanic*'s wealthiest and most prominent passengers had perished.

Passengers and Crew Lost and Saved

Passengers Carried

	Designed to Carry	Carried on Maiden Voyage
First Class	735	337
Second Class	674	271
Third Class	1026	712
Total	2435	1320

The Titanic also carried 892 crew members. This number does not include Thomas Andrews and the other members of the Harland & Wolff guarantee party, who were registered as second-class passengers.

Passengers and Crew Lost

	Men		Women		Children	
	Number	Percentage	Number	Percentage	Number	Percentage
First Class	118	67	4	3	1	17
Second Class	154	92	15	16	0	0
Third Class	381	84	89	54	53	67
Crew	674	78	3	14	–	–
Total	1327	80	111	26	54	50

Total Passengers and Crew Lost 1502 (68 per cent)

Passengers and Crew Saved

	Men		Women		Children	
	Number	Percentage	Number	Percentage	Number	Percentage
First Class	57	33	139	97	5	83
Second Class	14	8	79	84	23	100
Third Class	75	16	76	46	26	33
Crew	189	22	18	86	–	–
Total	335	20	314	74	54	50

Total Passengers and Crew Saved 705 (32 per cent)

These figures are based on the Board of Trade report, which is generally regarded as the most accurate accounting. See Daniel Allen Butler, 'Unsinkable': *The Full Story of RMS Titanic* (Mechanicsburg, PA: Stackpole Books, 1998), pp. 238–39. For a full list of those saved see Appendix 1, below, pp. 291–319.

Also on the 18th, the first stories appeared indicating that the *Titanic* had not carried sufficient lifeboats for all its passengers and crew. This fact had been ferreted out by an enterprising reporter from the *New York Times*, who had discovered that the *Olympic* carried only twenty boats, with a total capacity of 1180, on a ship with a capacity of over 3300 passengers and crew. It was likely that the *Titanic* had carried the same number, since the two ships were virtually identical. The British press was quick to pick up on these accusations. 'Why were there only twenty lifeboats for 2207 people on board the ill-fated *Titanic*?' asked the *Daily Mirror* on its front page on 19 April. The insufficient number of lifeboats gave the press a piece of solid information as well as a potential explanation for the massive loss of the life that the disaster had caused. Numerous editorials appeared over the next several days condemning the British government for antiquated regulations that had allowed such an appalling tragedy to occur.[15] Still, there was plenty of room for speculation, and accounts of the collision and its aftermath made frequent use of the conditional tense. Lead stories were supplemented with interviews with experts about icebergs, biographical information about Captain Edward J. Smith and some of the more notable passengers, and accounts of previous maritime disasters. Some papers devoted considerable space to blaming Franklin and White Star for misleading the press and the public into thinking that the *Titanic* was safe, while others expressed righteous indignation and voiced demands that measures be taken to prevent such an appalling calamity from occurring in the future.[16] Details about the sinking itself, however, were still extremely scanty.

In the first days after the sinking, the press was forced to make a very small amount of information stretch a long way. Only a few scraps of information offered anything beyond the bare facts of the time and place of the sinking and the number of survivors. One was the line in the *Olympic*'s wireless message stating that the survivors were 'nearly all women and children'. Another was that the names of a number of wealthy and socially prominent passengers were missing from the survivors list. From these tiny foundations would be constructed a mighty edifice: the story of the *Titanic* that is still in many respects with us today. 'It is clear', declared the *Daily Graphic* on 17 April, 'from the fact that women and children form by far the greater majority of the saved, that in this dire emergency the imperilled rose to supreme heights of courage and devotion. Millionaires and steerage emigrant alike were called up: alike they have presented us with that most inspiring of all spectacles – the inherent nobility of mankind.' [17] The *Evening News* announced on 16 April that 'the old rule of the sea has been observed to the letter, and one more record of splendid heroism and self-control has been added to a roll already rich in such glories'.[18] Both of these quotations, and many other virtually identical ones, appeared prior to the arrival of the *Carpathia*, which meant that very little was known at the time about what had actually occurred on the night of the sinking. But the press was determined to tell a story that, although not altogether divorced from reality, often emphasized what ought to have happened rather than what actually did. And it was a story that proved extremely resilient even when facts that directly contradicted it began to emerge.

Once the *Carpathia* docked on 18 April, the press could have opted to retreat from its earlier claims and to construct a more realistic version of events, for it turned out that women had died and first-class passengers had survived in considerably greater numbers than the initial reports had suggested. Moreover, some survivors told stories of the *Titanic*'s final moments – stories of male passengers rushing the lifeboats and of officers using revolvers to hold them back, of men putting on women's clothes and trying to sneak into boats – that did not fit with the vision of chivalry and stoicism that had been constructed over the previous several days. There was a moment, as the newspapers for 19 April were being prepared, that reporters and editors could have chosen to stress the less noble aspects of the story that were emerging from the survivors' accounts, which frequently emphasized the chaos, the terror and the panic that had increased as the night wore on. But they did not make that choice; instead they carefully selected the parts of the accounts that fitted with the vision of first-class men standing calmly aside while women and children of all classes were loaded into lifeboats. Such an appalling calamity as the sinking of the *Titanic* required an explanation and a meaning; the acceptance of chaos and random acts of destruction that would come to characterize western culture after two devastating world wars was not yet in place. Beginning on 20 April, the sinking of the *Titanic* departed – at least partially – from the realm of documented history and passed into a realm of myth.

The myth of the *Titanic* contained three significant aspects. First, it emphasized that the 'law of the sea' – 'women and children first' – had universally prevailed. The male passengers had done their duty by standing quietly and calmly aside while their wives, mothers, sisters and female friends were placed in the lifeboats. They had assisted when they saw an opportunity or when asked to do so by a crewman, but their heroism rested primarily on the way in which they stoically faced their own fate.[19] 'One supreme fact', claimed the *Daily Chronicle* on 17 April, 'stands out in the story of this wreck which makes for the glory of Anglo-Saxon manhood, and that is that out of the nearly 800 passengers saved only seventy-nine were men, the rest women and children.'[20] This claim would turn out to be patently false: in fact more men were saved from the *Titanic* than women, largely because 189 of the 207 crew members who survived were male.[21] But that did not matter, for the 'law of the sea' had prevailed. 'It is good to know that the women and children were first to leave the doomed vessel', declared the *Daily Mirror*. 'The best traditions of the sea were observed.'[22] The *Daily Mail* concurred:

> For what do we see from such testimony as the broken fragments of wireless messages have vouchsafed to us? The roll of survivors is mainly a list of the names of women and children. Those who are saved are not the strong and able-bodied but the weak and the dependent ... The captains of industry, the lords of money, the men of letters, the hard-mouthed seamen have gone quietly to their doom in twelve thousand feet of blue water, in order that the women whose lives were in their care might come perchance to a haven of safety.[23]

Such accounts were extremely influential in shaping views of the disaster beyond the press. Prime Minister Herbert Asquith was clearly convinced by them; in a speech to the House of Commons, he expressed his 'admiration that the best traditions of the sea seem to have been observed in the willing sacrifices which were offered to give the first chance of safety to those least able to help themselves'.[24] Thus, as initially defined by the press and refined in subsequent interpretations of the disaster, 'women and children first' became a – and perhaps *the* – central component of the myth of the *Titanic*.

Secondly, the myth of the *Titanic* emphasized not only 'manly' but 'gentlemanly' conduct, associating heroism with class as well as gender. In virtually every instance that was described afterwards, the kind of manly virtue described above was displayed by passengers travelling first class. Second and third class, meanwhile, were all but ignored, except in the instances where their women and children were permitted to serve as recipients of the *noblesse oblige* of the first-class men who stood aside while they entered the lifeboats. Upper-class men, the myth claimed, had sacrificed themselves so that socially inferior women and children could live.[25] Again, this assertion was ultimately proven false, as a much higher percentage of first-class passengers survived than second- or third-class ones. Again, the truth made little difference in the way that the myth of the *Titanic* took shape.

There were, to be sure, frequent claims that the *Titanic* had levelled social distinctions, since all men, no matter what their class, had died as equals. 'All on board the doomed liner, from the millionaire to the poorest deck hand, were knit together and made equals by courage which neither bent nor broke in the face of ... catastrophe', asserted the *Daily Chronicle*.[26] The inherent assumption in such claims, however, was that it was only *upper*-class men who had made a noble sacrifice, for they were the ones who had 'given up' their rightful places in the boats. 'Death levels all', claimed the *Daily Mirror* in pointing out that the American millionaire John Jacob Astor, the wealthiest man on the ship, had 'gone to his death just as though he were the poorest steerage passenger'.[27] But it is Astor's demise that is being lamented here, and his self-sacrifice that is being celebrated, not that of the 'poorest steerage passenger'.

Thirdly, the myth of *Titanic* featured a racial component. If almost all the heroes were upper-class men, they were also upper-class white men of American or British origin, 'Anglo-Saxons' in the contemporary parlance. The *Daily Mirror* claimed that 'women and children first' was not only the 'law of the sea' but the 'White Man's law'.[28] The *Daily Express*, meanwhile, stated that 'remarkable heroism was displayed by the great majority of men on board the ship, most of whom went to their death with a calmness and stoicism fully in accord with the traditions of the Saxon race'.[29] The *Titanic*, asserted the *Daily Mail*, proved 'the absolute insignificance of tremendous danger in the presence of the calm courage of the white man'.[30] To be foreign on board the *Titanic*, meanwhile, was to be a coward: if there were lapses in discipline, they were explained by the fact that the *Titanic*'s passengers and crew were 'not all Anglo-Saxon'.[31] Invariably, men who sneaked into lifeboats dressed as women or jumped in when the officers were not looking were described as 'Italians' or 'Chinese'.[32] Such claims were worse than fallacious; they were utterly ludicrous and based on not even the slenderest basis of factual information. In no other aspect of the myth of the *Titanic* did preconception and prejudice play such a dominant role.

All of this adds up to a story that was intended to bolster the status of the predominant gender, class and racial hierarchies in Britain. British accounts of the disaster were remarkably uniform in their reluctance to challenged established hierarchies. The only real dissent came from two members of the intelligentsia, Joseph Conrad and George Bernard Shaw.* In May 1912 Conrad published an essay entitled 'Some Reflections on the Loss of the *Titanic*' in the *English Review*. The essay argued that the commercial aspirations of the *Titanic*'s owners and builders had overreached their shipbuilding capabilities, and that the sheer size of the *Titanic* had not been its strength but its weakness, as its steel plates had not been as proportionately strong as they would have been in a smaller vessel. He also had harsh words for the regulations that had permitted the insufficient number of lifeboats. Conrad, however, refused to criticize the *Titanic*'s captain and crew, perhaps a lingering loyalty from his own days at sea. The ship's course and speed involved a risk, he admitted, but seafaring was an inherently risky enterprise, and even the best seamen found themselves in unavoidable difficulties on occasion.

Shaw, in contrast, allowed the *Titanic*'s crew no such quarter. His piece 'Some Unmentioned Morals' appeared in the *Daily News and Leader* on 14 May; in it he accused the press and public of failing to confront the real reasons for the tragedy and of promoting false heroism based upon 'outrageous romantic lying'. In a tone dripping with sarcasm, he questioned whether the rule of 'women and children first' had truly been obeyed: one lifeboat, he pointed out, had ten men in it and only two women. Whether Captain Smith had behaved nobly after the collision was not the key issue; the fact that he had driven his ship full speed into an ice field about which he had received repeated warnings was. 'Writers who had never heard of Captain Smith to that hour wrote of him as they would hardly write of Nelson', Shaw snorted. And

* See Appendix 2, below, pp. 321–35.

the band's 'heroism' in playing until the end had deterred many passengers from boarding lifeboats until it was too late because the music
had lulled them into a false sense of security.

Conrad and Shaw said things about the disaster that no other writers
in the British press did; Shaw's essay in particular is a unique blast of
invective in a hagiographic arena. It is worth noting that neither author
was of English descent: Shaw was Irish and Conrad was born in Poland
and became a naturalized English citizen only as an adult. Their origins
seem to have given them a perspective on the disaster that many Britons
could not share. In any event, their opinions had little impact on popular
perceptions, which remained stolidly in favour of the conventional,
heroic version of the *Titanic* story. Shaw admitted as much when he
wrote that the romantic view of the sinking that had been presented in
the press was precisely what the public believed and wanted to hear:
'Did the Press really represent the public? I am afraid it did. Churchmen
and statesmen took much the same tone ... It seems to me that when
deeply moved men should speak the truth. The English nation appears
to take precisely the contrary view'.[33]

The uniformity of *Titanic* narratives in Britain provides a contrast to
nature of the myth, or more accurately myths, of the *Titanic* that were
being formulated in the United States at the same time. To be sure, a
conventional narrative also developed in America that featured as its
primary motif 'a tale of first-cabin male heroism in which the men ...
willingly engaged in chivalric self-sacrifice'.[34] The best exemplars of this
type of heroism were John Jacob Astor and Benjamin Guggenheim,
both of whom were lionized after the sinking.

Born in Rhinebeck, New York, in 1864, John Jacob Astor IV was a
member of one of the wealthiest and most prominent families in
America. His great grandfather and namesake, who had arrived in the
United States from Schwabia in 1783, amassed a fortune in the fur trade,
with which he purchased vast amounts of real estate in New York City.
By 1912 the family's holdings included the elite Waldorf-Astoria Hotel,
but also some of the city's most notorious slums. The Astors had a
reputation for conducting their business with a certain ruthlessness, and
John Jacob IV lived up to it. 'He knew what he wanted and how to get
it', was the epitaph pinned on him by his family lawyer.[35] Immensely
wealthy through little effort of his own, Astor kept eighteen cars in the

garage of his Newport mansion. His attitude towards money was that of a man who had never lacked for it: he once remarked that 'a man who has a million dollars is almost as well off as if he were wealthy'. He could be vain. During the Spanish-American War he had raised a volunteer regiment and appointed himself its colonel; thereafter he preferred to be addressed by his 'rank' and frequently wore his uniform to political functions. But Astor also had an appealingly eccentric side. An inveterate tinkerer and inventor, he held patents on a bicycle brake, a pneumatic road construction machine and a storage battery, and he had written a science fiction novel entitled *A Journey in Other Worlds* about an attempt to straighten the earth's axis and thereby create perpetual springtime.[36]

Astor's reputation was shaky as he boarded the *Titanic* in Cherbourg on the evening of 10 April 1912. His decision three years earlier to divorce his wife of eighteen years so that he could marry Madeleine Force, who was more than thirty years his junior, had caused a public scandal that led to the couple being ostracised by their former friends. They had difficulty finding a clergyman willing to perform the wedding ceremony, which had not taken place until December 1911. (Astor was forced to offer a $1000 incentive to the reluctant pastor.) As part of a prenuptial agreement, Madeleine received $1,695,000 at the time of the marriage. The agreement also stipulated that, in the event of Astor's death, she would receive a $5 million trust fund and would continue to have the use of Astor's mansion on Fifth Avenue in New York and Beechwood Cottage in Newport, Rhode Island. (The agreement further stated that Madeleine would forfeit everything if she were to remarry, which she did in 1918.)

The newly-weds had spent the remainder of the winter abroad, hoping that the scandal would dissipate, but now it was time to return home. Tongues were still wagging, however, because Madeleine was visibly pregnant even though she had only been married for four months. The Astors were accompanied on the *Titanic* by John Jacob's manservant Victor Robbins, Madeleine's maid Rosalie Bidois and private nurse Caroline Louise Endres, and the couple's pet airedale Kitty. They occupied cabins C62 and 64, for which they paid £224 10s. 6d. The Astors seem to have kept a relatively low profile during the voyage, though John Jacob did make a significant purchase while on board. When the

Titanic reached Queenstown on the morning of 11 April, the ship was surrounded by a flotilla of small boats carrying vendors hawking all sorts of goods. Several of them were permitted to come on board, and the after Promenade Deck was transformed into an open-air market for Irish lace, linen and porcelain. Astor was so enamoured of a lace jacket that he paid $800 in cash for it.

After the collision with the iceberg, Astor left his suite and went up to the boat deck to investigate. He soon returned and informed Madeleine that the ship had struck some ice, but the damage did not appear to be serious. Not long afterwards, however, a steward informed them that all women should put on their lifebelts and go up on deck. Still not particularly alarmed, Madeleine took her time dressing. When she at last emerged from her cabin, she was wearing a black broadtail coat with sable trim, a diamond necklace and a fur muff. The Astors made their way to the A Deck foyer, where they encountered Captain Smith coming down the stairs. Astor spoke to him in hushed tones. Smith was calm, but when Astor returned to Madeleine, he told her and a group of other passengers who were standing nearby to put on their lifejackets. Some time later, the Astors were seen in the gymnasium sitting side by side on the mechanical horses. Astor was using his penknife to slice open a lifejacket in order to show Madeleine what was inside, presumably in an effort to reassure her. (Once the news of the disaster hit the press, accounts of this scene were printed in countless newspapers around the world.)

At 1.45 a.m. the Astors were among the group of passengers waiting to board Lifeboat 4. This boat had been a source of trouble for some time. At around 12.30 a.m., Captain Smith suggested to Second Officer Charles Lightoller that it be lowered to the Promenade Deck in order to make it easier for the passengers to get in. Lightoller duly sent the passengers below, but both he and the captain had forgotten that on the *Titanic*, unlike on the *Olympic*, the forward Promenade Deck was enclosed by windows. It was a passenger, Hugh Woolner, who reminded them: 'Haven't you forgotten, sir, that all those glass windows are closed?'

'By God, you're right!' Lightoller exclaimed. 'Call those people back.' The passengers duly returned to the boat deck, but by then Boat 4 had already been lowered to the Promenade Deck. Lightoller decided it would be easier to open the windows than to raise the boat again, so

the passengers were sent below for a second time. Exasperated by all of
the trooping up and down the stairs, Marion Thayer complained, 'Tell
us where to go and we will follow. You ordered us up here and now
you are taking us back'.[37]

Finally, the windows were opened, making it possible to begin loading
the boat. Astor helped Madeleine climb up the stack of deck chairs that
had been positioned to act as a makeshift set of stairs to allow the
passengers to climb over the window sills. 'Get into the lifeboat to please
me', he told her. Once she was safely on board, he turned to Lightoller
and asked if he could follow her, explaining that she was 'in delicate
condition'.

'No, sir', Lightoller replied, 'no men are allowed in these boats until
the women are loaded first.'

'Well, what boat is it?'

'Boat 4, sir.'

Lightoller was convinced that Astor wanted the number of the boat
so that he could lodge a complaint with the White Star Line later. Astor
made no further protests, however, and turned back to Madeleine and
told her, 'The sea is calm. You'll be all right. You're in good hands. I'll
meet you in the morning'. He handed her his gloves, and then stepped
away from the rail and made his way back up to the boat deck.[38]

That was the last confirmed sighting of Astor. Dr Washington Dodge
claimed to have seen him and Major Archibald Butt, aide to the American President William Howard Taft, standing side by side on the
bridge as the ship went down. Dodge was at least a half a mile away in
Lifeboat 13 at the time. The precise manner in which Astor met his
death is unknown, though the mangled condition of his body when it
was recovered suggested that he may have been one of those swimmers
who was crushed by a falling funnel as the *Titanic* underwent its
death throes. Astor's body could only be identified by the initials 'JJA'
on the collar of his shirt. He wore a gold watch and gold-and-diamond
cufflinks; in his pockets was over £200 and more than $2000. On
14 August 1912, four months to the day after the *Titanic* struck the
iceberg, Madeleine gave birth to John Jacob Astor VI.[39]

Prior to the *Titanic* disaster, Astor had not been a popular man; one
press account referred to him as 'the world's greatest monument to
unearned increment'.[40] After the sinking, however, views of Astor altered

dramatically. Although the precise nature of his death was unknown, the American press concurred, as the *St Louis Post-Dispatch* put it, that he had displayed 'wonderful fortitude and bravery'. A story circulated that, when Lightoller objected to ten-year-old William Carter Jr getting into Lifeboat 4, Astor had placed a girl's hat on his head and said, 'Now he's a girl, and he can go'.[41] Madeleine added to the heroic myths surrounding Astor by claiming that she saw Kitty running around the deck in the *Titanic*'s final moments, which she assumed was because her husband had gone to the kennel and released the dogs in order to give them a fighting chance. Other survivors bragged that Astor had personally assisted them as they boarded the lifeboats. 'Now when the name of Astor is mentioned', asserted the *Denver Post*, 'it will be the John Jacob Astor who went down with the *Titanic* that will first come to mind; not the Astor who made the great fortune, not the Astor who added to its greatness, but John Jacob Astor, the hero.'[42]

Astor's previous misconduct was not entirely forgotten, but it was widely believed that his heroic conduct during the sinking of the *Titanic* had redeemed him. When an Episcopal minister from Philadelphia, George Chalmers Richmond, preached that Astor's fate had been deserved due to his indulgence in 'personal pleasures' and 'sensual delights', the *Washington Post* leapt to his defence: 'Colonel Astor died like a brave man. He showed himself a true American ... It is not for Dr Richmond, or anyone else, to judge this man'. The *Religious Telescope* admitted that Astor had once been dismissed as a 'man without principle', but claimed that his behaviour during the disaster proved that 'there is a slumbering nobility in the heart of every man which but awaits the supreme occasion to be called forth'.[43]

Similarly elevated after the disaster was Benjamin Guggenheim, another plutocrat from one of America's wealthiest and most prominent families. Although he was not under a cloud of scandal as Astor was in 1912, Guggenheim was a notorious playboy who was travelling on the *Titanic* with his mistress, the French singer Leontine Aubart, while his wife and three daughters were at home in New York. Guggenheim had inherited an immense sum of money from his father, the mining magnate Meyer Guggenheim, but not his father's business acumen. He squandered over $8 million on bad investments and left his children only $450,000 each. In 1894 he had married Floretta Seligman, the daughter of a prominent New York City banker; the couple gradually became estranged and by 1912 Guggenheim was spending much of his time in Paris. In April, however, his business interests demanded his presence in New York. Guggenheim initially booked passage on the *Lusitania*, but transferred to the *Titanic* when the former ship was idled for repairs. He boarded in Cherbourg, along with Madame Aubart, her maid Emma Sägesser, his valet Victor Giglio and his chauffeur René Pernot.

After the sinking, Steward Henry Etches sought out Mrs Guggenheim at the St Regis Hotel (which ironically was owned by John Jacob Astor) and delivered an account of the way in which her husband had met his end. He reported that, following the collision, he had gone to Guggenheim's cabin, awakened him and told him to get dressed. He insisted that Guggenheim put on his lifejacket; at first, Guggenheim complained that it hurt his back, but after Etches made a few adjustments it felt better. Etches then demanded that Guggenheim wear a heavy sweater over his lifejacket before he went up on deck. He and Victor Giglio then left the cabin together. When they reached the boat deck, they first escorted Madame Aubart and Emma Sägesser to a lifeboat and then turned to rendering whatever assistance they could. Etches claimed that he saw them 'going from one lifeboat to another, helping the women and children. Mr Guggenheim would shout out, "Women first!" and he was of great assistance to the officers'. The next time Etches encountered Guggenheim and Giglio was about three-quarters of an hour later, at around 1.30 a.m. He was surprised to see them dressed in formal evening wear, without their lifejackets. Etches asked Guggenheim what they were doing. 'We've dressed up in our best', Guggenheim replied, 'and are prepared to go down like gentlemen.' 44 He continued:

> I think there is grave doubt that the men will get off. I am willing to remain and play the man's game if there are not enough boats for more than the women and children. I won't die here like a beast. Tell my wife ... I played the game out straight and to the end. No woman shall be left aboard this ship because Ben Guggenheim was a coward.45

That was the last that Etches saw of him; other survivor accounts claimed that Guggenheim and Giglio sat in chairs on the deck, sipping brandy and smoking cigars, as the ship went down. Guggenheim's body was never found; his six brothers publicly stated that there would be an extensive search using not only small steamships but aeroplanes as well, although it is unclear whether this was actually conducted.

Much like John Jacob Astor, Guggenheim was singled out for praise after the disaster. Etches's account of his demise appeared in countless newspapers around the world. Another, unverified story claimed that he, along with Astor and several other first-class male passengers, had held an impromptu conference on deck that culminated in a declaration that no man would enter a lifeboat 'until every woman and child is safe'. The *Baltimore Sun* declared that the 'chivalry and respect for the women and children' displayed by Guggenheim and his fellow millionaires 'showed that Anglo-Saxon men are made right'. (In adhering to contemporary racial stereotypes this writer ignored the fact that Guggenheim was Jewish.) Some writers acknowledged that Guggenheim's reputation had been something less than sterling prior to the disaster, but argued that his noble conduct had redeemed him. 'I did not guess your greatness', wrote the author and philosopher Elbert Hubbard. However he had been perceived previously, Guggenheim was now solidly on what the *Philadelphia North American* referred to as 'a roll of nobility that history will preserve'.[46]

In the United States, a standard account therefore emerged that told a similar story of upper-class male heroism to the one that emerged simultaneously in Britain. But, at the same time, America saw the development of other, often competing and conflicting versions that brought the sinking of the *Titanic* into a host of contemporary debates on gender, class and racial issues. In the United States, the meaning of the *Titanic* disaster was contested terrain. Supporters of women's suffrage protested the use of the sinking to promote the notion that men were women's natural protectors. Male chivalry, they argued, had done nothing to prevent the disaster, only to mitigate its effects. It would have been 'gross injustice', wrote one suffragist, 'to decree that the women, who have no voice in making and enforcing law on land or sea, should be left aboard a sinking ship, victims of man's cupidity'. Other suffragists praised the few women who had chosen to stay with their husbands rather than board a lifeboat. 'We honor the women who waive this sex advantage and choose to die like brave and conscientious human beings', wrote Charlotte Perkins Gilman.[47]

Nor did the class aspect of the conventional *Titanic* myth go unchallenged in America. Socialists and radical labour activists saw the disaster as yet another example of the oppression suffered by the working classes at the hands of the wealthy and powerful. Speaking to striking coal miners in West Virginia, Mother Jones gave her version of the story:

> I have been reading of the *Titanic* when she went down ... The big guns wanted to save themselves, and the fellows that were guiding below took up a club and said we will save our people. And then the papers came out and said those millionaires tried to save the women. Oh, Lord, why don't they give up their millions if they want to save the women and children? Why do they rob them of home, why do they rob millions of women to fill the hell-holes of capitalism? [48]

Jones and other radical critics turned the conventional myth of the *Titanic* on its head by claiming that it was third class not first who had been the heroes. The statistics backed them up: 63 per cent of first class survived but only 25 per cent of third.

Finally, African-Americans attacked the assumption of Anglo-Saxon supremacy that was a key element of the *Titanic* myth. Even though there had been no African-Americans on the ship, the black press quickly noted the racist implications of much of what was being written about Saxon heroism. When an apocryphal story surfaced about a black stoker who had tried to steal wireless operator Jack Phillips's lifejacket, the *Philadelphia Tribune* commented, 'We thought it would be strange if there were no coloured persons aboard the fated ship. Of course, he had to be made to appear in the light of a dastard'.[49] The great blues musician Hudie 'Leadbelly' Ledbetter began performing a song entitled 'Titanic' in 1912; in it he sang the lines, 'Jack Johnson want to get on board, / Captain said "I ain't haulin' no coal."' Johnson was the heavyweight boxing champion of the world at the time, and the lines were based on a real-life incident in which he had been denied a transatlantic passage because of his colour. Here, however, Ledbetter turns Johnson's defeat into an ironic triumph, for the captain's racism saves his life. In one version of the song Ledbetter took this theme even further, celebrating the absence of any African-Americans among the victims of the sinking: 'Black man oughta shout for joy, / Never lost a girl or either a boy'.[50]

These examples represent only some of the reactions to the *Titanic* disaster in the years immediately after the sinking. They provide a sharp contrast to what occurred in Britain, where the standard story was accepted and embraced with virtually no dissent. Only occasionally can an exception be found. On 19 April 1912, an editorial entitled 'Women First!' appeared in the *Daily Mail*. The author attempted to use the disaster to overturn suffragist's demands for equality between the sexes:

> It has become an integral part of the creed of Feminism to hold man in contempt. The whole body of Feminist literature reeks with disrespect for him. His selfishness, his 'intolerable airs of superiority', and his arrogant dominance on the one hand, and woman's self-sacrifice, her subjugation, her helotry on the other hand – these are the twin pillars of the Feminist creed. Man's chivalry to woman is not only denied as a fact; the sentiment itself is derided. Well, man has returned a titanic answer to those taunts.[51]

Three days later, the suffragist Lady Laura Aberconway responded in a long letter that rejected the editorial's arguments. 'Noble as was their devotion', she wrote, 'it is in my opinion a sacrifice which ought not to be demanded of the male sex nor accepted by the female ... An equal chance of life is all that women in danger should ask or take from men.' Lady Aberconway's letter drew a barrage of reactions. A few defended her; Alice Mary Dawson wrote that 'as a woman Suffragist, I claim the right equally with men to be regarded as a citizen of the Empire'. Most, however, disagreed. 'It is the privilege and duty of man to protect the weak', wrote one correspondent, while another declared that it was one thing for her to express such ideas 'from the calm shelter of her study table', but an open question 'whether she would still have maintained these views had she been on board the *Titanic*'. Another letter-writer, Ella Hepworth Dixon, declared that 'the imperishable heroes who went down to their graves in the sea and let the womenfolk be rowed away did so because civilised white people save the weakest first'.[52] This exchange reflected a variety of points of view about what the *Titanic* disaster had to say about gender roles, but it is important to note that the majority of opinions expressed took a conservative line, and that it is the only such debate that took place in the mainstream British press at the time.

Far more typical of British responses to the sinking of the *Titanic* was a volume of poetry on the disaster, edited by the Reverend Charles

F. Forshaw, that appeared in mid 1912. The volume, entitled *Poetical Tributes on the Loss of the RMS Titanic*, collected more than two hundred poems from all over Britain written by amateur and professional authors. Some of them were published here for the first time, while others had previously appeared in newspapers and other venues. In the introduction, Forshaw wrote:

> In addition to the effusions of minor poets, in this volume greater names are not unrepresented. Individual mention would perhaps be invidious; suffice it to say that here are poems written by well-known littérateurs of both sexes; learned members of the professions; university dons; pedagogues, ranging from the distinguished masters – past or present – of our chief public schools down to the village dominie; clerks; railway hands; tram conductors; postmen; shopkeepers; factory hands, and ploughboys; by venerable age; stalwart manhood; gracious womanhood, and school children of tender years.[53]

Despite the diversity of their authors, what is remarkable about these poems is their consistency. The same themes appear again and again: the chivalry of the crew and the upper-class male passengers; their adherence to duty in the most appalling circumstances; and the transitory nature of death as a moment of passage from earth to the afterlife for those who acted nobly. Gender and class are constant factors in the definitions of heroic conduct, as are national identity and race, while the heroes are always male, gentlemanly and Anglo-Saxon. In a typical example, the Reverend W. E. Vernon Yonge:

> 'To quarters men! Be smart and man the boats.
> God's Will be done! Women and children first.'
> So may it ever be. Tis manhood's right
> To give, and women's guerdon to receive.
> So be it England! In our social wrongs
> Let the strong bear the burden of the weak –
> 'Noblesse oblige!' Women and children first!
> Oh! deem not Ancient Chivalry be dead!
> E'en in a selfish and luxurious age
> Its spirit lives. 'Quit you like men, be strong.'
> Young England! Manhood calls protect your girls!
> Be true 'Knights Errant', and respect the flower
> Of womanhood and maiden purity![54]

The contrast between British and American interpretations of the *Titanic* disaster is further revealed by the distinction between the official inquiries into the disaster that took place in each country. The American inquiry began on 19 April, the day after the *Carpathia* docked. It was convened by the United States Senate and chaired by Senator William Alden Smith of Michigan. Smith inherently distrusted large corporations, which he felt all too often put profit ahead of the public interest; in his view the sinking of the *Titanic* was yet another product of corporate greed. Immediately upon the *Carpathia*'s arrival in New York, he came on board and informed J. Bruce Ismay that he would be expected to appear before his panel the following morning.[55] Having little choice, Ismay agreed, and was waiting in the Waldorf-Astoria Hotel's East Room when Smith opened the hearing at 10.30 a.m.[56] When Smith asked him to describe the night of the sinking, Ismay's reply was brief: 'I was in bed myself, asleep, when the accident happened. The ship sank, I am told, at two-twenty. That, sir, is all I think I can tell you'.[57] Smith was not content with this answer, and he launched into a long and gruelling cross-examination during which Ismay rapidly became aware that he was being made into a scapegoat for the disaster.

For the next four weeks, the inquiry continued in a similar vein. Eighty-two witnesses were called, including passengers, members of the crew and experts on various subjects. Second Officer Charles Lightoller, the highest-ranking surviving officer, did his best to establish that the sinking had been the unfortunate result of an unavoidable accident; he later dismissed the inquiry as a complete farce, 'wherein all the traditions and customs of the sea were continuously and persistently flouted'.[58] Smith, however, would not be dissuaded from his conviction that negligence was to blame. Only occasionally were the witnesses able to get the better of him, such as when Fifth Officer Harold Lowe, in response to a question about what icebergs were made of, laconically and sardonically replied, 'Ice'. Most of the time, however, Smith held the upper hand. He conducted almost all of the interrogations himself, uncovering a wealth of information about the disaster that has been invaluable to *Titanic* historians ever since.

In the end, though, Smith could find no clear proof of negligence under existing maritime laws, and he reluctantly was forced to concede that the sinking had been an 'Act of God'. But that does not mean that he let everyone off scot-free. In the summary of his report, Smith blamed the *Titanic*'s captain for going too fast and for taking inadequate precautions to deal with the ice that he knew was in the vicinity. In the future, he argued, ships should be made to slow down when entering areas of known ice and to post extra lookouts. There should be strict procedures for delivering navigational messages to the bridge and for posting them once they got there. Ships should be made to carry enough lifeboats for every person on board. And all ships that were equipped with wireless should be required to monitor it twenty-four hours a day.

Most of these conclusions were unassailable, but British opinion found plenty to criticize about Smith's inquiry. It was not so much the content of the proceedings that offended but the tone. They saw Smith as a bullying, bombastic bumpkin, and they lambasted his effrontery at detaining British subjects for his own political ends.[59] On London's music-hall stages, he came to be nicknamed 'Watertight', a reference to an unfortunate moment in Lightoller's testimony when Smith had asked if anyone could have survived by taking refuge in one of the *Titanic*'s watertight compartments.[60] One performer sang a mocking air to the tune of 'Lalago Potts':

> I'm Senator Smith of the USA,
> Senator Smith, that's me!
> A big bug in the enquiry way,
> Senator Smith, that's me!
> You're fixed right up if you infer
> I'm a cuss of a cast-iron character.
> When I says that a thing has got ter be,
> That thing's as good as done, d'yer see?
> I'm going to ask questions and find out some
> If I sit right here till kingdom come –
> That's me!
> Senator Smith of the USA.[61]

The British press was equally unfavourable towards Smith. Inquiries into maritime disasters were highly technical affairs, they asserted, and were best left to those with professional expertise, not a man who was ignorant 'in shipping matters or in law'.[62] 'The Senate Committee is not a body of experts', complained the *Daily Mail*, 'whose findings will carry universal assent ... It has no technical knowledge, and its proceedings ... show a want of familiarity with nautical matters and with the sea.'[63] The *Evening Standard* concurred, declaring that 'many of the questions ... suggest that the tribunal is as expert in investigating marine matters as a country magistrate's bench might have been'.[64] The *Daily Express* was most exercised, dubbing Smith 'a backwoodsman from Michigan', a state which the paper claimed was 'populated by kangaroos and by cowboys with an intimate acquaintance of prairie schooners as the only kind of boat'.[65] (This despite the presence of the Great Lakes.) The paper asserted that Smith's inquiry

> may have an effect positively injurious to judicial examination and the very opposite of that intended. A little more of this biased investigation, and a little more posturing by Senator Smith ... who is obviously seeking the limelight for his own interests, will swing public sympathy so heavily to the side of Mr Bruce Ismay and the White Star Line, as to create an unjudicial atmosphere.[66]

The inquiry planned by the Board of Trade, the British press agreed, would be a far more sober and constructive affair. 'We are sure that better results will be obtained by ... deliberate means than by the rather hurried methods of a not quite satisfactory body in America', declared the *Daily Chronicle*.[67]

More deliberate it clearly was. The British inquiry, unlike its American counterpart, was constituted as a court of law with full judicial powers. Its preliminary proceedings began on 29 April, when the *Titanic*'s surviving crewmen were taken from the liner *Lapland*, on which they had finally been allowed to return home, to a quarantine site so that their sworn statements could be taken down. The Board of Trade then reviewed these statements and decided which crewmen would be called upon to testify. The actual inquiry began on 3 May, in the Scottish Drill Hall near Buckingham Gate in London.

Presiding over the proceedings was John Charles Bingham, Baron Mersey of Toxteth, the Commissioner of Wrecks. Lord Mersey had a solid reputation as a tough inquisitor, first earned in 1896 when he had headed the inquiry into the Jameson Raid (though his critics noted that in the end Jameson had been allowed to wriggle off the hook).[68] From the start, however, the British inquiry faced a significant conflict of interest. It was being carried out under the auspices of the Board of Trade, the same Board of Trade that had allowed the *Titanic* to sail under outdated regulations with insufficient lifeboats. Lightoller was no more impressed by this inquiry than he had been by Smith's. 'A washing of dirty linen', he later wrote, 'would help no one. The Board of Trade had passed that ship as in all respects fit for the sea ... Now the Board of Trade was holding an inquiry into the loss of that ship – hence the whitewash brush.' [69] This was a harsh judgement, and one that was not entirely fair. The inquiry lasted for eight weeks, calling ninety-six witnesses and asking more than 25,000 questions. It was the longest court of inquiry ever held in Britain, and it cost nearly £20,000. (The American inquiry had cost only £1360.)

In the inquiry's findings, delivered on 30 June, Mersey concluded that the loss of the *Titanic* was due entirely to the collision with the iceberg. That collision, in turn, had come about because the *Titanic* was steaming at full speed in an area known to be hazardous with ice. The complacency of the officers had also been a contributing factor. Once the collision had occurred, the lifeboats were insufficient in number, and they had not been properly filled or manned by trained seamen. Mersey did not, however, condemn the White Star Line, the Board of Trade or Captain Smith as resoundingly as Senator Smith had done. *Titanic's* captain, he opined, had followed accepted practice, and any experienced master would have done the same. It was the practice that was faulty, not the captain's judgement. Smith's failure to slow down, he concluded, had been a mere 'mistake'; only if it were repeated would it be negligence.[70] Mersey stated in his findings, 'The importance of this Enquiry has to do with the future. No Enquiry can repair the past'.[71]

The British press was satisfied, viewing Mersey's report as the last word. No further questions needed to be asked, and the search for scapegoats could now end. 'It is difficult to suppose', wrote the *Daily Mail* on 31 July, 'that any court which had to inquire into the responsibility of the owners of the ship would disregard the expression of opinion of Lord Mersey and those who sat with him ... The report having, in effect, acquitted them of all blame, it is not likely that any attempt will be made hereafter to establish the contrary.' [72]

There is little point in proclaiming the superiority of one inquiry over the other. What is relevant here is to contrast the tone of the two reports. Every page of Smith's bristles with criticisms of established seafaring traditions and of the conduct of the *Titanic*'s builders, owners, officers and crew. Mersey's report, on the other hand, expresses itself in far quieter, more restrained language, and does not attempt to overturn long-standing convention. It focuses on technical details, not on subjective opinions about what should or should not have been done. It emphasizes the lessons to be learned from the disaster, not the apportionment of blame for it. It is the more learned and erudite of the two, while Smith's report reflects an inquiry that was in many ways poorly managed, disjointed and frequently distracted by irrelevant issues. But Mersey's report lacks Smith's sense of righteous indignation and his passion to right the wrongs that had been done to *Titanic*'s 1500 victims and to prevent such a tragedy from happening again. Smith chose to emphasize arrogance, complacency and culpability, whereas Mersey showed far greater tolerance for the inevitably of human error. The two interpretations present the sinking in very different lights.

What accounts for the difference between the two inquiries, and more broadly for the difference in the way that the *Titanic* story developed in Britain and the United States? In other words, what caused the British to be so much less willing to allow the *Titanic* disaster to challenge accepted hierarchies, traditions and practices? To answer this question, we must take into account a further discrepancy between interpretations of *Titanic* on the opposite sides of the Atlantic. For there is an element that features prominently in British accounts that is almost entirely absent from their American counterparts: patriotism. Even though many of the most-frequently cited acts of heroism on board the sinking *Titanic* were in fact carried out by Americans, there was little effort to turn this to patriotic account in the United States. To be sure, it was not uncommon for American interpretations to feature declarations of Anglo-Saxon racial superiority, but only rarely did they contain overt statements of national pride.

In Britain, however, patriotism played a prominent role. In the final moments before the *Titanic* sank, it was alleged that Captain Edward J. Smith had exhorted the passengers and crew who remained on board to 'Be British!'[73] Such a statement on Smith's part seems ludicrously chauvinistic and implausible today, but in 1912 it featured prominently in nearly every account of the sinking. Paul Pelham and Lawrence

Wright wrote a popular song entitled 'Be British!' to raise money for the *Titanic*'s widows and orphans. The song began:

> What a glorious thing it is to know that the breed is just the same
> As it was when the Anglo-Saxon race first gained immortal fame.
> What a glorious thing it is to know when danger there was nigh
> When the mighty liner sank to her rest our men knew how to die.

In a poem published in the *Rugby Observer*, John Butcher wrote: We hear, once more, high over all,

> The Captain's cry – a clarion call! –
> *'Be British, men, the women save!'*
> And British were they to their grave.[74]

In the *Bolton Observer*, William Cryer declared:

> The blackest cloud shows best the silver rim!
> Which is not lacking in this hour of gloom;
> Ne'er grows the British sun of glory dim,
> Supreme is duty in the hour of doom!
>
> Yet burns within us the just pride of race!
> And chivalry of never ceasing charm,
> Still finds for innocence a hiding place,
> And lends to weakness its protecting arm.
>
> 'Be British!' is the thought of valiant minds,
> And 'faithful to a trust' their best renown;
> And the great heart it true incentive finds
> In love that many waters cannot drown![75]

In the *Kent Messenger*, E. A. Lempiere Knight penned:

> 'Be British!' rang the stirring mandate out.
> They heard the call;
> With courage true, no coward's shrinking doubt,
> But Britons all
> Resolved their 'duty' high to carry out,
> Whate'er befall![76]

And James Simpson wrote in the *Alloa Advertiser*:

> O'er the mighty ship, 'Be British!'
> Lo, the fearless captain cried;

> Nobly, noble men responded,
> Nobly toiled and nobly died –
> Their country's pride.[77]

Other authors asserted that there had been no need for the captain to offer exhortations to behave nobly, for Britons were incapable of acting in any other way. In the *Huntingdonian*, Frank C. Greenwood declared:

> 'Women and children first!' was, as of old,
> The rule heroic;
> But when had son of Britain need be told
> To act the Stoic? [78]

The *Daily Mirror* proclaimed that 'amid all the inhuman scenes stand out deeds of heroism that make one thrill with pride for England and the English tradition that holds on both sides of the sundering ocean'.[79] The poet Louie Davoren asked his readers to:

> Heave a sigh for Britain's heroes who gave their lives to save
> The helpless women and children from the clasp of the cruel wave.
> Brave hearts of a brave old nation! Well have you proved your worth!
> Well have you done your duty for the land that gave you birth! [80]

In the *Banbury Advertiser*, James Slimming linked the sinking of *Titanic* to past examples of British heroism:

> The stranger may call us a hybrid race,
> And sneer at our insular pride,
> But where is the one who could take our place
> In ether, on land or on tide?
> Others may try to usurp the throne
> Which Britain has held so long;
> But Britain the Brave, and she alone,
> Can face even death with a song.
>
> Proudly we boast of our heroes of yore –
> Our Gordon, our Buller, our White,
> Our Blake, and our Nelson, who lived mid the roar
> And rattle of tumult and fight;
> But these are but samples of Britons to-day –
> We've heroes and heroines still,

Who wait but the signal to show us that they
Are ready such places to fill.

When death with his thirst and his hunger for blood,
Sweeps down in his horrible glee,
And chooses the mammoth that rides on the flood
His innocent death-trap to be,
The Briton looks on and waits for the end,
Undaunted he stands 'midst the throng:
That son of the sea e'en death cannot bend,
And he walks through death's portal with song.[81]

In order to make the case for a specifically British brand of heroism,
journalists and poets were forced emphasize the actions of the crew
rather than the passengers, for virtually all of the *Titanic*'s most prominent passengers were American, in particular the ones who were most
commonly cited as having behaved nobly. 'It is impossible not to realise
the magnificent heroism and sense of duty displayed by the officers and
crew', declared the *Daily Sketch*. 'All survivors speak in the highest terms
of the coolness and courage they displayed.'[82] The 'great majority of
the crew', claimed the *Daily Chronicle*, 'perished at their posts':

We have ever had reason, through centuries of history, to be proud of our
sailors, their courage and their unfailing devotion to duty. They have reared
the glorious traditions of our Royal Navy and no less raised to an unchallenged
height the credit and efficiency of our mercantile marine. And it is in times
of disaster such as this that were are forcibly reminded of that heroism which
has given us such proud sea fame. We have all too much reason for sadness,
but we have good cause for pride, in that spirit which has braved a thousand
fights, which is behind untold bravery, and which never droops, but rises
sublimely to its highest in the hour of sudden catastrophe, lives undimmed
in those who man the ships of Britain.[83]

Versifiers, too, celebrated the heroism of *Titanic*'s crew. In the *Southport
Visitor*, J. W. Stones wrote:

Then from the sea-swept bridge rang out,
Above the sinking deck, the Captain's cry.
'Be British!' – Like the immortal signal,
'England expects', so does this last command,
Of the doomed vessel's chief thrill every heart,

Of those who hear the tale; as e'er it will
Thro' all the rolling centuries to come,
Then, his last duty done, into the sea he leapt,
Striving to rescue others – not himself,
And, British to the core, gave up his life.
And, in one bond of willing sacrifice,
Stood millionaire and sturdy sailorman,
And all the gallant men who made that crew.
'True, true till death', they did their duty there,
And made Old England's heart beat high with pride! [84]

'List! To the voice of our Nation', James E. Penty demanded:

Give praise to the 'Titanic crew',
For they worked with determination,
As men Britannic, and true.[85]

This emphasis on the heroic conduct of the crew rather than the passengers represents another distinction between British and American interpretations of the sinking. American writers were far more willing to criticize the crew and to hold the captain and senior officers account-able for the disaster. For many British writers, however, lionization of the crew was a necessary component of their claims of British heroism. These claims were clearly ludicrous, as the Titanic carried people from a variety of nations and ethnic backgrounds, and neither noble nor ignoble behaviour was limited to persons from a particular country. All nations, of course, are keen to celebrate heroic deeds by their citizens, but in this particular case British writers were far more eager to do so, and to distort reality in the process, than their American counterparts. Why was this the case?

The short answer to this question is that Britain had more at stake than the United States. Since at least the sixteenth century, pride in maritime power has been a crucial component of British national ident-ity. Events such as the defeat of the Spanish Armada in 1588 and Nelson's victory at Trafalgar in 1805 were regarded as key events in British national history. This is the case partly because of geographical happenstance: island nations traditionally and almost inevitably have close relationships with the sea. It also has to do with the fact that the British have for centuries profited from the sea, not only in the form of military victories but in the form of the massive empire that was founded under the Tudors and only lost in the second half of the twentieth century. In 1694 Lord Halifax declared that 'the first article of an Englishman's political creed must be, that he believeth in the sea'.[86] Such sentiments only intensified as the centuries passed. Almost two hundred years later, Robert Louis Stevenson wrote that 'the sea is our approach and bulwark, it has been the scene of our greatest triumphs and dangers, and we are accustomed in lyrical strains to claim it as our own ... We should consider ourselves unworthy of our descent if we did not share the arrogance of our progenitors, and please ourselves with the pretension that the sea is English'.[87] Throughout the Victorian era, the need to maintain British maritime supremacy was the one thing on which politicians from across the spectrum could agree, and this consensus was bolstered by public opinion, which solidly supported the notion that Britain must continue its dominance of the seas as the guarantor of its industrial and imperial strength.

By the early twentieth century, Britain's maritime power was as significant a component of national identity as it had ever been, but it was also considerably less secure. In the eighty years after Trafalgar, no other country, or combination of countries, seriously challenged the supremacy of the Royal Navy, and Britain dominated merchant shipping as well: over one-third of the world's merchant fleet sailed under the British flag in 1860.[88] At the turn of the twentieth century this seafaring might was still formidable, as the Royal Navy was equal in power to the next two largest fleets put together. Beneath the surface, however, ominous forces were at work. Even substantial increases in the Royal Navy's budget could not keep up with the fleets being built up in the 1890s in France, Russia, Italy, Germany, Japan and the United States; the challenge from one country could only be met by weakening the navy's presence elsewhere.[89] By 1905, Britain's longstanding control of the seas had dwindled, and the Royal Navy was now focused on trying to maintain supremacy over the waters close to home rather than over the entire world's oceans. Fifteen years later, the Royal Navy had been equalled in strength by its American counterpart, and by 1930 Britain was the second-ranked naval power.[90]

The realm of merchant shipping was becoming equally competitive, and the North Atlantic passenger trade particularly so. In the final years of the nineteenth century, the British lines that had long dominated the trade began to face a serious challenge from the Germans, as the Hamburg-Amerika and Norddeutscher-Lloyd Lines began building ships that were bigger, faster and more luxurious than anything the British could offer. The British government was certainly concerned: it granted Cunard a substantial loan and annual subsidy to entice it to build the *Lusitania* and *Mauretania*, the largest and fastest ships afloat. The *Titanic* and *Olympic* represented White Star's counter-attack, intended to trump not only the internal competition offered by Cunard but the German lines as well. The Germans were, however, already preparing a response. Only five weeks after the sinking, Hamburg-Amerika launched the *Imperator*, which at 900 feet and 52,000 tons was larger than the *Titanic*. The *Titanic*'s claim to be the world's biggest ship would have been extremely short-lived, even if the end of its maiden voyage had been different.

This atmosphere of increased competition meant that, even if its naval and merchant fleets were as large and powerful in absolute terms as they had ever been, Britain's relative position had slipped. For the first time in nearly a century, they faced serious challenges from international rivals. This situation gave the sinking of the *Titanic* a significance beyond the level of tragedy represented by the largest maritime disaster in history. For it was possible to interpret the sinking as an indication of the erosion of Britain's maritime supremacy, particularly if it was found to be the product of negligence and incompetence rather than unfortunate circumstance. Britain's rivals were certainly well aware that this was the case. After the conclusions of Senator Smith's inquiry were announced, the *New York Times* proclaimed that 'England has been struck a blow in its tenderest and proudest spot. The mistress of the seas is indicted alike in its governmental administration and its seamanship, upon which the primacy of the island depends'.[91]

Other press accounts in the United States were less sensitive, however; as they rushed to point fingers at those responsible for the disaster, fingers that very often pointed at Britain. 'Old fogeyism!' thundered the *San Francisco Examiner*, once the news of the Board of Trade's antiquated regulations regarding lifeboats came out. 'What a commentary on national progress!' Equally scathing was an editorial by Hugo P. Frear, a naval contractor for the United Iron Works, that appeared in the late editions of several American papers on Tuesday 16 April: 'If the *Titanic* had been under United States government supervision, its owners would have been compelled to equip it with forty-two lifeboats at least ... The trouble with the English regulations is that they are behind the times. They have not kept up with progress'.[92] The general theme of such commentary was clear: Britain was an old nation whose time had passed, while the United States was the new, rising power in the world.

Not surprisingly, Britain responded defensively to such attacks. Instead of focusing on culpability and error, British commentators emphasized the heroism of the *Titanic*'s officers and crew, a heroism that linked them to maritime heroes of the past. 'Thank God! The spirit of our fathers still survives', wrote Sam Ffoulkes in the *St Helens Reporter*.[93] Similarly, Francis Thompson declared in the *Burton Observer*, 'Great Britain's sons are true Britons still, and worthy of her great name'.[94] A judge from Liverpool commented:

> We rejoice to think that Englishmen have once again proved to the world the courage, high sense of honour, and bravery, which has always distinguished them on occasions of this sort. There had been times lately ... when they had heard suggestions that the English race were not the men their fathers were; but when the full account of the *Titanic* disaster reached them they would know that England stood today as she always had done, as the home of the free-born, of men of courage, and of men who, in the hour of danger, proved themselves heroes indeed.[95]

An editorial in the *Daily Chronicle* proclaimed that 'the seed of decay has not yet entered' a nation whose men had behaved as heroically as those on the *Titanic* had done:

> It is still gloriously great; still worthy of the fine traditions of its past and of all the high hopes which we of to-day cherish for the generations of the future ... The Epic of the *Titanic* shows us that we still have in us the stuff of which strong nations are made. With this stirring story adorning the annals of our race we may rest assured that we still have that nobility of character, that courage, that nerve, that determination which we need so much if we are to face worthily and to achieve successfully the heavy national tasks which lie before us, if we are to raise still higher the standard of hope for the race.[96]

For all of these writers, the *Titanic* disaster confirmed the ability of British sailors to behave heroically even in the most difficult circumstances, a capability that would allow the nation's greatness to continue.

1. Poster advertising the *Titanic*. (*Mayfair Cards*)

2. The *Titanic* and *Olympic*. (*Harland & Wolff*)

3. The *Titanic* docked at Southampton. (*Harland & Wolff*)

4. The first-class staircase. (*Harland & Wolff*)

5. Thomas Andrews. (*Harland & Wolff*)

6. Captain Edward Smith. (*Southampton City Collections*)

7. The *Titanic*'s band, led by Wallace Hartley. (*Southampton City Collections*)

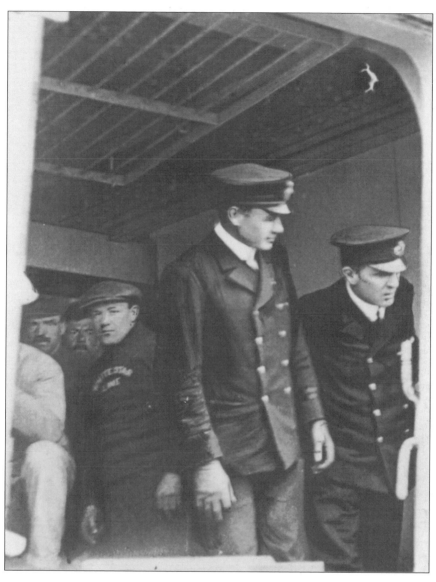

8. First Officer William Murdoch and Second Officer Charles Lightoller. (*Southampton City Collections*)

9. John Jacob Astor waits to board the boat train. (*Harland & Wolff*)

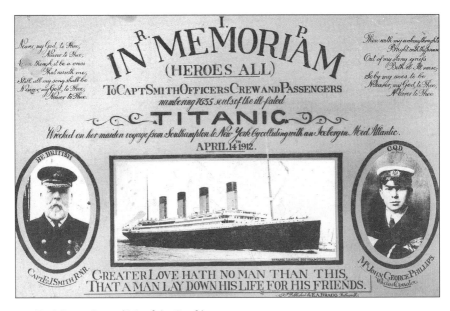

10. In Memoriam. (*Mayfair Cards*)

When seen in this light, it is small wonder that the British inquiry displayed a reluctance to criticize the actions of the crew or the conduct of the shipping line, and small wonder that the British press became highly incensed when the American inquiry did both. 'A schoolboy would blush at Mr Smith's ignorance', declared the *Morning Post*.

> While Mr Smith puts his farcical questions, and the flashlights are flared that photographers may get pictures of the witnesses, while outside the American Press retails the latest lie, the latest slander, about British seamen, honest Americans will feel with shame that not merely the White Star Line, but American civilization itself is on trial, and that the country is coming worse out of the ordeal than the company.[97]

This journalist recognized that the aftermath of the sinking of the *Titanic* had become an arena in which the relative maritime worth of nations was being assessed. Far more than just an accurate determination of the causes of the *Titanic* disaster was at stake: British national pride was on the line.

Indeed, many people in Britain were infuriated that the Americans were conducting an inquiry into the disaster at all. On 24 April the Member of Parliament Munro Ferguson asked the House of Commons what the precedent was for a foreign inquiry into the loss of a British ship. Joseph Conrad was also incensed. 'Why', he wrote, 'an officer of the British merchant service should answer the questions of any king, emperor, autocrat, or senator of any foreign Power (as to an event in which a British ship alone was concerned, and which did not even take place in the territorial waters of the Power) passes my under-standing.'[98] A letter writer to the *Daily Graphic* was equally indignant: 'What authority has a foreign power to inquire into the loss of a British ship? What authority has a foreign power to detain British subjects and compel them to appear as witnesses?'[99] Even a committed Irish nation-alist like Roger Casement was angry. On 20 April he wrote to his cousin Gertrude Bannister, 'The American Senate are going to make Sea Laws, it seems to me, for John Bull! What a situation! A foreign Parliament having an enquiry into the loss of a British vessel at sea, and subpoenaing witnesses!' Three days later, in another letter to Bannister, Casement added:

> I certainly think the USA Senate is a Beauty! I wonder no one has yet drawn

attention to these monstrous proceedings of a foreign Parliament enquiring into the loss of a British ship on the high seas, and issuing subpoenas and having 'flashlight' courts sitting – a fine body to elicit truth! No one [seems] to realize the enormous impertinence of these proceedings. Fancy the House of Lords hurrying down to Southampton with the Sergeant at Arms and ordering all the crew and the American owners of *St Louis* or *St Paul* to be confined and guarded ... and then commanding them to appear before it! 100

The problem with these defiantly Palmerstonian statements, however, is that they were not in point of fact accurate when they referred to the *Titanic* as a British ship. The ship had sailed under British registry, to be sure, but it was American-owned, for the White Star Line had been purchased by J. P. Morgan's International Mercantile Marine consortium in 1902. But that, as well, was not a subject about which British people wished to be reminded at the time of the *Titanic* disaster.

The anecdote that perhaps best encapsulates the British response to the sinking of *Titanic* was recorded by the writer Eva Anstruther, who was later made a Dame of the British Empire for her services in sending books to the trenches during the First World War. In an account of the British inquiry published in the *Westminster Gazette*, Anstruther described

ordinary men, doing their ordinary business in an ordinary way, intent on investigating facts, or elucidating the truth; shirking nothing, minimising nothing, exaggerating nothing, but all striving to the best of their power that blame should fall where blame was due, honour where honour; that disaster should be met with dignity.

As she watched a young seaman – a 'man trained for action and not for speech' – answer questions in his 'rough uneducated English', the following exchange occurred:

'What did you hear?'
'I heard the captain say, "Women and children first."'
'You remained at your post?'
'Yes, sir.'

Anstruther commented that 'it was all perfectly commonplace and ordinary. All in the day's work'. As she sat there observing, a 'little woman in black, a stranger to me' suddenly 'put her hand upon my arm'.

'"I'm glad I'm English", she said quietly. There was no more to be said.' [101]

Interpretations of the sinking of the *Titanic* in Britain thus took a more conservative line than their American counterparts. Conventional hierarchies of gender, class and race were all defended, with very few exceptions.[102] Moreover, as a comparison of the British and American inquiries reveals, there was a reluctance in Britain to criticize the conduct of the captain or crew, or to suggest that arrogance or negligence had played a role in bringing about the collision with the iceberg. It was far more comforting to see the disaster as the product of, as one journalist put it, 'a combination of circumstances that never occurred before and never can occur again'. Such sentiments were not only found in the popular press, but in more sober and scholarly forms as well. In his *A Modern History of the English People* (1912), the historian R. H. Gretton referred to the disaster as neither 'unforeseen nor unforeseeable', concluding his account with a dismissal of any suggestions of culpability: 'What suspicions emerged at the Inquiries of human failure in the crisis of the disaster may be left now unexplored'.[103]

The conservatism of British responses to the sinking of the *Titanic* resulted from national insecurity regarding the global situation at the time. An awareness of the increasing challenges which Britain faced to its longstanding maritime dominance created a need to deflect and defend any criticism of the seaworthiness of a British ship or the seafaring skills of its sailors. Instead of the questions and debates that characterized responses to the sinking in the United States, the British response was remarkably homogeneous. The *Titanic*'s officers and crew, it proclaimed, had behaved with the utmost chivalry and devotion to duty in appalling circumstances which they had done nothing to bring about and could do nothing to mitigate; the sinking was entirely the result of an unfortunate and unforeseeable accident. Contemporary Britons should thus feel proud that their men could conduct themselves as heroically as they had in the past; the sinking of the *Titanic* had indicated that there had been no weakening of the national fibre over the course of the centuries.

On a national level, a standard *Titanic* narrative quickly established itself in Britain, a narrative that in many ways has never been seriously challenged. Again, in contrast to America, there has been very little overt *Titanic* revisionism in Britain. In the United States, Walter Lord's classic account *A Night to Remember* (1955) represented the first substantial effort to address the problem of the fate of *Titanic*'s third-class passengers.[104] And in more recent years, James Cameron's blockbuster film reversed the conventional narrative's view of class relations by transforming the third-class passengers into heroes and the first-class passengers into villains. Cynthia Bass's novel *Maiden Voyage* (1995), meanwhile, offers a feminist view of the sinking by tracing the story of a fictional passenger named Sumner Jordan, a young boy who is the son of a leading American suffragist. During and after the sinking, Sumner is forced to confront the moral issues raised by the policy of 'women and children first'. Nothing comparable exists in Britain, where the standard, conservative narrative of the sinking continues to go largely unchallenged.

3

Heroes and Villains

On both sides of the Atlantic, heroism was a necessary component of the story of the *Titanic*, because it was a key element in allowing positive meaning to be extracted from the tragedy. If the *Titanic*'s victims could be shown to have behaved heroically, then their deaths had not been in vain. This need put the conduct of the dead virtually beyond reproach. But what precisely had they done in their moment of heroism? What were the traits of a *Titanic* hero? The answer to these questions can be approached by examining three of those heroes: Jack Phillips, *Titanic*'s senior wireless operator; Wallace Hartley, the leader of the ship's band; and Thomas Andrews, the managing director of Harland & Wolff, who was on board to assess the ship's performance on its maiden voyage. All three died, and all three were lionized afterwards for their conduct after the *Titanic* struck the iceberg. Phillips was lauded for continuing to send distress calls until the ship's wireless set lost power; he remained at his post even after Captain Smith released him from duty. Hartley (in some accounts, anyway) led the band as they played on deck until the waves washed them off. And Andrews attempted to get as many passengers into the lifeboats as possible; after there was no more to be done, he was last seen standing alone in the first-class smoking room calmly awaiting his fate.

In 1912, and thereafter, Jack Phillips, Wallace Hartley and Thomas Andrews were regarded as heroes, and their conduct on the night of 14–15 April was virtually unquestioned. There were other figures, however, whose actions were seen as less heroic. Great Britain did not experience the rush to identify scapegoats that occurred in the United States, but nonetheless there were several characters in the *Titanic* story who were seen as, if not quite villains, then as potentially culpable. Certainly, some men were looked upon as having betrayed their gender and to have fallen short of the standard of masculine heroism embodied by Phillips, Hartley and Andrews. They did not, according to the conventions of the time, do their duty, chivalrously sacrificing themselves for women and children while displaying a spirit of calm fortitude until the end. Instead, these men took the decision to board lifeboats when the opportunity arose. It did not matter that they had occupied places that would have otherwise gone unfilled. It was their duty to stand aside as long as there was still a single woman or child left on board. But they chose not to do that, and they would suffer the penalty of being regarded as cowards for the rest of their lives.

Almost every man who boarded a lifeboat found his conduct questioned afterwards, but two men in particular – J. Bruce Ismay and Sir Cosmo Duff Gordon – suffered particularly close scrutiny from the press and public. If anyone could be regarded as the 'villains' of the *Titanic* story, they could, and often were. In addition, however, there were two other men whose actions were more ambivalent: Captain Edward J. Smith and First Officer William Murdoch. In some accounts, Smith appeared as a brave and forceful commander who had gone down with his ship, but in others he seemed strangely passive and hapless. The question of Smith's culpability for the disaster was and is not easily resolved. It was difficult to exonerate him completely from all responsibility for the collision with the iceberg, but perhaps it had been primarily the product of bad luck or of interference from Ismay, who was himself under a cloud for his own conduct. Murdoch, meanwhile, was a capable seaman with a promising career ahead of him, but he was also the officer who had been in command of the *Titanic* at the time of the collision. It was not altogether clear that any action on his part would have enabled the ship to avoid the iceberg, but the possibility that he could have done something differently was the source of considerable speculation by both maritime experts and the general public.

Before we turn to the individual stories of what *Titanic*'s heroes and villains did – or were believed to have done – it is useful to see what characteristics they had in common. First, we will examine the qualities of *Titanic* heroism. Most obviously, Phillips, Hartley and Andrews were all men. In the United States, it was possible for the story of the *Titanic* to have heroines as well as heroes. Ida Straus, who chose to remain with her husband rather than board a lifeboat, became an exemplar of wifely loyalty in an age when social conservatives decried the breakdown of families. 'In this day of frequent and scandalous divorce', declared the *New Orleans Times-Picayune*, 'when the marriage tie once held so sacred is all too lightly regarded, the wifely devotion and love of Mrs Straus for her partner of a lifetime stands [*sic*] out in noble contrast.'[1]

The most famous of the *Titanic*'s American heroines, however, was Margaret Tobin 'Molly' Brown, immortalized after the disaster as the 'Unsinkable Molly Brown' due to her plucky conduct during the sinking.[2] Born into humble circumstances in 1867 to Irish immigrant parents in Hannibal, Missouri, Margaret Tobin headed west at the age of eighteen, following her brother Daniel and her half-sister Mary Ann. Like many Americans at the time, they saw the West as a place where fortunes could be made. Margaret moved into Daniel's home in Leadville, Colorado, a mining camp that was booming due to the presence of substantial deposits of silver-bearing lead ore, or carbonate. At first, she tended the house and cooked meals for Daniel, but before long she found work as a saleswoman in the carpet and drapery department of the dry goods store Daniels, Fisher & Smith. In 1886 she married James Joseph Brown, a tall, personable young Irishman who worked as a superintendent for the Moffat and Smith mining conglomerate. The couple had two children: a son, Lawrence, who was born in 1887, and a daughter, Catherine, who was born in 1889. The Browns were far from wealthy; 'I loved Jim', Margaret wrote in her memoirs, 'but he was poor'.[3] J.J. was ambitious, though, and in 1893 he struck it rich when he discovered gold in the Little Jonny Mine. The mine was soon producing 135 tons of gold ore per day, and J.J. became one of the most successful mining men in America. He and Margaret moved into a large house – known as the 'House of Lions' because of the two stone lions that guarded the front steps – on Pennsylvania Street in Denver. They also built a summer home, Avoca Lodge, in the countryside nine miles from the city. The Browns were not, as subsequent popular accounts of their lives claimed, ostracised from Denver society due to their lack of proper bloodlines. On the contrary, they regularly appeared in the society pages of local newspapers and were listed on the Social Register, though they, along with other members of the *nouveau riche*, were excluded from the 'Sacred Thirty-Six', a contingent of Denver's most elite families.

As a wealthy woman of leisure, Margaret devoted her time and money
to a variety of social and political causes. She worked with Judge
Benjamin Lindsey to establish the first Juvenile Court in the country,
which eventually became the basis for the juvenile justice system in the
United States. She was an ardent advocate of women's rights and was
a charter member of the Denver Woman's Club, which promoted
literacy, education and suffrage for women. The night of 14–15 April
1912, however, brought Brown her greatest fame. By that point, she and
J.J. had become estranged: she enjoyed being a globetrotting socialite,
whereas he preferred the simple life of a mining camp. Other contributing factors were his increasingly uncontrollable temper (aggravated
by a stroke he suffered in 1903) and his dalliances with the opposite sex.
Margaret now spent most of her time staying with friends in New York,
Paris and Newport, Rhode Island, and she also indulged her fondness
for travel. In the spring of 1912 she was touring Egypt with her daughter
Helen, who was a student at the Sorbonne, and her friends John Jacob
and Madeleine Astor when she received word that her first grandchild,
Lawrence Palmer Brown Jr, was ill. She immediately booked passage on
the first ship that was leaving for New York, the brand new White Star
liner *Titanic*, which she boarded, along with the Astors, at Cherbourg.
Margaret was well acquainted with Captain Smith, with whom she had
crossed the Atlantic twice before, most recently two months earlier on
the *Olympic*. As Margaret stood by the rail as the *Titanic* made ready
to depart from Cherbourg, her friend Emma Bucknell, widow of the
founder of Bucknell University in Pennsylvania, said, 'I have a premoni-
tion about this ship'. 'Nonsense', Brown replied, knowing that Emma
had four children anxiously awaiting her return, 'you're just anxious to
see your family.' 4

On the morning of Sunday 14 April, Brown rose early and followed
her daily exercise regimen, which included a brisk walk around the ship
and a half-hour workout in the gymnasium, where she rode the sta-
tionary horse and boxed. (Boxing was gaining popularity as a physical
activity for women in 1912, as it firmed the waist and upper body,
making a corset unnecessary.) At 10.30 a.m., she attended the church
service led by Captain Smith in the first-class dining saloon, then had
lunch in the Verandah Café, where she indulged in a small plate of
cheshire and gorgonzola cheese in addition to her main course of corned

beef. She then went for another bracing walk on deck and spent two hours reading and writing before retiring to her cabin to dress for dinner. She dined that evening in the *à la carte* restaurant, where at 7.30 p.m. she saw Captain Smith enter and sit at the long table reserved for the private party hosted by George Widener. As Smith passed by, Emma Bucknell whispered, 'Shouldn't he be on the bridge? I've heard rumours of icebergs and such'. 'Nonsense', Margaret told her, 'he often dines with first-class passengers.'⁵ Afterwards, she and Emma, along with their friend Dr Arthur Jackson Brewe, a physician from Philadelphia, retreated to the Palm Court and listened to the *Titanic*'s band play ragtime. At around 10 p.m., Margaret went to bed.

She was still awake and reading at 11.40 p.m. when she felt a crash and was knocked to the floor. Startled but accustomed to the unpredictability of ocean travel, she put on her dressing gown and ventured out into the corridor. A few other passengers were also poking their heads out of their cabins, but nothing seemed obviously amiss, so she returned to her cabin and picked up her book again. Hearing more sounds from the corridor, she opened the door to her cabin a second time and looked around, but she saw only an officer and a few stewards talking and decided that, whatever was going on, it was hardly an emergency, though she did think it somewhat unusual that the ship's engines had stopped. Once again she returned to her bed and her book.

After a few minutes, she was jolted by loud pounding on her cabin's small window. Parting the curtains, she saw the panicked face of James McGough, a buyer for Gimbels department store whom she had met earlier on the voyage. 'Get your life preserver!' he shouted. Brown reacted with typical hardheaded pragmatism. She dressed in her warmest clothing, a black velvet two-piece suit. She then pulled on seven pairs of woollen stockings and wrapped a sable stole around her neck. From the safe in her room she took $500 in cash and tucked it into a wallet she wore around her neck under her clothes. She strapped on her lifejacket and took the blanket from the bed. As she turned to leave her cabin, she slipped a small turquoise statue that she had purchased in Cairo into her pocket for good luck. She left behind the twenty-five gowns, fourteen hats and thirteen pairs of shoes she had acquired in Paris.

Once she was out on the Boat Deck, Brown watched the lifeboats being loaded until she was grabbed by two men and dropped into Lifeboat 6. The boat contained only two seamen, Quartermaster Robert Hichens and Lookout Frederick Fleet, and one male passenger, Major Arthur Peuchen; the twenty-one other occupants were women or children. Hichens took command and ordered his charges to row away from the *Titanic* as fast as they could, warning that, when the ship foundered, it would 'pull everything down for miles around'. Brown and Margaret Martin, a cashier from the *à la carte* restaurant, fitted the oar into the rowlock and began pulling with all their might; Brown told Martin to 'row like a galley slave!' From his position at the tiller, Hichens continued to berate them. 'Faster! Faster!' he shouted. 'If you don't make better speed with your rowing, we'll be pulled down to our deaths!'

'Wouldn't it be more profitable,' Major Peuchen asked, 'if you were to come down here and row and let one of these women steer the boat?'

'You row, sir,' Hichens replied, 'and I will remain in command of this boat'.

As Brown and the others looked on, the *Titanic*'s stern rose higher and higher out of the water. The ship's lights flickered and went out, and across the calm sea the occupants of Lifeboat 6 could hear the terrified shouts of those still on board. Suddenly, Brown wrote later, 'there was a rift in the water, the sea opened up, and the surface foamed like giant arms that spread around the ship'. For a long moment after the *Titanic* disappeared, there was silence in Lifeboat 6. Then several of the women, including Brown, began demanding that they return and try to save some of those flailing in the freezing water. 'We must go back!' demanded first-class passenger Helen Candee.

Her opinion was seconded by Julia Cavendish, who cried, 'There are a great many people in the water!'

Hichens was unmoved. 'No! It is our lives now, not theirs. Row, damn you. Our boat will immediately be swamped if we go back into all that confusion.'

'We have to go back,' Brown pleaded. 'We can't leave them!'

Hichens still refused to relent, telling the women that 'there's nothing in the water but a bunch of stiffs'.[6]

Brown and the other occupants of Lifeboat 6 continued to row, with only an occasional flare from another boat to let them know that they were not alone in the pitch darkness. One by one, Brown removed her six extra pairs of stockings and distributed them to the other women. From the stern, Hichens uttered a continuous barrage of gloomy predictions: 'We're likely to drift for days. There is no water in the casks, and we have no bread, no compass and no chart. If a storm should come up, we are completely helpless! We will either drown or starve. That is our fate'. Brown shouted at him to be quiet, telling him to 'keep it to yourself if you feel that way. For the sake of these women and children, be a man. We have a smooth sea and a fighting chance'. After several hours, they encountered Lifeboat 16; Hichens ordered them to tie up alongside, which prevented further rowing. For a moment, Brown and the other exhausted women enjoyed the respite, but soon the cold became unbearable. 'If I sit here for one more minute I'll utterly freeze to death!' declared Helen Candee.

'Yes, let's keep rowing', seconded Julia Cavendish.

'I'll decide when we row', Hichens snarled, though he did allow a stoker to transfer to Lifeboat 6 in order to give them another able-bodied man. The stoker wore only a thin jumper which exposed his legs from the knees down, and Brown took her sable stole and wrapped it around his calves, tying the tails around his ankles.

'Cut us loose!' Brown called to Lifeboat 16.

'I'll decide when to cut loose!' Hichens shouted. 'Indeed, if we do, I'll likely be thrown overboard.'

'I'll toss you over myself', Brown retorted, and rose from her seat.

'Sit down, damn you!' Hichens squawked. 'By damn, I wish you'd keep your place.'

The stoker protested at Hichens's choice of language: 'Say, don't you know you're talkin' to a lady?'

'I know to whom I am speaking, and I am commanding this boat!' Hichens snapped.

Despite Hichens's protests, Lifeboat 16 cut them loose. Brown began exhorting the others to row to keep themselves warm. As dawn broke, they saw a flash on the horizon; as its source drew closer, it was revealed to be a ship. Frederick Fleet, who until this point had not uttered a word, informed them that it was most likely the *Carpathia*, which had been the closest ship to respond to the *Titanic*'s distress call. With difficulty, they manoeuvred alongside, and the women and children were hauled up one by one in a wooden seat.

Once she was safely on board the *Carpathia*, Brown immediately sent a wireless message to her daughter Helen informing her that she was safe. (It was never received; nor were the numerous messages that Brown later sent from second- and third-class survivors who did not have enough money to pay for telegrams themselves.) She then began helping to distribute supplies to the numerous women and children who were sleeping in dining rooms, corridors and other public areas of the ship. When the *Carpathia*'s doctor tried to stop her by telling her that they already had been given blankets, she angrily replied, 'You can't calm these tortured minds with blankets!'⁷ Brown's ability to converse in French, German and Italian proved immensely useful as she attempted to comfort distraught survivors from steerage who spoke little or no English. At breakfast the morning after her rescue, Margaret discussed with several of her friends from first class that something needed to be done for those poor women and children who had lost everything they owned in the sinking. One women responded with a pronounced lack of enthusiasm: 'Why, Mrs Brown, why worry? I will be met by representatives of the Waldorf, who will take me at once to the hotel, and you, of course, will be greeted by the Ritz-Carlton, so why bother?' Shocked by the woman's ignorance, Brown informed her that 'all of these people will not have a Ritz-Carlton or a Waldorf to receive them', but the woman still refused to help.⁸ Undaunted, Brown continued her efforts, and by that afternoon a committee had been formed, with her in the chair. They started a subscription list, with the names of the contributors and the amounts they had contributed tacked on the wall in a prominent place. By the time the *Carpathia* reached New York, nearly $10,000 had been pledged.

After the *Carpathia* docked on the night of 18 April, Brown remained on board until the following day to help survivors reach their destinations. She then transferred her efforts to the Ritz-Carlton, where she, with the assistance of her son Daniel, continued to assist foreign-born survivors by directing them to their consulates in New York and contacting their friends and relatives. She also worked for almost a week to make sure that donations of cash and clothing went to those who needed them. Only then did Brown go home to Denver. At the end of May 1912 she returned to New York for a formal ceremony at which the Survivors' Committee presented each crew member of the *Carpathia* with a medal and Captain Arthur Rostron with a silver cup. She also gave Rostron the turquoise Egyptian statue that had remained in her pocket throughout the sinking and rescue.

Brown continued to chair the *Titanic* Survivors Committee for the next twenty years. Between 1912 and 1923, she spent most of her time in Newport, where she rented a twenty-six room 'cottage' called Mon Etui, though she often wintered in Denver. In Newport, her lavish parties, exotic décor and preference for newfangled inventions such as an 'eclectric automobile lunch buffet' (a four-wheeled electric cart with cookers, warmers, a refrigerator and space for dishes, silverware and food that was invented by Brown herself) ensured her continued notoriety. She also continued her efforts on behalf of women's rights. In 1914, six years before women had the right to vote on a national level, she nearly ran for the United States Senate, withdrawing from the race only when the First World War broke out, because her sister Helen was married to a German count serving on Kaiser Wilhelm II's staff, and it was thought that the connection would scuttle Margaret's chances of electoral success. During the First World War, she served as a director of the American Committee for Devastated France, which helped to rebuild houses and distribute clothes, food and other necessities in the areas that had suffered the most damage. She was awarded the Legion of Honour by the French government in 1932 in recognition of her wartime work as well as her other humanitarian and philanthropic activities.

In 1922 J.J., who had continued to support Margaret's lavish lifestyle despite their separation, died at the age of sixty-eight. To the astonishment of his family, he left no will, and the ensuing complications kept the settlement of his estate in the court for the next six years as Margaret was forced to do battle with her own children over J.J.'s wealth, which was still substantial though considerably diminished from its peak. She ultimately received half the estate, but her relationship with her children was all but destroyed by accusations on both sides of financial chicanery and mental instability. She rewrote her will, removing Lawrence and Helen completely. Her own financial state, meanwhile, changed dramatically, for what remained of J.J.'s fortune was not sufficient to support her in the style to which she had become accustomed. Forced to vacate Mon Etui, she spent the remainder of her life travelling from hotel to hotel in the United States and Europe.

In 1925, Margaret was staying at the Breakers Hotel in Palm Beach, Florida, when a fire broke out. Just as she had done during the sinking of the *Titanic*, she kept her nerve and calmly led a group of other guests down a fire escape. Afterwards, one of her friends declared, 'She must be a combination of fish and phoenix. She's been through fire and water before; she's hit the high spots of danger and come through unharmed'.[9] Even 'the unsinkable Molly Brown' was not immortal, though. On 26 October 1932, she died suddenly at the Barbizon Hotel in New York. She had been suffering from migraine headaches for some time, and an autopsy revealed the presence of a large brain tumor. She was buried next to J.J. in Holy Rood Cemetery in Westbury Village on Long Island.[10] At the time of her death, her estate was valued at less than $50,000.

As the stories of Brown's conduct during the sinking of the *Titanic* and her subsequent efforts to assist needy survivors filtered into the popular press, she came to be regarded in America as a heroine of epic proportions. Wildly exaggerated accounts depicted her as nursing a nearly dead Madeleine Astor back to health or commanding Lifeboat 6 single-handedly. It was not until after her death, however, that the legend of the 'Unsinkable Molly Brown' was truly born. The legend was created from two main sources – Gene Fowler's *Timberline* (1932) and Caroline Bancroft's *The Unsinkable Mrs Brown* (1936) – neither of which depicted Brown's life at all accurately. Instead, they presented her life story in a highly fictionalized form, emphasizing colourful episodes that had never occurred. In them, Brown became an earthy, rough and ready exemplar of quintessentially American virtues such as resilience and forthright-ness. This became the standard image of Brown in American popular culture. At the height of the Cold War in the 1950s the Advertising Council and the Magazine Publishers of America sponsored a full-page advertisement for United States Savings Bonds headlined 'Mrs Brown Refused to Sink' and featuring a photograph of a formidable-looking Molly. The text related the tale of Brown's survival and then moved into the sales pitch: 'Asked how she'd done it, she replied, "Typical Brown luck. I'm unsinkable".[11] But it wasn't luck. It was pluck. And Americans have always had plenty of that smiling, hardy courage. When you come to think of it, that's one reason why our country's Savings Bonds rank among the world's finest investments'.12 Similar versions of Brown would be immortalized in the Broadway musical and film *The Unsinkable Molly Brown* in the 1960s, and more recently in James Cameron's blockbuster film *Titanic* (1997).

After the *Titanic* disaster, Molly Brown became a uniquely American hero. Women could identify with her as a strong female who refused to adhere to social conventions that limited her role during the sinking to passive acceptance of male chivalry, while men could see in her the tough, individualistic spirit that had settled the West and made America great. In neither of these guises, however, was she likely to appeal to British audiences. And beyond that, in Britain it was not possible for a woman's conduct during the sinking of the *Titanic* to be viewed in the same heroic light. Noëlle Leslie, the Countess of Rothes, had been equally stalwart as Brown in the face of disaster, taking charge of the tiller in Lifeboat 8 so that Able Seaman Thomas Jones, who was in command of the boat, could row. He later told the *Sphere*, 'When I saw the way she was carrying herself and heard the quiet, determined way she spoke to the others, I knew she was more of a man than any we had on board'.13

The Countess of Rothes, however, was never embraced by the British press and public in the way that Brown was in America, for in Britain the brand of heroism depicted in accounts of the *Titanic* disaster was exclusively masculine. The popular song 'Be British!' proclaimed tauto-logically that on the *Titanic* 'men behaved like men should do'.14 This suggests that not only did the *Titanic*'s heroes have to be men, but they had to be 'manly' as well; the word recurs over and over again in responses to the sinking. In the *Shanklin Guardian*, W. H. Cumpston wrote:

> Into the depth of Ocean's waters cold,
> The strong, the faithful, and the manly brave,
> Willing to lose themselves, the weak to save,
> Denied in fond farewell their loved to enfold.

Willie Horner in the *Halifax Courier* also used the word 'manly' to describe *Titanic*'s heroes

> 'Let women be first' were the words that thrilled
> Each manly heart to its core.

In the *Alloa Advertiser*, James Simpson concurred that heroism and masculinity went hand in hand:

> The chivalrous and manly,
> Who in hundreds stood aside,
> That the weaker might be rescued
> From the all-devouring tide.[15]

But what, more specifically, did it mean to be 'manly' in the Britain of 1912? In the final decades of the nineteenth century, concepts of manliness underwent a metamorphosis from earlier incarnations that emphasised piety, earnestness and intellectual attainment to what historians have termed a 'neo-Spartan virility' characterized by stoicism, physical hardiness and endurance. This new ethos of masculinity derived from an ideal developed in the late Victorian public schools, where physical and mental toughness supplanted more traditionally academic areas as the focus of the curriculum. Sports and other forms of physical activity were favoured over intellectual development; in 1857 the *Spectator* described Tom Brown, the contemporary *beau idéal* of the public schoolboy, as 'a thoroughly English boy. Full of kindness, courage, vigour and fun – no great adept at Greek and Latin, but a first-rate cricketer, climber and swimmer, fearless and skilful at football, and by no means adverse to a good stand-up fight in a good cause'.[16] Boys were expected to conform to this ideal, and to take their medicine without complaint. The public school, declared the *Dublin Review* in 1865, was 'a miniature world; and certainly, the world is in many respects a big public school. The training it gives is of the rough and ready order, with plenty of hard blows and little allowance for sentiment'.[17] Boys indoctrinated by this ethos often found it difficult after leaving school to adapt to marriage and domestic life, whose characteristics were difficult to reconcile with the notions of manliness that had been instilled in them. Too much time in the company of women, they feared, would lead to effeminacy, so they immersed themselves in the all-male world of the club and constructed all-male preserves in their country houses in the form of libraries, smoking rooms and billiard rooms. In the most extreme cases, young men fled abroad and sought careers in the Empire as a means of preserving the masculine domain to which they had become accustomed.[18]

Nor was this new conception of masculinity limited to the elite in its influence. For the less privileged, it was diffused through Edwardian society by institutions such as the Boy Scouts, which demanded that men relinquish their personal comforts and desires for the good of the nation and the Empire. Robert Baden-Powell minced no words when he declared in *Rovering for Success* (1922), 'God made men to be men ... We badly need some training for our lads if we are to keep up manliness in our race instead of lapsing into a nation of soft, sloppy, cigarette suckers'.[19] This view was further spread by the adventure stories that were a staple of contemporary literature; men who could not transplant themselves to the Empire could at least read about the masculine world it offered. Robert Louis Stevenson, H. Rider Haggard, G. A. Henty and other authors presented stories in which men could set off into the unknown unencumbered by feminine or domestic constraints.

In order for Phillips, Hartley and Andrews to be regarded as heroes, they had to be made to conform to contemporary notions of manly heroism. Their depictions in accounts of the *Titanic* disaster featured a number of traits that were key components of Edwardian conceptions of masculinity. First, they all performed their duty, or 'stayed at their posts', until the bitter end. In the most commonly accepted version of the *Titanic*'s last moments, all three continued to do their jobs – to send wireless messages, to play music, or to assist in the saving of lives in any way possible – until it became impossible to do them further.

Duty was a recurring concept in interpretations of *Titanic* heroism. 'They nobly answered duty's call', wrote Charles Davidson, 'and like true heroes died.' In the *Caithness Courier*, H. Henderson wrote:

> Heroes were they, each and all,
> With the *Titanic* lost,
> Well they answered duty's call,
> Each died at duty's post! [20]

Duty was not only linked to masculinity, but to patriotism as well; by staying at their posts, the *Titanic*'s heroes had proved the nation's worthiness as well as their own. William Cryer in the *Bolton Journal* declared that

> The blackest cloud shows best the silver rim!
> Which is not lacking in this hour of gloom;

> Ne'er grows the British sun of glory dim,
> Supreme is duty in the hour of doom! [21]

The second trait that Phillips, Hartley and Andrews shared was that they maintained strict control over their emotions – kept a 'stiff upper lip' – even in the most adverse circumstances. There was never any suggestion in the press or elsewhere that any of the three men showed signs of panic or despair as the *Titanic* sank. This was again in keeping with contemporary notions of masculinity, which emphasized self-control. Men of the late Victorian and Edwardian eras grew up in homes in which the overt expression of emotion was considered to be an exclusively feminine trait; they would have been accustomed to seeing their fathers suppress the need to give or receive affection.[22]

Phillips, Hartley and Andrews also showed a willingness to sacrifice themselves for others, in particular 'weaker' women and children. In the standard version of the *Titanic* story that evolved in the period after the sinking, Hartley and Andrews made no attempt to save themselves, and Phillips did so only after the failure of the *Titanic*'s power supply made it impossible to send further distress calls. (In any event, his effort came too late and he did not survive.) Chivalric selflessness was another key component of *Titanic* heroism, and of contemporary masculinity. Edwin Holdsworth told his readers:

> Oh, think of it – the terror of the grave
> Awaiting them! the rush and fight for life,
> With hopelessness the barrier in the strife!
> Yet midst it all, how eagerly the brave
> Relinquish self, their weaker ones to save,
> And stay the purpose of the threatening knife
> That severs heartfelt ties of love and home!
> Oh, what a sacrifice for others' sake!

In the *Westminster Gazette*, James Rhoades linked self-sacrifice to duty and to the maintenance of a stiff upper lip:

> No frantic scream; no frenzied strife;
> Unflinching gave their sacrifice;
> Unflinching stood that noble host,
> Each man at his appointed post.[23]

Finally, Phillips, Hartley and Andrews were all self-made men who had worked hard to attain their positions. Phillips and Hartley, both under thirty, had risen from undistinguished backgrounds to posts on the largest and most prestigious ship afloat. Andrews, for his part, had been born in somewhat more comfortable circumstances, but he had started as a lowly apprentice at Harland & Wolff and worked his way up the ladder to become managing director, with only his own talents to propel him. Samuel Smiles's concept of self-help hovered behind much of the writing on popular manliness in the late Victorian and Edwardian eras, combined with a healthy dose of Social Darwinism that proclaimed the virtue of allowing the fittest to prove their ability to survive and flourish.[24] As the *Saturday Review* declared in 1860:

> To the boy or to the community alike, the constant reliance upon another for aid in difficulties, guidance in perplexities, shelter from temptations, fatally weakens the fibre of the character. Boys, like nations, can only attain to the genuine stout self-reliance which is true manliness by battling for themselves against their difficulties, and forming their own characters by the light of their own blunders and their own troubles.[25]

Phillips, Hartley and Andrews perfectly fitted the mold of a contemporary masculine hero. Not all the men board were seen as heroes, however, as the disaster's two most-criticised survivors, J. Bruce Ismay and Sir Cosmo Duff Gordon, readily demonstrate.

For J. Bruce Ismay, the fall from grace was swift and far. Prior to the sinking of the *Titanic*, he had been master of all he surveyed: managing director of White Star, since his father's retirement in 1892, and president of International Mercantile Marine, J. P. Morgan's massive consortium of shipping lines, since 1904. A handsome man well over six feet in height, Ismay was forty-nine in 1912, old enough to appreciate his accomplishments but still sufficiently young to anticipate a succession of future triumphs. His managerial style was autocratic, but the results he had obtained earned him respect if not affection. Over the last few years, White Star's profits had soared and were now threatening to outstrip even Cunard's. For Ismay, the *Titanic* was the ship that would provide emphatic confirmation of his longstanding belief that size and comfort were what mattered in passenger liners, not speed. He had paid close attention to the ship's construction and even suggested a few of the refinements that made this latest vessel superior even to the *Olympic*. The glass windows along the first-class Promenade Deck that protected passengers from sea spray had been his idea, being nicknamed the 'Ismay screen' by the ship's builders.

All of this was wiped away in the three hours after the *Titanic* struck the iceberg. Initially, Ismay behaved as the standards of the time dictated for a man of his class and position, assisting as best he could in the loading of the lifeboats. He appeared near Boat 5 as Fifth Officer Harold Lowe was preparing to lower it and, noticing that the boat was not full, called out, 'Are there any more women before this boat goes?'

A female voice replied, 'I am only a stewardess'.

'Never mind', said Ismay, 'you are a woman – take your place.' As the boat was being lowered, however, Ismay became a bit over-enthusiastic in his eagerness to help. Hanging onto one of the davits, he leaned out over the ship's side and watched the boat's slow progress towards the water. Impatient, he began swinging his arms in circles and shouting, 'Lower away!' Furious at such interference from a non-seaman, Lowe screamed at Ismay, 'If you get the hell out of the way, I'll be able to do something! You want me to lower away quickly? You'll have me drown the lot of them!' Thoroughly chastised, Ismay slunk off towards Boat 3. As he left, the first distress rocket went up; Lowe always retained the memory of Ismay's face – his mouth open, eyes staring upwards in disbelief.[26]

From there, it was all downhill for Ismay. At around 1.45 a.m., he made a decision that he almost certainly regretted for the rest of his life. He was on the starboard side of the ship helping First Officer William Murdoch and Purser Hugh McElroy in the loading of Collapsible C. A scuffle broke out as a group of stewards and male passengers tried to rush the boat, and McElroy was forced to draw his revolver and fire it twice into the air, while Murdoch shouted at the mob to stay back. Two stewards managed to jump into the boat, but they were dragged back out by two passengers, Hugh Woolner and Bjorn Steffanson. The loading of the boat then proceeded in a more orderly fashion, and, when there were no more women and children to be found, McElroy gave the order to lower away. As the boat's gunwale reached the level of the deck, Ismay stepped forward and climbed into an empty place near the bow.[27]

Almost immediately, Ismay began to suffer the consequences of his decision. When he came on board the *Carpathia* at 6.30 a.m. on the morning of 15 April, he requested to be taken to 'some room where I can be quiet'. The ship's doctor escorted him to his own cabin, where he remained sequestered until the *Carpathia* reached New York. His behaviour did not endear him to his fellow survivors. 'I know many women who slept on the floor in the smoking room', the newly widowed Mary Smith declared, 'while Mr Ismay occupied the best room on the *Carpathia*.' Eleanor Widener, who had also lost her husband, was even harsher in her judgement: 'Better a thousand times a dead John B. Thayer than a living J. Bruce Ismay'.[28]

For Ismay, this was only the beginning of the ignominy that would be heaped upon him once it was confirmed that he had survived. From the minute he stepped on board the lifeboat, his reputation was ruined. He had failed to obey the code of masculine, gentlemanly behaviour that dictated that no man should live if a single woman or child died. Combine this with the fact that he was head of the shipping line that had allowed the *Titanic* to sail with lifeboats that were clearly woefully inadequate, and the revelation at the American inquiry that he had possibly encouraged Captain Smith to maintain full speed even though the ship was entering a known area of ice, and Ismay was doomed. If a scapegoat was what the public wanted, here was one served up ready-made on a platter.

The British press was certainly not kind to Ismay. 'You were the one person on board', *John Bull* indignantly proclaimed, 'who ... had a large pecuniary interest in the voyage, and your place was at Captain Smith's side till every man, woman and child was safely off the ship. The humblest emigrant in the steerage had more moral right to a seat in the lifeboat than you.' *Truth* commented, 'I cannot help regarding it as "providential" that the chairman of the company happened to be standing where he was at the moment when the last boat – or was it the last but one? – left the ship, and there were no women or children at hand to claim the place into which he was thus enabled to jump'.[29]

This level of criticism was nothing, however, compared to what Ismay faced in the United States. He was the first witness called to testify in the American inquiry, and the smug and supercilious manner with which he answered the questions did little to help his cause. By the next day,

Ismay was being universally pilloried in the American press. 'Mr Ismay', declared the *New York American*,

> cares for nobody, but himself. He cares only for his own body, for his own stomach, for his own pride and profit. He passes through the most stupendous tragedy untouched and unmoved. He leaves his ship to sink with its precious cargo of lives and does not care to lift his eyes. He crawls through unspeakable disgrace to his own safety, seizes upon the best accommodation in the *Carpathia* to hold communion with his own unapproachable conduct.

On the editorial page of the same newspaper was a cartoon of Ismay cowering in a lifeboat with the sinking *Titanic* visible in the background. The text was 'Laurels of Infamy for J. *Brute* Ismay', with caption below reading 'It is respectfully suggested that the emblem of the White Star Line be changed from a White Star to a White Liver'.[30]

Throughout America, Ismay was singled out as a representative of the greed and disregard for safety that had led directly to the disaster. The *Denver Post* referred to him as 'the Benedict Arnold of the Sea', the Worcester, Massachusetts, preacher H. Stiles Bradley called him 'a skulking coward', and the Reverend Baker P. Lee of Los Angeles described him as 'one of those human hogs whose animal desires swallow up all finer feelings'. The Boston historian Brooke Adams summed up the groundswell of anti-Ismay sentiment in a letter to Senator Francis Newlands, who sat on Smith's inquiry committee:

> Ismay is responsible for the lack of lifeboats, he is responsible for the captain who was so reckless, for the lack of discipline of the crew, and for the sailing directions given to the captain which probably caused his recklessness. In the face of all this he saves himself, leaving fifteen hundred men and women to perish. I know of nothing at once so cowardly and so brutal in recent history. The only thing he could have done was to prove his honesty and his sincerity by giving his life.[31]

The town of Ismay, Texas, considered changing its name to 'Lowe', in honour of the *Titanic*'s Fifth Officer, who had castigated Ismay for his interference with the lowering of Boat 5. Ismay, Montana, also wanted to change its name, but the citizens had difficulty agreeing on a suitable alternative. They did not 'favor the name of Astor', and 'Butt' and 'Smith' were thought 'too insignificant a designation for a growing town like Ismay'.[32]

In the eyes of the British press and public, however, some of the wrath directed at Ismay went too far. 'He must be glad he is an Englishman', declared the *San Francisco Examiner.* 'He is no gladder than we are.' [33] It was one thing to criticize Ismay, but to turn him into a symbol of Britain's inferiority to the United States was a bit much for the British public to swallow. 'The American press', complained the British Ambassador to the United States, 'has been perfectly hysterical over the disaster, and has published the wildest and most untruthful statements without taking any trouble to justify the same. The particular butt has been Mr Bruce Ismay, whose conduct has been savagely criticized.' [34] 'The Deathless Story of the *Titanic*', a special supplement to *Lloyd's Weekly News* published two weeks after the disaster, saw Ismay as 'a tragic figure' who had done all he could to help the women and children to the boats and then, when 'there were no passengers on the deck', had climbed into the last lifeboat. The popular historian Filson Young also defended Ismay, claiming that he was 'among the foremost in helping to sort out the women and children and get them expeditiously packed into the boats'. Afterwards, he bore the grievous insults hurled at him 'with a dignity which was proof against even the bitter injustice of which he was the victim'.[35] In the report of the British inquiry into the disaster, Lord Mersey went out of his way to defend Ismay, who, he concluded, had helped many passengers into the boats and then, when there were no more to be found, had climbed into a place in Collapsible C that would otherwise have gone empty. He was under, Mersey asserted, 'no moral obligation' to go down with the ship: 'Had he not jumped in he would merely have added one more life, namely, his own, to the number of those lost'.[36]

The contrast between Ismay's treatment in Britain and the United States suggests that his behaviour became a bone of contention in the Anglo-American tensions that resulted from the disaster. To Americans, Ismay represented everything that they saw as inferior about Britain: he seemed an effete and incompetent product of a too-rigid adherence to an archaic class system, a man who had obtained his position through heredity rather than merit. But in Britain those selfsame qualities made it necessary to defend him, at least from the most blatantly unfair – and anglophobic – assessments of his conduct. After the initial shock of the disaster dissipated, many people in Britain began to urge a more balanced view of Ismay.

Even if the British press and public would not allow Ismay to serve
as a symbol of Britain's supposed inferiority to the United States, this
did not mean that they viewed his conduct in a positive light. The *Daily
Express* defended him from the worst of American invective, but admitted that 'he fell short of that sublime valour of which so many
examples were given in the *Titanic*'.[37] Even less sympathetic were Ismay's
fellow members of the elite, who would never again invite him to their
parties or greet him warmly on the street. Less than a year after the
disaster, Ismay resigned from his positions at White Star and International Mercantile Marine and moved to western Ireland, spending the
rest of his life as a virtual recluse. In the years prior to his death in 1937,
he was often heard to remark that the *Titanic* had ruined his life.[38]

There was another man on *Titanic* whose behaviour was questioned as
much as, if not more than, Ismay's. He was Sir Cosmo Duff Gordon,
who made the decision to board a lifeboat alongside his wife and then
compounded his subsequent difficulties by offering five pounds each to
the crewmen in the boat. Duff Gordon claimed that he was only giving
them the replacement value for the possessions they had lost, but it was
all too easy for the public to view his action as a bribe intended to deter
the men from returning to pick up swimmers in the water, which they
could well have done since the boat was less than half full. Like Ismay,
Duff Gordon found that his reputation never recovered from the damage
done to it that night.

Sir Cosmo Duff Gordon was a Scotsman from a branch of the Gordon
family, whose head was the Marquess of Aberdeen. He was tall and
good-looking, as well as unusually talented by the standards of the
British elite. In his younger days, he was noted for his beautiful singing
voice, and he was also a superb athlete who had once been a member
of the British Olympic fencing team. In 1900 he had married Lucy
Wallace, sister of the scandalous novelist Elinor Glyn and proprietress
of 'Lucile', a fledgling couture house specializing in naughty lingerie.

After his marriage, Sir Cosmo settled into the life of a sporting country
gentleman. At Maryculter, the family house in Aberdeenshire, one of
his favorite pastimes was to shoot at his guests with wax bullets, though
he did allow them to don fencing masks in a concession to ocular safety;
he himself had previously lost an eye in a shooting accident. Initially,

he and Lucy seem to have been very much in love, but Sir Cosmo's staid lifestyle soon grew tiresome to his more adventurous wife. She complained to her mother that he was 'most extraordinarily dull to be with' and that he 'never makes a joke'. They spent an increasing amount of time apart as Lucy's business expanded; by 1912 she was employing more than a thousand people and her designs were sought after by some of the most socially prominent people on both sides of the Atlantic. She made frequent and extended trips to London, Paris and New York while he stayed home in Scotland; both found the arrangement perfectly amicable.[39]

In the spring of 1912, Lucy was in Paris setting up a new branch of Lucile when urgent business demanded her presence in New York. On such short notice, and with the coal strike's reduction in the number of crossings, the only available berth was on the *Titanic*, but she was extremely reluctant to travel on an untested ship. She initially refused to book the passage, but, when she told him of her fears, Sir Cosmo volunteered to go with her. This was unusual, for by that point the couple rarely travelled together. At Cherbourg, the Duff Gordons boarded as 'Mr and Mrs Morgan', for reasons that remain unclear, since their familiarity to many of their fellow first-class passengers made any effort to travel incognito pointless.

On the first days of the voyage, Lucy's fears seemed groundless: 'Everything aboard this lovely ship reassured me, from the Captain with his kindly, bearded face and genial manner ... to my merry Irish stewardess with her soft brogue and tales of the timid ladies she had attended during hundreds of Atlantic crossings'. Still, she felt apprehensive and refused to undress completely at night, keeping her fur coat and jewelry case close at hand. On Sunday, 14 April it was so cold that she had her secretary, Miss Laura Francatelli, switch on the electric heater in her stateroom. Dinner that night was splendid: 'We had a big vase of beautiful daffodils on the table the table which were as fresh as if they had just been picked. Everyone was very gay, and at the neighbouring tables people were making bets on the probable time of this record-breaking run'.[40]

On the night of 14 April at 11.40 Lucy was in bed when she was awakened by 'a funny rumbling noise'. Soon thereafter, she heard people running along the deck outside her cabin, joking about the ice lying on the ship's forward decks. She went across the corridor to Sir Cosmo's cabin, but he had heard nothing and was annoyed at being awakened. He reassured her by reminding her of the ship's watertight compartments and told her to go back to bed. Still nervous, she went out on deck and looked over the side, but could see nothing amiss and so returned to her cabin. Suddenly, the noise of the steam being vented from the boilers erupted, and she rushed back to Sir Cosmo, who agreed to get up and go to see what was happening. He encountered John Jacob Astor near the bridge, and they agreed that their wives should get dressed and come up on deck.[41]

Lucy put on the warmest clothes she could find, a squirrel coat and a mauve silk kimono. When they got up to the boat deck, a 'scene of indescribable horror' greeted them: 'Boat after boat was being lowered in a pandemonium of rushing figures fighting for places ... trampling women and children under foot. Over the confusion, the voices of the ship's officers roared "Women and children first. Stand back" and I heard the sharp bark of a revolver'. Lucy was offered a place in a lifeboat but refused to go without Sir Cosmo. 'Promise that whatever you do you will not let them separate us', she demanded.[42] Along with Miss Francatelli, they went over to the starboard side. Again, officers tried to force her into a boat, and again she refused to go without Sir Cosmo.[43]

Lucy later testified at the British inquiry that the number of people in their vicinity suddenly diminished sharply, leaving only a handful of seamen launching Boat 1. Sir Cosmo asked First Officer Murdoch if he could get into the boat along with Lucy and Miss Francatelli and was told that he could. The Duff Gordons and Miss Francatelli jumped in, and the boat was lowered. As they rowed away, Lucy could hardly stand to look back at the *Titanic*:

> I could see her dark hull towering, like a giant hotel with lights streaming from every cabin porthole. As I looked, one row of those shining windows was suddenly extinguished. I guessed the reason ... When I forced myself to look again, yet another row disappeared. After what seemed like long hours of misery a sharp exclamation from my husband aroused me from the stupor into which I was sinking. 'My God, she is going now!' he cried.

After the ship had disappeared beneath the waves, Lucy could hear the 'terrible cries of despair from the poor souls she had carried down with her'. Then there was only 'the plash of the oars as the men rowed harder than ever, seeking perhaps to get away from their thoughts'.⁴⁴

Boat 1 contained only twelve people – one seaman, five firemen and six passengers – though it had a capacity of forty. This was to be a major source of controversy later, for it was the lowest number of occupants in any boat. Why had they not gone back and attempted to rescue some of those in the water? This question became the source of considerable speculation in the press, and the British inquiry into the disaster ultimately spent several days trying to answer it.

After the *Titanic* had disappeared beneath the waves and Boat 1 was left bobbing in the calm sea, Lucy commented to Miss Francatelli about her bedraggled appearance, 'There's your beautiful nightdress gone'. The firemen were appalled by her priorities.

'Never mind, madam', one of them told her, 'you were lucky to come away with your lives.'

Another firemen chimed in, 'You people need not bother about losing your things, for you can afford to buy new ones when you get ashore. What about us poor fellows? We have lost all our kit and our pay stops from the moment the ship went down'.

Sir Cosmo's next action ultimately turned out to be a colossal blunder, open as it was to a variety of interpretations. 'Yes, that's hard luck', he told the crewmen. 'But don't worry, you will get another ship. At any rate, I will give you a fiver each towards getting a new kit.'⁴⁵ Lucy later recorded, 'It was said with his characteristic impulsiveness, and I don't think anybody thought much of it at the time, but I remember every word of the conversation, for it had a tremendous bearing on our future. I little thought that because of those few words we should be disgraced and branded as cowards in every corner of the civilised world'.⁴⁶

Once they were safely on board the *Carpathia*, Sir Cosmo remembered his promise to the crewmen and, two days before the ship docked in New York, presented each of them with a cheque for five pounds. After asking the men to sign her lifebelt as a memento of 'our wonderful escape', Lucy proposed that a photograph be taken of the group, and they all posed wearing their lifebelts. Nearby survivors expressed indignation when Sir Cosmo requested everyone to 'Smile, please!'⁴⁷

When they reached New York, the Duff Gordons had no inkling of the storm of controversy that was about to break over them. They drove immediately to the Ritz, where they celebrated their survival with friends. 'We were all very gay, and drank champagne', Lucy recalled. Never one to minimize drama, she described her adventure in colourful and somewhat romanticized terms. One of the dinner guests was the editor of the *Sunday American*, one of William Randolph Hearst's papers. The next day, he telephoned Lucy and told her that Hearst very much wanted her story for tomorrow's edition. 'May I tell your story as I heard it?' he asked. Without thinking, she agreed. When the story appeared, it presented Lucy and Sir Cosmo as upper-class twits who viewed the tragedy as a splendid diversion from the tedium of transatlantic travel. Among other things, the story claimed that Lucy had told Sir Cosmo, 'We might as well get into a boat, although the trip will only be a little pleasure excursion until the morning'.[48]

This story was soon followed by an interview with Able Seaman Robert Hopkins, who claimed to have overheard an 'American millionaire' telling the crew of his lifeboat that he would 'make it all right with them' if they would 'get right away from the ship'. Hopkins asserted that this promise had been carried out on the *Carpathia*, when each member of the boat's crew had received a cheque for five pounds. Although Sir Cosmo was not American, it did not take long for the press to connect Hopkins's story to the Duff Gordons. The headlines in the press were unflinching: 'Duff Gordon Scandal', 'Cowardly Baronet and his Wife Who Rowed Away from the Drowning', 'Sir Cosmo Duff Gordon Safe and Sound While Women Go Down in the *Titanic*'.[49] The accusations were harsh: not only had they escaped in a less than half full lifeboat, but they had bribed the crewmen in that boat five pounds each to persuade them not to go back for those dying in the water and then to keep their mouths shut afterwards. Boat 1 was now commonly being referred to in the press as 'the Money Boat'.[50]

The Duff Gordons were called to testify at the British inquiry into the disaster on 20 May. (They were the only passengers who testified.) The scandal had attracted so much interest that the hall was filled with spectators, more than had attended on any previous day. The event was treated as if it were part of the social calendar; Lucy wrote that 'it was difficult to believe that we were not going to some pleasant social function, for there were such rows of cars outside'.[51] Two German princes, relatives of the royal family, were present, along with the Russian ambassador, several Members of Parliament and Margot Asquith, the wife of the Prime Minister. Few of those present were without an opinion on the Duff Gordons' behaviour: some had come to defend them, others to see their cowardice confirmed once and for all.

As Sir Cosmo gave his evidence, Lucy sat nearby with bowed head. He denied that there had been any conversation in Boat 1 'while the cries of the drowning people were heard', and that in 'a dead silence' the crewmen had rowed away from the wreck site. He also denied that he or Lucy had objected to going back to try and pick up survivors. W. D. Harbison, the attorney for *Titanic*'s third-class passengers, cross-examined Sir Cosmo about the £5 'gifts' to the crewmen. 'Was this not', he asked, 'rather an exceptional time, twenty minutes after the *Titanic* sank, to make suggestions in the boat about giving away £5 notes?'

'No, I think not. I think it was a most natural time. Everything was quiet; the men had stopped rowing; the men were quite quiet lying on their oars doing nothing for some time, and then the ship having gone I think it was a natural enough remark for a man to make.'

'Would it not have been more in harmony with the traditions of seamanship that that should have been the time that you should have suggested to the sailors to have gone and tried if they could rescue anyone?'

'I have said that I did not consider the possibility – or rather I shall put it that the possibility of being able to help anybody never occurred to me at all.'

'That is to say, would I accurately state your position if I summed it up in this way, that you considered when you were safe yourselves that all the others might perish?'

'No, that is not quite the way to put it.'

At this point, Lord Mersey intervened and asked Harbison, 'Do you think a question of that kind is fair to this witness? The witness's position is bad enough. Do you think it is fair to put a question of that kind to him? I do not!' Lord Mersey went on to remind Harbison that 'your duty is to assist me to arrive at the truth, not to try to make out a case for this class against that class'. Lucy followed her husband onto the stand; her testimony corroborated Sir Cosmo's in every detail.[52]

In the inquiry's report, the Duff Gordons were, like Ismay, exonerated of any impropriety, but for years afterwards Lucy would overhear strangers whispering, 'That is Lady Duff Gordon, the woman who rowed away from the drowning'. Most of the public calumny, however, fell on Sir Cosmo, who was supposed to adhere to conventions of masculine conduct that did not apply to Lucy. She quickly rebounded, relocating first to Paris and then, when the First World War broke out, to New York. She and Sir Cosmo separated in 1916 and never lived together again. When Lucile went bankrupt in 1923, it was not because of any lingering effects of the *Titanic* scandal, but because Lucy proved a hopeless business manager when left to her own devices. After the collapse of her business, she lived in London in straitened financial circumstances, publishing her memoirs, entitled *Discretions and Indiscretions*, in 1932. She died three years later at the age of seventy-one.

For the rest of his life and beyond, Sir Cosmo's name remained associated with cowardice. To be sure, he had his supporters, for there were many people with a vested interest in maintaining the class system whose top tier he represented. Many of the members of the social elite who witnessed Sir Cosmo's testimony at the British inquiry were there to support him; when Lord Mersey castigated Harbison for his over-aggressive cross-examination, a spontaneous burst of applause erupted from the spectators' gallery. Ultimately, though, Duff Gordon had fewer defenders than Ismay. Criticism of Ismay was more muted in Britain than it was in America not only because of greater social conservatism when it came to denigrating the class system, but because to criticize Ismay was to criticize White Star, and to criticize White Star was to criticize the entire British shipping industry. Duff Gordon, however, benefited from no such protection. He could be attacked as an isolated case of a man failing to behave in a 'manly' fashion; as such, complaints about his behaviour supported the conventional gender and social code. His character had been found to be sorely lacking, and public judgement was harsh and unforgiving. After the disaster, Sir Cosmo lived at Mary-culter in relative seclusion until he died in 1931. Long after his death, the stigma of public disapprobation was still upon him. In 1947, Evelyn Waugh wrote to Nancy Mitford about whether she had heard about a mutual friend's 'Duff Gordon escape from drowning'. As recently as 1984, an article by Bernard Levin in the *Times*, entitled 'In Extremis and Character', declared that, during the sinking of the *Titanic*, 'the cool and brave behaved more coolly and bravely than ever before, the weak and the cowardly more like weaklings and poltroons'. Second Officer Charles Lightoller, Levin asserted, displayed 'bravery and selflessness' in 'exceptionally great measure, which – to put it with positively excessive moderation – Sir Cosmo Duff Gordon did not'.[53]

In the sinking of the *Titanic*, heroism and villainy were defined by how well a man – for in Britain the main characters of the story were exclusively male – adhered to contemporary standards of 'manly' conduct. Survival in and of itself was often sufficient to remove a man from the ranks of *Titanic* heroism, as J. Bruce Ismay and Sir Cosmo Duff Gordon discovered. There was no way for them to reconcile their decisions to board a lifeboat with the code of masculine behaviour that required a man to stand calmly aside and sacrifice their places to 'weaker' women and children. Those men who died on the *Titanic*, on the other hand, could far more easily be elevated to heroic status. After the sinking, three men in particular – Jack Phillips, Wallace Hartley and Thomas Andrews – came to be regarded as *Titanic* heroes.

4

Jack Phillips

John George Phillips, whom from an early age everyone called 'Jack', was born on 11 April 1887 in Farncombe, Surrey, a small village that was incorporated into the borough of Godalming in 1892. Godalming is most famous today as the home of Charterhouse School; it is a genteel, attractive town that exemplifies Surrey's sedate, conservative, upper middle-class prosperity. Until the mid nineteenth century, however, it was an industrial town whose fortunes were dependent on the manufacture of cloth, paper and leather goods. *Black's Guide to Surrey* recorded in 1864 that 'the trade of Godalming is chiefly maintained by the large paper-mills at Eashing and Catteshall; its tanneries, flour mills and hoisery manufacturers'. The *Guide* hinted at changes to come, however, when it added that 'the recent opening of the direct Portsmouth railway may probably communicate to this somewhat sleepy borough a fresh impetus'.[1]

Indeed, following the arrival of the railway in 1849, Godalming began to take on a genteel and residential character, as the town's proximity to London enticed wealthy city dwellers to purchase country houses nearby. The old tenements and workshops were gradually torn down, and the high street shops began to cater for a more upmarket clientele. This more congenial atmosphere was a key factor in luring Charterhouse to move from London to Godalming in 1872. In 1900, Craddock's *Godalming Almanac and Directory* declared that 'during the last few years building operations have been carried on very extensively in the town and neighbourhood. The demand for residences is daily increasing – the general salubrity of the locality, and the facility of railway accommodation, offering great inducements for families desiring convenient country residences'.[2]

The Phillips family was typical of the local tradespeople who catered to the needs of Godalming's wealthy new arrivals. In the late 1940s H. A. Haskell, a former schoolmate of Jack's, recalled them as 'very respected business people'. Jack's father and mother managed a drapery shop called Gammons, a flourishing business with branches in several towns in Surrey, Sussex and Hampshire. As a boy, Phillips attended Farncombe School and then later Godalming Grammar School. Haskell, who was four years his senior, remembered him as 'a pale-faced, modest boy looking through the iron gates at us bigger and more rugged boys'. Haskell also recalled that Phillips was a not very adept pupil, who 'could not learn as well as the other boys in his class', until his father arranged for him to be tutored privately. After that, he began to do 'exceptionally well'.[3]

Upon leaving school, Phillips became a telegraphist for the Godalming Post Office. After three years there, Phillips recognized that wireless radio was the way of the future, and in March 1906 he enrolled at the Marconi Training School in Liverpool. In the early twentieth century, wireless operators were perceived as being on the cutting edge of new technology; by choosing such a career, Phillips was displaying a clear desire for advancement beyond his lower middle-class origins. Marconi's recruiting material appealed to ambitious young men by encouraging them to escape from 'blind alley careers' and acquire a practical, modern skill. In October 1911, the Marconi-produced magazine the *Marconigraph* offered these words of advice to the prospective applicant: 'Let him not for one moment suppose that in the operating side of wireless telegraphy he has discovered an El Dorado; but without painting an alluring picture, let me unhesitatingly say that the attractions and remunerations are such as make a favourable bid for the entry of capable and zealous young men'.[4] The rate of pay, however, was not commensurate with the glamour that Marconi offered: a senior wireless operator on a passenger liner could expect to earn a little over £4 a month, a junior operator half of that. (This was less than the lowly firemen and trimmers who shovelled coal below decks earned.) Nevertheless, many young men were seduced by Marconi's promise of a brighter occupational future. These students tended to be a confident lot. The mock public-school jauntiness that was the preferred style of professional wireless communications illustrates the breezy bravado that was characteristic of the early days of radio; messages commonly began with the salutation, 'I say, old man', which was so frequently used that it was abbreviated 'ISOM'.

Jack Phillips spent six months at the Marconi School studying the theory and practice of wireless, including lessons in the elementary principles of electricity, magnetism and telegraphy, as well as instruction in the use and repair of various kinds of equipment. He would also have learned about the general routine and discipline of life on a ship, as wireless operators were technically crew members with the rank of junior officer, though in practice they were largely left to their own devices. After completing his course of study, Phillips received a certificate confirming his proficiency at wireless operations. For the next two years, he served on board a number of ships for both the White Star and Cunard Lines, including the *Lusitania* and *Mauretania.*

The fact that Phillips was posted to such prestigious vessels suggests that he was perceived as being good at his job. Marconi operators required self-confidence and independence, for they frequently worked long and irregular hours alone, making snap decisions about the priority of certain messages over others. Their employment by the Marconi Company rather than the shipping lines created a sense of distance from the rest of the crew that was seldom breached. They wore a different uniform and spent almost all of their time in the wireless cabin, where they ate and slept as well as worked. Wireless operators also had to face the scepticism of their captains and senior officers, who often distrusted the new technology. The public may have seen wireless as exciting and glamorous, but many sailors saw it as little more than a gimmick. In terms of the day-to-day operations of a ship, wireless was an ancillary – and often unessential – form of technology, not an integral and vital source of information about weather conditions, the position of other ships and other navigational matters.[5]

After two years at sea, Phillips was transferred in 1908 to the Marconi transatlantic station at Clifden on the west coast of Ireland, where his job was to handle messages to and from the Marconi station at Glace Bay, Nova Scotia. In 1911, he was posted to the White Star liner *Adriatic,* on which he served until being sent to Belfast as senior wireless operator on the brand-new *Titanic.* By that point, although only twenty-five years old, Phillips was one of the most experienced wireless operators in the world. He would have arrived on the *Titanic* confident in his ability to deal with any situation that might arise.

As the *Titanic* underwent its sea trials on 2 April 1912, Phillips, assisted by junior officer Harold Bride, worked to get the ship's brand-new

wireless apparatus up and running. The equipment had just been received from the Marconi Company and was not yet fully operational.
The set was one of the most powerful afloat, with a 400-mile daytime
range and treble that at night; it even featured a battery-operated backup
system in case the main power failed. Above the top deck an antenna
ran three-quarters of the ship's length, suspended from two masts 200
feet in the air.[6] Phillips and Bride spent a busy day connecting wires
and making adjustments. During the voyage from Belfast to Southampton that night, they handled a number of messages to and from White
Star's home office in Liverpool as the anxious owners sought information
about the ship's performance. They also communicated with several
other vessels as they tested the *Titanic*'s transmitter. As the *Titanic*
rounded Land's End, freak atmospheric conditions enabled the ship's
signals to be heard as far away as Tenerife and Port Said.[7]

Once the *Titanic*'s maiden voyage was underway, Phillips and Bride
were swamped by a deluge of messages.[8] Most were from passengers
eager to use the new technology and to boast of their presence on the
world's largest and most luxurious ship. After they boarded at Cherbourg, the Ryerson family sent a message home to Cooperstown, New
York: 'Meet us Wednesday on arrival. Dock or Belmont. Bring mail'.
Messages came in as well as went out. Paris milliner George Rheims,
on a business trip to New York, received a loving farewell from his wife
Marie: '*Bons voeux tendresses*'. Passing ships also sent messages wishing
the *Titanic* success; Captain Murray of the *Empress of Britain* signalled,
'Officers and self send greetings and best of luck to the *Titanic*, her
officers and commander'.[9]

Phillips and Bride worked staggered shifts so that one of them was
on duty at all times. In addition to sending and receiving messages, they
were responsible for monitoring the news from shore, which on White
Star vessels was incorporated into a shipboard magazine called the
Atlantic Daily Bulletin. Most of the magazine was prepared prior to
departure, but whatever titbits Phillips and Bride could pick up were
incorporated into it, providing a further demonstration of the wonders
of wireless technology.

On the afternoon of Friday 12 April, the *Titanic* received its first
warning of ice from the French liner *La Touraine*; the warning was
acknowledged by Captain Smith, who replied 'thanks for your message

and information' along with details of the *Titanic*'s position and the weather conditions.[10] That night at around 11 p.m. the *Titanic*'s wireless set broke down, requiring Phillips and Bride to make repairs that took about seven hours. The trouble was determined to be in one of the leads running from the transformer to the transmitter, and by Saturday morning the apparatus was functioning once again. No ice warnings were received on Saturday, though numerous ships that lacked wireless capability reported seeing ice in the North Atlantic shipping lanes once they reached port. As we have seen, on Sunday 14 April the *Titanic* received seven ice warnings via wireless communication, along with a message sent by Morse lamp from the *Rappannock*. Of these, three – those sent by the *Amerika*, the *Mesaba* and the *Californian* – seem never to have made it to the bridge.

In retrospect, it would appear that there was considerable room for criticism of Phillip's conduct prior to the moment when the *Titanic* struck the iceberg. Although he presumably based his judgements on his substantial experience as a shipboard wireless operator, he prevented information from getting to the bridge that might have altered the decisions made by the *Titanic*'s officers. The priority established by the Marconi Company for the transmission and reception of different kinds of messages was quite specific: navigational messages were to be regarded as more important than private correspondence. Phillips, however, probably reasoned that numerous warnings regarding ice had already been delivered to the bridge, and that a few hours' delay in delivering another would make no difference. He was also exhausted; Bride had agreed to relieve him at midnight, two hours early, because of the long hours Phillips had spent dealing with the backlog of messages created by the set's malfunction. Moreover, it seems highly unlikely, given the standard seafaring practice of the day, that Captain Smith would have reduced speed even if he had been in possession of the information contained in the additional ice warnings. Still, a public anxious to identify scapegoats in the wake of the disaster could easily have fixed on Phillips. Why did they not do so?

They did not do so because Phillips's conduct after the collision with the iceberg made him virtually unassailable, according to contemporary standards of heroic conduct. At the time of the sinking of the *Titanic*, a model already existed that defined how a wireless operator should act in case of a disaster at sea. That model had been created three years earlier by Jack Binns, wireless operator on the White Star liner *Republic*. At 5.30 a.m. on 23 January 1909, the *Republic* was steaming through fog off Nantucket when it was rammed by the Italian liner *Florida*. The collision ripped a huge gash in the *Republic*'s side and damaged the ship's wireless set. The *Florida* was in better shape but had no wireless capability. As the doomed *Republic*'s passengers were transferred to the *Florida*, Binns struggled to repair the apparatus and finally managed to send out a distress call. Several ships responded, including the *Baltic*, which brought all of the *Republic*'s 461 passengers safely to New York. The *Republic* later sank as it was being towed into shore; the captain and crew barely managed to escape in time.

Afterwards, Binns was hailed as a hero, as press accounts described how he had waded through icy water to get to the storage room where the extra batteries for the wireless set were kept, and how he had held the damaged transmitter together with one hand while signalling with the other. 'CQD Binns' quickly became a national celebrity; while attending a musical review on 29 January he was made to come up on stage and give a speech, surrounded by adoring chorus girls. His actions convinced the public of the value of the miraculous new technology and inspired countless young boys to take up wireless as a hobby. They also established a pattern that accounts of Phillips's actions during the sinking of the *Titanic* would emulate. There was no real evidence that Binns's actions had actually saved anyone's life, since the ship's passengers and crew were able to be transferred to the still-seaworthy *Florida*. His true contribution was to accelerate the arrival of other ships on the scene and thereby to minimize the survivors' discomfort. What mattered, though, was that he had done his duty and stayed at his post, much as Phillips would do three years later.

The public first learned the story of Phillips's heroism on the *Titanic* from the account of Harold Bride, who was interviewed by *New York Times* reporter Jim Speers as soon as the *Carpathia* docked. The lead story on the front page of the *Times* on the morning of 19 April 1912, Bride's account was the first direct testimony by a *Titanic* survivor to appear in the press. (It appeared in the British press the following day.) Bride established the foundation of Phillips's heroism. He described how he was preparing to relieve Phillips at midnight on 14 April when Captain Smith 'put his head in the cabin' and informed the two wireless operators that the *Titanic* had struck an iceberg: 'I'm having an inspection made to tell what it has done for us. You better get ready to send out a call for assistance. But don't send it until I tell you'. About ten minutes later, Smith returned and ordered Phillips to send the distress call. 'What call should I send?' asked Phillips as he put on his headphones.

'The regulation international call for help. Just that.' Phillips began transmitting 'CQD', the international signal for distress, followed by the *Titanic*'s call sign, MGY, and approximate position.

'He flashed away at it', Bride recalled, 'and we joked while he did so. All of us made light of the disaster. We joked that way while he flashed signals for about five minutes. Then the captain came back.'

'What are you sending?' Smith asked.

'CQD', replied Phillips.

Bride 'cut in with a little remark that made us all laugh, including the Captain. "Send SOS", I said. 'It's the new call, and it may be your last chance to send it.' With a laugh, Phillips changed the signal to SOS. Over the next few minutes, Phillips and Bride 'said lots of funny things to each other', although by that point they were becoming aware of the *Titanic*'s increasing list.[11]

Today, the jokes that Phillips and Bride made as they transmitted the distress call seem inappropriate, and their conduct seems to be that of two callow young men unaware of the gravity of the situation. In 1912, however, their conduct was interpreted as an exemplar of manly heroism, reflecting an ability to maintain a cool head in a crisis. Phillips further demonstrated his steadiness by telling Bride to get dressed; the younger man had forgotten that he was still in his pyjamas. As the ship's list increased

> there was a great scramble aft, and how poor Phillips worked through it I don't know. He was a brave man. I learned to love him that night, and I suddenly felt for him a great reverence to see him standing there sticking to his work while everybody else was raging about. I will never live to forget the work of Phillips for the last awful fifteen minutes.

Recognizing that the end was near, Bride went and retrieved his lifebelt from under his bunk; when he returned Phillips was 'standing out there still sending away, giving the *Carpathia* details of just how we were doing'. As Phillips continued to transmit, Bride strapped his lifebelt on him and tried to figure out a way to 'get him into his boots' as he worked. Still showing good humour, Phillips 'suggested with a sort of laugh that I look out and see if all the people were off in the boats, or if any boats were left, or how things were'. Bride went out and became caught up in the frantic struggle to launch Collapsible A, then returned and informed Phillips that 'the last raft had gone'.

It was at this point that Captain Smith paid the wireless shack one final visit and ordered, 'Men you have done your full duty. You can do more. Abandon your cabin. Now it's every man for himself. You look out for yourselves. I release you. That's the way of it at this kind of a time. Every man for himself'. Still, Phillips 'clung on sending and sending. He clung on for about ten minutes, or maybe fifteen minutes, after the Captain had released him. The water was then coming into our cabin'. As he worked, a stoker crept into the wireless shack and tried to slip Phillips's lifebelt off his back. Phillips was 'too busy to notice what the man was doing', but Bride saw him. Bride was a small man, but he 'remembered in a flash the way Phillips had clung on' and fought the stoker off, leaving him unconscious on the floor. Shortly afterwards, Phillips finally abandoned his post and ran aft: 'That was the last I ever saw of him alive'. In the conclusion to his account, Bride said that he remembered two things from the sinking: 'the way the band kept playing' and 'the way Phillips kept sending after the Captain told him his life was his own, and to look out for himself'.[12]

From start to finish, then, Phillips's conduct was impeccable. He responded to the initial news of the disaster with humour, and even as he had become more serious he had never lost his composure, staying calm while 'everybody else was raging about'. He had taken charge, as the senior wireless operator should, remaining at the apparatus while issuing clear and forceful orders to his subordinate. Above all, even after he had been released from duty by his captain, he had remained at his post, desperately trying to find another ship closer to the *Titanic*'s position than the *Carpathia*. The whole story has a *Boys' Own* quality to it, culminating as it does with the fight over the lifebelt with the stoker.[13] (Even that did not distract Phillips from his duty!)

Thanks to Bride's account, which became one of the most frequently cited of all the survivor's stories, Phillips was universally hailed as a hero. 'There is no finer thing in chivalry', asserted the *Daily News*, 'than the fidelity of the telegraphist who kept to his work till the end.'[14] The *Daily Mirror* declared that 'he remained nobly at his post and sent out messages with coolness and despatch'.[15] '[Phillips's] name is imperishable; his death a glorious tradition', wrote Philip Gibbs in 'The Deathless Story of the *Titanic*', a special supplement in *Lloyd's Weekly News* published two weeks after the disaster. He became 'Phillips the brave; Phillips the true', the man who 'helped the helpless in the hour of gloom' and 'saved the weak from a yawning tomb'. Agnes Campbell wrote of how the

> Wireless operator, whose heart was filled with dread,
> Sent out the urgent message, 'We are sinking by the head!'
> And Philip's hand
> By sticking to the wireless, saved seven hundred fellow men.
> Such heroism could never be pictured by a pen,
> For it was grand.

In the *St Helens Reporter*, Annie Hampton wrote:

> Mourns England her lost son,
> Phillips, whose fame has won,
> Love's tears and orison,
> A deathless name!
> *Carpathia*'s aid he sought,
> His life for others bought
> Sweet aid. Himself was caught.
> Played out life's game.[16]

Putting it most succinctly was the headline in the *Daily Chronicle* on 17 April: 'Jack Phillips – Hero'.[17]

In Godalming, a previously undistinguished native son had suddenly become one of England's biggest heroes; no townsman had earned such fame since James Edward Oglethorpe had founded the British colony of Georgia in 1733.[18] First to respond was the Post Office where Phillips had once worked as telegraphist. By the end of April 1912, the postmaster, W. R. Williams, had commissioned a copper plaque in Phillips's honour. The plaque was eighteen inches by twelve inches and divided into eight sections, with a portrait of Phillips in the centre. Over the portrait were the initials 'J.P.' surrounded by a wreath; underneath was a depiction of the *Titanic*. On the left side was an inscription reading 'Duty First'. According to the *Surrey Advertiser and County Times*, 'the memorial is excellently designed, and will be a handsome and lasting record of a brave deed'. The paper also reported that the postmen were collecting funds for a 'large framed portrait' of Phillips that would be hung 'in their room'.[19]

Nor was the Godalming Town Council slow to commemorate the heroism of their famous son. A memorial honouring Phillips was first discussed on 26 April, when Mayor Bridger stated that 'this Council expresses its deep sympathy with those bereaved by the loss of the steamship *Titanic* and especially with Mr and Mrs Phillips in the loss of their son who died bravely doing his duty'. A Phillips Memorial Committee was established to choose a suitable location and design for the memorial, and a subscription fund was opened. The committee soon determined that the 'only practical site' was a small piece of common land between the Technical Institute and the home of one Mr Nash, a member of the Council. The site had the further advantage of being in Farncombe, Phillips's place of birth. Nash was sent a letter requesting permission for the memorial to be erected on the piece of land in question. He agreed, but expressed concern that the memorial might attract noisy children who would cause 'some annoyance' to his family. To alleviate these concerns, the committee agreed to erect a fence thirty feet from the boundary of Nash's property.[20] For the time being, Nash made no further objections.

Meanwhile, ideas as to what form the memorial should take were solicited from the noted garden designer Gertrude Jekyll, who lived nearby. The committee had proposed a drinking fountain embossed with a portrait medallion, but Jekyll had other ideas. On 7 September, she sent a letter to the committee expressing her views. Regarding the fountain and medallion, she stated that 'what has been attempted in this way has nearly always resulted in expensive and useless failure'. She pointed out that a medallion 'executed by a first-rate sculptor' would be 'a very costly matter', while 'no other would be worth having'. She further argued that 'an effigy of a young man of Phillips's age could rarely be of that pronounced character that could be satisfactorily rendered in bronze or marble'. As an alternative scheme, Jekyll, in consultation with the local architect Thackery Turner, proposed 'a rectangular cloister of some hundred and twenty feet square':

> Entering the enclosure there would be a wide paved space with a small square middle garden consisting of beds and dwarf shrubs and flowers with grass between. The centre circle shown on the plan could be either a shallow fountain or another planted bed. The sides to right and left would be unbroken cloister. The further side would have the wall not cloistered but arcaded to the meadow, with a wide central solid panel where the memorial tablet would be placed. Seen through the arches, the view of meadow and hill would be singularly beautiful. There would be seats under the cloisters, and, according to wind and weather, there would always be some portion affording comfortable protection. It would be of special utility to nurses with young children, providing a safe place for air and exercise in threatening weather, as well as of pleasure to the many who would be glad of such a spot of reposeful beauty and harbourage. The style of structure that we contemplate is that of the older of the local farm buildings, buildings that have the merit and beauty of a simple aim and the dignity that comes of the use of local material in the excellent traditional way of the county.

Jekyll further proposed that the remainder of the land be 'enlarged and made more useful as a possible children's playground by the diversion of the stream'. She suggested that any negative impact on Nash's property be mitigated by providing him with 'a separate entrance which gives access to the back of his premises'. She offered no estimate of the cost, but stated that such a scheme, 'promising both beauty and use to Godalming', would be likely to 'bring in new contributions ... from original subscribers and even from a wider circle afield ... For though we of Godalming and the near neighbourhood feel that to perpetuate the memory of a splendid act of duty is a debt of honour that we are glad to acknowledge, yet it may well be regarded as a national concern and not merely one of local interest'.[21]

The Memorial Committee and Town Council responded to Jekyll's proposal with enthusiasm, but they were concerned about the cost, which the Borough Surveyor estimated at £700. They had already collected £420 in subscriptions, which left an additional £280 to raise. The committee stated that it was of 'the unanimous opinion that inasmuch as the scheme ... will add to the attractiveness of Godalming, and provide a spot suitable for rest and recreation of both young and old, further efforts should be made to obtain the remainder of the sum required to carry out the whole scheme'. The five members of the Council present at the meeting of 9 November concurred; they consented to the common land being used to build a Phillips Memorial Cloister and invited further subscriptions to the memorial fund.[22] Everything seemed to be humming along nicely.

Nicely, that is, until Councillor Nash started causing trouble. On 11 January 1913 the committee received a letter from him stating that

> I have given this matter further consideration and regret that I feel compelled to withdraw my consent to the erection of the proposed building and the laying out of a playground on the piece of Lammas land surrounding my property as such a building would obfuscate the view from my house, and the playground would be such an intolerable nuisance as to necessitate my removal elsewhere, and further, I should feel obliged to ask you to compensate me for the serious depreciation of my property should you ultimately decide to carry out your scheme.

The committee was furious, and objected strenuously to Nash on the grounds that 'the bulk of the money' for the memorial had been subscribed on the supposition that the cloister would be built on that particular piece of ground in accordance with Jekyll's plans. They entered into further negotiations with Nash, who agreed to sell the relevant piece of land if the corporation would sell him another piece near his house that was approximately equal in size. Nash had clearly realized that he was in the driver's seat, and he was not prepared to surrender his rights to the common land without getting something in return. The committee pondered his proposal and went so far as to draw up a draft agreement, but in the end they decided that there were 'fatal objections' and rejected it. Nash then tried an alternate approach, suggesting that if the corporation was not willing to sell the other piece of land to him he would accept a lease of twenty-one years. Once again, however, the committee refused. Nash then proposed a third deal: he would convey to the corporation two additional pieces of land that he owned nearby and allow them to construct the memorial on them, if the corporation would convey to him in return a one-acre site between the Technical School and his house. The committee visited the proposed new location for the memorial and found it acceptable, though 'not such a good one as the proposed original site'.[23]

Nash therefore won a double victory: the memorial was not built adjacent to his house, and he was able to arrange a deal for a piece of land that he had his eye on. In any event, the land that the corporation obtained from him in the deal was not ultimately used for the Phillips Memorial Cloister, because in November of 1913 the town purchased about three acres of land adjoining Godalming parish church. Initially, it was proposed that the land be used not only for the cloister but also for a bathing place and recreation ground.[24] Mayor Harry Colpus, however, objected to the construction of a bathing place because there was insufficient space, because the land was boggy due to its proximity to the River Wey and would be expensive to drain, and because 'the idea of the Phillips Memorial Cloister is the provision of a quiet resting place for people wishing to use it'.[25] In the end, only the recreation ground was built; it can still be found next to the cloister today.

The cloister was complete by the spring of 1914. The dedication ceremony was held on 15 April, the second anniversary of the sinking of the *Titanic*. Inside the cloister was a small fountain provided by the Postal Telegraph Clerks' Association; the inscription reads:

> This Cloister is Built in Memory of
> John George Phillips
> A Native of This Town
> Chief Wireless Telegraphist of
> The Ill-Fated S.S. *Titanic*
> He Died at His Post
> When the Vessel Found-
> ered in Mid-Atlantic
> On the 15th Day of
> April 1912

Over the years, as vandalism became an increasing problem, it became necessary to make alterations to the original design. In the 1960s, one wall of the cloister was removed and replaced by a timber pergola in order to open it up. One night in the 1980s, a prankster removed 140 goldfish from the pond, which was subsequently filled in and planted with shrubbery. In 1993 the Waverly Borough Council and Surrey Garden Trust renovated the cloister to repair the damage caused by almost eighty years of neglect. Today, Godalming proudly proclaims it to be the largest *Titanic* memorial in the world.

Even that, however, was not considered sufficient commemoration of Jack Phillips's heroism. On 29 June 1913 Farncombe parish church unveiled a brass tablet in Phillips's honour, bearing the inscription: 'In memory of John George Phillips, aged 26 years, formerly a chorister of this Church, Chief Marconi Operator on RMS *Titanic*, which sank at sea, April 16th [*sic*] 1912. Faithful to his duty till the last'.[26] The Mayor, Town Council, Post Office officials and Fire Brigade were all present for the unveiling, along with a 'large congregation'. In the evening service that followed the ceremony, the rector held up Phillips's conduct as a model for his parishioners:

> Noble deaths in all ages should act as incentives for us all to nobler aims of duty. Such a one was that commemorated by the tablet which has been unveiled and dedicated ... in memory of one who, in that great disaster at sea more than a year ago, remained at his post and was faithful to his duty till the last ... The thought of his steadfastness and self-sacrifice should have an uplifting effect on us all. His devotion to duty helps to swell the great catalogue of honourable deeds, which we should not be content merely to admire, but strive in our degree to imitate.[27]

As this example illustrates, Godalming's commemorations of Jack Phillips all focused on a common theme: his devotion to duty. Indeed, this theme has remained a prominent part of the town's memory of Phillips down through the years. In the early 1930s, the *Godhelmian*, the magazine of Godalming Grammar School, declared:

> Looking back on the disaster, one feels that something more should have been done, some greater effort made. Yet in one way the utmost possible had been achieved: Phillips and his fellow workers had stayed, sending out messages which were bringing several other ships at top speed to the rescue. Without their efforts the loss of life would have been infinitely greater, for those in the boats would have died from exposure in the intense cold. Scorning to seek his own safety, Phillips died at his post when the vessel foundered.[28]

In honour of the eighty-fifth anniversary of the sinking in April 1997, Godalming Museum held an exhibition entitled 'Jack Phillips and the *Titanic*'; so many people attended that the museum reopened the exhibition in May. Curator Adela Goodall asserted that Phillips 'showed a real devotion to duty and strength of character by continuing to signal for help even as the ship went down'.[29] And a new Wetherspoon pub named after Phillips recently opened on Godalming High Street. Just inside the door, a poster proclaims: 'When the [*Titanic*] went down after hitting an iceberg, Jack Phillips stayed at his post sending out the Mayday message'.

Phillips thus remains a true Edwardian hero in Godalming, a man who refused to abandon his post even though he knew his own life was in danger. The story of his heroism lives on in the town. As part of the festivities for the eighty-fifth anniversary, *Titanic* survivor Millvina Dean was invited to lay a wreath at the fountain in the memorial cloister. When asked what she would like to say to Phillips, Dean replied, 'Thank you, Jack, for saving my life'.[30]

5

Wallace Hartley

The second member of the *Titanic*'s heroic triumvirate was Wallace Hartley, the bandleader who, according to several survivor's accounts, kept the ship's eight-member orchestra playing until the water literally washed them off the deck. By doing this, Hartley displayed the key characteristics of a *Titanic* hero: a commitment to duty, a maintenance of a stiff upper lip and a display of chivalrous self-sacrifice. In the immediate aftermath of the sinking, Hartley became the most lionized of all the *Titanic*'s victims in the British press. Story after story told of how the brave bandleader had played until the last possible moment, with the hymn 'Nearer My God to Thee' as his final musical selection. Today the story of Hartley and the band remains one of the most enduring aspects of the *Titanic* myth, an episode that is well known even to people with only a passing familiarity with the details of the sinking. Whether it actually occurred in the form in which it is traditionally imagined or even at all is very much an open question, but that has mattered little in popular *Titanic* memory. No other part of the story has the weight of so much sentiment behind it: we believe it to be true because we want it to be true. Nor did any doubts about what actually happened during Wallace Hartley's final moments affect his commemoration in his hometown of Colne in Lancashire. Just as Jack Phillips became a local hero in Godalming, Hartley was celebrated – and continues to be celebrated – in Colne, where his conduct on the night of the sinking was held up as an exemplar of civic virtue.

Wallace Hartley was born in Colne on 2 June 1878 and spent his childhood and adolescence in the town, though by 1912 his family had moved to Dewsbury in Yorkshire. Nicknamed 'Bonnie Colne' because of its scenic setting between the Yorkshire Dales and the Ribble Valley, the town occupies an attractive hilly position in the north-eastern corner

of Lancashire. Colne's economic fortunes have not, however, traditionally depended on the beauty of the surrounding region, but on the
textile industry. Since the sixteenth century, when it first emerged as a
centre for woollen cloth manufacture, Colne has been a textile town.
The introduction of spinning mills in the 1780s brought about a shift
from wool to cotton; by 1824 there were twenty-two cotton mills in the
town. The arrival of the power loom in the 1830s sparked further
expansion, and by the time of Hartley's birth Colne was truly ruled by
King Cotton.

The king's crown, however, rested somewhat uneasily on his head.
Throughout the nineteenth century north-east Lancashire suffered from
the consequences of rapid industrialization, which brought about considerable economic distress and social unrest. In 1827 the *Liverpool
Commercial Chronicle* described the state of the weaving districts:

> The cotton weavers who reside principally in the neighbourhood of Bolton,
> Chorley, Wigan, Blackburn, Haslingden, Padiham, Burnley, Colne and Tod-
> morden are by far the most wretched body in this part of the country. The
> number of cotton weavers in the places above-mentioned must exceed 60,000
> and probably is near 100,000 and the utmost sum they can earn per week, on a
> fair average, working diligently from six til eight ... is only four shillings.[1]

On his tour of the Lancashire manufacturing districts in 1842, W. Cooke
Taylor stopped at Colne, where he visited 'eighty-three dwellings selected
at hazard':

> They were destitute of furniture, save old boxes for tables and stools, or even
> large stones for chairs; the beds were composed of straw and shavings,
> sometimes with torn pieces of carpet or packing canvas for a covering, and
> sometimes without any kind of covering whatever. The food was oatmeal
> and water for breakfast, flour and water with a little skimmed milk for dinner;
> oatmeal and water again for a third supply for those who went through the
> form of eating three meals a day. I was informed in fifteen families that their
> children went without the 'blue milk', or milk from which the cream had
> been taken, on alternate days. I was an eye witness to children appeasing the
> craving of the stomach by the refuse of decayed vegetables in the root market.
> I saw a woman in the very last stage of extenuation suckling an infant which
> could scarcely draw a single drop of nourishment from her exhausted breast.
> I enquired the child's age? Fifteen months. Why was it not weaned? Another
> mouth would be added to the number of those for whom the present supply

of oatmeal was insufficient. I was told that there had been several instances of death by sheer starvation.[2]

Such acute distress bred discontentment. Riots and outbreaks of violence were common, and radical political movements such as Chartism found widespread support. In the mid 1840s, mobs pulled boiler plugs out of machines to stop work in the mills and even set one mill on fire. In 1860 Colne experienced an eleven-month strike, the longest in the history of the Lancashire cotton industry. The strike brought 1500 mill workers to the brink of starvation before it collapsed.

By the time of Wallace Hartley's birth, however, conditions had improved. Wages for mill workers had increased, and the working week had been cut to fifty-six hours, with a half day on Saturday. Infant mortality had declined, and the number of schools had grown. Along with those of the town, the Hartley family's fortunes had improved. Wallace's grandfather Henry was a weaver, and his father Albion was listed in the census of 1871 as a cotton 'sizer'. Ten years later, however, Albion Hartley had risen to mill manager, and by 1891 he had escaped from the mills altogether and become an insurance superintendent for the Refuge Assurance Company.

Like many families in Colne, the Hartleys were Nonconformists. They attended Bethel Independent Methodist Chapel, which had been built in 1857 to serve the growing working-class area of Primet Bridge, close to the Hartleys' house. Albion was an active member of the congregation: he led the choir and supervised the Sunday school. On the day of Wallace's birth, the doctor who performed the delivery joked that he would donate five shillings to the collection if the choir would sing 'Unto Us a Child Is Given' at the service. Albion replied, 'Let me have your five shillings; we have been rehearsing it, and will sing it to-day'.[3]

Details about Wallace Hartley's pre-*Titanic* life are scant, and precise dates in particular are in short supply. He attended the day school at Bethel Chapel, where music was seen as an important component of the education of young Methodists. His musical talents were also encouraged by his father, an amateur violinist who played in local orchestras. Hartley began receiving violin lessons at the age of twelve, and by fifteen he was giving solo concerts. In the mid 1890s Albion Hartley's job necessitated a move to Dewsbury in West Yorkshire, where

Wallace became a clerk in the Union Bank. He pressed his parents, however, to let him pursue a musical career, and they reluctantly agreed. Hartley was able to get positions in a number of ensembles in Bridlington, Harrogate and Leeds before a more prestigious position opened up in the orchestra of the Carl Rosa Opera Company, with which he toured the country for three years. He then joined the Moody-Manners Opera Company for two years.

Hartley's big break came when he was hired by Cunard as an orchestra leader; he served on a number of the line's most prestigious ships, including the *Lusitania* and the *Mauretania*, suggesting that the tall, handsome violinist was popular with first-class passengers. Certainly, the rival White Star Line seems to have thought so. For the new *Titanic*, White Star wanted to hire the best musicians available, and they offered Hartley a substantial increase in pay if he would agree to serve as bandmaster. There is some evidence that Hartley was of two minds about accepting the post. In 1912 he had become engaged to Elizabeth Robinson of Ballston Spa, and his forthcoming marriage may have caused him to consider a return to life on land. It seems, however, that the pay raise and the prestige of serving on the *Titanic* won out, and he accepted the job. He spent the week prior to the ship's departure in Yorkshire with Elizabeth, before hastening down to Southampton to take up his new post. In his last letter home, which was posted from Queenstown, he expressed his regret to his parents that he had been unable to see them before he left.

The life of a ship's musician was a somewhat odd one. Prior to 1912, the steamship lines dealt directly with musicians, hiring them for individual voyages, just as they signed up other members of the crew. The pay was a union scale, which worked out to £6 10s. a month, plus a monthly uniform allowance of 10s. But in 1912 a talent agency from Liverpool run by C. W. and F. N. Black entered the picture. They promised the shipping lines that they would streamline the process by hiring the musicians themselves and contracting them out. One by one, the lines signed contracts with the Blacks, giving them the exclusive right to supply bands to their vessels. The musicians were still required to sign the ship's articles, which meant that they were subject to the authority of the captain and other senior officers while on board, but they were now employed and paid by the Blacks and could only get jobs through the agency. Since the musicians now worked for the Blacks or not at all, they had to take whatever pay they could get, which in many cases turned out to represent a sharp cut in wages. Instead of £6 10s. per month, they now got only £4, with no uniform allowance.

The Amalgamated Musicians Union protested, to no avail. In March 1912 they met J. Bruce Ismay, White Star's managing director, to complain about band members being paid at less than union scale, even though they were members of the ship's crew. Ismay's solution was simple: if the union objected to the bandsmen being paid less than other comparable crew members, he would turn them into passengers. On the next voyage of the *Olympic*, the five musicians were listed as second-class passengers and were issued regular second-class tickets, though they still occupied the same cramped quarters on E Deck, next to the potato washer. When the ship reached New York, they each had to produce $50 in cash, just like other second-class passengers, in order to prove that they were not destitute. There was one benefit of the change in status, however: the musicians now got to dine in the second-class saloon, rather than the more utilitarian crew's dining room.

On board the *Titanic*, Hartley had seven musicians under his direction: pianists Theodore Brailey and P. C. Taylor, violinist Jock Hume, cellists Roger Bricoux and J. W. Woodward, bass-violist Fred Clark and violist George Krins. Although *Titanic* histories contain frequent references to 'the band' or 'the orchestra', in reality there were two separate ensembles of musicians. A quintet consisting of piano, violin, cello, viola and bass-viola played at teatime, after dinner and during religious services on Sunday, while a trio consisting of piano, violin and cello played in the reception room on B Deck as well as outside the Café Parisien and the *à la carte* restaurant. The two bands maintained completely separate musical libraries and arrangements, and it is likely that they did not play together until the night of the sinking.

As the *Titanic* steamed away from Cherbourg and the first-class passengers sipped their coffee and liqueurs, the quintet, led by Hartley, performed its first after-dinner concert. The music was selected from a range of light melodies taken from operettas, waltzes, music-hall tunes and ragtime. The concert lasted until around 11 p.m., by which time most of the passengers had drifted off to their cabins, a pattern that would be repeated on subsequent evenings, including Sunday 14 April.

Hartley's musicians had almost certainly retired for the evening when they were summoned by Captain Smith, following the collision with the iceberg, and ordered to begin playing in the first-class lounge; it is unknown how much Smith told them about the extent of the damage to the ship. At around 12.15 a.m., they launched into a set of lively tunes, including Irving Berlin's 'Alexander's Ragtime Band' and 'In the Shadows', the big British hit of 1911. Surviving passenger Jack Thayer remembered them playing for the restless crowd that milled in and out of the room, with no one paying them much attention.

Later, though the exact time is unclear, the musicians moved up to the Boat Deck level of the Grand Staircase, and then eventually out onto the deck itself, where they played near the forward entrance to the Grand Staircase, seemingly oblivious to the growing chaos around them. (It is unclear whether the two piano players were with them at this point, as it is unlikely that they dragged their instruments out onto the deck.) Numerous survivors claimed that the band played until almost the last moment, when the slope of the *Titanic*'s deck would have made it impossible for them to stand upright. Harold Bride recalled hearing music as he struggled to free Collapsible Lifeboat B from the roof of the officers' quarters. Greaser Thomas Ranger could still hear them when he came up from the engine room after the last boat had gone. And perhaps most poignantly, Steward Edward Brown, when he was asked at the British inquiry how long the band had played, replied, 'I do not remember hearing them stop'.[4]

Others, however, reported that the musicians stopped playing well in advance of that point. Colonel Archibald Gracie claimed that they put down their instruments about half an hour before the ship sank, an account that was confirmed by first-class passenger A. H. Barkworth, who recalled, 'I do not wish to detract from the bravery of anybody, but I might mention that when I first came on deck the band was playing a waltz. The next time I passed where the band had been stationed, the members had thrown down their instruments, and were not to be seen'.[5]

Whatever time the band stopped playing, there must have been a final tune. The identity of that tune has become one of the most abiding controversies of the *Titanic* story. According to popular tradition, as well as several survivor accounts, the choice was the hymn 'Nearer My

God to Thee', which has been featured in the vast majority of literary and cinematic versions of the sinking, including the 1997 James Cameron film. These claims are bolstered by the fact that Hartley had once told fellow musician Ellwand Moody that, if he were ever to be on a sinking ship, 'I don't think I could do better than play "Oh God Our Help in Ages Past" or "Nearer My God to Thee". They are both favourite hymns of mine, and they would be very suitable to the occasion'.[6]

There is, however, a problem with firmly establishing 'Nearer My God to Thee' as the final tune played that night, for there were three different settings of the hymn available at the time of the *Titanic* disaster. In the United States, the preferred version was set to the tune 'Bethany', composed by Lowell Mason. In Britain, there were two versions: John Bacchus Dykes's 'Horbury', which was favoured by the Church of England, and Sir Arthur Sullivan's 'Propior Deo', favoured by British Methodists. Hartley was a Methodist who was well versed in the musical traditions of his faith, and thus it seems likely that he would have selected Sullivan's 'Propior Deo'. Indeed, that is the tune inscribed on his grave in Colne Cemetery. But on British liners religious services would have followed the Church of England liturgy, which makes it likely that the only tune that the band members would all have known was Dykes's 'Horbury'.

To add to the confusion, a number of survivors claimed that the last tune they heard was not 'Nearer My God to Thee' at all, but another one entirely. Colonel Gracie, who was on the ship almost until the final moment, insisted that he heard only lively tunes: 'If "Nearer My God to Thee" was one of the selections, I assuredly would have noticed it and regarded it as a tactless warning of immediate death, and more likely to create a panic that our special efforts were directed towards avoiding'. Two other passengers – Peter Daly and Dick Williams – who were on board until the end also claimed that the band played only light, cheerful music.[7] In his account, wireless operator Harold Bride described the *Titanic*'s final moments: 'From aft came the tunes of the band. It was a ragtime tune, I don't know what. Then there was "Autumn"'.[8] Bride's account is generally regarded as accurate, and he was certainly on the ship almost until the last moment, but it is difficult to establish precisely to which piece of music he was referring. The *New York Times*, where Bride's account first appeared, claimed that the tune in question was an Anglican hymn called 'Autumn', which included in its third stanza the highly appropriate lines:

> Hold me up in mighty waters;
> Keep my eyes on things above.

But if this is what Bride was referring to, it was odd for him to call it 'Autumn', for in both Britain and America hymns are usually known by their first line ('Onward, Christian Soldiers'), not by the name of their tune ('Saint Gertrude'). There is no British hymn that begins 'Autumn'.

So to what song was Bride referring? There was a major hit in London in 1912 entitled 'Song d'Automne', composed by Archibald Joyce. Bride would almost certainly have known it well, though it was probably unfamiliar to the readers of the *New York Times*, as it was never very popular in America. The British press, however, identified the song Bride heard as a 'ragtime air' rather than a hymn, which may mean that they assumed that he was talking about 'Song d'Automne'.

Since neither Hartley nor any of the other seven musicians survived, it is impossible to determine with certainty what was the final song they played that night. What is more certain is that, in the weeks after the sinking, the band, and Hartley in particular, came to be celebrated as the *Titanic*'s greatest heroes. The first survivor reports of the band playing 'Nearer My God to Thee' as the ship slipped beneath the waves arrived with the *Carpathia* on 18 April, and the first published version appeared in the *New York Times* on the following day. In her account of the sinking Vera Dick recalled, 'What I remember best was that as the ship sank we could hear the band playing "Nearer My God to Thee"'.[9] On 20 April British newspapers were full of stories with headlines such as 'The Musician Heroes of the *Titanic*', 'Music on the Sinking Ship' and 'The Band Goes Down Playing'. 'Not since the deathless story of the wreck of the *Birkenhead*', declared the *Daily Chronicle*, 'has there been so strong an exhibition of sublime heroism as that shown by the bandsmen of the ill-fated *Titanic*. It was a fitting end to a solemn and terrible tragedy, and could not have failed to have brought consolation to all.'[10] Similarly, the *Daily Mirror* asserted:

> It was the bandsmen who sounded what was probably the most poignant note of heroism during the last tragic minutes on the *Titanic*. In the whole

history of the sea there is little equal to the wonderful behaviour of these humble players. In the last moments of the great ship's doom, when all was plainly lost, when presumably braver and hardier men might have been excused for doing practically anything to save themselves, they stood responsive to their conductor's baton and played a recessional tune.[11]

Hartley, in particular, was singled out for praise. Alongside a story entitled 'Till the Water Closed Over Them', the *Daily Sketch* printed a photo of him with the caption 'Musician Hero'. In its story 'Nearer My God to Thee', the *Daily Graphic* referred to the 'young Yorkshireman' who called 'his band together to play as they go to their death'.[12]

The heroism of Hartley and the band was celebrated not just in the press but in books, postcards and, appropriately, popular music. The Colne Public Library preserves a number of these commemorative items. In 'Memoriam Lines to Wallace Hartley and the Brave *Titanic* Band', W. H. Tanner of Burnley wrote:

> Ever shall their names be written on the fadeless scroll of fame,
> And their deed be rich emblazoned in each living heart aflame,
> On the roll of honour deeply carve the brave *Titanic* band,
> For the hero claims the homage of all hearts in every land.[13]

The Rotary Photograph Company produced a postcard displaying four verses and four bars of 'Nearer My God to Thee', while Millar and Lang's version provided the music and lyrics in their entirety. Bamforth and Company of Holmfirth, Yorkshire, produced a series of six postcards on the theme of 'Nearer My God to Thee', replete with weeping angels, Christ appearing over a dark sea and a sinking *Titanic*. Other postcard companies opted for photos of the musicians, with the example from Joe Dixon of Hull including crowns over each man's head. A song entitled 'The Band Was Playing as the Ship Went Down' was written by Robert Donnelly and printed for sale as sheet music; the cover featured a portrait of Hartley with no identification of him as the *Titanic*'s bandleader, suggesting that the public were expected to recognize him.[14] The third verse of the song contains the lyrics:

> Fancy a band playing knowing that death
> Would come in a few minutes time
> 'Nearer my God to Thee', how true these words
> To that brave band of men in their prime.[15]

Within weeks of the sinking, Wallace Hartley had become a hero, and commemorations of his conduct took place all over Britain. In Dewsbury, the town to which Hartley's family had moved in 1908, the Amateur Light Operatic and Dramatic Society performed the light opera *The Geisha* to raise funds for a memorial, and the local orchestra and military band gave a joint concert that concluded with the singing of 'Nearer My God to Thee'. In Leeds, local professional musicians arranged a concert that collected over £100; the funds were used to commission a painting of the *Titanic* in the band's memory that now hangs in the Leeds City Art Gallery. And in London, over five hundred musicians played in a memorial concert on 24 May in the Albert Hall, which was filled to capacity. At the end of the concert, Sir Henry Wood led the orchestra and the audience in singing 'Nearer My God to Thee'. Later, memorials to the *Titanic*'s musicians were erected in Southampton and in Liverpool. It was in Colne, however, where the greatest efforts to commemorate Hartley were made.

The news of Hartley's death first appeared in the local press in Colne on the 19 April 1912. 'A former Colne man named Mr Wallace Hartley is believed to be a victim of the disaster to the *Titanic*', reported the weekly *Colne and Nelson Times*. The tone of the report suggests that Hartley was not particularly well known in Colne prior to the sinking, which was not surprising given that he had last resided in the town seventeen years earlier. Even these early reports, however, acknowledged the benefits of claiming one of the *Titanic*'s greatest heroes as a native son. 'If Mr Hartley has gone down with the ship', the story concluded, 'much sympathy will be felt in the town with the family in their bereavement.' [16]

By the time that the next edition of the paper appeared a week later, Hartley was a full-blown national hero, and Colne rushed to join in the celebration. The *Colne and Nelson Times* featured an account of the band's heroic conduct that duplicated the stories found in the national press:

> After the terrible nature of the disaster had become known, the band of which Mr Wallace Hartley was the leader assembled on the after deck and played lively opera airs to keep the spirits of the crowded passengers bright as they thronged to the boat deck. Calmly, as if in the concert room, they went on

playing while slowly the great ship dipped her bows deeper into the water
and one by one the lifeboats were launched. Then, when the last lifeboat had
got clear away, as the floods of icy water crept higher and higher up the decks
of the sinking ship, the tune was changed. Out over the dark waters there
crept the moving strains of King Edward's favourite hymn, 'Nearer My God
to Thee'. Never since the early Christian martyrs went to their death singing
hymns has sacred music been heard in more moving and memorable circumstances. On the very brink of a terrible death this band of heroic musicians
played their very souls out of Time and Eternity for their strange and
wonderful music was still stealing over the water, and up to the star lit sky
when the lifeboats had left the *Titanic* behind, and the great ship had taken
her last plunge beneath the waves.[17]

Much of this account is debatable, and some of it, in part the final claim
that the strains of 'Nearer My God to Thee' could still be heard after
the *Titanic* sank, is clearly hyperbole. Colne, though, clearly had an
interest in viewing their local man's conduct in as heroic a light as
possible.

But how, more specifically, to celebrate Hartley's local ties and to
commemorate him in an appropriate fashion? On 26 April a letter from
'Civis' to the editor of the *Colne and Nelson Times* suggested that some
form of permanent memorial was in order:

As all the world knows now of the heroic conduct of Wallace Hartley, would
it not be fitting if his native town of Colne put up some memorial in his
memory? I would suggest that the Mayor call a town's meeting to consider
the matter. Not only his fellow townsmen, but, I feel sure, hundreds in his
native country, would be glad to subscribe ... The conductor has set an
example which all ought to emulate and one of which Colne, particularly,
ought to be proud.[18]

The town was quick to act on this suggestion. At the May meeting of
the town council, Deputy Mayor J. Smith announced that, 'at the request
of several gentlemen in the town', Mayor Turner Hartley (no relation
to Wallace) had opened a memorial fund to commemorate Hartley's
'heroic deeds'. It was the duty of the townspeople, Smith declared, 'to
assist the Mayor in making the memorial as good as they possibly
could ... so that it would be something for the young and rising
generation to look at and learn lessons from in the future'.[19]

Before detailed plans for a permanent memorial could be formulated, however, events necessitated a more immediate act of commemoration. On 30 April Hartley's battered body was found and brought to Halifax, Nova Scotia; his face was bruised and discoloured almost beyond recognition, but the violin case strapped to his back and his band uniform made a positive identification possible. The body was shipped back to England on the *Arabic*, and Albion Hartley travelled to Liverpool to claim it. According to the *Liverpool Daily Post and Mercury*, as Albion signed the receipt for the delivery of the body, 'his hands quivered with emotion' and 'he walked away broken with grief'.[20] Hartley's body was then conveyed the sixty miles to Colne by horse-drawn hearse, with the journey taking place at night in order to avoid public attention. The coffin was placed on a purple-draped bier in Bethel Chapel that bore the inscription:

Wallace Hartley
Died April 15th 1912
Aged 33 Years
'Nearer My God to Thee'

The funeral of one of the *Titanic*'s biggest heroes was bound to be of great interest to the public, not just in Colne but throughout Britain. Plans were made for the body to be interred in the Hartley family plot in Colne Cemetery on Sunday 18 May. After consulting with the Hartley family, the local authorities announced that a memorial service would take place in Bethel Chapel that would conclude with those in attendance singing 'Nearer My God to Thee'. The service was to be followed by a procession to the cemetery led by five brass bands. Next would come a battalion of the East Lancashire Regiment, buglers from the Boy Scouts, the town's ambulance brigade, the congregation of Bethel Chapel, the Colne Orchestra, the Bethel choir, the Colne Town Council and, at the end, the carriages carrying the coffin, wreaths and mourners. The gates of the cemetery would remain closed until the procession had entered in order to prevent the expected throng from impeding the mourners' progress to the gravesite. 'As it is expected that a large crowd will follow them to the grave', reported the *Colne and Nelson Times*, 'we are asked to make a request to the public that they will keep on the paths in the Cemetery, and not step on to other graves.'[21]

On the day of the funeral, over a thousand people jammed into pews meant for seven hundred in Bethel Chapel, and the press estimated that 40,000 people lined the route of the procession, half of them from out of town. (At the time, the population of Colne was around 26,000.) If this total is accurate, Wallace Hartley's funeral was the largest single *Titanic* memorial event on either side of the Atlantic. It took over an hour for the cortège, which stretched for half a mile, to reach the cemetery. As it passed, men doffed their hats, and people spoke in hushed tones. The blinds of every house were drawn, and the cotton mills shut for the day. After the last rites were pronounced at the graveside, the Bethel choir sang 'Nearer My God to Thee' as the coffin was lowered into the ground. Hartley's tombstone, one of the largest in the cemetery, took the form of a broken column with a bas-relief violin on the bottom of the pedestal, and just above it the words 'Nearer My God to the Thee' along with the first bars of the Sullivan setting of the hymn. The inscription reads:

In
Loving Memory
Of
Wallace Henry,
The Beloved Son of
Albion and Elizabeth
Hartley,
Formerly of Colne,
Who Lost His Life in the
SS *Titanic* Disaster
On April 15th, 1912,
Aged 33 Years,
And Was Interred
On May 18th, 1912

After the funeral, discussions for a more public memorial to Hartley continued. In announcing the opening of the memorial fund, Mayor Hartley declared that 'it has been deemed most fitting that a Water Fountain or other suitable Memorial should be erected in front of the Municipal Hall or in the Library Grounds'.[22] This suggestion did not, however, meet with favour from the local populace. 'Drinking fountains are a nuisance, and they also help to spread disease', wrote one correspondent to the *Colne and Nelson Times*, while another commented,

'Surely there has been enough water in this sad affair'.[23] Public opinion prevailed, and instead of a fountain the memorial, which cost £265, took the form of a bust of Hartley on a pedestal, flanked by two figures representing Music and Valour. It still stands today on its original site in the centre of Colne. The inscription reads:

> Wallace Hartley
> Bandmaster of the R.M.S. *Titanic*
> Who Perished in
> The Foundering
> Of That Vessel
> April 15th 1912
> Erected by Voluntary
> Contributions to Com-
> Memorate the Heroism
> Of a Native of This
> Town

By the time the memorial was unveiled in 1915, the First World War had distracted British attention from the *Titanic* disaster, and Hartley's heroics soon faded from the forefront of local consciousness. For a few years after the disaster memorial services were held on the anniversary of the sinking, but gradually active efforts to commemorate him ceased. As the decades passed, both the memorial and the gravestone fell into disrepair. In the last twenty years, however, as interest in the *Titanic* has revived, Colne's pride in its native son has returned. In 1982 Mayor Fred Melling laid a wreath in the shape of a violin on Hartley's grave in honour of the seventieth anniversary of the sinking. Ten years later, the eightieth anniversary was marked by a concert, an exhibition in the local library and a commemorative postcard. In 1996 the bust of Hartley, which had turned green with oxidation over the years, was refurbished and rededicated, funded by a grant from English Heritage. Following the release of the James Cameron film in 1997, a visit to Colne from the actor Jonathan Evans Jones, who played Hartley, received extensive coverage in the local press, which featured numerous photos of Jones placing a wreath on Hartley's grave. In 1999 a second Hartley exhibition opened at Colne Library, and a fund was set up to cover the cost of renovating the headstone on Hartley's grave, which had lost much of its lead lettering. The completion of the repairs, which cost £350, was marked by a ceremony in March of 2000 in which Mayor Ian Gilhespy laid a wreath in the shape of the music to 'Nearer My God to Thee' on the grave.

The commemoration of Wallace Hartley in Colne, therefore, followed a similar trajectory to the commemoration of Jack Phillips in Godalming. Once the news of the local man's heroism reached his hometown, it was decided almost immediately that there should be a public memorial, and the process of collecting funds for and erecting it was fairly straightforward, with only minor debates over design and location. After 1912, although never completely forgotten, little attention was paid to Phillips and Hartley, and their hometown memorials suffered from neglect and vandalism. The resurgence of interest in the *Titanic*, which began in the 1980s with the discovery of the wreck and which peaked in 1997 with the release of the James Cameron film, however, revived awareness of the two heroes' local connections, and the relevant authorities sought to capitalize on the tourist potential they represented with public ceremonies, exhibitions and commemorations.

6

Thomas Andrews

Neither Jack Phillips nor Wallace Hartley features prominently in the current wave of *Titanic* mania. Although *Titanic* experts are still familiar with their stories, the fan whose interest derives primarily from the film would almost certainly not be, for they play very minor roles and are accorded minimal screen time. Neither, in fact, is even identified by name in the film's dialogue. Instead, it is another *Titanic* hero who has been given a much more prominent place in recent versions of the story: Thomas Andrews, the managing director of Harland & Wolff, who was on board to ensure that the ship had been handed over to its owners in perfect working order. Andrews did not feature particularly prominently in national accounts of the sinking in 1912 – or indeed for decades afterwards. In the late twentieth century, however, he came to be treated as the *Titanic*'s greatest hero, or at least as its most tragic figure, a man whose creation was responsible for his own death.

As in the cases of Jack Phillips and Wallace Hartley, Andrews became the focus of intense local attention and admiration in the period following the disaster, culminating in the construction of a memorial in his hometown of Comber in the north of Ireland. Unlike Phillips and Hartley, however, Andrews did not simultaneously become a national hero, for little notice was taken of him in the press outside of his native Ulster. It was not until the most recent burst of *Titanic* mania, which began in the mid 1980s following the discovery of the wreck on the bed of the North Atlantic, that Andrews was elevated to a figure of national – and even international – renown. Why did his apotheosis take so long? The answer lies in evolving conceptions of heroism over the course of the twentieth century. As we have seen previously, Phillips and Hartley fitted perfectly the mold of the Edwardian hero: they were celebrated in 1912 because they stuck to their duty even in the most adverse circumstances. But by the late twentieth century this kind of heroism was no longer so highly regarded; in our more cynical view, the actions of Phillips and Hartley still retain a certain nobility, but what also stands out is their futility. What is the point, we ask, of continuing to send wireless messages when no other ships can hear them or of playing soothing music on the sloping decks of a doomed ship?

In contrast, Thomas Andrews seems better suited to our sense of what makes a tragic hero. To be sure he, like Phillips and Hartley, did his duty until the bitter end, helping to load lifeboats and throwing deck chairs overboard in the hope that they might serve as flotation devices. That is not, however, why we have come to admire Andrews so much in recent years. Instead, it is for the image conjured up by the last reported sighting of him: a figure standing alone in the first-class smoking room, unresponsive to attempts to persuade him to try and save himself. At that moment, the real tragedy of Thomas Andrews comes into focus: the creator of a technological marvel destroyed by his own creation. To a modern audience, this moment cannot help but resonate with our own fears about a world that is increasingly dependent on technology and, at the same time, increasingly at its mercy.

Thomas Andrews junior was born on 7 February 1873 in the town of Comber, which lies on the north-west shore of Strangford Lough in County Down, in the Irish province of Ulster (now Northern Ireland). The Andrewses were a prominent local family, proprietors of a linen mill that employed around six hundred people in the early twentieth century. The family's status is confirmed by the number of local positions held by Thomas's father, Thomas Andrews senior. He was President of the Ulster Liberal Unionist Association, Chairman of the Belfast and County Down Railway Company, a Privy Councillor, a Deputy Lieutenant and a High Sheriff of County Down and Chairman of the County Down Council. In 1870 Thomas Senior married Eliza Pirrie, the sister of Lord Pirrie, later the managing director of the Harland & Wolff shipyard and a man who would go on to play a role of great significance in the life of Thomas Junior. Thomas and Eliza's first child, John, was born in 1871, followed by Thomas Junior two years later. Two more sons and a daughter were born subsequently.

By all accounts, Thomas enjoyed an extremely happy childhood; his elder brother recalled that 'we were never treated than with more than kindness and devotion, and we learned the difference between right and wrong rather by example than by precept'. Although the family were strict Presbyterians – Eliza offered a prize to her sons if they made it to their twenty-first birthdays without having indulged in alcohol or tobacco – their religious devotion does not seem to have produced a stifling domestic atmosphere. Young Thomas sported a cheerful demeanour and sunny disposition; a childhood playmate recalled that 'he was always happy'. As a boy, he was educated by a private tutor, but at eleven he was enrolled in the Royal Academical Institution in Belfast, which his father had also attended. In best *Tom Brown's Schooldays* fashion, he was a mediocre scholar, but he excelled at sports, cricket in particular.[1]

From an early age Thomas showed an interest in boats, earning from his friends the nickname of 'Admiral' due to his skill in building models of them. Unlike his other childhood pursuits, which had included beekeeping and horsemanship, this one was to last. When he left school at sixteen, he entered the Harland & Wolff shipyard as a premium apprentice. Although he was Lord Pirrie's nephew, he was afforded no preferential treatment and proceeded through the same rigorous, five-year training period as his fellow apprentices. He spent three months in the joiners' shop, followed by a month with the cabinet makers, two months working in ships, two months in the main store, five months with the shipwrights, two months in the moulding loft, two months with the painters, eight months with the iron shipwrights, six months with the fitters, three months with the pattern-makers, eight months with the smiths and finally a long stint of eighteen months in the drawing office. During his time as an apprentice, his bright personality made a very favourable impression on his co-workers. 'I can remember how encouraging his cheery optimism and unfailing friendship were', recalled a fellow apprentice. By the end of training period, Andrews was a strapping young man of twenty-one who stood six feet tall and weighed nearly fourteen stone, with broad shoulders and handsome features.

Once his apprenticeship ended in 1894 and he became a manager at Harland & Wolff, Andrews quickly established a reputation as a skilled repairer of damaged ships. It was in the construction of new ships, however, where he would truly make his mark, beginning with the building of the *Celtic* between 1899 and 1901. He went on to assume responsibility for the construction of more than a dozen ships, and in 1905 he was promoted to the head of Harland & Wolff's design department. The qualifications for the job included:

> A knowledge of [the firm's] fifty-three branches equal to that of any of the fifty-three men in charge of them; the supervising of these, combining and managing them so that all night, smoothly and efficiently, work to the one great end assigned, the keeping abreast with the latest devices in labour-saving appliances, with the newest means of securing economical fitness, with the most modern discoveries in electrical, mechanical and marine engineering – in short, everything relative to the construction and equipment of modern steamships.[2]

In 1907 Andrews, still only thirty-four years old, became managing director of Harland & Wolff. As a mature man, he seems to have been, like his family, solidly Unionist in his politics; he believed, according to his biographer, that 'Home Rule would spell financial ruin to Ireland'.[3] (His brother John became Prime Minister of Northern Ireland in the 1920s.) He was a member of Ulster Reform Club, a bastion of Unionist privilege in Belfast, and was urged at various times to accept the presidency of a number of Unionist clubs and to stand for election to Belfast City Council as a Unionist candidate. He turned down all such entreaties, however, for politics was not the primary focus of his life. He was also appalled by the extremes to which some Unionists were prepared to go, and opposed those 'who strove to influence British elections by appeals to passion rather than by means of reasoned argument'.[4] His moderation in political questions is attested to by the admiration with which he was regarded by the prominent Irish nationalist Erskine Childers, who after his death praised his 'combination of power and simplicity'.[5]

In 1908 Andrews married Helen Reilly Barbour, and the couple moved into an impressive new house, Dunallan, on Windsor Avenue in Belfast, not far from Queen's University. A daughter, Elizabeth, was born in 1910. By that time, Andrews was thoroughly immersed in the construction of the *Olympic* and the *Titanic*. One night he brought Helen down to the yard to see his new creations as they stood shrouded in scaffolding in their huge slipways. As they stood on the *Titanic*'s half-finished deck, Andrews's pride in his latest and greatest shipbuilding accomplishment must have been immense, and the future must have seemed as bright as Halley's Comet, which the happy couple could see blazing across the night sky.

When the newly completed *Titanic* sailed from Belfast on 2 April 1912, Thomas Andrews accompanied it as head of the Harland & Wolff guarantee party. During the overnight journey to Southampton, Andrews walked ceaselessly around the ship, taking copious notes and assigning workers to last-minute tasks. From Southampton, he wrote to Helen of a 'very satisfactory trip'. 'The weather was good and everyone most pleasant. I think the ship will clean up all right before sailing on Wednesday.' He worked tirelessly over the next several days. His secretary Thompson Hamilton recalled that 'through the various days that the vessel was at Southampton, Mr Andrews was never for a moment idle. He generally left his hotel about 8.30 for the offices, where he dealt with his correspondence, then went on board until 6.30, when he would return to the offices to sign letters'. While still in port, Andrews noted only a few minor problems with the *Titanic*: the pebble dashing on the private promenade decks was too dark, and the coathooks in the staterooms used too many screws. In general, however, he was pleased with his new creation. On 9 April he wrote to Helen that 'the *Titanic* is now about complete and will I think do the old Firm credit tomorrow when we sail'.6

On sailing day, Andrews boarded at 6:30 a.m. and conducted a last-minute inspection of the ship. As he bade good-bye to Hamilton, he told him to 'keep Mrs Andrews informed of any news of the vessel'. From Cherbourg, he wrote to Helen that 'the weather is fine and everything shaping for a good voyage'. His last letter home was posted the following day, 11 April, from Queenstown; it reported that everything was still proceeding splendidly.

Once the *Titanic* was out in the North Atlantic, Andrews could relax a bit, but he continued to comb the ship for imperfections during the day and pore over drawings and calculations in his stateroom, A36, in the evening. As he moved around the ship, he was frequently sighted by both passengers and crew. May Sloan, a stewardess from Belfast, recalled:

He came from home and he made you feel on the ship that all was right. It was good to hear his laugh and have him near you. If anything went wrong it was always to Mr Andrews one went. Even when a fan stuck in a stateroom, one would say, 'Wait for Mr Andrews, he'll soon see to it', and you would find him settling even the little quarrels that arose between ourselves. Nothing came amiss to him, nothing at all. And he was always the same, a nod and a smile or a hearty word whenever he saw you and no matter what he was at.

Two of his table companions at dinner, Vera and Albert Dick, got to know Andrews and to admire his character. To them, his immense pride in the ship was obvious, but what he really wanted to discuss over dinner was how much he missed his family: 'Upon every occasion ... he talked almost constantly about his wife, little girl, mother and family, as well as of his home'. Other passengers observed that Andrews looked a bit haggard; perhaps the strain of ensuring that the *Titanic* was perfect in every detail was weighing upon him. By Sunday 14 April, however, he seemed to have relaxed somewhat. Chatting with Andrews on the way to dinner, May Sloan noted that 'he was in good spirits, and I thought he looked splendid'.[7]

After dinner, Andrews went to thank the baker for some special bread he had made for him, then retired to his cabin, where he commenced his customary perusal of the *Titanic*'s plans, searching for ways to improve the ship. He had noticed that the writing room, to which first-class ladies were supposed to adjourn in the evenings, was getting little use, and he was thinking of converting it to additional staterooms. He was still pondering various matters regarding the ship at 11.40 p.m., when the collision with iceberg occurred. High above the waterline on A Deck, the impact would have been barely perceptible, and Andrews, immersed in thought as he was, seems not to have felt it at all. He was still working diligently at his desk when he was summoned to the bridge by Captain Smith shortly before midnight. He and Smith made a thorough inspection of the damage, and Andrews knew immediately that the *Titanic* was doomed. Smith asked how much time the ship had left, and, after some quick calculations, Andrews informed him that it had no more than two hours to live.

As the ship's officers began loading the lifeboats, Andrews, who was not part of the crew and therefore had no formal assignment, assisted in any way that he could. 'He was here, there and everywhere', recalled May Sloan, 'looking after everybody, telling the women to put on lifebelts, telling the stewardesses to hurry the women up to the boats, all about everywhere, thinking of everyone but himself.'[8] It was a delicate task to convey a sense of urgency without causing a panic, which may explain why Andrews gave different – and sometimes false – information to different passengers. He told the Thayers that the ship did not have 'much over an hour to live', but he told the Dicks that 'she will not sink if her bulkheads hold'. Andrews also encouraged the crew to set a good example. When he encountered stewardess Annie Robinson, he scolded her for not wearing her lifebelt: 'Put it on – walk about – let the passengers see you'.

'It looks rather mean.'

'No, put it on! If you value your life, put it on. Now, I want you to open up all the spare rooms. Take out all the lifebelts and spare blankets and distribute them.'[9]

Later, out on the boat deck, Andrews continued to convey a sense of quiet urgency, with perhaps a hint of exasperation: 'Ladies, you must get in at once! There is not a moment to lose! You cannot pick and choose your boat! Don't hesitate, get in!'[10] Once all the boats had been launched, he began throwing deck chairs over the rail, hoping that they might serve as flotation devices for those in the water.

Eventually, however, there was nothing more to do. Andrews was last seen by Steward John Stewart when he looked inside the first-class smoking room at around 2.10 a.m. He was surprised to see Andrews standing in the centre of the room with his arms folded across his chest. 'Aren't you even going to try for it, Mr Andrews?' Stewart called out. There was no response, as Andrews continued to stare at the painting of Plymouth Harbour that hung over the fireplace. As Stewart left the room, he saw Andrews's lifebelt, which he had worn all night in order to set a good example for the passengers, lying on a nearby card table. His body was never found.

In his native Ulster, the news of Andrews's death stood out even amidst the pervasive sense of shock generated by the disaster. 'There are few men who have such a thorough knowledge of the various branches of shipbuilding industry as he possesses ... He has gained the esteem of all with whom he has come in contact', wrote the *Belfast News-Letter* on 17 April.[11] (Presumably the use of present tense was due to faint hopes that Andrews would still be found alive.) In his sermon on 21 April at the Rosemary Street Unitarian Church, the Reverend H. T. Rossington declared:

> One deeply respected and loved ... had been taken from the roll of that congregation. He spoke to many who knew that the name of Andrews stood for integrity, stood for truthfulness, and stood for staunchness of principle far and wide in the North of Ireland. Their true friend who was gone was known for his ability, for his fidelity to duty, for his unshrinking devotion to that which he believed to be true.[12]

Once more details about the precise circumstances of Andrews's death began to emerge, he was quickly elevated to the status of a hero in Belfast and the surrounding area. In response to requests from the Andrews family for information about Thomas's fate, his mother's cousin, James Montgomery, who lived in New York, wired on 19 April: 'Interview *Titanic*'s officers. All unanimous Andrews heroic unto death, thinking only safety others'. Two days later, White Star's New York office cabled its counterpart in Liverpool:

> After accident Andrews ascertained damage, advised passengers to put on heavy clothing and prepare to leave vessel. Many were skeptical about the seriousness of the damage, but impressed by Andrews's knowledge and personality, followed his advice, and so saved their lives. He assisted many women and children to lifeboats. When last seen, officers say, he was throwing overboard deck chairs and other objects to people in the water, his chief concern the safety of everyone but himself.[13]

The Ulster press quickly seized upon this information. 'Everyone was confident that Mr Andrews would play a heroic part, and that he would remain on the ship until all the others had been saved or the vessel had sunk', declared the *News-Letter*. 'His death has caused his friends to be overwhelmed with grief, but they have the consolation of knowing that he died as he had lived – sacrificing himself for others and thinking only of their safety'.[14] The *Belfast Evening Telegraph*, meanwhile, commented that 'all accounts tell of his heroism and his strenuous exertions to save others'.[15] The *Northern Whig* added that 'if anything can soften the grief of friends in a terrible bereavement', it was that Andrews had been 'truly a hero, who gave his life for others'.[16] These were all Unionist newspapers which were likely to be sympathetic to someone of Andrews's political and religious orientation, but admiration of him was not limited to the Unionist press. The nationalist *Irish Weekly* wrote of Andrews in equally glowing terms, referring to the 'high courage and grand self-sacrifice' that he 'conspicuously displayed in the awful last hours of the *Titanic*'.[17]

In Comber, resolutions of sympathy were offered to the Andrews family from a variety of sources, including the Protestant churches, the employees of the family's linen mill and the local government council. Almost immediately, discussions began of the possibility of erecting a memorial, but when it was announced that a memorial to all of the Ulster victims would be put up in Belfast, Comber temporarily shelved its plans. By the autumn of 1912, however, the discussion was revived. According to the *Herald and County Down Independent*:

> It has been recognized more particularly in recent years that Comber has been suffering from the want of a suitable public hall which would be available for general purposes. Any buildings in the town which have been utilized for public meetings are either connected with the churches or with the Orange body, and it is felt that the accommodations and arrangements are not adequate to meet the requirements of the town, and that the erection of a public hall on neutral grounds would be appreciated by the inhabitants generally.[18]

In other words, there was a need in Comber for a meeting hall without sectarian associations, and an 'Andrews Memorial Hall' would serve this purpose nicely. A deputation was sent from the local government to the Andrews family in order to secure their approval, which was readily granted. A committee was then established to take charge of raising the £5000 that was required to build, equip and endow the hall. Contributions came in quickly, and the project was given an additional boost when a local citizen donated a piece of land on Ballygowan Road, not far from the town square.

The groundbreaking ceremony took place on 2 October 1913, with the first piece of sod cut by Andrews's three-year-old daughter Elizabeth. The Thomas Andrews Junior Memorial Hall was officially opened on 29 February 1915. The ceremony was small and informal due to the First World War; Andrews's widow Helen gave a brief address in which she thanked all those who had contributed to its cost as well as the committee that had overseen the project. She extended the hope that it would be of use to the people of Comber. In its original state, the hall contained a billiard room, a reading room, a committee room and a kitchen on the ground floor, with the main hall, which held about seven hundred people, on the first floor. After several decades of use as a venue for community events, the hall was taken over by the local school board and converted to an elementary school, the Andrews Memorial Primary School. As the town's population grew, a new school building was constructed next door, and the hall became an annex that was – and continues to be – used for various school functions. Every ten years, the hall serves as the site for an exhibition of the students' work that tells the story of Thomas Andrews and the *Titanic*. Still in its original place on the first floor is a plaque commemorating Andrews's heroism during the sinking: 'When with tragic suddenness the call came he died, as he lived, faithful to his duties, and gave his life that others might be saved'.

Andrews was commemorated not only in stone but also in print in his native Ulster. Soon after the disaster, Sir Horace Plunkett, the noted advocate of agricultural cooperation in Ireland, suggested to the Ulster writer Shan F. Bullock that he prepare a short biography of Andrews. Bullock received the eager cooperation of the Andrews family and of the Harland & Wolff shipyard, and the biography appeared in print before the end of 1912. Given the circumstances in which and the purpose for which it was written, it is not surprising that the book is extremely hagiographic, but it does provide valuable information about Andrews's upbringing and pre-*Titanic* career. In his introduction, Plunkett referred to Andrews as 'one of the noblest Irishmen Ulster has produced in modern times'.[19]

In Comber, and indeed throughout Ulster, Thomas Andrews was thus commemorated as a hero in the period immediately following the sinking of the *Titanic*. The press in the North of Ireland was quick to celebrate his selfless actions, and his hometown of Comber constructed a lavish memorial hall in his honour. In the rest of the United Kingdom, however, Thomas Andrews was all but ignored. There was little mention of him in the London newspapers, which focused on the *Titanic*'s other heroes, in particular, as we have seen, Jack Phillips and Wallace Hartley. This relative inattention to Andrews may have resulted partially from the fact that he was Irish; the English press and public may have preferred their heroes to be English as well. Or it may have been caused by the fact that Andrews's actions were less clearly identifiable than those of Phillips or Hartley: he had obviously behaved heroically, but it was difficult to point to what precisely he had done.

On a national level, then, Andrews made little impact in 1912 and the years immediately thereafter, whereas other heroes like Phillips and Hartley ascended into the British, or certainly English, pantheon. Over time, however, their relative positions slowly reversed. Phillips and Hartley remained prominent parts of the *Titanic* story, but their self-sacrificing adherence to their duty was no longer quite as admirable as it once had been. In the modern, more cynical context of the late twentieth century, their actions came to seem increasingly pointless: what, after all, had either man truly accomplished? Phillips may have succeeded in summoning the *Carpathia* to the rescue of the *Titanic*'s survivors, but this required him only to send a simple wireless distress call soon after the collision with the iceberg. His insistence upon remaining at his station until the bitter end had been a futile gesture, for no other, closer ships had heard his frantic pleas for help. Likewise, Hartley's decision to continue playing music until the last possible moment had not lessened the extent of the catastrophe one iota; in fact it could be argued that the orchestra's actions had convinced some passengers that nothing was seriously wrong with the ship and therefore dissuaded them from promptly boarding the lifeboats. Furthermore, research has cast doubt on whether Hartley and his fellow bandsmen did indeed play until the end, and if they did, whether they really played 'Nearer My God to Thee'. Phillips and Hartley will always be seen as *Titanic* heroes, but today there is something archaic about the precise qualities of their heroism.

Andrews, on the other hand, displayed heroism of a sort more likely to appeal to our modern sensibilities. He, of all people on board the ship, knew that there was nothing to be done, and that at the minimum half of the *Titanic*'s occupants were going to perish in the icy waters of the North Atlantic. Yet he continued to do everything he could. What distinguishes him from Phillips and Hartley is that he *knew* that his actions were futile, that nothing within his power or anyone else's could avert the massive scale of the tragedy that was unfolding that night. He acted, unlike virtually anyone else on ship, in the full knowledge of what was going to happen, but he still acted heroically.

And when there was no more to be done, he simply stood quietly in the first-class smoking room, accepting his fate. It is for that moment, most of all, that we have come to admire Andrews. He stood there, having deliberately removed his lifebelt, and pondered what had occurred, and was still happening, and his role in it. He must have thought of how he had built the *Titanic*, bringing it into solid reality from the dreams of its owners and the plans of its designers. He had tried to create a ship that could withstand any foreseeable disaster at sea, but the precise nature of the damage to the *Titanic* had not been foreseen. For a man accustomed to pinpointing the tiniest design flaw, this must have been a painful realization, to discover that everything he thought he knew about maritime safety had been wrong. The *Titanic*'s critics had been right: the ship was too big, too cumbersome. In building it, Harland & Wolff had overreached humanity's engineering capabilities.

For this effrontery, Andrews paid the ultimate price. The creator was destroyed by his creation, and technology was once again proven inadequate in the age-old struggle with nature. As we struggle with the impact of technology upon our own world, a world in which we live increasingly at the mercy of machines, a world in which giant skyscrapers can crumble into dust in a matter of seconds, we understand the pain that Andrews must have felt as the *Titanic*'s end approached. Many of us felt it too, albeit vicariously through a television screen, on the morning of 11 September 2001.

It is therefore not surprising that, in the most recent wave of *Titanic* mania, Thomas Andrews has come to be regarded as the disaster's most tragic hero. After playing only a minor role in previous novels and films about the *Titanic*, he was elevated to far more prominent status in the two most significant fictional treatments of the story in the 1990s: the 1996 Broadway musical and the 1997 Hollywood film. Phillips and Hartley, meanwhile, were reduced to brief appearances.

In the musical, Andrews is one of three main characters, along with Captain Smith and J. Bruce Ismay. Peter Stone, author of the story and the book, conceived of this triumvirate as collectively adhering to 'the Greek concept of a tragic figure'. Each man would have a flaw of character – for Andrews, compromise; for Smith, compliance; and for Ismay, greed – that when combined 'with the ineluctable forces of nature' would send the *Titanic* to its doom. In the case of Andrews,

Stone chose to focus on his decision to extend the *Titanic*'s watertight bulkheads only to D Deck, a compromise that, in Stone's view, 'would prove to be disastrous'.[20] Andrews acknowledges his responsibility for the disaster in the song 'The Blame' when he sings, 'My doing / No one else's'.[21] By the end, the burden has become unbearable. The final scene on board the ship features Andrews in the first-class smoking room at 2.19 a.m. He pores over the *Titanic*'s plans one last time, seemingly 'unaware of his surroundings or even the tilt of the ship'. In the song 'Mr Andrews' Vision', he acknowledges the design flaws that have sealed the *Titanic*'s fate:

> Just a cursory look at the blueprints here
> Shows the weaknesses that we have missed,
> How the water poured in,
> A three-hundred-foot gash,
> And caused the bow to flood and to list.

> And then it filled, to the top
> Of our sep'rate watertight compartments
> And began to overflow ...
> Because the walls in-between the compartments
> Are too low!
> She's only sinking because these bulkheads
> Stop a deck too low!

For a brief moment, he begins to formulate ideas to improve the ship, and the *Titanic* is back in the Great Gantry at Harland & Wolff:

> But here's a thought! take a line ...
> And extend up the walls to the brink ...
> It's just a small redesign ...
> But once it's done, then I know she can't sink!
> Like this! ... and like this! ...

But, as he wildly erases and redraws the lines on the *Titanic*'s plans, a bellboy enters and asks, 'Mr Andrews! Aren't you going to make a go of it?' The interruption restores him to reality, and when he renews his song, he sings not of the flawless, unsinkable ships that he will build, but of what will occur in the *Titanic*'s final moments:

> The ship will start to plunge beneath the surface,

> The water lapping at our feet,
> Down sinks the bow, up flies the stern
> To the sky ...
> The panicked people in retreat.[22]

In his final moments, he goes mad, unable to bear his sense of responsibility for the loss of so many lives, before he is put out of his misery by a piano that crushes him against a bulkhead.

James Cameron's 1997 film reached an even wider audience. In it Andrews, portrayed by the Canadian actor Victor Garber, serves as the focus of some of the film's most poignant and powerful moments. After the collision with the iceberg, he arrives on the bridge, where he uses a blueprint of the *Titanic* to explain the extent of the damage to the captain, ship's officers and J. Bruce Ismay:

Andrews	Water fourteen feet above the keel in ten minutes ... in the forepeak ... in all three holds ... and in boiler room six.
Smith	That's right.
Andrews	Five compartments. She can stay afloat with the first compartments breached. But not five. Not five. As she goes down by the head the water will spill over the tops of the bulkheads ... at E Deck ... from one to the next ... back and back. There's no stopping it.
Smith	The pumps –
Andrews	The pumps buy you time ... but minutes only. From this moment, no matter what we do, *Titanic* will founder.
Ismay	But this ship can't sink!
Andrews	She is made of iron, sir. I assure you, she can. And she will. It is a mathematical certainty.[23]

As the ship sinks, Andrews functions as a stand-in for the film's audience, as the one person on board who understands the extent of the disaster that is unfolding. We share his frustration as he moves around the ship, feeling, according to Cameron's script, as if he is 'in a bad dream'. When he sees lifeboats being launched with considerably under their full capacity of passengers, he angrily confronts Second Officer Charles Lightoller:

Andrews	Why are the boats being launched half full?!
Lightoller	Not now, Mr Andrews.
Andrews	There, look ... twenty or so in a boat built for sixty five. And I saw one boat with only twelve. *Twelve*!
Lightoller	Well ... we were not sure of the weight –
Andrews	*Rubbish*! They were tested in Belfast with the weight of seventy men. Now fill these boats, Mr Lightoller. For God's sake, man! [24]

In the ship's final moments, Andrews stands alone in the first-class smoking room, where Rose, the film's heroine, encounters him and urges him to try and save his own life. With a tear trickling down his cheek, he apologizes to her for not building 'a stronger ship', and then, handing her his lifebelt, wishes her luck. After she departs, he leans against the mantel, head bowed; in this moment the viewer experiences the enormity of the tragedy filtered through Andrews's personal anguish. In contrast to the musical, however, Andrews does not go mad under the strain of his heavy burden. Instead, he remains the consummate engineer. In perhaps the saddest moment in the film, he takes out his pocket watch to check the time and finds that the clock on the mantel is slightly incorrect. He opens the clock's face and adjusts it to the correct time. It is 2.12 a.m., and the *Titanic* has precisely eight minutes to live.[25]

Numerous critics singled out Garber's performance for praise, and Cameron's film, along with the Broadway musical, helped to generate new interest in Thomas Andrews around the world. For the first time, he moved to the front rank of *Titanic* heroes. A new edition of the Shan Bullock biography appeared in 1999, and Andrews has also been featured in a series of collectible *Titanic* dolls. There have also been more eccentric manifestations of Andrews enthusiasm. William Barnes, a purveyor of exotic birds from Arizona, claims to have discovered under hypnosis that he is a reincarnation of Andrews. In 2000 he published a 'biography' using his 'memories', entitled *Thomas Andrews Voyage into History: Titanic Secrets Revealed through the Eyes of Her Builder*.[26] Neither Jack Phillips nor Wallace Hartley, meanwhile, has played such a prominent role in the recent outburst of *Titanic* mania. Their dutiful heroism was of a particularly Edwardian type; it still seems admirable but at the same time somewhat archaic today. Andrews, however, was a hero of a more modern stripe, a man who thought he had mastered technology only to have its limits tragically revealed in a chance encounter with the power of nature. As we see him standing in the *Titanic*'s first-class smoking lounge in the ship's final moments, it is easy for us to share his pain.

7

Edward Smith

In Beacon Park in the city of Lichfield, a statue of Captain Edward John Smith, master of the *Titanic* on its first and only voyage, stands with arms folded, chin held high and one leg thrust confidently forward. On the whole, he looks rather pleased with himself. And well he should. After decades of not being wanted in his hometown of Hanley, Stoke-on-Trent, or in Lichfield, Captain Smith has in recent years found himself the object of a fierce competition between the city of his birth and the city where his statue currently stands.

As we have seen, J. Bruce Ismay and Sir Cosmo Duff Gordon were the most obvious targets of the wrath of the British press and public in the aftermath of the *Titanic* disaster. Other men, however, had questions raised about their conduct. Certainly, Captain Smith's decisions and behaviour became the subject of much debate, as it was difficult to avoid pinning at least a portion of the blame on the *Titanic*'s master. Smith also had his defenders, however, particularly among a loyal group of passengers who had travelled with him on numerous occasions during his long and – at least until 14 April 1912 – distinguished career.

When those passengers decided to erect a public memorial to Smith, his birthplace of Hanley in Staffordshire did not exactly rush to volunteer itself as a suitable location. Nor, for that matter, did any other town. Ultimately, the city of Lichfield, also in Staffordshire, accepted the Smith memorial, but only in the face of vociferous protests from a number of prominent citizens. But if neither Hanley nor Lichfield was particularly eager to give the memorial a home in 1912, in more recent years their attitudes have changed dramatically. As both communities have become aware of the potential for a *Titanic* connection to attract tourism, the memorial that nobody wanted has become the memorial that everybody wants.

Edward John Smith was born in Hanley on 27 January 1850.[1] Until the

mid eighteenth century Hanley had been a small agricultural village, but
the construction of the Wedgwood pottery works at Etruria in 1769
sparked rapid industrial growth, accompanied by a corresponding surge
in population. By the 1830s Hanley was the largest town in the Potteries
and the second largest in Staffordshire.

As Wedgwood's presence indicates, the key industry in Hanley, and
in the surrounding region, was pottery-making. In 1861 almost half of
the inhabitants of the Potteries worked in the pottery industry.[2] They
worked in twelve-hour shifts from 6.30 a.m. to 6.30 p.m., except on
Saturdays when they were let off at 2 or 4 p.m., depending on the
manufactory. Wages varied widely, but were generally relatively high:
in the early 1860s approximately nine out of ten adult men earned more
than twenty shillings per week, whereas in the cotton industry only
around half of adult men earned that much. Nevertheless, poverty was
common, with around one in ten families unable to afford basic
necessities.[3]

The rapid growth of the pottery industry led to serious problems in
Hanley with overcrowding and unsanitary conditions. Privies were uncommon and unclean, and many houses were badly ventilated, a surefire
recipe for outbreaks of disease. A pall of smoke from the potteries hung
over the town at all times, along with noxious fumes from the numerous
metalworks that were also located in Hanley. Most workers lived in rows
of terraced houses that were caked with soot from the kilns, with little
separation between their homes and their places of employment. A
reporter from the *Morning Chronicle* described a typical residential
district:

> The older houses are sometimes built on all sides of a small airless square,
> with a narrow passage leading to the street. Occasionally the common ash-pits
> and conveniences are erected in this delectable quadrangle. More generally,
> each house has its backyard – these places being too often, however, in a
> filthy state of dirt and neglect ... Even in the poorest class of dwellings it
> was curious to observe how the fashion in furniture prevailing in the district
> was perceptible; wretched imitations of sofas – all rickety boards and torn
> and dirty calico – were often drawn near the fire. In more than one instance
> they served as day beds, and probably night beds too, for sick children.[4]

All of this contributed to a death rate that was a quarter higher than
that of England and Wales as a whole; the mean age of death for men

was forty-six, ten years less than the English average. In particular, the seared lungs that workers suffered as they retrieved pottery from the kilns often severely shortened their lives.[5]

To outsiders, Hanley could be a frightening place. The landscape was dominated by 'bottle ovens' of the potteries, so named because of their convex chimneys that belched out acrid black smoke and flames day and night. When H. G. Wells visited Hanley, at the invitation of the novelist Arnold Bennett, who was from the town, he was so shocked by the inferno-like vista created by the ovens at night that he later used Hanley as his model when he described the devastation wrought by the Martian invasion in *The War of the Worlds*.

This, then, was the world into which Edward Smith was born, a far cry from the glittering world of the luxurious passenger liners on which he would spend much of his life. The Smith family's house, a typical, two-up, two-down, Victorian working-class dwelling, still stands at 51 Well Street. Smith's father, who was forty-five at the time of his birth, was also named Edward; he had been born in Hanley as well and was, not surprisingly, a potter. Three years before, he had married Catherine Hancock, a widow with two children. Her daughter Thirza was still living at home, but her son Joseph had joined the merchant navy at seventeen; he was to play a prominent role in Edward's future.

Shortly after Edward's birth, his father quit his job as a potter and set up as a grocer. This was unusual, for very few men moved out of the pottery industry after the age of thirty.[6] In this case, however, self-help worked and the business flourished. Although his 'working-class origins' were often referred in later press accounts, Edward grew up in comfortable middle-class circumstances as the son of a successful small entrepreneur. The Smiths were Primitive Methodists, a splinter sect known for its fiery style of worship. Primitive Methodist preachers, nicknamed 'Ranters' because of their energetic delivery, could often be seen in working-class areas of Britain's industrial cities, haranguing crowds from the back of a cart. By 1850 they had garnered considerable support among the working classes in the Potteries.

The Smith family, however, decided to send Edward to a mainstream Wesleyan Methodist school, the Etruria British School. The school had been founded by the Wedgwood family to provide for the education of their own children as well as those of their workers, and their continued supervision ensured that the teaching was of a high standard. Edward was remembered by his classmates as 'a quiet, respectable, courageous lad who never put himself to the front too much', but also as a boy who did not shy away from a scrap.⁷

At the age of twelve, Smith left school and took a job at the Etruria Forge, a metal smelting and pressing concern. He quickly proved himself a capable worker, and was trusted to operate the huge Naysmith steam hammer that shaped large wrought-iron components. By the mid 1860s, however, the iron industry was suffering from decreased demand, and Smith decided to seek better opportunities elsewhere. His half-brother Joseph Hancock had risen through the ranks of the merchant navy to become the captain of the American sailing ship *Senator Weber*, and Smith decided to follow the trail Joseph had blazed. He quit his job and went to Liverpool, where Hancock allowed him to sign on to the *Senator Weber* as a boy, the lowest rank of ordinary seaman.

Over the next five years, Smith climbed through the ranks of the merchant service, acquiring along the way experience on a variety of vessels. In 1871, he earned his certificate of competency as a second mate, followed two years later by his first mate's certificate, and then, in 1875, his qualification as a master mariner, which enabled him to command his own ship. His first command was the *Lizzie Fennell*, a 1000-ton three-master that carried goods to and from South America. Only twenty-six at a time when a man was lucky to get his first captaincy by forty, Smith was frequently teased about his youth, but he responded good-naturedly, saying that it was something he would soon grow out of.⁸

Early achievement of a command was not enough to satisfy Smith's ambitions. He knew that in the merchant navy the most prestigious posts were on the big passenger steamers that plied the North Atlantic route. As he brought the *Lizzie Fennell* into Liverpool one day in 1880, Smith pointed out to the harbour pilot the White Star liner *Britannic*. The 5000-ton steamer was a famous ship, for at the time it held the record for the fastest crossing of the North Atlantic. Smith told the pilot that he would not mind 'going down a rung or two' – in other words giving up his captaincy and serving as a junior officer – in order to get on board such a fine vessel.⁹ He meant what he said, for shortly thereafter he resigned command of the *Lizzie Fennell* and joined the White Star Line. He was to spend the rest of his career on the North Atlantic.

Now thirty, Smith had to go through a second apprenticeship in order to learn the skills required of an officer on large passenger ships. These skills were not exclusively – or even primarily – related to seafaring, but to social etiquette as well. White Star's officers were expected not only to get their vessels from one port to another in a safe and timely fashion, but also to entertain wealthy passengers so that they would make all of their crossings on the line's ships. It was customary in those days for first-class passengers to have favourite captains or even favourite officers, whom they would follow from ship to ship. Officers who had charm and polish were therefore preferred by the line, and without such qualities a man was unlikely to go far.

As he had done on sailing vessels, Smith rose rapidly through the ranks, suggesting that he possessed both the seafaring and the social skills that the North Atlantic passenger trade demanded. His roots in the Staffordshire Potteries were left far behind as he mingled with the rich and famous. In 1882 he became second officer of the *Coptic*, and three years later he was promoted to first officer of the *Republic*. In 1887 he married Eleanor Pennington, the daughter of a farmer from Winwick. Despite the prolonged separations that the couple endured while Edward was at sea, the marriage seems to have been a happy one. In her letters, she referred to Smith as 'Teddy', while he called her 'my only dear one'.[10] At first the Smiths lived in Liverpool, but when White Star moved its main port of embarkation to Southampton in 1907 they followed, settling into a large red brick house on Winn Road in the upmarket Westwood Park district. In 1902 they had a daughter, Helen Melville Smith, their only child.[11]

In 1888 Smith applied for the extra master mariner's certificate that would qualify him to command a large passenger steamer, but for the first time in his career he failed a competency examination. He took the test again a week later, however, and passed. White Star was clearly pleased with his progress: they gave him his first command, of the *Republic*'s twin sister *Baltic*, at the end of the year. That same year, Smith joined the Royal Naval Reserve, which meant that in wartime he could be called up to active duty.

The *Baltic* was an ageing vessel, but Smith quickly proceeded to more prestigious commands, including the *Republic*, the *Cufic*, the *Coptic*, the *Adriatic*, the *Runic*, the *Britannic* and the *Germanic*. As captain, he had to be host, diplomat, confidant and counsellor as well as master mariner, but he proved up to the task. He was highly regarded by his crewmen. The *Titanic*'s second officer, Charles Lightoller, later wrote that 'he was a great favourite and a man any officer would give his ears to sail under'. Others concurred. The *Titanic*'s sixth officer James Moody wrote to his sister, 'Though I believe he's an awful stickler for discipline, he's popular with everybody', and a White Star steward described him as 'a good, kind-hearted man' who was looked upon 'as a sort of father'.[12]

Smith's passengers were equally fond of him. After Smith's death, Mr and Mrs John Thalton of the United States wrote:

> We always felt so safe with him, for one knew how deeply he felt the responsibility of his ship and all on board. He has been a deeply cherished friend on sea and land all these years, and we hold him in love and veneration, and are proud that we could count so noble a man among our closest friends.[13]

J. E. Hodder Williams of the publishing firm Hodder and Stoughton recalled:

> We crossed with him on many ships and in many companies, through seas fair and foul, and to us he was, and will ever be, the perfect sea-captain. In the little tea parties in his private state-room we learned to know the genial warm-hearted family man; his face would light as he recounted the little intimacies of his life ashore, as he told of his wife and the troubles she had with the dogs he loved, of his little girl and her delight with the presents he brought her and the parties he had planned for her ... He was amazingly informed on every phase of present-day affairs, and that was hardly to be wondered at, for scarcely a well-known man or woman who crossed the Atlantic during the last twenty years but had sometime sat at his table. He read widely, but men more than books. He was a good listener, ... although he liked to get in a yarn himself now and again, but he had scant patience with bores or people who 'gushed'. I have seen him quell both.[14]

In 1895 Smith took the helm of the 10,000-ton *Majestic*, a post he held for the next nine years, the longest command of his career. During the Boer War, he was called up for active duty in the Royal Navy and made two voyages carrying troops to South Africa. For his military service, he earned the Transport Medal, which he wore proudly on his uniform for the rest of his life. Restored to civilian duty, Smith was given command in 1904 of the brand-new *Baltic*, the largest ship in the world at 23,000 tons. This inaugurated White Star's tradition of giving Smith command of its new ships, a tradition that would continue for the remainder of his career. In May 1907 he took command of the even larger *Adriatic*. After the ship docked in New York, Smith told a reporter from the *New York Times*:

> When anyone asks me how I can best describe my experience of nearly forty years at sea, I merely say, uneventful. Of course there have been winter gales, and storms and fog and the like, but in all my experience, I have never been in an accident of any sort worth speaking about ... I never saw a wreck and have never been wrecked, nor have I been in any predicament that threatened to end in disaster of any sort.[15]

By 1910 Edward Smith had attained every goal to which a captain in the merchant navy could aspire. Now sixty, he was the most respected master on the North Atlantic, and earned a commensurate salary: £1250 per annum, plus a £1000 bonus if he brought his ships into port in good order. He was extremely popular with first-class passengers, who went out of their way to travel on his ships. He was, as Charles Lightoller described him, the '*beau idéal* of a western ocean mail boat captain'.[16] There was no question that he would be given command of White Star's new flagship, the *Olympic*, when it went into service in 1911, and no question that he would also command its sister, the *Titanic*, on its maiden voyage the following year.

In Belfast, on 2 April 1912, Smith took command of the RMS *Titanic* for its sea trials. He put the ship through its paces: turning to port and starboard, slowing down and speeding up and stopping. One test measured the distance it took the ship to stop. With the *Titanic* at full speed, around twenty knots, Smith ordered the telegraph to be shifted to 'full astern'. It took around half a mile – and about three minutes – for the ship to come to a complete stop. The tests continued until 7 p.m., when the *Titanic*'s owners and builders and the Board of Trade representative pronounced themselves satisfied with the ship's performance. At 8 p.m., the *Titanic* left Belfast, sailing through the night in order to reach Southampton by the noontime high tide the following day. It was precisely one week until sailing day.

As the ship was being loaded with the requisite provisions for its maiden voyage, Smith stayed at home in Winn Road with his wife and daughter. He returned to the *Titanic* on the morning of 10 April, boarding at 7.30 a.m. He was joined by Maurice Harvey Clarke of the Board of Trade, whose function was to clear the *Titanic* as an immigrant ship under the Merchant Shipping Acts. With all the requisite paperwork in order, Smith submitted his final report to the White Star Line: 'I herewith report this ship loaded and ready for sea. The engines and boilers are in good order for the voyage, and all charts and sailing directions up to date. Your obedient servant, Edward J. Smith'.[17]

At 11 a.m., harbour pilot George Bowyer came on board and conferred with Smith about the draught, displacement and turning radius of the huge ship. Shortly before noon, a blast on the *Titanic*'s whistles signalled that anyone on board who was not planning to travel must go ashore. A few minutes later, three more blasts indicated that the *Titanic* was ready to depart. The lines from the tugs were made fast, and the mooring lines securing the *Titanic* to the dock were released. Slowly, the ship was towed to the River Test's turning circle and then manoeuvred in a ninety-degree turn to port. Now, at last, the *Titanic* could move forward under its own power. The telegraph signalled 'ahead slow', and the ship's propellers began to spin.

It was as this point that the near-collision with the *New York* occurred. One wonders if the incident gave Smith a moment of pause. At the very least, it must have brought back unpleasant memories of an accident that had occurred seven months earlier as he was taking the *Olympic* out of Southampton. The Royal Naval cruiser *Hawke* had been proceeding up the Solent towards its home base in Portsmouth when it had come up on the *Olympic*'s starboard quarter. The *Hawke* slowed and turned to port as if it intended to pass under the *Olympic*'s stern, but the massive suction generated by the *Olympic*'s engines drew the smaller ship into the liner's starboard side, opening a substantial gash in the *Olympic*'s hull and damaging its propeller shaft. The accident did not endanger the ship, but the *Olympic*'s voyage to New York had to be cancelled and its passengers offloaded. The ship then returned to Belfast for repairs. In the inquiry into the matter by the British Admiralty, the *Olympic* was faulted for drawing the *Hawke* into its wake. Smith was exonerated from blame, since the *Olympic* had been under the command of the harbour pilot at the time, but it had still been an unnerving episode, revealing as it did the unforeseen navigational problems that such enormous ships could create.[18] Now, as the *Titanic* crossed the English Channel on the way to its first port of call at Cherbourg, Smith spent the better part of the afternoon conducting S-turns and other manoeuvres. He was already almost an hour behind schedule, due to the delay caused by the *New York* incident, but he clearly wanted to get the feel of his new ship before he headed out into the more treacherous waters of the North Atlantic.

Smith's concerns must, however, have quickly faded. The *Titanic* was performing beautifully, and the weather was ideal. Still, he kept a watchful eye on things, and the passengers saw little of him during the first two days of the voyage. He even took his meals in his cabin, and it was not until the evening of Friday 12 April that he finally appeared in the first-class *à la carte* restaurant. He also began to mingle more with the passengers during the day. Seven-year-old Eva Hart encountered him while she was carrying a very large teddy bear; Smith genially compared her height to that of the bear and found the bear to be slightly taller.[19]

Smith spent most of Sunday 14 April on the bridge. At 10.30 a.m. he presided over a religious service in the first-class dining saloon, but returned to the bridge upon its conclusion. At 7.30 p.m., he attended a private party given by George Widener in the *à la carte* restaurant. He smoked two cigars during the evening but drank nothing alcoholic.[20] Shortly before 9, Smith excused himself and returned to the bridge, where he discussed the conditions and the likelihood of ice with Charles Lightoller, the officer of the watch. Then, at around 9.20, he retired to his cabin.

Immediately after the collision with the iceberg at 11.40 p.m., Smith reappeared on the bridge. He ordered the watertight doors to be shut (Murdoch had already shut them) and then told Fourth Officer Boxhall to make an inspection while he sent for Thomas Andrews, who could make a more thorough assessment of the extent of the damage. He knew from his glance at the commutator, which showed that the *Titanic* was already listing to starboard and down slightly by the head, that the situation was serious. Once Andrews arrived, he accompanied him on his inspection of the damaged areas, and together they determined that the ship was doomed. Upon his return to the bridge, he issued a series of orders to his officers: Murdoch was told to muster the passengers, Sixth Officer Moody to find the list for the lifeboat stations, and Boxhall to wake the other officers. Chief Engineer Joseph Bell was summoned, and Smith asked him to keep power flowing to the lights and to the wireless set for as long as possible. When Boxhall returned, Smith ordered him to work out the ship's position so that the wireless operators could begin transmitting a distress call. Smith delivered the coordinates to the wireless room himself; as he was leaving he encountered Lightoller, who recalled that his face looked 'stern but haggard'.[21] Lightoller asked if the lifeboats should be swung out, and Smith told him that they should be and that passengers should be directed to their boat stations. A few minutes later, Lightoller found Smith a second time and asked if the boats should be filled; Smith again told him to proceed, saying, 'Yes, put the women and children in and lower away'.[22]

It was now 12.20 a.m., forty minutes after the collision. Once the boats were being filled, there was little else for Smith to do. He moved back and forth from the bridge to the deck, doing his best to reassure anxious passengers. Spotting Mary Compton getting into a lifejacket, he smiled and said, 'They will keep you warm if you don't have to use them'.[23] He was standing near Boat 6 as it was being lowered when the women in the boat called up that they had no seamen on board. 'Here's one', said Smith, grabbing a boy by the arm and shoving him into the boat.[24] Smith directed the crewmen in charge of the boats to pull for the ship's light they could see off the starboard bow. Once they reached the other ship, they should unload their passengers and return to the *Titanic* as quickly as possible. As she waited to board Boat 8, the Countess of Rothes heard Smith tell crew member Tom Jones to 'row straight for those lights over there, leave the passengers aboard and return as soon as possible'. Turning back to the crowd on the deck, Smith asked three times if there were 'any more ladies?' When there was no response, he assisted a steward in lowering the forward falls.[25]

For the most part, however, there was little Smith could do, and he is curiously absent from most survivor accounts. At 2.05, he made his last visit to the wireless room, releasing operators Jack Phillips and Harold Bride from duty. A few minutes later, Steward Edward Brown heard Smith tell the crew, 'Well, boys, do your best for the women and children and look out for yourselves'. The captain then headed back to bridge, still holding his megaphone.[26] This was the last reliable sighting of Edward J. Smith. His body was never found.

Afterwards, there were a number of versions of how Smith met his end. The first press accounts claimed that he had shot himself on the bridge. This story was first reported on 19 April by the Reuters news agency, and it appeared in every major British newspaper. No reliable witness to the incident could be identified, however, and, as soon as the *Carpathia* docked in New York, the suicide story was quickly repudiated. The *Daily Mail* described it as 'a cruel slander on one of the noblest of the dead we mourn', while the *Daily Sketch* declared 'of all the cruelly heartless fabrications which the sensation-mongers have woven about this tragedy of the *Titanic*, the most stupid and senselessly false is the tale that Captain Smith killed himself on the bridge'.[27]

Alternative versions of Smith's end depicted him as opting to stay with his doomed ship. The last reliable sighting of Smith was by Steward Edward Brown, who reported seeing him on the bridge only minutes before the *Titanic* sank. This was corroborated by crewman G. A. Drayton, who stated that he saw Smith swept off the bridge by the onrushing water, but that he swam back onto the sinking ship: 'He went down with it in my sight'.[28] A British press eager to depict Smith's death in an heroic light quickly endorsed these accounts. 'Many personal statements ... have been made by survivors bearing witness to the cool courage with which the captain went down with his ship', declared the *Daily Express*.[29] The *Daily Chronicle* proclaimed that Smith had 'died bravely on the bridge', thereby displaying 'unparalleled self-sacrifice and heroism'.[30] The *Daily Mirror* referred to Smith as the 'noble captain', who went to 'a hero's grave' as 'an Englishman among Englishmen'.[31] On 20 April the cover of the *Daily Sketch* featured a full-length portrait of Smith in his dress uniform on what was described as the bridge of the *Titanic*, though Smith had never been photographed there. 'Where the British Captain Stood Till Death', read the caption, while the text underneath contained passenger testimony that Smith had stayed on the bridge until the end. Inside were more pictures of the captain beneath a headline reading 'Captain Smith Dies Like a British Sailor'. On 23 April, the *Daily Graphic* included an artist's rendering of Smith superimposed on a photograph of *Titanic*'s bridge, with the caption, 'A Tribute to the Man Who Remained on the Bridge to the End'.

In some eyes, however, a captain deciding to stay on the bridge until the bitter end was not heroic enough. The captain of a sinking ship had a duty not only to stand aside and let others be saved, but actively to bring about their salvation. Smith's behaviour that night, however, contained few examples of active heroism. Once he had completed his flurry of initial orders, he seems to have done little more than offer encouragement as the crew loaded and launched the lifeboats. His apparent passivity may have been because there was nothing else for him to do, but it still threatened to undermine the nation's belief in the heroism of its sea captains. Britons wanted Smith to do something more than shout encouragement through his megaphone or offer reassurances to anxious passengers.

But how to do this? There were a few witnesses who were certain that they had seen Smith in the water after the ship sank. Harold Bride, who looked back at the *Titanic* as he clung to overturned Collapsible B, said that he saw Smith jump from the bridge wing into the sea. Lookout G. A. Hogg thought he saw Smith swimming alongside Boat 7 and yelled, 'There's the skipper! Give him a hand!' But Smith resisted their entreaties to come on board, telling them, 'Good-bye boys, I'm going to follow the ship', as he swam away. Greaser Walter Hurst heard an authoritative voice from the water shouting encouragement to the oarsmen: 'Good boys, good lads!' Hurst was convinced for the rest of his life that the voice was Captain Smith's. A seaman also claimed to have seen Smith in the water, telling the crewmen in the boat, 'Don't mind me, men. God bless you', before he vanished under the waves.[32]

With a little embellishment, these accounts could be used to transform Smith into precisely the kind of hero that the British public wanted him to be. The *Daily Chronicle* asserted that, after being swept off the bridge, Smith 'was seen in the act of helping those struggling in the water'.[33] The *Daily Express* quoted Sir Cosmo Duff Gordon as claiming to have seen Smith rescue an infant from the freezing water and delivering it to a lifeboat.[34] This story was repeated in 'The Deathless Story of the *Titanic*', a special issue of *Lloyd's Weekly News* that was published within two weeks of the disaster. In it the journalist Philip Gibbs claimed that Smith had remained on the bridge until he was swept off. Once in the water, he had spotted an infant floating in the waves and had carried him or her over to a lifeboat:

'Take the child!' he gasped.

A dozen hands reached forth to grasp the baby which was taken into the boat. They tried to pull the captain into the boat, but he refused.[35]

There was some evidence for this actually having occurred: both Fireman Harry Senior and Charles Williams, a racquets coach from Harrow School, claimed to have seen Smith swim up to a lifeboat clutching a child. The problem was, however, that no one could point definitively to the child in question. It seems certain that, even amidst all the confusion, someone would have remembered the captain handing him or her a child, but no one did.

No reliable survivor account, therefore, showed Smith to be acting in an actively heroic manner, as the captain of a doomed vessel should have done. And as time went on, British writers began to show increasing discomfort with the subject of the captain's conduct. In the more than two hundred poems on the disaster contained in Charles Forshaw's collection, many authors chose not to mention him at all; he appears far fewer times than do more obviously heroic figures such as Wallace Hartley and Jack Phillips, and he is almost never referred to explicitly by name, only as 'the captain'.

Smith's primary difficulty in being depicted as a hero derived not from anything he had done, or not done, after *Titanic* struck the iceberg, but from before. He was, after all, was the man who bore the responsibility for seeing the ship safely into port, and he had failed utterly in fulfilling that responsibility. He may have followed accepted practice, he may have been caught up in unforeseeable circumstances, but at the end of the day he was the man who had sunk the *Titanic*. In the *Whitby Gazette*, Robert Hey wrote:

When this great ship drew near to mid-ocean,
The brave captain, no doubt, used every precaution,
For just about here many icebergs appear,
And his duty it was to steer the ship clear.[36]

Hey's lines present an obvious paradox: the 'brave' Smith may have 'used every precaution', but it was still his 'duty' to 'steer the ship clear', a duty which he had evidently failed to carry out. It was this issue which led to the debate over the location of his memorial.

The story of Captain Smith's statue began in early 1913, when a committee was formed 'with the object of arranging a fitting Memorial' as 'a tribute to his strenuous career, his patriotism, his self-sacrifice and his heroic end'.[37] Unlike many other *Titanic* memorials, however, this one was not the product of a local desire to commemorate one of their own. Instead, the group who wanted to memorialize Captain Smith consisted primarily of an international contingent of wealthy Britons and Americans who had sailed with him during his long career as a White Star skipper. They remembered him fondly and wished to provide tangible evidence of their affection. The nature of the Smith Memorial Committee, however, created an awkward situation when it came to choosing a spot for the memorial. The committee had not only to decide what place would be most suitable, it also had to convince that town to accept a monument that was intended to honour the man who had sunk the *Titanic*.

The most obvious choice of location was Smith's birthplace in Hanley. Somewhat oddly, however, the committee decided not to approach the town. Instead, they went to Lichfield, a place with which Smith had absolutely no connection. This strange decision has caused considerable controversy in recent years, but at the time no one thought much about it. Officially, Lichfield was selected for several reasons. According to Francis Seymour Stevenson, the secretary of the memorial committee:

> Being about half-way between Liverpool and London, Lichfield would be convenient alike to British and American subscribers, and its selection would enhance the interest they already feel in the City owing to the beauty of its Cathedral and the wealth of its literary and historical associations. It is situated in the county, and is the Cathedral City of the Diocese in which the Captain was born ... The reason why Hanley was not also included was because a tablet had already been put up at the Hanley Town Hall ... and because Lichfield appeared to the Memorial Committee to be more accessible, and in other respects more suitable.[38]

Indeed, as Stevenson indicated, Hanley had previously put up a brass tablet in Smith's memory in the apse facing the entrance to the Town Hall. The plaque read:

This tablet is dedicated to the memory of Commander Edward John
Smith, RD, RNR. Born in Hanley, 27th Jany 1850, died at sea, 15th April
1912.

Be British.

Whilst in command of the White Star SS *Titanic* that great ship struck an
iceberg in the Atlantic Ocean during the night and speedily sank with
nearly all who were on board. Captain Smith having done all man could
do for the safety of passengers and crew remained at his post on the
sinking ship until the end. His last message to the crew was 'Be British'.

At the dedication ceremony of the plaque on 13 April 1913 many tributes
were paid to Smith; the Mayor proclaimed that he 'always carried out
his duties faithfully and honestly, and on every occasion justified his
appointment even in that lamentable disaster to the *Titanic*'.[39] The
following week, a portrait of Smith was unveiled at his old school in
Etruria, now relocated to a new building. Another, smaller version of
the portrait was unveiled on the same day in the building occupied by
the school at the time Smith had attended.

Even though Hanley did in fact already have several memorials to
Smith, there may have been more to the Smith Memorial Committee's
decision to put the statue in Lichfield. Although this was never explicitly
stated, the type of people who were Smith's most ardent admirers were
also the type of people who would be inclined to turn up their noses
at Hanley's industrial grime and to prefer instead the genteel cathedral
city of Lichfield. Perhaps the memorial committee wanted to complete
the rags-to-riches story of Smith's life by removing him from Hanley
once and for all.

That the memorial committee felt this way is not altogether surprising.
What is more curious, however, is that Hanley's civic leaders voiced no
objection to the decision to put the statue in Lichfield. If they truly felt
pride in their local hero, why did they not protest? A closer look at the
efforts Hanley did make to honour him suggests that this pride was
tempered – and possibly even overcome – by embarrassment that it had
been one of their own who had been in command of the *Titanic* on
that fateful night. Despite the Mayor's presence at the dedication ceremony for the plaque, and despite the plaque's location in the Town
Hall, the initiative behind it had not come from the town's government.
Instead, it had been a private citizen, William Hampton, who had started

the subscription campaign that had provided the necessary funds. Hampton, an old friend of Smith's, was determined to see him properly commemorated in the town of his birth. Only two days after the disaster, he had written to the *Stoke Sentinel* to start a subscription list:

> Sir, Might I suggest it would be a gracious act to place a memorial tablet in some public building in Hanley to the memory of the late Captain E. J. Smith of the *Titanic*?
>
> It is well known that he was a native of Hanley, and I have (amongst the many others who are now with us) known him personally since his schooldays, and have watched his career and have been proud that Hanley has produced such an eminent seaman. There are no doubt many who would like to show respect to his memory by subscribing towards the memorial.[40]

Contributions were a little slow to come in, however, and Hampton's son Thomas was forced to post another solicitation a few weeks later: 'I am sure there are hundreds of people in the Potteries who would only be too pleased to subscribe to such a fund to show our appreciation of Captain Smith's gallant conduct in this terrible disaster. Not only are "we Potters" proud that he was an Englishman, but that he was a Potteryman and a Briton to the backbone'.[41] This blatant appeal to local pride did the trick, and total contributions of just over £210 were received from around ninety subscribers.

One can imagine the dilemma that Hampton's efforts caused Hanley Town Council. A local man had played a prominent but also dubious role in the biggest maritime disaster in history, and here was someone wanting a public memorial to him, and offering the funds to pay for it. Smith, they must have felt, was not the best advertisement for the town, but to reject the memorial would have created a tremendous stir by making it clear that they felt that he had contributed to the sinking, thereby casting the town in an even more unfavorable light. The most prudent course seemed to be to go along with Hampton's scheme, and to put a brave face on things and proclaim Smith a hero.

They could not, however, entirely ignore the tensions surrounding Smith's conduct. 'It was very proper, he was sure all present would agree with him', stated the Mayor at the plaque's dedication ceremony, 'that some memorial should be erected in Hanley to the memory of Captain Smith. He was a Hanley boy, and prior to the *Titanic* disaster, had done so much to make a name for himself, and in that way to glorify the

11. Memorial to the disaster in the grounds of Belfast City Hall. (*Stephanie Barczewski*)

12. The *Titanic* under construction in Belfast. (*Harland & Wolff*)

13. Harland & Wolff workers with *Titanic* in the background. (*Harland & Wolff*)

14. The dry dock specially built to accommodate the *Titanic* and *Olympic* in case they needed repairs. (*Stephanie Barczewski*)

15. *Titanic* Crew Memorial, Holyrood Church, Southampton. (*Stephanie Barczewski*)

16. *Titanic* Engineers' Memorial, East Park, Southampton. (*Stephanie Barczewski*)

WALLACE
HARTLEY
BANDMASTER OF
THE R.MS TITANIC
WHO PERISHED IN
THE FOUNDERING
OF THAT VESSEL
APRIL 15TH 1912.
ERECTED BY VOLUNTARY
CONTRIBUTIONS TO COM-
MEMORATE THE HEROISM
OF A NATIVE OF THIS
TOWN

17. Memorial to Wallace Hartley, Colne. (*Stephanie Barczewski*)

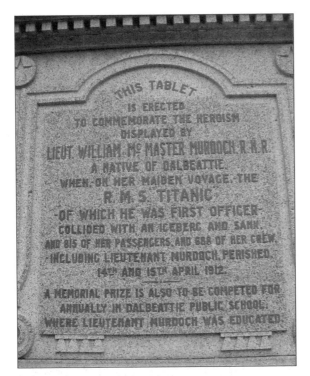

THIS TABLET
IS ERECTED
TO COMMEMORATE THE HEROISM
DISPLAYED BY
LIEUT. WILLIAM McMASTER MURDOCH R.N.R.
A NATIVE OF DALBEATTIE,
WHEN, ON HER MAIDEN VOYAGE, THE
R. M. S. TITANIC,
OF WHICH HE WAS FIRST OFFICER,
COLLIDED WITH AN ICEBERG AND SANK,
AND 815 OF HER PASSENGERS, AND 688 OF HER CREW,
INCLUDING LIEUTENANT MURDOCH, PERISHED,
14TH AND 15TH APRIL 1912.

A MEMORIAL PRIZE IS ALSO TO BE COMPETED FOR
ANNUALLY IN DALBEATTIE PUBLIC SCHOOL,
WHERE LIEUTENANT MURDOCH WAS EDUCATED.

18. Memorial to William Murdoch, Dalbeattie. (*Stephanie Barczewski*)

19. The Jack Phillips Memorial Cloister, Godalming. (*Stephanie Barczewski*)

20. Memorial to Edward Smith, Lichfield. (*Stephanie Barczewski*)

21. Painting of the *Titanic* leaving Southampton. (*Southampton City Collections*)

town to which he belonged'. Here, the Mayor emphasized Smith's achievements before he took command of the *Titanic*, as if the event which had made him famous had nothing to do with the plaque being placed in the town hall. Regarding the sinking of the *Titanic*, the Mayor minimized Smith's role, stating that 'whenever a disaster of that magnitude overtook them the individual played a small and insignificant part'.[42]

Similarly, in his speech at Etruria British School, Major Cecil Wedgwood, who unveiled the portrait, spoke primarily of Smith's successful career as a White Star captain: 'He meant to make the most of his life, and he not only had a high sense of duty but a very laudable ambition to do the best he could by the profession he entered'.[43] In both ceremonies, Smith was presented as someone who had deserved a memorial even without – or perhaps in spite of – his role in the *Titanic* disaster. Indeed, this theme was so prevalent that, as we shall see, a myth grew up in Hanley that a statue of Smith had been commissioned *before* the *Titanic* sank, in recognition of his status as the best-known captain of passenger liners in Britain. After the disaster, the story went, the town had been too embarrassed to put it up, and so they had given it to Lichfield.

Certainly the tone of the two ceremonies suggests that Hanley's civic leaders were far from eager to commemorate Smith, and one wonders if they would have done it at all if Hampton had not pushed them into it. In reading the words spoken by the Mayor as he unveiled the plaque, one can still feel him struggling to express sentiments that neither praised Smith excessively nor criticized him unduly. And there are other indications, as well, that Hanley was uncertain of how to handle Smith's sudden notoriety. When the memorial committee announced a public subscription for the statue in Lichfield, a project that was far more grandiose than Hanley's efforts, only three people from Hanley contributed. As the years passed, the town continued to downplay Smith's local connections. In 1961, when alterations were made to the town hall, it was decided to remove the plaque in his honour. It was given to the Etruria British School, which displayed it until it closed in 1978. It was then returned to the town hall, but, instead of being placed in the entrance where it would be easily visible, it was moved further into the interior of the building, where it stills hangs today.

All of this has been a roundabout way of suggesting that, when the Smith Memorial Committee opted to put the statue in Lichfield, the civic authorities in Hanley probably felt relief, not jealousy. In contrast, the Mayor of Lichfield, H. J. C. Winterton, eagerly accepted the statue when he was first approached by the committee:

> The Council and ... the citizens generally would welcome a Memorial to the late Commander E. J. Smith being placed [in Lichfield], and would consider it an honour to the City ... There is some fitness in the thought that Lichfield, the 'field of the dead', may help to keep alive for the sake of future generations the memory and example of one who was foremost among many in courage, devotion to duty, regard for others, self-abnegation and heroism.[44]

Perhaps Winterton had a less ambivalent attitude towards Smith's conduct than did his counterpart in Hanley, or perhaps it was less problematic for a town that had no previous associations with Smith to accept his statue, as its presence would be less of a reflection on the surrounding community. Whatever the case may have been, in May 1913 the memorial committee was given preliminary approval to proceed, pending the selection of a sculptor and a suitable site. More specific plans for the memorial were announced in October. The plans called for a 'two-fold' monument, with the statue in Lichfield plus a stained-glass window in the new cathedral in Liverpool. A public subscription was announced, with any surplus funds to be donated to the Seaman's Orphanage for Boys in Southampton.

The collection campaign was a success, and at its meeting on 19 November the memorial committee felt that the time had come to commission a sculptor. The committee chose Lady Kathleen Scott, widow of the explorer Robert Falcon Scott, who had died in March 1912, only two weeks before the *Titanic* sank, on the return journey from the South Pole. The eight-foot-high bronze statue cost the memorial fund £740. As it neared completion in the spring of 1914, a place for it still had to be found. At its meeting on 26 May Lichfield City Council voted unanimously to put the statue in Museum Gardens, in close proximity to a memorial to the late King Edward VII. The unveiling ceremony was set for 29 July.

At the eleventh hour, however, a campaign was launched to stop the statue from being placed in Lichfield. On 3 June a letter from the

Reverend Wilfrid Fuller, vicar of the local parish church of St Chad's, appeared in the *Lichfield Mercury*:

> A few persons, strangers to our City, have made a request for permission to erect a statue in our Museum Grounds to the memory of the late Captain Smith, who was in command of the White Star liner, the *Titanic*, on her first and last voyage. It seems to me a fair question, which should first be answered, 'What are we going to memorialise?' It can truthfully and heartily be said, 'A seaman and an officer who died most manfully at his post of duty'. But a brave death is not so very uncommon, we are thankful to know; and on board the *Titanic* and from the ship many died equally bravely that night. I would write with great caution, and not say a word against a person now no more in this world ... But, as a statue erected in a public place is intended to praise a man and his work, we ought to bear in mind some of the findings of the Court of Enquiry. If my memory serves me clearly, it was proved that on the day of the disaster the officers received warning of the existence of ice in the region they were to enter that night, and that the speed of the ship was not reduced. I think, therefore, that the point of view should not be lost sight of from which the relatives of the 1500 lost lives may regard this proposal.[45]

Fuller had hit upon the key difficulties impeding the campaign to transform Smith into a hero. Nothing he had done after the collision with the iceberg, including dying 'most manfully at his post of duty', was unique; instead it had been a fate shared by many other men. And, more significantly, there was the issue of his culpability for the accident, in particular his failure to reduce the ship's speed despite repeated warnings about ice in its path.

A few days later, Fuller's opinion was seconded by 'A Layman':

> I, as another citizen of Lichfield, was delighted to see Mr Fuller's letter in your issue of 5 June ... The 'monument' in question may be a work of art – but whether or not it should find its home in Lichfield is another question ... It would be a pity to allow our gardens to become a dumping ground for monuments of men who have no connection with the City, and are unknown to fame. We must face facts; and I believe it is a fact (and I say this at the risk of being labelled uncharitable) that the late Commander of the *Titanic* was unknown to fame before he committed the error of judgment, which, humanely speaking, led to one of the greatest catastrophes of modern times. He was no doubt plucky, and met his death in a truly British and seaman-like manner – but so did many others.[46]

Once again, it was pointed out that, whatever Smith had done in dying
bravely was done by many others as well, and that Smith had committed
a serious 'error in judgment' in his navigation of the ship. Fuller had
been careful to voice his opposition to the memorial in terms that only
indirectly criticized Smith's conduct on the night of the sinking, but 'A
Layman' was far less circumspect, and his comments reveal that there
were Britons who felt that Smith bore considerable responsibility for
the disaster.

Those two letters marked the start of a formal protest campaign
against the statue being placed in Lichfield. Two weeks later, a petition
signed by Fuller and seventy-three others was presented to Lichfield City
Council. The petitioners, while stating that 'we do not in the least suggest
any sense of reproach upon the memory of an admittedly brave sailor',
declared that the plan to put the statue in Museum Gardens was
'undesirable' on three grounds. First, Smith was not from Lichfield and
therefore had 'no claim upon the City'. Secondly, monuments erected
in Lichfield should be reserved for 'distinctly eminent men'. Thirdly,
there was no 'particular historical reason warranting the perpetuation
of Captain Smith's memory'. The petitioners were clearly trying to be
tactful. They avoided condemning Smith's conduct overtly, recognizing
that maligning the dead was a strategy likely to backfire. Only their third
argument hinted at Smith's culpability, and even it did so in extremely
veiled terms. The first two arguments, on the other hand, focused on
less contentious issues: Smith had no connection to Lichfield and had
not been sufficiently famous to warrant commemoration with something
so grandiose as a statue.

In discussing the petition, Lichfield City Council found itself in an
unenviable position. The signatories included a number of prominent
citizens, but by this point the statue was complete and the unveiling
ceremony was less than six weeks away. To reject the statue now would
be a serious embarrassment, so they chose the lesser of two evils and
rejected the petition instead. Councillor Raby was the most vehement
in his comments, complaining that the petition had been 'particularly
ungracious' in its denunciation of 'a Staffordshire man and a Staffordshire hero'. Raby's motion that the petition be rejected was seconded
by Councillor Harrison, who stated that 'he thought it an honour to
have the statue in Lichfield'. Councillor Jones added that 'as an old

sailor, he had great pleasure in supporting Councillor Raby's motion'. Councillor Longstaff was the only member to express any sympathy with the petition, although in the end he, too, voted for Raby's motion. He declared that if the petition had been received a year earlier, it would have received more serious consideration: 'A year ago, it might have been arguable whether it would not be better to put the statue at Hanley, or elsewhere in the Potteries, rather than in Lichfield ... but it seemed to him now, in spite of the undoubted weighty names on the petition, too late to go into the question'.[47]

Raby's motion to reject the petition passed unanimously, and the unveiling ceremony took place as scheduled on 29 July 1914. In attendance were Lady Scott, many members of the memorial committee and numerous local luminaries. The Queen Mother sent a message of support, as did the Marquess of Salisbury, the Dowager Countess of Arran and other prominent persons from both sides of the Atlantic who harboured fond memories of crossings with Smith. Smith's daughter Helen, who was now twelve years old, performed the unveiling. Only once during the ceremony was the controversy surrounding the statue's placement in Lichfield alluded to, when the Bishop of Willesden stated that 'although it may cause trouble in the hearts of some, yet if it teaches us the lesson to remember those who have gone before it will be good'.[48]

The statue was therefore installed, but not without some debate. Looking at it today, it seems that, for all of their official enthusiasm for the project, Lichfield City Council may not have been quite so keen in their hearts. Certainly the position selected for the statue was neither highly visible nor easily accessible. There is no path directly leading to it, and anyone wishing to stand in front of it has to snake through a series of flowerbeds. Moreover, the statue stands on the edge of a manicured lawn, and the low fence surrounding the lawn comes so close to the statue's base that it is impossible to get a good look at it without stepping on the pristine grass, something many people are doubtless reluctant to do. Of course the park may not have been configured in this way in 1914, but it has been since at least 1958, when a story in the *Lichfield Mercury* described its location: 'The statue is situated behind some neatly maintained turf, the type which is so immaculate that only the innocent child or the naughty dog dare to tread. No direct path is laid to the memorial, and visitors, finding the approach uninviting, neither dare or bother to study the dark, heavy carving'.[49] Lichfield, it seems, was not interested in showing off its memorial to the *Titanic*'s captain. On the contrary, its placement suggests that the city was not altogether comfortable with the statue.

Nor, perhaps, was the memorial committee quite so certain of Smith's heroism. The bronze tablet on the granite plinth on which the statue stands bears this inscription:

> Commander
> Edward John Smith, RD, RNR,
> Born January 27th, 1850,
> Died April 15th, 1912,
> Bequeathing to his countrymen the
> Memory and Example of
> A Great Heart,
> A Brave Life, and
> A Heroic Death.

One key word is missing from the inscription, the one word with which Smith will forever be associated: '*Titanic*'. A charitable interpretation would be to argue that in 1914 there was no need to mention Smith's association with the *Titanic* because everyone would have known that he was the ship's captain. It seems more likely, however, that the memorial committee did not want to refer to the incident that had made Smith as infamous as it had made him famous.

For decades, Smith's statue stood in Museum Gardens, unloved and for the most part ignored. By the mid 1980s, however, times had changed. Robert Ballard had discovered the wreck of the *Titanic* on the floor of the North Atlantic, creating a surge of interest that peaked with the release of the James Cameron film in 1997. A growing number of '*Titanic* tourists' from around the world began travelling to sites with links to the disaster.

Suddenly Lichfield recognized that what long had been the statue's greatest liability – its association with the *Titanic* – was now its greatest asset. In 1985 the words 'Captain Smith was Captain of the *Titanic*' were added to the plinth in order to identify the statue, in the hope that it would help to lure visitors to the city. Lichfield Chief Executive John Thompson found himself swamped with questions and requests for interviews about the statue, so much so that he embarked upon a research trip across England to find out all he could about the man it commemorated. Using the information Thompson uncovered, Lichfield District Council published a booklet about Smith which they continue to distribute today. The statue was also featured on the front of 60,000 leaflets distributed at the National Garden Festival in 1986.

This flurry of interest in Smith did not go unnoticed in Stoke-on-Trent. It was one thing to ignore Smith's Hanley origins when he was a bit of an embarrassment, but entirely another one when he was the subject of tourist interest. Stoke offers few obvious attractions to tourists: the only memorial in the town centre is a statue of Sir Stanley Matthews, the famous Stoke City footballer, who is not likely to lure visitors from very far away. As *Titanic*-mania spread in the 1980s and 1990s, it seemed time at long last to stop de-emphasizing the connection with Smith. In the new Potteries Shopping Centre, he was featured in a mural of people and events from local history, alongside Matthews, the novelist Arnold Bennett, and Reginald Mitchell, the designer of the Spitfire. On the occasion of the eightieth anniversary of the sinking in 1992, a local pottery firm turned out a limited edition Smith figurine, and a brewery began producing a *Titanic* ale with a picture of Smith on the label.[50] That same year, the Potteries Museum and Art Gallery put on an exhibition devoted to Smith, the first time he had been so honoured.

The Smith memorial, however, was still in Lichfield, and the wheels in the minds of Stoke's tourist development officers began to spin. The old rumours about the statue being originally commissioned by Hanley prior to Smith's death recirculated, and in November 1985 they became the basis of an official request by Stoke-on-Trent City Council for Lichfield to 'return' it to Stoke. In a letter to Lichfield District Council, Stoke Council claimed that the statue had been commissioned by Hanley 'in recognition of Smith's prominent status' as the best-known captain of passenger liners. They claimed that when the *Titanic* sank Smith had fallen into disgrace, and thus Hanley had rejected the statue; but now they wanted it back.

Not surprisingly, Lichfield District Council was unsympathetic. A quick search through press cuttings from 1913 and 1914 revealed that the statue had always been destined for Lichfield, and Stoke Council was told emphatically that there was no chance of it being moved from its present location. Lichfield Councillor Bob Blewitt said that Stoke should be given a flat refusal, since Lichfield had been responsible for cleaning the pigeon droppings off the statue for the past seventy years. Councillor Doug Constable was even more blunt, accusing the Stoke Council of 'not doing its homework' and telling it to 'go to hell'.[51]

The Smith statue therefore stayed put. In the mid 1990s, however, schoolchildren at Ball Green Primary in Stoke-on-Trent launched another campaign to bring Smith back to Hanley after their teacher, Pat Bailey, included the story of the *Titanic* in their lessons. The children started a petition calling for the statue to be moved and wrote letters to the *Stoke Sentinel* voicing their opinions. 'We have been wanting Captain Smith's statue back in Stoke-on-Trent for a long time', wrote six-year-old Alex Malpass. 'I think it should stand next to Stanley Matthews in the middle of Hanley.' The children were aware of the controversy that had traditionally surrounded Smith, but they defended him ardently. 'We want to get Captain Smith's statue back', asserted Laura Heath Jones, aged seven, 'It was not his fault. It was the builder's fault. The *Titanic* was too big to manoeuvre and that is why it hit the iceberg and sank'. These heartfelt pleas from Stoke's schoolchildren fell on deaf ears in Lichfield. 'Several bids have been made in the past for the statue', Chief Executive Thompson declared, 'and our response is the same. It was never intended for Stoke – so hard luck.'[52]

In 1997, not uncoincidentally the year in which the blockbuster James Cameron film was released, Stoke tried yet again to 'reclaim' the statue. For the third time, however, the campaign ended in failure. 'This is another unwelcome approach to take our statue away from us', declared John Thompson. 'It was always intended that Lichfield be the statue's home and I am very surprised that Stoke have bid for it after previous unsuccessful attempts to prise it away from us.'[53] The reason for Lichfield's recalcitrance was clearly the potential to attract tourism that the statue now represented. 'Before the film, no one wanted to know him', declared Lichfield Council Leader Peter von Hagen. 'All of a sudden he's become very popular in the film and he may well be a popular tourist attraction.'[54] Stoke City Council, meanwhile, vowed to commission its own statue. 'In the years to come we will look at ways of commemorating him', stated Council Leader Barry Stockley.[55] To date, however, no statue has appeared, and Stanley Matthews continues to dribble his football alone in Hanley town centre.

The evolution of Captain Edward Smith's relationship to his home-town of Hanley, Stoke-on-Trent, parallels the evolution of the *Titanic* from a source of controversy and sorrow to a subject of popular enthusiasm. In the period immediately after the sinking, no place was particularly eager to commemorate Smith. Hanley's local authorities put up a plaque in the town hall only because an old friend of Smith's took the initiative, and they did not protest when the Smith Memorial Committee announced their intention to put Smith's statue in Lichfield. Lichfield, meanwhile, accepted the statue only over the protests of some of its most prominent citizens, and it stood all but ignored in Beacon Park for nearly three-quarters of a century. It was only when the statue began to have the potential to attract tourism in the 1980s and 1990s that the two cities began to compete for it. Based on erroneous infor-mation regarding the history of the statue, Stoke-on-Trent argued that the statue rightfully belonged to them and should be returned. Lichfield, however, mounted a spirited defence in which they made it clear that the statue was staying put. No improvement in Smith's reputation brought about the change in attitude towards the statue; no new evidence has been uncovered that exonerates him from blame for the disaster. But when profits from tourism are at stake, local government is capable of overlooking even the most dubious conduct.

8

William Murdoch

The story of the efforts to commemorate Captain Edward J. Smith in Lichfield and Stoke-on-Trent is a story of a memorial that neither city was particularly eager for in 1912 but that both cities want now. The doubts about Smith's conduct on board the *Titanic* have been overcome by the potential which any local association with the world's most famous shipwreck has to bring in tourist revenue. The story of the memorial of the *Titanic*'s First Officer William Murdoch, on the other hand, is the story of a town that overcame its hesitation about their native son's conduct much more quickly. Murdoch, who had the misfortune to be on watch at the time of the *Titanic*'s collision with the iceberg, was born in Dalbeattie, a small town in south-western Scotland, about fifteen miles from Dumfries. As soon as Murdoch was cleared of any wrongdoing by the two inquiries into the disaster, the town put up a memorial to him. In Murdoch's case, however, the surge of interest in the *Titanic* that reached a peak with the release of the James Cameron film in 1997 created a difficult situation for his hometown, for the film did not depict Murdoch in a positive manner. Once again, as they had done in 1912, the people of Dalbeattie rallied to Murdoch's defence, this time taking on a major Hollywood studio in a battle to restore their hero's good name.

William McMaster Murdoch was born on 28 February 1873. At the time, Dalbeattie was barely a century old; it had been founded in 1781 as a planned town beside the Dalbeattie burn, which supplied the water power for the mills that were the main local industry. Strict conditions were imposed on the size, standard, design and layout of the houses, although Dalbeattie was not as formal as other planned towns such as Gatehouse and Castle Douglas. The inhabitants enjoyed a considerable improvement in their quality of life over that which they had experienced in Galloway's traditional villages, as housing was generally superior, with stone, slate-roofed cottages replacing the single-roomed bothy.[1]

By the late nineteenth century, when William Murdoch was born, Dalbeattie was no longer primarily a mill town. Instead its main industry was granite quarrying, the profits from which triggered a population boom which saw the town grow from 1600 inhabitants in 1858 to almost 4000 by the 1880s. Granite from Dalbeattie went into houses all over England and Scotland, as well as roads and railway beds. The need to transport the granite led to the expansion of Dalbeattie's harbour, which in the late nineteenth century enjoyed steady traffic from vessels carrying the stone to Liverpool and other English ports. With its strong tides and hidden sandbars, Urr Water and its entrance, the Rough Firth, were extremely difficult to navigate, and as a result Dalbeattie sailors earned a reputation as some of the best in the world.

The Murdochs were prominent seafarers along the Solway Coast, having intermarried with a number of other maritime families such as the Cummingses, the Raes, the Wilsons and the Hallidays. They may even have been distantly related to the most famous local sailor, John Paul Jones, naval hero of the American Revolution, who was born in Kirkcudbrightshire at Kirkbean.[2] Even in difficult economic times, a Murdoch could rely on family connections to get a berth on a ship. A sailor's life was a dangerous one in the nineteenth century, and the Murdochs were well acquainted with its hazards. During William's boyhood, both his uncle John and his great-uncle Andrew perished at sea.

William's immediate family managed to avoid such tragedy. His grandfather was sufficiently prosperous to acquire part-ownership of a small sailing vessel that traded with the Continent, and his father Samuel was a master mariner who captained tall ships all over the world. Samuel's profession meant that he was rarely home for more than a few weeks a year, but it enabled his family to enjoy a financially comfortable existence. Shortly after William's birth, they moved from a small terraced house at 3 Sunnyside to a larger home at 341 High Street and then to a handsome twin-gabled granite dwelling called Oakland Cottage, also in the High Street. The house had been custom built for Samuel, who named it after Oakland, California, one of his favourite ports of call.

Like many local boys, William learned to sail at a young age, and seems to have decided early on to pursue a career at sea. After leaving

Dalbeattie High School at the age of fifteen, he served an apprenticeship with William Joyce & Company of Liverpool on board the barque *Charles Cotesworth* for four voyages to the west coast of North and South America. During his apprenticeship, Murdoch would have learned many things, including how to tie sailor's knots, how to identify every rope in the rigging even in the dark, and how to pinpoint the ship's location by various navigational methods. He would have also learned the importance of getting a ship from place to place as quickly as possible, for the faster the journey, the greater the profits to the owners. In order to compete with the steamships, the captains of sailing vessels followed a practice known as 'cracking on', in which they used as much sail as the masts could stand, even in a full gale. This increased speed but also the potential for catastrophe, as the slightest miscalculation would snap a mast. The best 'crackers on', however, came to be highly regarded and received higher wages than their more cautious colleagues. Many of these captains later switched to steamships, where they continued the practice, running the engines at full speed regardless of weather conditions. Some critics felt that a disastrous accident was inevitable, but until one occurred 'cracking on' continued to be the order of the day.

In 1892 Murdoch completed his apprenticeship, having accumulated almost four years at sea. Now nineteen, he took and passed the examination for his Second Mate's certificate, and he quickly gained a berth on board the full-rigger *Iquique*, which was captained by his father. He remained in that post for three years and made his first voyage around the world. On one stop in Rotterdam, he met a young apprentice seaman named Stanley Lord, who later played a prominent – and controversial – role in the *Titanic* disaster as the captain of the *Californian*. In March 1895 Murdoch passed his First Mate's examination and shortly thereafter took a berth on the iron-hulled barque *Saint Cuthbert*. The following year, he earned his Master's and Extra Master's certificate, which meant that he now possessed all of the qualifications necessary to follow in his father's footsteps and become a captain.

Captaincies were hard to come by, however, and Murdoch was forced to take another berth as First Mate on board the *Lydgate*, a slow sailing ship that plied the route between New York and Shanghai. It may have been this experience with an inferior vessel that convinced Murdoch that the future of ocean travel lay with steam. When the *Lydgate* discharged its crew in Antwerp in May 1899, Murdoch decided to apply for a position with a passenger steamship line. While awaiting a berth, he served as a lieutenant in the Royal Naval Reserve on board troop transports ferrying British, Canadian and Australian soldiers to South Africa to fight in the Boer War. After completing his military duties, Murdoch was hired by the White Star Line, which had just expanded its service to Australia and needed additional officers. It is unclear to which White Star vessel he was posted first, but by September 1900 he was on board the *Medic*, a new ship, as Second Officer. On a dinner menu signed by all the ship's officers, Murdoch added a quotation from the Scottish author John Henry Mackay that reflected his ambition and determination: 'Whatever obstacles control, go on, true heart, thou'lt reach the goal'.[3] His choice may also have reflected some unusual political views: Mackay was a notorious anarchist.

By 1901 Murdoch was serving as Second Officer on the *Runic*; his rapid advance to senior rank suggests that he was regarded as a capable officer. In June 1903 Murdoch transferred from the Australian to the North Atlantic service, where he would get the chance to serve on some of the most prestigious ships afloat. He was assigned to the maiden voyage of the *Arabic*, a further indication of White Star's confidence in him. (Charles Lightoller, who later served with Murdoch on the *Titanic*, was the *Arabic*'s Fourth Officer.) Their trust was rewarded when Murdoch's quick thinking avoided a collision with a large sailing vessel on the *Arabic*'s fourth voyage. Murdoch had just come onto the bridge to relieve the Chief Officer when the lookout spotted a light bearing down on the ship from the port side. The Chief Officer shouted an order to port the helm, but Murdoch realized that if the order were followed the other vessel would strike the *Arabic* amidships. With no time to argue, he shoved the quartermaster aside, seized the wheel and kept the *Arabic* steady on its course. His action was vindicated when the sailing vessel slipped by with only a few feet to spare.

Over the next four years, Murdoch served on a number of other White Star vessels, including the *Celtic*, the *Germanic*, the *Oceanic* and the *Cedric*. In May 1907, he joined the *Adriatic* for its maiden voyage. The *Adriatic* was captained by Edward J. Smith, under whom Murdoch would later serve on the *Titanic*. Now thirty-four, Murdoch was a handsome man with a thick moustache, powerful physique and ready smile that made him popular with his fellow officers. More than one woman had succumbed to his charms, and on one of his first voyages with White Star he had met a teacher from New Zealand named Ada Florence Banks, who was travelling with her father on a business trip to Britain. They had exchanged letters ever since, but had not seen each other since Murdoch had transferred to the North Atlantic route. The relationship survived the long separation, however, and on 2 September 1907 William and Ada were married in Southampton, the city to which White Star had recently moved its North Atlantic passenger service. Soon afterwards, the couple settled into a semi-detached house on Belmont Road, but their time together was to be brief, as Murdoch was back at sea only three weeks after the wedding. For the duration of their marriage, William and Ada saw each other perhaps one week a month. With the couple already in their mid thirties, children were unlikely, and Ada continued to work as a teacher, an unusual decision for a married woman. Murdoch remained on the *Adriatic* until May 1911, when he followed Captain Smith to the brand-new *Olympic*, on which he served as First Officer. The fact that he was given an important post on the maiden voyage of such a famous ship demonstrates that at this point in his career he was regarded as one of White Star's best officers. This was further confirmed a year later when he again followed Smith, this time from the *Olympic* to the *Titanic*. He also received a promotion from First to Chief Officer, one step below Captain. His new status was short-lived, however. When the *Titanic* reached Southampton in early April 1912, the *Olympic*'s Chief Officer, Henry Tingle Wilde, was transferred to the *Titanic*, bumping Murdoch back down to First Officer and Charles Lightoller, who had been the *Titanic*'s First Officer, to Second Officer. The *Titanic*'s original Second Officer, David Blair, lost his berth altogether and remained behind in Southampton. None of the affected officers were very pleased. Lightoller later recalled that 'this doubtful policy threw both Murdoch and me out of our stride; and, apart from the disappointment of having to step back in our rank, caused quite a little confusion'.[4] For his part, Murdoch accepted his fate, but he was eager for a future chance of advancement. He wrote to his sister Margaret on 8 April, two days prior to the *Titanic*'s departure, that White Star had 'as much as promised that when Wilde goes I am to go up again'.[5]

Once the voyage was underway, Murdoch seems to have harboured no resentment about his unexpected demotion. He made no reference to it in his last letter to his parents, which was posted from Queenstown, the *Titanic*'s final port of call, on 11 April:

> Only a short note to let you know that we are this length alright. We have had clear & squally weather ever since we left & it looks very well now ... I left Ada quite well yesterday morning ... We are getting things pretty straight now, but owing to the coal strike we are only going out at 19 or 20 knots per hour. I sincerely hope that you are both keeping very well ... With fondest love & looking forward to hearing from some of you at Q'town.[6]

On Sunday 14 April Murdoch relieved Lightoller on watch at 1 p.m., when he was informed that Captain Smith had received a wireless warning regarding ice only a few miles north of the *Titanic*'s course. Later that afternoon, Smith ordered the *Titanic*'s course to be altered to the south, which the officers interpreted as a precaution to avoid the ice. Still, Murdoch remained concerned. At 7.15 p.m., he told Trimmer Samuel Hemming to shut the forward hatch cover and the skylight over the crew's galley in order to prevent the glow from interfering with the night vision of the lookouts. At 10 p.m., he came on the bridge to relieve Lightoller; while Murdoch waited for his eyes to adjust to the darkness, the two men chatted. Lightoller later recalled the conversation:

> Murdoch and I were old shipmates, and for a few minutes – as was our custom – we stood there looking ahead, and yarning over times and incidents past and present. We both remarked on the ship's steadiness, absence of vibration, and how comfortably she was slipping along. Then we passed on to more serious subjects, such as the chances of sighting ice, reports that ice had been sighted, and the positions. We also commented on the lack of definition between the horizon and the sky – which would make an iceberg all the more difficult to see – particularly if it had a black side, and that should be, by bad luck, turned our way.

Lightoller then wished Murdoch 'joy of his watch' and went on his rounds before retiring to his cabin.[7]

For the next hour and a half, Murdoch stared into the darkness from his position on the *Titanic*'s bridge wing. The precipitous drop in temperature would have warned him that the ship was possibly entering an area of ice. The *Titanic* was still steaming forward at over twenty knots an hour, but Murdoch had no authority to reduce the ship's speed even if he had thought it warranted. In any event, he almost certainly would not have thought the *Titanic*'s speed unusual or reckless; ships slowed down only for actual hazards, not potential ones. The visibility appeared to be excellent, and Murdoch was confident that any large object in the ship's path would be spotted in time to manoeuvre around it.

He was, of course, wrong. At 11.40 p.m., Murdoch and the other crew members on the bridge heard the crow's nest bell ring three times, indicating an object directly in front of the ship. The telephone linking the crow's nest to the bridge rang and was picked up by Sixth Officer James Moody, who heard lookout Frederick Fleet shout, 'Iceberg right ahead!' Moody turned to inform Murdoch, but he seemed to have already spotted the berg, for he was running from the bridge wing to the engine-room telegraph even before Moody hung up the phone. 'Hard-a-starboard!' he yelled to Quartermaster Robert Hichens, who was at the wheel. As Hichens began spinning the wheel as quickly as he could, Murdoch grabbed the handle of the telegraph and signalled 'full astern'.

Now Murdoch could only wait and hope that the *Titanic* would turn in time to clear the iceberg. He was attempting a manoeuvre called a 'port around', an attempt to swing the *Titanic*'s bow to port in order for it to miss the iceberg and then swing the stern back to starboard so that it too could pass by unscathed.[8] The bow continued to plow straight ahead, however, for it took between twenty and thirty seconds for the steam-powered steering mechanism completely to turn the *Titanic*'s massive rudder. Fearing the worst, Murdoch flipped the switch that closed all the watertight doors. At the last minute, the bow swung a few degrees to the left, and above the waterline the hull scraped by the iceberg, dislodging about two tons of ice that fell onto the *Titanic*'s forward decks. Far below, Murdoch could hear a grinding sound that lasted about ten seconds. When it ceased, he ordered Quartermaster Alfred Olliver to note the time of the collision and told Moody to enter it in the ship's log. Captain Smith, who had been in his cabin adjacent to the bridge, immediately appeared and asked, 'What have we struck?'

'An iceberg, sir', Murdoch replied. 'I hard-a-starboarded and reversed the engines, and I was going to hard-a-port around it, but she was too close. I could not do any more.'[9] After Smith and Thomas Andrews conducted their inspection of the damage and determined that the

Titanic was doomed, Smith ordered Murdoch to muster the passengers and take charge of loading the lifeboats on the starboard side. At first, Murdoch had difficulty persuading any passengers, male or female, to leave the apparent safety of the warm and comfortable *Titanic* and get into the boats. At 12.45 a.m., after half-an-hour of trying to fill Boat 7, he gave up and ordered it to be lowered with only twenty-five occupants out of a capacity of sixty-five.

Next, Murdoch moved to Boat 5, which he filled with forty people and then told Fifth Officer Harold Lowe, 'That is enough before lowering. We can get a lot more in after she's in the water'. He may have harboured concerns that a fully-loaded boat might buckle as it hung from the davits. Putting Third Officer Herbert Pitman in charge of the boat, Murdoch ordered him to row to the after gangway door to take on more passengers once the boat reached the water. As Pitman climbed into the boat, Murdoch shook his hand and said, 'Good-bye, good luck', which Pitman later interpreted to mean that Murdoch had already decided to go down with the ship.[10]

Amidst the chaos, there were still occasional moments of levity. As Murdoch was loading Boat 1, two Americans, Abraham Solomon and C. E. Stengel, appeared and were told to board. Stengel had difficulty negotiating the railing and tumbled clumsily into the boat; Murdoch laughed and said, 'That's the funniest thing I've seen all night!' He then ordered six stokers to get in and put Lookout George Symons in charge, telling him to 'stand off from the ship's side and return when we call you'. Boat 1 was then lowered with twelve occupants out of a capacity of forty.[11]

Murdoch then headed aft to load the remaining boats on the starboard side. On the way, he encountered Wilde, who asked him where the firearms were stowed. Murdoch, Wilde, Lightoller and Captain Smith all proceeded to Murdoch's cabin, where the guns were kept in a locker. Each of the senior officers took a revolver and several rounds of ammunition. Murdoch returned to the Boat Deck and supervised the lowering of Boats 11 and 13, which were fully loaded. As he filled Boat 15, a group of around six men rushed forward and tried to force their way in. Shouting 'Get back! Get back! It's women first!' Murdoch, assisted by Steward Ray Hart, fought to hold them back as the crew barely managed to get the boat away. Murdoch then turned to Collapsible C, which had been fitted into Boat 1's davits. A mob of stewards and third-class passengers rushed the boat, but, with the assistance of Purser Hugh McElroy, Murdoch managed to launch it. Around this time, Murdoch encountered Steward John Hardy, whom he told, 'I believe she is gone'.[12] Hardy assumed he meant the lifeboat; only later did he realize that Murdoch meant the *Titanic.*

The last reliable sighting of Murdoch was by Lightoller, who saw him on the roof of the officers' quarters trying desperately to attach Collapsible A's falls to the davits. As Lightoller watched, the water rolled up the Boat Deck, engulfing Murdoch and sweeping him off the ship. There were other witnesses, however, who claimed that Murdoch had met with a very different fate. Thomas Whitely, a waiter, asserted that Murdoch 'shot one man ... and then shot himself', though he admitted that 'I did not see this, but three others did'. Eleanor Widener stated that as her lifeboat was rowing away from the *Titanic* she saw 'one of the officers shoot himself in the head'. And third-class passenger Carl Jansen declared that he 'glanced toward the bridge and saw the chief officer place a revolver in his mouth and shoot himself. His body toppled overboard'.[13] Two other passengers, Eugene Daly and George Rheims, later wrote to their families about how they had seen a senior officer put a gun to his head and pull the trigger.[14]

When the news of the sinking reached Murdoch's wife and family in England, they were given a brief moment of hope by the presence of the name 'William Murdock' on the list of surviving crew members. This man turned out to be a stoker, however, and they were forced to accept that the William Murdoch who had been the *Titanic*'s First Officer had perished. To make matters worse, Ada and Murdoch's parents had to deal with more than just their grief; they also had to deal with accusations that William had been at least partially responsible for the disaster, and that he had not behaved in an heroic manner during the sinking. There were three actions on Murdoch's part which were thought to be questionable. First, he had been the officer on watch at the time of the collision and had ordered the manoeuvre that had ultimately caused the fatal damage to the *Titanic.* Could he or should he have done something else? This question was raised on the first day of the American inquiry, when J. Bruce Ismay had testified that 'if this ship had hit the iceberg stem on, in all human probability she would have been here today'.[15] Ismay based this opinion on the fact that the *Titanic* had been designed to withstand a head-on collision, but not the sort of glancing blow that the sudden turn to port that Murdoch had ordered caused.

Some modern *Titanic* historians concur. Wyn Craig Wade is critical of Murdoch's order to reverse the engines, claiming that this was a direct contradiction of standard practice at the time, which was to continue full speed ahead while making a sharp turn to avoid the object. He cites the 1910 edition of *Knight's Modern Seamanship*, which reads, 'To turn away and slow is the surest possible way of bringing about a collision'. Wade adds that the *Titanic*'s design compounded Murdoch's alleged error, because only the two reciprocating engines that turned the ship's outer propellers were reversible, and not the turbine that turned the centre propeller. This meant that when Murdoch reversed the engines the turbine shut off, depriving the rudder of the slipstream of water from the centre propeller and seriously reducing its efficiency. Wade asserts that Murdoch's 'best course of action would have been to reverse the port screw full astern, keep the starboard screw full ahead, and put the helm hard astarboard'. Wade also concurs with Ismay's point that it would have been preferable for the *Titanic* to strike the iceberg stem-on, again citing *Knight's Modern Seamanship*: 'Any vessel in danger of collision ... should present her stem to the danger rather than her broadside'.[16]

The second aspect of Murdoch's conduct that was questionable was his procedure while loading the lifeboats, and in particular his launching of several boats at considerably less than full capacity. The chairman of the American inquiry, Senator William Alden Smith, was very interested in this issue and thoroughly grilled Fifth Officer Harold Lowe, who had assisted Murdoch with the loading of the lifeboats on the *Titanic*'s starboard side. Lowe tried to deflect him by suggesting that the 'floating capacity' of a lifeboat was greater than its capacity 'in the air', or in other words when it was hanging from the davits, but Smith was clearly not convinced. Although he did not explicitly accuse Murdoch of incompetence in his supervision of the loading process, he clearly felt that Murdoch had made the final determination as to whether a boat was full, and thus he was the one ultimately responsible for those boats that were lowered at less than total capacity.

The third questionable action that Murdoch performed that night was his alleged suicide. As we have previously seen, the standard of heroic conduct during the sinking of the *Titanic* demanded calm acceptance of one's fate and a stoic acceptance of suffering and self-sacrifice; suicide was seen as a cowardly, unmanly act. Of the witnesses who purported to have seen Murdoch shoot himself, however, only one, Thomas Whitely, specifically identified him as the officer in question, and Whitely admitted that he had not seen the incident himself but was reporting what he had heard from other sources. None of the other witnesses named Murdoch and referred only to 'a senior officer' or 'the chief officer'. Some early press accounts did feature sensational headlines about a high-ranking officer's suicide, but they identified the culprit as Captain Smith. Gradually, however, the story came to be associated with Murdoch, perhaps because assumptions were made that he must have been feeling considerable guilt about the fact that the collision with the iceberg had occurred on his watch.[17]

In Dalbeattie, the earliest press accounts noted only that a local man had been the *Titanic*'s First Officer without further comment.[18] As time passed, however, the local press began presenting Murdoch in a more heroic light:

> Mr Murdoch ... won high praise by his splendid behaviour throughout the trying hours that followed [the collision]. No idea of leaving the vessel seems to have been in Mr Murdoch's mind ... A large, powerful man, Mr Murdoch proved invaluable in handling the crowds. He was imperative but self-controlled. It was he who met the frightened crowd of emigrants at the head of the steerage ladder and quelled the incipient disorder. Mr Murdoch did his duty admirably in the difficult task of filling his boats. He collected the women, sometimes using positive force to part them from their men. He saw to it that all the women and children on deck were safely placed in the boats, and drove back men who would have slipped in or forced or cajoled their way on board. Then he supervised the difficult operation of launching the lifeboats.[19]

Similar in tone was the account that appeared in the *Kirkcudbrightshire Advertiser* on 26 April: 'Lieutenant William Murdoch has added a noble name to the list of our Galloway sailors ... It is a glorious thing to have given to the whole world an example of how a man should die, and it is a fine thing to know that in that list of heroes whose names history will preserve, a representative of one of our most noted seafaring families distinguished himself for coolness and bravery'.[20] In these two accounts can be found all of the standard elements of *Titanic* heroism: manly strength, self-control, the performance of one's duty under the most difficult circumstances, noble self-sacrifice, and a clear commitment to the principle of 'women and children first'.

The rumours of Murdoch's suicide were beginning to spread, however, so much so that Charles Lightoller, the *Titanic*'s highest-ranking surviving officer, felt compelled to write a letter to Ada Murdoch that was printed in the *Dumfries and Galloway Standard and Advertiser* on 11 May. After expressing his sympathies for Ada's loss, Lightoller declared that

> I was practically the last man, and certainly the last officer, to see Mr Murdoch. He was then endeavouring to launch the starboard forward collapsible boat. I had already got mine from off the top of our quarters. You will better understand when I say that I was working the port side of the ship, and Mr Murdoch was principally engaged on the starboard side of the ship, filling and launching the boats. Having got my boat down off the top of the house, and there being no time to open it, I left it and ran across to the starboard side, still on top of the quarters. I was then practically looking down on your husband and his men. He was working hard, personally assisting, overhauling the forward boat's fall. At this moment the ship dived, and we were all in the water. Other reports as to the ending are absolutely false. Mr Murdoch died like a man doing his duty.[21]

The letter was signed not only by Lightoller but by the *Titanic*'s three other surviving officers: Third Officer Pitman, Fourth Officer Boxhall and Fifth Officer Lowe. It did not explicitly refer to the stories of Murdoch's suicide, but was clearly written to refute them. Although it was addressed to Ada, the letter was obviously intended for publication, as is indicated by its formal tone and detailed account of the *Titanic*'s final moments. Lightoller invoked his authority as an officer in order to suggest that his version of events was more accurate and authoritative than those of other witnesses.

Questions about Murdoch's conduct still lingered, however. A few months after the disaster, Ada Murdoch left Southampton and moved to Dalbeattie, where Murdoch's parents and sisters still lived, apparently to escape from the hostility of family members of the *Titanic*'s crew.

She later relocated to Brittany, where she remained until the outbreak of the First World War, when she moved to London. In 1918 she returned home to New Zealand, where she spent the rest of her life.

Back in Dalbeattie, the concerns about Murdoch's conduct were reflected by the town's cautious approach towards the construction of a memorial to him. The public meeting to discuss a memorial did not occur until 20 August, over four months after the disaster, a delay caused by the desire of the local authorities to wait for the outcome of the American and British inquiries, which would, they hoped, exonerate Murdoch from blame. Although neither inquiry specifically cleared Murdoch, they did not specifically condemn him either, instead pinning the blame on others or on factors beyond the crew's control. Local officials in Dalbeattie interpreted their verdicts as providing sufficient absolution for the memorial to proceed. At a public meeting, which was held in the town hall, Provost McLaurin admitted that 'many no doubt thought that the meeting should have been called earlier' and that 'those who, like himself, knew Mr Murdoch intimately never for a moment doubted that he did his duty faithfully and well', a statement that met with a burst of applause from the audience. McLaurin continued, however, that he had thought that 'it was well ... to postpone the meeting until after the [British] inquiry was held, because although a good many of those in Dalbeattie knew what Mr Murdoch would do in the circumstances, others to whom an appeal would be made would not know so well'. McLaurin then asked the Town Clerk, James Little, to read a number of extracts from the report of the British inquiry that 'showed that Mr Murdoch did all that was humanly possible immediately before and after the contact with the iceberg' and that 'Mr Murdoch not only did his duty, but ... did it well ... Duty performed as he performed it was nothing short of heroism – (applause) – and it was only such heroism that was in keeping with the best traditions of British seamanship (applause)'. The disaster, McLaurin asserted, was caused by the fact that the *Titanic* was 'going at too great a speed', but 'the captain alone was responsible for the speed of the vessel, and Mr Murdoch had nothing to do with it'. It was thus 'their duty' to commemorate 'in some tangible form' a townsman who had occupied 'such a high position in his profession'.[22]

McLaurin then called upon Little to move the following resolution: 'That steps be taken to raise a memorial to the late Mr Murdoch, the First Officer of the ill-fated *Titanic*'. The motion carried unanimously, and a committee, consisting of Provost McLaurin, several town councillors and a handful of prominent local businessmen, was established to make the necessary arrangements. By April 1913 the committee had collected £157, with most of the donations coming from the people of Dalbeattie. It was resolved that the memorial should take the form of a granite plaque that would be attached to an exterior wall of Dalbeattie's town hall. The memorial was in place by the end of 1912. It reads:

> This tablet is erected to commemorate the heroism displayed by Lieutenant William McMaster Murdoch, RNR, a native of Dalbeattie, when, on her maiden voyage, the RMS *Titanic*, of which he was First Officer, collided with an iceberg and sank, and 815 of her passengers, and 688 of her crew, including Lieutenant Murdoch, perished, 14th and 15th April 1912.

Underneath the main inscription, a footnote adds that a 'memorial prize is also to be competed for annually in Dalbeattie Public School'. The prize of £4 was awarded – and continues to be awarded to this day – to the best student under the age of fourteen at any school in the Stewartry of Kirkcudbright, as determined by a special examination given at Dalbeattie High School. Over time, inflation has seriously eroded the value of the prize, and so efforts have been made in recent years to increase the fund's endowment. Originally the target was set at £1000, but, following a donation of £5000 from the film studio Twentieth Century Fox in 1998, the administrators have set a more ambitious goal of £10,000.

Why did a major Hollywood studio give such a generous sum to the Murdoch Memorial Fund? The studio was responsible for the blockbuster film *Titanic* (1997), in which Murdoch is played by the actor Ewan Stewart. In the film, director James Cameron not only chose to depict Murdoch's death as a suicide, but added a few details that made Murdoch's conduct on the night of the sinking appear even more problematic. In Dalbeattie, where for eighty-five years Murdoch was viewed as a local hero, the response was swift and furious. The town mounted a spirited defence of Murdoch, a defence which resulted in a formal apology from Fox as well as the hefty donation to the memorial prize fund.

In Cameron's film, Murdoch is shown as the officer in charge of the *Titanic*'s helm at the moment of the collision, but there is no attempt to blame him for the accident. A deleted close-up of his face in the moment immediately afterwards, however, suggests that Cameron did want the audience to assign him at least partial responsibility: 'The alarm bells still clatter mindlessly, seeming to reflect [Murdoch's] inner state. He is in shock, unable to get a grip on what just happened. *He just ran the biggest ship in history into an iceberg on its maiden voyage.*' [23]

Later, as Murdoch is supervising the loading of the lifeboats on the starboard side, he encounters the film's fictional villain, Caledon Hockley, played by Billy Zane. Hockley attempts to bribe Murdoch into letting him into the boat. The screenplay reads, 'Cal slips his hand out of the pocket of his overcoat and into the waist pocket of Murdoch's greatcoat, leaving the stacks of bills there'. Cal then asks Murdoch, 'So we have an understanding then?' In the original screenplay, Murdoch nods curtly and responds, 'As you've said', but this line was later cut from the finished film because Cameron 'did not want Murdoch accepting Cal's bribe outright' and instead wanted to make the scene 'ambiguous territory': 'I wanted to imply that he was too preoccupied with other matters to deal with it at that moment'. As staged, Murdoch glances at Hockley's money in his pocket and then walks off. A few minutes later, as he prepares to launch Collapsible C with spaces still remaining, he asks, 'Any more women and children?' When no one comes forward, he looks meaningfully at Hockley, apparently acknowledging the bribe, and says, 'Any one else, then?' Hockley is unwilling to leave without his fiancée Rose, however, and does not avail himself of the place in the boat.[24]

In a subsequent scene, Murdoch struggles to maintain order as he tries to launch Collapsible A. A crowd threatens to rush the boat, pressing forward and 'yelling and shouting at the officers'. Murdoch fires his revolver twice into the air, then points it at the crowd, saying, 'I'll shoot any man who tries to get past me'. Cal steps towards him, protesting that 'we had a deal, damn you'. Murdoch shoves him back, pointing the pistol at his chest and thrusting his money back at him, telling him, 'Your money can't save you any more than it can save me'.[25] Suddenly, the Irish emigrant Tommy Ryan is jostled from behind by someone in the crowd and Murdoch shoots him. He crumples to the deck in the arms of his friend Fabrizio, who shouts curses at Murdoch. Murdoch then turns to the other crew members who are helping to launching the boat and 'salutes smartly'. He 'puts the pistol to his temple and ... BLAM! He drops like a puppet with the strings cut and topples over the edge of the boat deck into the water only a few feet below'. In the published screenplay, Hockley 'stares in horror' at Murdoch's floating body as the money floats out of his coat pocket and spreads across the surface of the sea, though this part of the scene was cut from the finished film.[26]

In Dalbeattie this depiction of Murdoch was anathema to a community that had made a considerable investment in his status as a hero. In early 1998, even prior to the film's release in the United Kingdom, several local citizens began voicing their displeasure. Linda Kirkwood, head teacher at Dalbeattie High School, recalled that

> people were incensed. I've got relatives who died at sea, and so have many other families around here. It was the bribe that galled us most. We know the codes of honour men have to follow at sea. Murdoch's was an honourable death and to have that thrown at him was an enormous insult. If they wanted something like that for the sake of the story, why couldn't they have invented a character instead of smearing Murdoch?[27]

Kirkwood's pupils, who compete for the Murdoch Memorial Prize each year, wrote a letter of protest to Twentieth-Century Fox. The previous year's recipient of the Murdoch Memorial Prize, Lyndsay Moffat, complained that the film was not 'very fair because [Murdoch] risked his life to save other people and they made him look like an evil and selfish character'.[28]

Most incensed by the film's depiction of the *Titanic*'s First Officer was eighty-year-old Scott Murdoch, William's nephew. After seeing a copy of the film's script prior to its release, Scott Murdoch wrote two letters to Cameron asking him to 'set the record straight'; neither received a reply.[29] Murdoch was joined in his publicity campaign by Tommy Henderson of the Dalbeattie Museum, who put together an exhibit about William. 'Dalbeattie is such a quiet, wee backwater', said

Henderson. 'All of a sudden they have went and besmirched this man's name. That's what got up our noses. He was held in very high esteem in this town and all of a sudden the poor soul was a coward. Well, we're going to make sure people know he wasn't.'[30]

Rapidly the protest against the film's depiction of Murdoch began to spread beyond his home-town. In February 1998 *Scotland on Sunday* inaugurated a campaign to clear Murdoch's name. 'So far', wrote Dorothy Grace Elder in her weekly 'Rattling the Cages' column,

> Hollywood cowards haven't replied to protesting letters from the townspeople and from Murdoch's relatives. They want something put on the film separating their true local hero from a made-up ponce defiling his heroic name. Before this heartless, rotten film – quite bad enough to win umpteen Oscars – triumphs in March at the odious Oscar ceremony, may I urge readers to back Ayrshire people by sending strong protest letters and faxes to me ... which I'll forward to the Hollywood creeps. We might just be able to put a little guilt on the Oscar gingerbread.[31]

At the end of February several Scottish politicians joined the fray: Members of Parliament from the Scottish National Party put forth a motion in the House of Commons to protest at the film's treatment of Murdoch. The motion read: 'This house notes with dismay the inaccuracies in the film *Titanic* in which William McMaster Murdoch is portrayed as a coward who shoots and kills a passenger and then takes his own life'. It further called on Cameron and Twentieth-Century Fox to apologize to Murdoch's family and the entire community of Dalbeattie. Alasdair Morgan, MP for Galloway and Upper Nithsdale, which includes Dalbeattie, introduced the motion. 'I felt something should be done to protect this local man's good name', he stated.[32] Morgan also sent a letter to Fox requesting that the studio make a donation to the Murdoch Memorial Prize fund as a compensation for besmirching Murdoch's reputation.

Dalbeattie's response to the depiction of William Murdoch in the film *Titanic* became a major news story not just in Scotland but in Britain as a whole, because, much as in 1912, British national pride was at stake. The film's critics complained not only that the reputation of a local man had been besmirched, but that the entire nation had been insulted. And they did not, interestingly, define the nation in question as Scotland but as Britain. The *Mirror* featured an editorial entitled 'It's a *Titanic* Liberty with the Truth' in which the paper complained that Murdoch would be unfairly remembered as 'a brutal murderer' by 'millions of people around the world'.[33] The *Independent,* meanwhile, ran an editorial by Trevor Phillips that made a similar point: 'In the movie [Murdoch] is portrayed as a craven coward, panicked into shooting two passengers, and then himself ... As a result there are now literally hundreds of millions of people who probably believe that Murdoch was a villain, and who, were they ever to meet any of his relatives, would treat them accordingly'.[34]

The defence of Murdoch's reputation became a small battle in a bigger cultural war between the United States and Britain. The issue reflected an increasing resentment of the dominance of the American film industry around the world, with Dalbeattie's efforts to challenge the veracity of the biggest-grossing film ever made and the power of the studio that had made it interpreted by the British press as an heroic struggle of David versus Goliath. A recurring theme on the British side of the argument was the failure of James Cameron to consult any British authorities on *Titanic*. 'We think he has been fed by the *Titanic* societies in the States which are really anti-British', complained Linda Kirkwood, while Dorothy-Grace Elder grumbled that her queries about the research done for the film had met with no response: 'It was American. America's *Titanic* Historical Society is "credited" ... The British *Titanic* Society wasn't consulted'.[35] Elder's implication was clear: British *Titanic* experts would never have allowed the truth to be overwhelmed by commercial pressures in the way that their American counterparts clearly had.

In April 1998 Fox caved in. In a letter to Alasdair Morgan, the studio's executive vice-president, Scott Neeson, conceded that there was 'no irrefutable link' between Murdoch and the officer whom survivors reported as committing suicide.[36] In recompense, Fox made a £5000 donation to the memorial prize fund, which Neeson delivered personally on the eighty-seventh anniversary of the sinking on 14 April 1998. Neeson also gave Dalbeattie High School an engraved plaque honouring Murdoch and presented Scott Murdoch with a framed dinner plate used on the set of the film. The studio refused, however, to issue a clear public statement announcing that the depiction of Murdoch in the film had been inaccurate. 'There is no indisputable set of events for what happened on that night. There have been so many different versions it is not quite clear', Neeson stated. No attempt would be made, he added, to alter the film or to add a correction to its credits.[37] In 2002, however, James Cameron went some ways towards making restitution for the damage done to Murdoch's reputation in his film *Ghosts of the Abyss*, a three-dimensional exploration of the *Titanic* wreck site, produced by the Walt Disney Corporation. In the film, the narrator, Bill Paxton, states that Murdoch's decision to allow men as well as women and children in the lifeboats on the starboard side resulted in many additional lives being saved. Paxton describes Murdoch's conduct that night as 'heroic'; it is clear that this time Cameron wanted to ensure that Murdoch was depicted in a far more positive light than he had been in *Titanic*.

The fight over Murdoch's character in *Titanic* was not so much over the reputation of one man as it was over the cultural predominance of American cinema and of American culture as a whole. In the eyes of British critics, *Titanic* was yet another example of the Hollywoodization of history, in which accuracy is regarded as far less significant than entertainment. Cameron had opted for a more sensational interpretation of Murdoch's death even if it meant sacrificing veracity and the real man's reputation. When Dalbeattie objected, the British press rallied to its side, for they recognized that the battle was over something far more significant than William Murdoch's good name.

9

Belfast

Belfast – there are few other cities in the world that have such a negative image. To people on both sides of the Atlantic, the name immediately conjures up pictures of sectarian violence, of death and destruction brought about by religious bigotry and political conflict. The casual visitor – if there is such a thing as a casual visitor to Belfast – arrives with a suitcase full of expectations, few of them optimistic.

Certainly, Belfast can be a disconcerting place to visit. On my first trip two years ago, I stayed in South Belfast on one of the leafy avenues near Queen's University, an area abounding with trendy new cafés and restaurants, seemingly far from the murals and barricades of Shankill and the Falls, the working-class Protestant and Catholic neighborhoods that have traditionally been the flashpoints of sectarian strife. My husband and I were walking back from dinner one evening when suddenly a British Army patrol came around the corner: four soldiers wearing camouflage, carrying machine guns and looking as if they meant serious business. It was a shock, after an excellent meal at a superb restaurant, to be jolted into recalling that I was in a city experiencing a military occupation. Sirens are still a common part of the soundscape here, and the police carry guns and travel in armoured vehicles. At night, observation helicopters hum ominously overhead.

But if the tensions of the past continue to be readily apparent, there is also an ongoing – and in many ways successful – struggle to move beyond them towards a new vision of Belfast's future. Belfast is not a closed, tense city that is mistrustful of strangers, but a warm and vibrant place eager to dispel the misconceptions of its visitors. During my time there, I was repeatedly asked, 'Were you nervous about coming here?' A negative answer produced big smiles from a people who have waited for decades to show off their city's charms. Located between – both geographically and in terms of cultural identity – two of the most popular tourist destinations in the world, Great Britain and the Republic of Ireland, Northern Ireland gets relatively little tourist traffic; it seems to exist in a parallel universe to the rest of the British Isles. It is like Britain only more Irish: strangers chat with you in circumstances – in shops and restaurants, on the street – that would be viewed as intolerably intrusive in England. But it is also like Ireland only more British: you will see more Union Jacks flying in a week in Belfast than you will see in a year in London.

A quick stroll around Belfast's compact city centre reveals much about the city's history, and its present as well. Perhaps most noticeable is that nothing in Belfast is very old, befitting a city whose importance has always derived from its industrial might. Although the Normans built a castle here in the twelfth century, the town was of no great size or significance until textile manufacturing at the end of the eighteenth century and shipbuilding in the middle of the nineteenth created a prosperity that attracted people from all over Ireland. By 1910, when the *Olympic* and *Titanic* were under construction at Harland & Wolff, the world's largest shipyard, Belfast could boast of supremacy in a variety of other industrial categories as well, as it was home to the biggest ropeworks, tobacco factory and linen factory in the world. Virtually all of Belfast's most impressive buildings date from the late Victorian and Edwardian eras, including the Grand Opera House (1895), St Anne's Cathedral (1899) and City Hall (1906).

Today these grand edifices can seem out of proportion in a city whose industrial base and population have been in steady decline and in which very little economic development has taken place over the last half century. Belfast suffered major bombing damage in the Second World War (the Luftwaffe missed the docks but levelled several residential and commercial areas instead), and in the 1960s and 1970s sectarian tensions brought about further decline and decay. Shipbuilding, the city's core industry, has all but collapsed; Harland & Wolff is down to less than five hundred employees from a peak of 30,000 in the 1920s.

The success, albeit precarious, of the peace process that commenced in the early 1990s, however, has generated a new spirit of optimism that is visible in new, ultramodern buildings such as the Odyssey and Waterfront Hall entertainment complexes on the banks of the River Lagan, in the upscale chain stores that line Donegall Place and Royal Avenue, and in the posh restaurants and cafés along the Golden Mile near Queen's University. To be sure, Shankill and the Falls are still divided by the corrugated metal 'Peace Line', but now tour buses drive through on a regular basis, their guides pointing out the most striking examples of loyalist and nationalist mural-painting. This is not to suggest that sectarian tensions have disappeared entirely, for they most assuredly have not, but these days Belfast can look forward to a future in which they might – a far cry from the hopelessness that prevailed twenty or thirty years ago.

That future will be in many ways determined by the past, as Belfast seeks a heritage that can be embraced by all of its residents, Protestant and Catholic, Nationalist and Unionist, as well as lure tourists to the city. To fulfil this goal, Belfast's civic leaders have been looking more and more to the *Titanic*, which was launched here in 1911 and completed in April of the following year. For much of the twentieth century, the *Titanic* was, as Michael McCaughan of the Ulster Folk and Transport Museum has written, a symbol of the 'thwarted pride' of Ulster Unionists, thanks in large measure to the timing of the ship's construction and destruction.[1] As the *Titanic* departed from Belfast for the last time on 2 April 1912, ferment over the third Home Rule Bill reached a fever pitch in the House of Commons. In Belfast, the epicentre of the conflict between Ulster Unionism and Irish nationalism, the timing of the disaster meant that it represented more than the loss of the latest and greatest creation of Harland & Wolff's craftsmen. Instead, the *Titanic* disaster came to represent a challenge to Unionist identity, for industrial accomplishment in 1912 was inextricably intertwined with Unionist political aspirations. For Protestant Belfast the sinking was a fearful blow, and for decades afterwards the *Titanic* was a difficult subject, at times submerged as deeply as the wreck on the floor of the north Atlantic.

But just as the wreck lay patiently awaiting discovery two and a half miles beneath the ocean's surface, the *Titanic* remained a ghostly presence beneath the surface of Belfast memory. Indeed, its adaptability as a symbol has proven itself yet again in the unique context of the conflict-ridden city of its birth. At the end of the twentieth century, the *Titanic* ceased to be a sectarian symbol and instead became a symbol of the decline of the entire community, Protestant and Catholic, as Belfast's industrial prosperity gave way to economic collapse, a collapse that simultaneously fed and was fed by religious and political schism. To the citizens who lived through the 1970s and 1980s, it must have seemed as if they were being made to atone for the failure of their most famous industrial product.

With the revival of Belfast's fortunes, as peace has become a reality, the *Titanic* can at long last emerge from the depths. A city whose image in the eyes of the outside world has been for decades that of a bloody battleground desperately needs to emphasize other aspects of its past, and what could be better for this purpose than the ship for which people everywhere seem to have an insatiable appetite? The *Titanic*'s loss may prove Belfast's gain after all: as the city prepares to move beyond the Troubles into a brave new twenty-first-century world of high technology and economic growth, the ship's association with the city is being pushed more and more to the forefront of the local heritage industry. In 1912, the *Titanic* was an incarnation of Belfast's technological mastery, a mastery that seemed to herald a bright future. Perhaps, nearly a century after its destruction, the *Titanic* can be that again, in symbolic if not physical form.

In Donegall Square in the heart of Belfast stands Belfast City Hall, a potent symbol of Edwardian municipal pride. Completed in 1906, the building was intended to represent more than the city's industrial and commercial aspirations; it was also meant to serve as an 'expression of embattled Unionism, and of an effort ... to convert a brash and sprawling industrial centre into a politico-religious capital city'.[2] By the early twentieth century, Roman Catholics made up more than a third of Belfast's population of around 350,000, and with each passing year the Protestant majority felt themselves more threatened, to which they reacted by becoming more determined to proclaim their separate identity. This was the era of the signing of the Solemn League and Covenant and of the founding of the Ulster Volunteer Force.

Today City Hall remains a powerful symbol of the Ulster Protestant ascendancy, dominating Donegall Square with its 173-foot-high dome, a dome that less than a decade ago was festooned with a banner reading

'Belfast Says No' in response to the Anglo-Irish peace negotiations. Inside, the less than subtle political message is delivered by numerous references to key events in the Unionist pantheon. A stained-glass window in one corridor honours the Royal Ulster Constabulary, while a painting in another shows the 36th Ulster Division in action at the Battle of the Somme. The portraits of Belfast's Lord Mayors that line the walls reinforce the point; only one, Alban Maginess in 1997, has been a Catholic.

These days, as Belfast tries to move beyond the sectarian divisions of the past, the tour guides who show visitors around City Hall carefully avoid mention of the blatantly Unionist iconography of the building. They do, however, refer repeatedly to another aspect of Belfast's history, the construction of the *Titanic* at the Harland & Wolff shipyards on Queen's Island between 1909 and 1912. This is commemorated in a variety of ways. (Indeed, the building is sometimes referred to as the 'Stone *Titanic*'.) Inside one of the public reception rooms is a portrait of Lord Pirrie, chairman of Harland & Wolff at the time of the *Titanic*'s construction. Outside in the grounds is a statue of Sir Edward Harland, one of Harland & Wolff's founders. The statue of Queen Victoria that stands before the main entrance is supported by two figures, Spinning and Shipbuilding, representing Belfast's two major industries. And, most obviously, there is the official *Titanic* memorial, dedicated in 1920, to the twenty-two Belfast men who died in the tragedy.[3]

The presence of so many references to the *Titanic* at Belfast City Hall provides powerful evidence of the ship's centrality to the city's identity, an identity that has been largely created (at least in its official, public manifestations) by Unionist Protestants. This centrality is best revealed, however, by something that visitors do not see on the daily tours. At the end of a long corridor can be found the Lord Mayor's offices, a palatial suite befitting a position in which so much Unionist pride has traditionally been vested. And within this suite is the Lord Mayor's cloakroom. To the casual observer, the link with the *Titanic* is not obvious, but those familiar with photographs of the interiors of the great ship will immediately feel a sense of recognition, for the wood panelling in the cloakroom is virtually identical to that which was installed in many of the first-class areas of the *Titanic*. The resemblance is no coincidence. The cloakroom was completed not long before construction of the *Titanic* and *Olympic* began, and many of the craftsmen who carved its woodwork also worked on the two ships.⁴ Here, then, we see the *Titanic* and the Unionist cause joined in the most intimate way. On the day I saw the bathroom, it still smelled of soap and toothpaste, as if the current Lord Mayor had recently showered and dressed there. No better symbol could be found of how the *Titanic*'s place in Belfast's history stretches beyond the realm of public commemoration, to the very heart of Ulster Unionism.

For decades afterwards, the fate – and failure – of the *Titanic* in April 1912 made it a difficult subject for Unionists to broach. The greatest accomplishment of Belfast industry, the ship represented the most impressive gift to the Union that the city could make and a tangible indication of Ulster's commitment to remaining in it.⁵ But that gift was rejected when the ship's British owners and crew smashed it at full speed into an iceberg, causing it to sink. The men of Belfast who built the *Titanic*, and indeed the entire Unionist population of the city, were left empty-handed, their skills and their sacrifice seemingly unwanted by the country of which they so desperately wished to remain a part. Their precious gift – into which they had poured thousands upon thousands of hours of their labour – had been discarded by the very people whom they hoped would value it most.

In the spring of 2002, however, *Titanic* returned to a place of prominence in Belfast's civic culture, as Belfast City Hall became the focal point of a ten-day celebration entitled *Titanic: Made in Belfast*. The festival marked the first large-scale effort to remind both local residents and tourists of Belfast's associations with the most famous ship ever built. Featuring exhibits, talks by the world's leading *Titanic* experts, re-enactments of the ship's launching day, tours of the Harland & Wolff shipyard by boat and by bus, theatrical presentations, film screenings, and numerous other activities, *Titanic: Made in Belfast* attracted thousands of visitors, many of them local but a sizeable number from all over the world. This event vividly demonstrated how the *Titanic* is a significant part of Belfast's hopes for the future. The *Titanic* is big business all over the world, and Belfast has a more direct claim on its legacy than almost anywhere else. In order for the city to reap the maximum benefit, however, the *Titanic* will have to shed its sectarian associations with Ulster Protestantism and become, for the first time, a symbol of the entire Belfast community.

In the spring of 1912, as the *Titanic* neared completion at Harland & Wolff, Rudyard Kipling's poem 'Ulster 1912' appeared in the *Morning Post*:

> The dark eleventh hour
> Draws on us and sees us sold
> To every evil power
> We fought against of old.
> Rebellion, rapine, hate,
> Oppression, wrong and greed
> Are loosed to rule our fate,
> By England's act and deed.

Intended as a protest against the third Home Rule Bill currently before the House of Commons, Kipling's poem presents the Unionist case aggressively and angrily, as the struggle over Home Rule between Unionism and Irish nationalism that had begun almost three decades earlier reached its culmination. The failure of the first two Home Rule Bills in 1886 and 1892 had been followed by a decade of relative calm, as British politics was dominated by the pro-Union Conservative Party, but the respite was temporary. The Liberal landslide of 1906 brought to power a party committed to Home Rule, and five years later the stripping of the House of Lords' ability to veto parliamentary legislation seemingly removed the last obstacle. H. H. Asquith's government, however, underestimated the recalcitrance of the Unionists, who were determined to remain within the United Kingdom even if it no longer wanted them. The anti-Home Rule campaign in Ulster was officially launched on 23 September 1911, when 50,000 spectators marched from Belfast to Craigavon, the home of Unionist leader Captain James Craig, where they heard Edward Carson, head of the Irish Unionist Party, pledge to defeat 'the most nefarious controversy that has ever been hatched against a free people'.[6] Six months later, on Easter Tuesday, more than 100,000 Unionists gathered in Balmoral, a suburb of Belfast, in order to provide further confirmation of their resolve. In two columns, the crowd marched past a giant Union Jack measuring forty-eight feet by twenty-five feet, claimed to be the largest ever woven.

In spite of these emphatic demonstrations of Unionist determination, the Liberal government proceeded with its plan to introduce a Home Rule Bill, which they duly did on 11 April 1912, the day before the *Titanic* set sail on its ill-fated maiden voyage. Six days later, the first vote on the Bill, which was carried by a majority of about a hundred, took place amidst angry scenes in the House of Commons. That same day, however, the news of the *Titanic* disaster hit the British and Irish press, sweeping everything else aside. For the Ulster Protestant community, the timing was to give *Titanic* a symbolic significance that it continues to possess to this day.

Belfast's rapid growth in the nineteenth and early twentieth centuries, which saw the city's population rise from under 20,000 in 1801 to almost 400,000 in 1911, was sparked by two industries: textiles and shipbuilding. Prior to the 1830s, cotton mills lured workers from the Irish countryside, a demographic trend that continued after Belfast became the centre of the global linen industry in the second half of the nineteenth century. The emergence of shipbuilding, however, made Belfast into the biggest and most prosperous city in Ireland, and one of the most important ports in the United Kingdom. In the 1830s and 1840s, the harbour commission ordered two cuts to be made to straighten the River Lagan and allow easier access to Belfast Harbour; the resulting mud was dumped on the County Down side of the river, where it formed a seventeen-acre island. The harbour commission constructed a slipway on the south side of the island that could be used for shipbuilding and repairs, and in 1851 the first shipyard opened. This arrangement allowed the separation of commercial and shipbuilding activities in Belfast Harbour, which avoided the problems encountered by other British ports, where the docks and quays constricted the growth of shipyards.

In an effort to lure shipbuilders to what came to be called Queen's Island, the commissioners advertised in English and Scottish newspapers, offering land and infrastructure. Their efforts attracted the attention of an ironmaster named Robert Hickson, who saw shipbuilding as a market for his boilerplates. In 1853 the commissioners fitted out a new yard for Hickson at a cost of £1100. Needing an overseer with expertise in shipbuilding, Hickson hired a twenty-three-year-old engineer from Yorkshire named Edward James Harland. The firm flourished, largely thanks to Harland's ability and ruthless determination to maintain the highest standards of quality. He prowled constantly around the yard with a ruler and a piece of chalk in his pocket, measuring work and circling defects.[7]

In 1858 Hickson sold Harland his share of the firm for £5000, most of which Harland borrowed from his friend G. C. Schwabe, a partner in Liverpool's Bibby Line. Schwabe's nephew Gustav Wolff joined the company as Harland's personal assistant, and the relationship between the two families transformed the business into a major shipbuilding enterprise. Eighteen of the first twenty-five ships that Harland & Wolff built were for the Bibby Line; Harland's unique design, featuring exceptional length and narrowness of beam that increased their speed, stability and capacity, earned them the nickname 'Bibby coffins'. It was the relationship with another Liverpool shipping firm, however, that was to transform Harland & Wolff into the largest shipbuilding yard in the world. Over a game of after-dinner billiards in 1869, Schwabe challenged a young shipowner named Thomas Henry Ismay, who had recently acquired the bankrupt White Star Line, to shift the line's focus from Australian to North Atlantic routes. The rapid growth of the American economy after the Civil War was attracting an influx of European immigrants, creating a huge demand for transatlantic passenger shipping. Schwabe promised that, if Harland & Wolff was given the contract to build the ships, he would ensure that Ismay got the necessary financing.[8] Ismay took up the challenge, and the following year he placed an order with Harland & Wolff for five 420-foot steamers of just under 4000 gross tons each.

Decades of expansion followed as White Star and the other transatlantic shipping lines competed to attract passengers with larger, faster and more luxurious ships. By 1900 Harland & Wolff was the biggest shipbuilding firm in the world, employing over nine thousand workers and producing an average of 100,000 tons of shipping each year. Edward Harland and Gustav Wolff gradually retired from the business, leaving it in the hands of William James Pirrie, a Belfast native whose enormous energy and intelligence led the company to its greatest heights. In 1907 Pirrie hosted a dinner at his London home for J. Bruce Ismay, who had inherited the White Star Line upon his father's death in 1897. At the dinner, the main topic of conversation was the two ships, the *Lusitania* and *Mauretania*, about to be launched by White Star's main rival, Cunard. They would be by far the biggest and fastest ships afloat, and

Ismay knew that White Star had to respond. At twenty-six knots, the
speed that the Cunarders' turbine engines generated would be difficult
to exceed, and in any event Ismay had never felt that speed was the
primary concern of his passengers. The most important thing was to
provide them with a sense of security and comfort, and what better way
to do that than to build ships so large that it would be virtually
impossible to conceive of them sinking? He thus proposed a bold plan
to Pirrie: White Star would commission from Harland & Wolff three
huge liners, each 50 per cent bigger than the *Lusitania* and *Mauretania*
in gross tonnage and a hundred feet longer. The three ships would also
set a new standard for passenger luxury. The only area in which they
would be inferior to the *Lusitania* and *Mauretania* was in their speed,
which would be a maximum of twenty-one knots, sufficient to allow
them to make the crossing in less than a week's time, but considerably
slower than the Cunard greyhounds.

In early 1908 Harland & Wolff received an order from White Star to
build the first two ships at a total cost of over £3,000,000. 'So the pride
of place, for everything in mercantile marine construction but speed,
has come back to Belfast', reported the *Belfast News-Letter*.⁹ In order to
build these leviathans, the yard was forced to convert three berths –
berths that had previously seen the construction of some of the world's
largest ships – into two. The world's largest overhead gantry was erected
to accommodate the massive hulls, and the world's largest floating crane
was installed to lift boilers, engines and funnels on board. The keel of
ship No. 400 – the *Olympic* – was laid on 16 December 1908, and that
of No. 401 – the *Titanic* – followed on 31 March 1909. During construction, the *Olympic* received most of the attention, although when
completed the *Titanic* was technically the larger of the two sisters – and
thus the biggest ship in the world – because of minor modifications that
resulted in a slightly greater length and gross tonnage.¹⁰

Between three and four thousand of Harland & Wolff's fifteen thousand workers were employed in *Titanic*'s construction. A reporter from the
Northern Whig visited the shipyard in November 1911 and heard the dinner
horn sound: 'Down the gangways ... began to pour streams of hurrying
workmen – streams that seemed inexhaustible ... Watching these human
streams, one got an idea of what the construction of the *Titanic* means
in enterprise, sustained effort and money'.¹¹ Almost all these workers

were Protestants, although religion was only one component of a system of exclusion based upon craft union traditions in which skilled workers fought fiercely to defend their privileges and relatively high rates of pay from the flood of predominantly Catholic emigrants pouring into Belfast from the Irish hinterland.[12] It is also difficult to draw a clear line of demarcation between the religious and political identities and the community loyalties of the workers. The vast majority of them lived in the East Belfast community of Ballymacarrett, in the shadow of Harland & Wolff's gantries and cranes, and much of their pride in their craft stemmed from a local sense of family and kinship.[13] But, from the Catholic point of view, the reasons for their exclusion from the shipyards were irrelevant, for the result was the same as if it had been the product of blatant bigotry: a shortage of opportunities for employment in skilled trades. The census of 1901 reveals that only 9 per cent of Belfast's Catholic population was employed in shipbuilding or engineering at a time when Catholics represented 24 per cent of the city's inhabitants.[14]

The limited number of Catholics who did manage to secure employment at the shipyards suffered from periodic and often violent efforts to expel them. In August 1864 a substantial number of Belfast's Catholics journeyed to Dublin to attend the unveiling ceremony for a statue of Daniel O'Connell. In retaliation for this display of nationalist sympathies, Protestant shipwrights from Harland & Wolff attacked Catholic navvies employed in carrying out a series of improvements to the docks. They then went on strike, demanding the dismissal of the firm's small number of Catholic employees. Edward Harland reacted swiftly, posting notices all over the yard stating that if any Catholics were turned out he would shut operations down until they were permitted to return.[15] The stern warning put an end to the expulsions, but only for the time being. Eight years later on 15 August 1872, 500 men from the yard stopped work early so that they could participate in efforts to evict Catholics who were living in Protestant parts of Belfast.[16] After the defeat of the first Home Rule Bill in 1886 and in the wake of the huge Conservative victory in the subsequent election, shipyard workers roamed the streets armed with pieces of scrap metal nicknamed 'Queen's Island Confetti'. At Harland & Wolff 190 of the 225 Catholics employed at the time left due to the fears for their personal safety, although Edward Harland continued to claim that the firm was nonsectarian in its hiring practices. 'Some of our best men – some of the men who are paid the best – are Catholics', he declared when called to testify before the Belfast Riots Commission the following year.[17] Nevertheless, by early 1887 only seventy-seven Catholics had returned to work, and periodic attacks on Catholic shipyard workers continued.

Following Harland's death in 1896, William Pirrie's ascension to the leadership of Harland & Wolff offered hope that the discrimination against Catholics might be curtailed. His pleas for tolerance notwithstanding, Harland had been a committed Unionist who had campaigned vigorously against Home Rule during his stint as Lord Mayor of Belfast in the 1880s. In contrast, Pirrie was a supporter of Home Rule who in 1906 was rewarded with a peerage by the Liberal Party. This made him unpopular with Belfast's Protestant majority; the *Times* reported that he had 'deserted Unionism about the time the Liberals acceded to power, and soon afterwards he was made a peer; whether *propter hoc* or only *post hoc* I am quite unable to say, though no Ulster Unionist has any doubts on the subject'.[18] In February 1912, as the *Titanic* neared completion, Pirrie chaired a meeting of the Ulster Liberal Association at which Winston Churchill presented the case for Home Rule. Originally scheduled for the Ulster Hall, where Churchill's father Randolph had made his famous 'Ulster will fight, and Ulster will be right' declaration in 1886, the meeting had to be moved to the Celtic Park football ground after Unionists threatened to pack the building.

In this instance, Pirrie's pro-Home Rule views had little impact upon his employees. As Churchill attempted to make his way to the ground, a group of shipyard workers surrounded his car and threatened to turn it over; they were only dissuaded from doing so when they saw Mrs Churchill sitting next to her husband. Nor did the efforts of labour leaders to convince Belfast workers to set aside sectarian divisions and recognize their common class interests have much effect. The participation of Protestants and Catholics together in the 1907 dockers' strike led by Irish nationalist James Larkin was seen by the labour movement as pointing the way towards a future in which class rather than religion would determine workers' primary loyalties. The strike, however, represented an anomaly and not an indication of things to come. When Home Rule resurfaced after 1911, traditional sectarian attitudes quickly scuttled any prospect of a recognition of mutual class interests by

Protestant and Catholic workers. Most Protestant workers were convinced that their economic self-interest lay within the Union, an attitude
that was particularly prevalent in the shipyards. The yards were thus
fertile ground for recruitment efforts by the Unionist leadership as they
sought to encourage working-class resistance to Home Rule. When the
Ulster Unionist Council began to organize Unionist Clubs in 1911, they
focused on the shipyards because effective mobilization of the labour
elite there would be a major factor in gaining the support of the rest
of the working classes. By April 1912, the month in which the *Titanic*
sank, six thousand shipyard workers were actively involved in the clubs,
many of which were engaged in military-style drilling in preparation for
armed resistance to Home Rule.[19]

Only three months after the sinking, shipyard workers provided an
aggressive demonstration of their fiercely Unionist loyalties. In the wake
of an attack by the nationalist Ancient Order of Hibernians on a
Presbyterian Sunday school outing at Castledawson, Protestant workers
began 'making the rounds', or evicting all Catholics from the yards.
After a number of physical assaults, virtually every Catholic – two
thousand in all – left. The attacks were so vicious that even the Unionist
leadership was embarrassed by them; the Ulster Unionist Council passed
a resolution appealing to 'Unionist workmen who have so staunchly
supported their leaders in the past to continue to bear themselves as
men worthy of the great cause in which their whole future and that of
the community is involved'.[20] In the aftermath of the expulsions of July
1912, the Belfast Commissioner of Police drew up a report that emphasized the history of sectarian violence at the shipyards and the extent to
they were outside effective police control: 'They did not do duty in the
shipyards and their presence there was regarded as an intrusion and an
insult. Even in ordinary times, a policeman in uniform has missiles
frequently thrown at him if he has to go down about the Queen's
Road'.[21] The reluctance of the police to enter the shipyards shows that
in 1912 Harland & Wolff must have been a difficult place to work for
anyone who did not share the Protestant beliefs and commitment to
the Union of the majority of the workforce.

It was in this context of sectarian tension that the *Titanic* was built;
and, more significantly, it was in this context that the ship sank.[22] The

hull was launched on 31 May 1911, the same day that the newly completed *Olympic* was handed over to White Star. Thousands of shipyard workers and members of the general public attended the ceremony, while the owners' box was packed with luminaries, including J. P. Morgan, the American plutocrat whose International Mercantile Marine consortium had purchased White Star in 1905. 'The stands were by no means adequate for all who had assembled', reported the *Belfast News-Letter*, 'and hundreds of people took up positions in various parts of the yard from which they could see the ship enter the water.'[23] At 12.14 p.m., the *Titanic*'s massive hull, propelled by a hydraulic launching ram and aided by almost twenty-five tons of tallow and grease, slid gracefully down the slipway into the Lagan. The journey took sixty-two seconds; the *Belfast News-Letter* reported that 'she took to the water as though she was eager for the baptism':

> If the circumstances under which the launch took place can be accepted as an augury of the future, the *Titanic* should be a huge success. The weather was glorious, a multitude of people assembled to bid the vessel 'God speed', and it would be impossible to conceive of a launch for which the whole of the conditions could be more ideal.[24]

One of the witnesses was a young boy from Bangor named William MacQuitty, who went on to produce the film version of Walter Lord's *A Night to Remember* in the 1950s. Eighty years later, MacQuitty still vividly recalled the scene:

> At five minutes past noon, a red flag was hoisted to warn the fleet of boats in the River Lagan to stand clear. Another five minutes went by before a rocket was fired and workers began to hammer at the restraining chocks. At 12.14 the firing of a second rocket reduced the vast crowd to silence. Would this huge vessel ever really move? All at once the workers on board gave a cheer in which the crowds on shore joined. The slide had begun. Every ship in the lough sounded its siren, the noise drowning the roar of the piles of restraining anchors as they were dragged along the ground. Slowly gathering speed, the *Titanic* moved smoothly down the ways, and a minute later was plunging into the water and raising a huge wave. I felt a great lump in my throat and an enormous pride in being an Ulsterman.[25]

That final sentence – with MacQuitty taking pride in being an Ulster-man, not an Irishman – doubtless reflects what the majority of the onlookers felt on that bright spring day. For them, the *Titanic* represented not only Ulster's greatest shipbuilding accomplishment, but also a tangible reminder of Ulster's commitment and worth to the British Empire.

Indeed, Lord Pirrie's pro-Home Rule views notwithstanding, the *Titanic*'s builders saw their role in a British, rather than Irish context. Following the launch, the White Star Line treated the press and VIPs to lunch at the Grand Central Hotel, where the theme of the congratulatory speech by White Star's spokesman John Shelley was one of cooperation between 'the Anglo-Saxon nations' of Great Britain and the United States. When a toast was drunk in honour of Harland & Wolff; the company's Assistant Secretary, Saxon J. Payne, responded by incorporating Ulster into this racial elite:

> He ... looked upon the building of the *Titanic* and the *Olympic* as a great Anglo-Saxon triumph ... The two vessels were pre-eminent examples of the vitality and progressive instincts of the Anglo-Saxon race, and he did not see anything which need give them alarm, regarding the prospects for the future. As a race they were young and strong and vigorous, and by what it had done in assisting the White Star Line in its great and commendable enterprise Belfast could lay claim to no small share in the maintenance and prosperity of the British Empire.[26]

Implicit in Payne's words, as in all of the speeches at the lunch, was a disdain for the Celtic peoples of Ireland and an opposition to sharing a political realm with them. Ulster, he asserted, belonged with its Anglo-Saxon brethren and had proven its right to do so by its valuable contribution to the Empire.

Payne's British racial pride was duplicated in the accounts of the launch that appeared in the Unionist press. The *Ulster Echo* wrote:

> It is impossible to over-estimate the service rendered to the Anglo-Saxon race by the enterprise of our ship owners and builders. The *Olympic* and *Titanic* are not only the largest vessels in the world, they represent the highest achievements in naval architecture and marine engineering; they stand for the pre-eminence of the Anglo-Saxon race on the ocean.[27]

In contrast, Irish nationalists saw the *Titanic* as an Irish, rather than British, achievement. In its coverage of *Titanic*'s launch, the Catholic *Irish News* boasted proudly of the fact that, with the *Titanic* and *Olympic* both at Queen's Island, Belfast 'enjoyed for one day the world's record of having over 90,000 tons of shipping in her port'.

> The greatest ship building centres of the world have never come within measurable distance of this feat of local industry; and Ireland generally, and our city especially, have every reason to be proud of this most convincing of proofs of Irish brains and Irish industry. That Ireland can beat the world in the second decade of the Twentieth Century is perhaps a sign of the times, which cannot be taken too seriously by her sons. All over the world the hearts of our countrymen will be gladdened at the news of yet another signal victory of the old country.[28]

Unionists saw the *Titanic*'s construction in Belfast as an argument for why Ulster must remain a part of the United Kingdom; the nationalist writer, in contrast, saw it as an argument for Irish independence.

As the crowd melted away from the launch site, the *Titanic* was towed to Harland & Wolff's deepwater basin for 'fitting out', in the course of which its engines, boilers and other machinery were installed, its four funnels put in position, and its magnificent interiors completed. Activity was frantic as the shipyard scrambled to meet their 1 April deadline, necessary so that *Titanic* could make its debut crossing, scheduled for 10 April. Now in his mid nineties, John Parkinson was five years old when his father, a joiner and woodworker who worked on the *Titanic*, took him to see the ship at Harland & Wolff's finishing wharf in January 1912, where he remembers seeing the men 'working feverishly away at it'. Three months later, his father took him back to the shipyard to see the *Titanic*'s final departure from Belfast:

> On 2 April 1912 ... my dad Frank, mother Ellen, sister Agnes and brother Jim boarded a train to Greencastle and took up a good vantage-point on the Shore Road. Although the crowds were enormous we got a great view of the ship moving off. It was unbelievably big ... She was so big she had to be towed down the lough. Her propellers couldn't be started till she was in really deep water. Some tug-boats had actually come over from Liverpool to pull her. People sang 'Rule Britannia' and waved handkerchiefs as they shouted their goodbyes.[29]

At that moment, the crowd was simultaneously expressing its pride in Belfast's shipbuilding accomplishments and, with the singing of 'Rule Britannia', its defiance of Home Rule.

That pride and defiance, however, quickly turned to shock, when two weeks later the news of the disaster that had befallen the *Titanic* reached Belfast. The story quickly shunted the Home Rule controversy off of the front pages. 'Nobody talks of Home Rule – it is not thought of here at the moment, as everyone is thinking of the *Titanic*', wrote the Irish nationalist Roger Casement to his cousin Gertrude Bannister in a letter written in Belfast on 20 April. Three days later, he added in another letter to Bannister that 'this dreadful *Titanic* disaster over-hangs all minds here in Belfast'.[30] The city's churches were packed with people searching for an explanation, and shipyard workers stood in the streets and wept openly. 'For those of us in Belfast, especially, this news was beyond all comprehension', John Parkinson recalled. 'My father couldn't believe it. Later he broke down and cried. He was big shipyard man and he just cried like a child. You see, his pride was broken. They had great pride in that ship. It had taken them four years to build and now it was gone.'[31] At Harland & Wolff, the news was almost incomprehensible. In the 1980s, John Ned Quinn, who worked in the yard at the time, described the moment when he first heard about the disaster:

> I was coming with two buckets of water from the well down the orchard for the horses and this man was after coming out from Newry and he was coming up to the gate when I was coming out of the orchard.
> And he says, 'Jack', he says, 'there's shocking bad news this morning'.
> I says, 'What's wrong?'
> He says, 'This big ship', he says, 'the *Titanic* that sailed. She's to the bottom this morning'.[32]

In a recent BBC documentary, the son of a Harland & Wolff employee who helped build the *Titanic* recalled that after the sinking there was 'a period of withdrawal and denial. They couldn't believe that ship went down. It was the same sort of grief that hit East Belfast the night they heard about the Battle of the Somme'.[33] Similarly, Margaret Steed, the great-granddaughter of *Titanic* carpenter James McDowell, remembers, 'When the *Titanic* went down ... an awful feeling of gloom came over the entire city and that sense of pride soon turned to shame. [The shipyard workers] rarely talked about *Titanic* again because they felt that in some way they were to blame for the tragedy'.[34]

Beyond the shipyards the sense of shock was similar. On 17 April, the *Belfast News-Letter* reported:

> The details of the loss of the *Titanic*, as published in our columns yesterday, created a profound impression in Belfast, and the disaster was the main topic of conversation throughout the day. Indeed it cast quite a gloom over the city, and on every side, and amongst all classes of the community, one heard expressions of deep regret and genuine sympathy for those who have suffered through the sinking of the huge vessel. There were few, if any, of the citizens who did not take a keen personal interest in the *Titanic* by reason of the fact that, like all the vessels of the White Star fleet, she was built at Queen's Island ... No language can describe the pity and horror of such a tragedy nor express all that one feels in its contemplation ... All the hopes which were centred on her when she was launched in the presence of thousands of cheering spectators, who were proud of her because she was the product of one of our local shipbuilding yards and because she marked the beginning of a new era in naval architecture, have been violently shattered – shattered in a manner which has brought grief into hundreds of homes.[35]

A week later, the city was still grappling to make sense of what had occurred: 'Neither time nor achievement can dispel the memory of the catastrophe or heal the grief that has taken possession of the hearts of men'.[36]

In Unionist eyes, the *Titanic* had symbolized the city's great achievements in industry, achievements that provided more than just Belfast's economic lifeblood. Industrial accomplishment had a political meaning as well, for it distinguished Ulster from the rest of Ireland, and for many Protestants it provided both the rationale and the justification for remaining within the Union. Ulster must remain within the Empire, they argued, because without access to markets its industries would collapse. In Ulster, industrialism and Unionism were often two sides of the same coin. How could Irish Catholics from the south possibly be expected to understand this, the argument went, when their economic horizons had never stretched beyond their small agricultural plots?

When the *Titanic* left Belfast Lough and set sail for Southampton in early April 1912, it represented not what the *Belfast News-Letter* called 'the very latest achievement in the mercantile shipbuilding world',[37] but also Belfast's economic and political commitment to the Union.[38] 'If Britain rules the waves, Belfast builds the ships', was a well-known adage in the first half of the twentieth century.[39] The predominantly Protestant shipyard workers of Harland & Wolff had laboured for years to build the *Titanic*, an effort into which they had expended all the expertise, craftsmanship and strength they could muster. In the days of the *Titanic*, writes local historian David Hammond:

> The pride was enormous, connected with Britishness, with the Empire, with Protestantism. The notions of Home Rule were an affront and the *Titanic* was a symbol of their resistance, a statement of their values. The very name *Titanic* had a god-like ring. By their origins in the hills around Craigantlet, Conlig, Upper Ards and Comber, the workers were most likely in the configuration of Calvinist Celts, but their affirmations were to a white, Anglo-Saxon Protestantism, and they were anti-Catholic.[40]

The workers watched the *Titanic*'s departure with pride, assuming that its new owners and crew would recognize the size and significance of their gift. But the ship sank, leaving Belfast Protestants to feel that their offering to the Union had been rejected.

The timing of the construction of the *Titanic* caused it to become a symbol of the industrial achievement that was a key component of Ulster Unionism.[41] Certainly, Ulster Catholics had little difficulty in seeing it as a Unionist emblem; in the years after 1912 – and particularly after the partition of Ireland in 1922, when they found themselves marooned in a Protestant-dominated and often discriminatory state – the sinking was frequently interpreted as the consequence of Protestant pride and arrogance. Legends arose that a shipyard worker had painted 'Let God sink this vessel if he can!' on the *Titanic*'s hull before erasing it prior to the launching date, and that the *Titanic* had been assigned the registration number 3909 04 or 3606 04 or 3909 ON, which when held before a mirror spelled 'No Pope'. An angry – and presumably pro-Catholic – God, so the argument goes, sank the ship in retribution for such effrontery.[42] And if some Ulster Catholics interpreted the sinking as divine retribution by a God angered by Protestant arrogance, others saw it as another act of deliberate injustice visited upon the Irish poor by a British/Ulster Protestant conspiracy. Far more Catholic than Protestant Irishmen and Irishwomen died in the disaster, making it possible to argue Catholics had suffered yet again at Protestant hands.[43]

Certainly, by the 1920s popular myths regarding the *Titanic* had emerged in Irish Catholic culture that displayed a profound sense of

resentment and alienation. John Wilson Foster records that a friend's
teacher at a National School in Tipperary in the 1950s explained the loss
of the *Titanic* as retribution for loyalist bigotry.[44] The literary critic
Jeremy Hawthorn reports that a friend from Belfast gave him a book
on the *Titanic* inscribed 'Built by Prods, sunk by Brits'.[45] Such episodes
reveal that the *Titanic* continued for decades after the sinking to be
regarded as Protestant property in Belfast.

The timing of the ship's sinking, however, meant that its ability to
function as a Unionist symbol was severely problematic. The initial
shock that greeted the sinking in Belfast was quickly replaced by a feeling
that can only be described as shame. There were, after all, only a limited
number of explanations available for the disaster. First, the sinking could
be interpreted as the result of faulty engineering or craftsmanship.
Secondly, it could be interpreted as the result of negligence or complacency on the part of the *Titanic*'s British crew. Or thirdly, it could
be interpreted as the result of divine intervention.

   None of these explanations was likely to provide much comfort to
Unionists. The first would require an acknowledgement that the shipyards, the heart and soul of Belfast industry, had failed at the task of
building the world's largest ship. That possibility continued to haunt –
and was fiercely denied by – the men who had worked on the *Titanic*
for decades afterwards. 'Whatever happened to her, it wasn't my rivets
that put her down', declared Sam McLaughlin, the *Titanic*'s last living
riveter, in 1986.[46] The second explanation required an acknowledgement
that the British, whom Unionists by necessity saw as superior to Irish
Catholics in order to justify their continued loyalty to the Union, had
failed at the task of sailing that same ship. Such an acknowledgement
was unthinkable in the political context of 1912, for it undermined the
case against Home Rule. And the third explanation was perhaps the
most unsatisfactory of all, for it required an acknowledgement that the
Protestant denizens of Ulster had somehow done something to incur
God's wrath. Certainly, a number of local churches held memorial
services, but they emphasized a religious message that had little to do
with the immediate context, preferring to focus instead on more universal themes. The Reverend Patterson's sermon at May Street Presbyterian
Church was typical: he asserted that it often took such a disaster to

make man realize his responsibilities and open his pockets to the less fortunate.[47] Ulster Protestants of a more evangelical type were, like their counterparts in Britain and the United States, hostile to the luxury and material greed that *Titanic* had seemed to embody; they, too, saw the hand of a vengeful God in the sinking.[48] There was no effort, however, to apply this blame on a local level; it was humanity in general whose sins were responsible for the disaster.

Given the nature of the readily available explanations, it is not surprising that Ulster Unionists faced a difficult struggle to comprehend what had happened to the *Titanic* and to extract meaning from it. In the public commemorations held in the weeks and months following the disaster, local authorities instead stressed the heroism of the twenty-two men from Belfast who had died in the sinking, including the eight members of the Harland & Wolff guarantee party. On 1 May Belfast City Council passed a resolution stating that 'the City of Belfast recognises with unbounded pride that in the hour of trial the fortitude of her sons failed not; and while she mourns for her dead, she rejoices in having given to the world men who could so nobly die'.[49] This was the city council's first meeting since the disaster; it is odd that in Belfast, a city connected more intimately with the *Titanic* than any other, the local governing body did not call a special meeting to pass a resolution of sympathy. In contrast, in many other places in Britain that had no direct connection to the ship local councils held special meetings exclusively for that purpose.

Two days after the resolution was passed, Lady Mayoress Julie McMordie called for a meeting in City Hall to discuss the construction of a *Titanic* memorial. Again, the emphasis was to be on the heroism of the local victims, not on tragedy and certainly not on culpability. At the meeting, a resolution was passed proclaiming that 'this tribute to the memory of those who acted so nobly in the tragic circumstances attending the loss of the SS *Titanic* shall take the form of an appropriate public Memorial, to be erected on the most prominent site available, so that it may keep green their memory and serve to tell succeeding generations of their heroism and devotion to duty'.[50] Within a month, over a thousand pounds had been collected, with the bulk of the funds coming from three sources, the Andrews family (£360), Harland & Wolff's employees (£231), and the White Star Line (£105). Now with sufficient money in hand for construction, the Lady Mayoress led a deputation to the 30 July 1912 meeting of the council's Improvement Committee, which was charged with handling such matters. She asked them to provide a site in Donegall Square North, across from Robinson and Cleaver's department store, or alternately at Castle Junction, another highly visible location. The chairman of the committee, Councillor Crawford McCullagh, promised that the request would receive 'careful consideration' and referred it to the city surveyor, who was directed to give a report at the next meeting.[51] On 6 August, the surveyor duly reported that Donegall Square North site was acceptable, 'provided a design suitable to the position suggested be submitted'.[52]

The Lady Mayoress and her delegation then turned to the task of choosing a sculptor. They opted to give the memorial commission to Sir Thomas Brock, who had already produced the statues of Queen Victoria and Sir Edward Harland in the grounds of City Hall, as well as the Queen Victoria Memorial in front of Buckingham Palace in London. Following approval by the surveyor, authorization by the improvement commission, and a positive vote by the city council on 2 January 1913, Brock commenced work. As in the case of numerous other *Titanic* memorials, the First World War delayed completion, and Brock's sculpture was not erected until 1920. The twenty-two foot high memorial is dominated by a figure of Thanatos, the Greek personification of death, whose right hand holds a laurel wreath over the head of a drowned man being borne up by two mermaids. Engraved on two sides of the pedestal is the following inscription:

> Erected to the imperishable memory of those gallant Belfastmen whose names are here inscribed and who lost their lives on the 15th of April 1912, by the foundering of the Belfast-built RMS *Titanic*, through collision with an iceberg, on her maiden voyage from Southampton to New York. Their devotion to duty and heroic conduct, through which the lives of many of those on board were saved, have left a record of calm fortitude and self-sacrifice which will ever remain an inspiring example to succeeding generations. 'Greater love hath no man than this, that a man lay down his life for his friends.'

The other two sides of the plinth display the names of the twenty-two men from Belfast who died, in order of shipboard rank rather than alphabetically.[53]

Apart from its brief reference to the *Titanic* as 'Belfast-built', the memorial focuses exclusively on the heroism of the local victims, even engaging in the unsubstantiated hyperbole that their 'devotion to duty and heroic conduct' saved 'the lives of many of those on board'.[54] An anonymous poem published in the press at the time of the dedication of the memorial offers a similar emphasis on the heroism of the Belfast-men:

> It was my own men who built her, the mighty ship of pride,
> To take the seas with strength and grace, a new Atlantic bride.
> I sat, the lusty city, snug between sea and shore,
> And clear above my clatt'ring streets, above my workshops' roar,
> I listened to the iron's clang that sang how fast she grew;
> My own men built her, heads and hands, they built her stout and true.
> It was my own men sent her, the greatest ship of all,
> To fight the seas for mastery and brave the winds at call.
> There fell a sudden silence. My busy lough at gaze
> Held breath to watch her stir and move and glide along the ways.
> Then loud from all my people there rose a triumph cry;
> Their thundered praise of her and me flung challenge to the sky.
> It was my own men built her, the fated ship of woe,
> That fell with snapped and maiden sword before an ambushed foe.
> I sat, the stricken city, bruised between grief and shame,
> Until I caught a healing thought to sear my wound with flame:
> High among all heroic souls upon the death-bound deck,
> Those men of mine who died with her snatched honour from the wreck.
> Those men of mine who sailed with her and share her trackless grave,
> Send home to mend my tattered pride the glory of the brave.
> I weep, the mother city, unshamed to all the world;
> My own men wrought, my own men died, my flag is yet unfurled.
> And proudly in my proudest place be set my people's sign
> How gain was wrested out of loss and courage still is mine.[55]

The poet admits to feeling 'shame' when he first heard the news of the sinking before lighting upon the idea that the men of Belfast behaved heroically, thereby redeeming the entire city. The mere fact that he feels a need to promote such heroism, however, implies that Belfast has something to answer for, that the city is indeed in need of such redemption. Although he avoids tackling the question of blame directly, it is clear that he feels uncomfortable with the notion that it might be placed upon the birthplace of the great ship. When he proclaims Belfast to be 'unshamed before the world', there is a shrill tone to his words, as if even he himself does not fully believe them.

It could be argued that Belfast's immediate response to the sinking differed little from the responses of other British communities in attempting to extract a positive meaning from the disaster by emphasizing the heroic conduct of the victims. That, however, is precisely the point. By reacting no differently from anywhere else, Belfast implicitly sought to deny its unique relationship with the *Titanic*, and to de-emphasize its role as the city of the ship's birth. In July 1912, three months after the sinking, a special report appeared in the periodical *Engineering* entitled 'Harland & Wolff's Works at Belfast'. The lengthy report dealt with the yard and its history in depth and detail, but alluded to its most recent – and famous – product in only a single sentence: 'a great step was made in 1911, when there were completed two more ships of the *Olympic* type, with a tonnage of over 45,000 tons'. The *Titanic* is not even named; the report, as John Wilson Foster writes, is like '*Hamlet* without the Prince'.[56] Although there is no way to confirm this, it seems likely that an agreement was reached with Harland & Wolff that, in return for access to the yard, the *Titanic* would not be mentioned. Certainly, there was a clear effort in the article to demonstrate that the sinking was of no economic consequence to Belfast, and that the city had quickly moved on: 'From the industrial point of view, Belfast is very prosperous; it was probably never more so, especially as regards shipbuilding and engineering'.[57] These words were by and large true, but they also concealed the very real trauma that the city had suffered.

There were, to be sure, a handful of plays, paintings and other cultural effusions related to *Titanic* produced in Ulster in the years following the sinking. Most of these, however, failed to confront the complex and uncomfortable legacy that the ship bequeathed to the city of its birth. The year after the sinking, Samuel Cowan published a loyalist ode, entitled 'De Profundis', which treated the disaster as the consequence of an unhappy and unpreventable accident:

> In what wise didst thou, O Fate!
> Make our proud Sea-Giant die?

Cowan's avoidance of blame of the ship's crew is necessary to support his claims of British heroism, a heroism which he encourages his fellow Unionists to celebrate:

> Mother! teach thy child to give
> Homage to each British Brave! [58]

Cowan makes no attempt to identify a distinctive role for Ulster in the *Titanic* story; Belfast's contribution is simply to pay tribute to the dead heroes alongside the rest of the Union. Once again, what is distinctive about Belfast's response to the sinking is its very lack of distinctiveness. The pride seen at *Titanic*'s launch had given way to a desire to ignore all connection between the ship and the city.

Few other Ulster authors, meanwhile, wished to draw attention to the disaster, which could only revive painful memories of loss and humiliation in a context in which pride was often Ulster's most potent weapon. The actor Jimmy Ellis, a Belfast native whose father helped build the *Titanic*, claims that the disaster became 'a shadow over the city ... They couldn't believe it, they just never got over it. There was this collective blame that nobody would ever get to the bottom of'.[59] In the years before and immediately after partition, Ulster Unionists proved extremely adept at ignoring reality – a reality that left them an anomalous and, in some eyes, unviable statelet that the rest of the United Kingdom, to which they so ardently proclaim their allegiance, often wished would simply disappear.

It was therefore preferable to ignore the *Titanic*'s Ulster origins, given the ignominious end to which the ship had come. In 1922 the playwright St John Ervine, who was from Ballymacarrett, the working-class district of East Belfast where many of Harland & Wolff's employees lived, published a play entitled *The Ship*. The play tells the story of the world's largest ship, which is supposedly unsinkable but which hits an iceberg and sinks on its maiden voyage. Ervine, however, changed the name of the ship to the *Magnificent* and moved the shipyard that built it to the fictional English city of Biggport. This was only one of many attempts to downplay the connection between Belfast and the *Titanic*. In the mid 1930s, BBC Northern Ireland was asked to broadcast a radio programme called 'I Was There – *Titanic* Survivor'. The regional director, however, wrote to London in protest: 'The *Titanic*, and everything to do with it,

is an exceedingly sore point in Belfast history, as not only were some
forty Belfast people drowned – mostly rather important people – but
also it was a very grave set-back to civic pride when this much-vaunted
ship went out from Harland & Wolff's yard to sink on its maiden
voyage'. This was not the last time that BBC Northern Ireland would
clash with London over this issue. In 1947, the Northern Ireland Prime
Minister Sir Basil Brooke requested that another programme on the
Titanic be delayed for a week so that it would not coincide with
the launch of a new Cunard White Star liner from the Harland & Wolff
shipyard.[60] The intervention of a prominent politician like Brooke suggests the lengths to which people in Ulster were still willing to go to
prevent the old *Titanic* wounds from being opened again. In the 1950s,
the Belfast *Titanic* Memorial was moved, ostensibly because it had
become a traffic hazard, to what a local historian refers to as 'an obscure
corner of the City Hall grounds, where no one ever sees it'.[61] (This claim
was confirmed in the spring of 2002 when I was photographing the
memorial and a local resident wandered over to see what I was so
interested in. He had never noticed it before.) At the time, in fact, there
were proposals to move the memorial out of Belfast altogether.[62]

Meanwhile, Unionists looking for ways to prove their loyalty to and
willingness to sacrifice themselves for Britain found an alternative that
was not fraught with the tensions of the *Titanic* story. During the First
World War, the 36th Ulster Division, comprised heavily of men from
the Unionist paramilitary group the Ulster Volunteer Force, suffered
5500 casualties out of a total strength of 11,000 on the first day of the
battle of the Somme on 1 July 1916. For future Unionist generations,
this would be the 'blood sacrifice' that was accepted; the decimation of
the 36th Ulsters became a major complicating factor in postwar negotiations about the future of Ireland, playing a significant role in ensuring
the partition that kept Northern Ireland within the United Kingdom.[63] In contrast, the *Titanic*, which produced no such ultimately
beneficial outcome in Unionist eyes, continued to be a subject best
avoided.[64]

As time passed and the trauma of the disaster became less immediate,
a few Ulster authors, including Louis MacNeice, Derek Mahon and John
Hewitt, began to tackle the *Titanic*.[65] None of their writings, however,

examines the question of what the sinking meant to the city that had built the ship. It was not until the 1970s and 1980s that increased sectarian violence created a context which forced Ulster to confront the ghosts of the past in order assess their continuing impact on the present.[66] In such an atmosphere, the legacy of the *Titanic* at long last began to be confronted in Belfast. In 1974, Stewart Parker's radio play *The Iceberg* offered one of the first literary attempts to deal with the legacy of the disaster. The play's main characters are Danny and Hugh, the ghosts of two Harland & Wolff workers who fall to their deaths in a shipyard accident shortly before the *Titanic* sets sail on its maiden voyage. The ship carries their spirits to Southampton; the fact that they are able to interact normally with the passengers and crew indicates that everyone on board has, like them, already crossed over into the afterlife. Parker acknowledges the symbolic status of the ship as a gift to the Union. 'This ship is our proudest offering – to the Empire – and to the world', says Thomas Andrews, portrayed here as a stereotypical dour Northern Irish Presbyterian who works compulsively, forswears alcohol and wants his creation to be 'perfect in every detail'.[67]

Parker also traces the inextricably intertwined relationship between Unionism and industry. 'Look at this boat,' says Danny, 'can you imagine them building it in Cork or somewhere? ... Belfast-built, that means something, you know it does, Hughie. Workmanship – all over the world. It wasn't bogtrotters that built this ship.'[68] And in two different scenes, Parker refers to the chronological confluence of the *Titanic*'s maiden voyage and the debate on the third Home Rule Bill. The first occurs when Danny obtains a copy of the shipboard newspaper, the *Atlantic Daily Bulletin*:

Danny	We're on the front page.
Hugh	What?
Danny	'Home Rule Bill Published'.
Hugh	Oh, is that all – I thought you meant you and me – 'Two Dead Riveters Missing, Feared Alive'.
Danny	Look at this headline, 'Mr Asquith's Explanation'.
Hugh	Sounds like a music-hall turn.
Danny	He can explain himself blue in the face, but he won't convince the loyal people of Ulster.[69]

Later, Thomas Andrews and the ship's surgeon, Dr O'Loughlin, a southern Irishmen, argue over Home Rule:

Andrews   You've got your Home Rule Bill launched anyway.

O'Loughlin   Not mine, Thomas. Ireland's. Ours.

Andrews   Oh, not me. Besides, she's only launched. I doubt you'll find that she'll ever make it into active service.

O'Loughlin   There's good stuff in her. Four-fifths of the votes of the whole Irish people.

Andrews   It's her cargo I was thinking of. The powers of taxation, invested in this putative Dublin parliament, for instance. You know as well as I do what's implied.

O'Loughlin   Irish taxes for Irish services.

Andrews   Dublin taxes on Northern industry to prop up its own peasant economy.

O'Loughlin   (EXAGGERATING ACCENT) Ah, Thomas, sure you're terrible suspicious of poor peasants.

Andrews   We're simply rationalists up in the North, doctor. We look at Belfast today, a city close to half a million souls employed in manufacturing industries that can compete with any in the world. Yet what was it before the Act of Union made us part and parcel of Britain? A scruffy provincial village.[70]

Here, encapsulated in microcosm, is the entire Home Rule debate as two men of the middle class see it, presented from both a northern and southern Irish point of view. O'Loughlin argues that independence and self-determination are what really matter, whereas Andrews counters by elevating economic interest to the forefront.

Parker's play represents a rare attempt to place the *Titanic* squarely in a Belfast context. What Parker does not do, however, is confront the sense of guilt and shame that the sinking produced in the city. Significantly, he ends the play on the afternoon of Sunday, 14 April, *before* the ship strikes the iceberg. Ironically if not surprisingly, it took a playwright from the Republic of Ireland to confront the meaning of the *Titanic* to Ulster Protestants head on. Frank McGuiness's 1986 play *Observe the Sons of Ulster Marching towards the Somme* depicts a group of Protestant soldiers from the 36th Ulster Division, soon to go into action – and be decimated – at the Somme. Two of the soldiers are home on leave shortly before the climactic battle that will kill all but one of them:

McIlwaine	Know what I'm thinking about? ... That boat.
Anderson	The *Titanic*? ... What brings the *Titanic* into your mind?
McIlwaine	The drum. The noise of it. It's like the sound she made hitting the Lagan.
Anderson	We weren't to blame. No matter what they say.
McIlwaine	Papists? (MCILWAINE SPITS ...)
Anderson	Every nail they hammered into the *Titanic*, they cursed the Pope. That's what they say.
McIlwaine	There was a lot of nails in the *Titanic*.
Anderson	And still he wasn't cursed enough.
McIlwaine	Every nail we hammered into the *Titanic*, we'll die the same amount in this cursed war. That's what I say.
Anderson	What are you talking about?
McIlwaine	The war's cursed. It's good for nothing. A waste of time. We won't survive. We're all going to die for nothing ... We're on the *Titanic*. We're all going down. Women and children first. Women and children. Damn the Pope. Let me die damning him ...
Anderson	The bloody *Titanic* went down because it hit an iceberg.
McIlwaine	The pride of Belfast went with it.
Anderson	You're not going to meet many icebergs on the front, are you? So what are you talking about?
McIlwaine	The war is our punishment.[71]

McGuiness is able to acknowledge the guilt felt in Unionist Belfast in the wake of the *Titanic*'s sinking in a way that no Northern Irish writer has had ever been able to. McIlwaine sees his predicament as a soldier about to go into battle as retribution for his city's crime in building the ship involved in the worst maritime disaster in world history. The *Titanic*'s fate, he predicts (accurately, as it turns out) has sealed his own; Belfast must atone for all of those deaths in those dark and icy waters on that fateful April night.

If Parker puts the *Titanic* in its proper Belfast context and McGuiness acknowledges the city's guilt for the disaster, then Robert Johnstone's poem 'Undertakers' establishes the link between past and present Northern Irish disasters. 'Undertakers' is part of a suite of poems entitled *Titanic* that appeared in Johnstone's collection *Eden to Edenderry*, published in 1989. It describes the voyage of the *Mackay-Bennett*, the ship sent on the macabre mission in April 1912 of collecting the bodies of the *Titanic*'s victims that were still floating in the North Atlantic. The poem connects the process of identifying the bodies and properly disposing of them to the grisly aftermath of a terrorist bomb blast:

> We identify, embalm, encoffin
> All first-class passengers. Second and third
> We wrap in canvas. Crew we pack in ice.
> A question of time and money, drawing lines,
>
> For even love, or grief, is relative.
> Which reminds me – of the bodies laid out
> At the Mayflower curling rink, visitors –
> Relatives – skidding from one to the next,
>
> That poster of the unrecognizable
> Remains of a person mummified, it seemed,
> In the fireblast of the hotel-bombing,
> Or the fireman gathering limbs in town,
>
> The weeping priest waving his handkerchief,
> A crowd of people walking, not running,
> In ones and twos away from a cloud of dust.
> Oddly, every one has her mouth open.[72]

By linking the *Titanic* disaster to the Troubles in this way, Johnstone implies a causal relationship in which the first tragedy led inexorably to the second. Indeed, in the 1970s and 1980s it must have seemed to many people in Belfast that the city was being made to continue to atone for the failure of its most famous product. The promise represented by the *Titanic*, as the greatest of Belfast's roster of impressive – and profitable – industrial feats, remained unfulfilled, as politico-religious strife and economic collapse became locked in a mutually parasitic relationship.

This context, however, allowed the *Titanic* to shed some of its old sectarian associations with Ulster Unionism, as it ceased to be a symbol of Protestant pride (or Protestant shame, as the case the may be) and became instead a symbol of the despair of the entire city. This transition can be seen in Mary Costello's memoir of her Belfast childhood, entitled *Titanic Town*, published in 1992. In the opening chapter, Costello reiterates a sectarian view of the sinking by identifying a link between the discrimination suffered by her Catholic forebears at Harland & Wolff and the ship's demise: 'Paddy Mohan worked on the *Titanic*, but only briefly. When his co-workers discovered that his name was not truly Victor or George or Robert they threw him into Belfast Lough, and a clatter of spanners after him ... So they were bound to have no luck of the ship'. But the next line is telling: 'Ill-fated. Like the city itself'.[73] Here, Costello shifts from referring to those affected by the sinking as only the Protestant shipyard workers who were so cruel to its relation to the entire city of Belfast. The film version of *Titanic Town* expands upon this theme. In one scene, two Catholic teenagers whose lives have been torn apart by sectarian strife visit the Harland & Wolff shipyards, which have fallen into a state of near dereliction. Dino points out to Annie, 'That's where they built the *Titanic*. They painted "No Pope Here" on the side'. Annie responds, 'Lucky Pope!'[74] The scene reveals how the disaster has gradually ceased to be metaphor of thwarted Protestant pride and become a metaphor for the fate of the entire city, Protestant and Catholic alike. 'In a retrospective way, the tragedy of Belfast's *Titanic* can be seen as mirroring that of the city itself', writes Michael McCaughan of the Ulster Folk and Transport Museum.[75]

If the *Titanic* can function as a symbol of Belfast's despair, it can also function as a symbol of the city's hope, hope that has grown in recent years as sectarian strife and postindustrial despair have retreated in the face of a tenuously successful peace process that has brought with it signs of economic rebirth. Responding to these changes, the *Titanic* has proven its mutability as a symbol of the city of its birth, this time shifting from a symbol of divisiveness and collapse to a symbol of unity and renewal. 'Today, despite our problems, there is a spirit of hope in Northern Ireland', writes McCaughan:

> New visions for the future include the reclamation of a proud *Titanic* past and Belfast as a player in the international *Titanic* heritage industry. As a world-wide brand, fusing profit, pleasure and memorialisation, *Titanic* is

now beginning to be celebrated in her homeland as an important signifier
of economic, social and cultural regeneration. No longer in denial, past and
present achievements are being linked together and their success projected
into the future.[76]

Former Lord Mayor Ian Adamson concurs: 'It is time to start celebrating
the magnificent achievement by the people of Belfast. In its day the
Titanic was the greatest feat of engineering the world had seen, but that
tends to have been overlooked'.[77]

Signs that Adamson's hopes may be realized have been appearing in
Belfast over the past decade. In 1992 the Ulster *Titanic* Society was
formed 'to research RMS *Titanic*, her sister ships, the White Star Line
and also the development of the Harland & Wolff shipyard. Of all the
different aspects of the *Titanic* story, her birthplace, where she spent
more time than anywhere else apart from her final resting place,
has gone largely forgotten'.[78] Over eighty people attended the first
meeting, including children, grandchildren and great-grandchildren
of the Ulstermen lost in the disaster. The first president, Marjorie
Wood MacCormick, was the daughter of Artie Frost, a member of the
Harland & Wolff guarantee group. Following her death in 1995, Mac-
Cormick was succeeded by John Parkinson, who had witnessed the
Titanic's departure from Belfast as a five-year-old boy. Membership
grew steadily over the next several years, and in April 1997 the society
sponsored a convention entitled '*Titanic* at Home'. The society's chair-
person, Una Reilly, wrote in the report on the convention that 'at long
last the great ship was given her rightful place in Ulster's history'.[79]
Today, membership in the Ulster *Titanic* Society stands at over three
hundred.

Such attempts to recover Belfast's pride in the *Titanic* are propelled
significantly by the potential profits that *Titanic* tourism could create in
a city economically devastated by the collapse of its major industries.
Local commercial entities that once tried to conceal their associations
with the *Titanic* now proudly advertise the fact that their wares were
selected for use on board. The web site for Belfast furniture makers
Gilbert Logan and Sons introduces their '*Titanic* Range' by trumpeting,
'The young Gilbert Logan crafted the original captain's table for the ship.
As well as the exact replica of the table and matching sideboard, Gilbert
Logan have created reproductions of other furniture from the vessel'.[80]

A new company called 'Titanic Irish Linen Plus' boasts that they 'have put together two world famous names – "Titanic" and "Irish Linen". Both these names represent a period of elegance from a bygone age.'[81] The Lagan Boat Company offers what it claims is 'the only authentic Titanic boat tour in the world', with commentary by members of the Ulster Titanic Society.[82] And, perhaps most significantly of all, the shipyard that once tried to conceal its construction of the world's most famous ship is now eager to build a replica of it, provided an investor with sufficient capital can be found. 'Marketing it as built in Belfast by Harland & Wolff rather than anywhere else would help because of the historical associations', said a spokesperson for the shipyard in June 2000.[83]

The economic motivations of Belfast's growing interest in the Titanic should thus not be overlooked. 'At last there are signs that Northern Ireland is waking up to the enormous potential of the Titanic story', began an editorial in the Belfast Telegraph in July 1999:

> The possibility of promoting Belfast as the birthplace of the doomed ship should have been spotted years ago. Imagine how America would have sold the story had the yard been located in the United States ... It is an ace card in our tourism pack, and should now be played with vigour ... The Titanic tragedy focussed world attention on Belfast in 1912, and now, almost a century on, it can again have the same impact. In marketing parlance, the story of the liner is a unique selling point for Northern Ireland, and could open the door to thousands of tourists.[84]

Two years later in April 2001, Belfast City Council unanimously passed a resolution calling for a new Titanic monument. Councillor Robin Newton, who proposed the resolution, asserted that 'Belfast has an opportunity ... to get even greater tourists coming. This memorial would be something people would be interested in visiting'.[85]

Newton's comments suggest that there is an increasing recognition that Belfast's industrial might is gone forever. Instead, the city's economic future rests on two potential sources of profit: high technology and heritage tourism. And, as a symbol of the new Belfast, the Titanic has the perhaps unique potential to represent both. 'For a long time people felt some kind of guilt about Titanic', says Maria Therese McGiven of the Belfast city government. 'But I think slowly as we've gained confidence in ourselves we've realized that the ship at that time represented the real cutting edge of technology and this city can again provide the cutting edge in technology for the world'. Similarly, Michael McCaughan declares that 'the downside of the disaster is being set aside. It's *Titanic* as built in Belfast as a supreme example of Edwardian shipbuilding technology. It's that aspect that's being adopted and projected into the future'.[86]

In some ways, Belfast is better positioned than other cities with close associations with the tragedy, such as Southampton, because it is associated more with the construction of the ship than with its destruction. If anywhere can actually view the *Titanic* as a source of celebration, Belfast can. 'The world commemorates the tragedy of the *Titanic*', ran a headline in a special supplement of the *Belfast Telegraph* in April 1998. 'Only in Belfast can we celebrate her triumph.' Or, as the motto of the Ulster *Titanic* Society puts it, 'What happened was a disaster, but she was not'. In April 2002 as Belfast celebrated the ninetieth anniversary of the *Titanic*'s departure from the city, Lord Mayor Jim Rodgers declared:

> While never forgetting those who died in the disaster ... Belfast can uniquely celebrate the magnificent technological achievement that was *Titanic* ... It is therefore highly appropriate that Belfast City Council should be taking the lead in helping the people of Belfast, and beyond, to celebrate not only the magnificence of the *Titanic* herself, but also the vision, the skill and dedication of the people of this city who brought her to life.[87]

Rodgers's words concerning the 'skill and dedication' of the workers who built the *Titanic* suggest that Belfast is beginning to take pride once again in the industrial accomplishment that the ship represented, and in the people who were responsible for that accomplishment. For much of the twentieth century, Irish cultural achievement has been measured in an exclusively rural, preindustrial idiom in which modernity and machinery have had no role, and indeed have often been viewed with antipathy.[88] In this scenario, Ulster's industrial working class has been regarded as being full of men and women who were at best drab philistines and at worst loathsome bigots; this interpretation was so pervasive that even in Belfast itself it was scarcely challenged. At long last, however, there are signs that the shipyard workers are beginning to be celebrated, or at least recalled in a more sophisticated way. In 1997

Stewart Love's play *Titanic* was performed at the Ulster Hall; it offers the most complex view of the men who built the *Titanic* yet seen on the stage or in any other cultural venue.[89] Similarly, Michael Fieldhouse's play *The Song of the Hammers* (2002) provides a poignant requiem for the sufferings of the shipyard workers in the wake of the disaster:

> All those rivets, all those steel plates, all those hours of work, … the men who died, the men who were injured, the thousands who worked day after day – the thousands more in Belfast who made things for her, the painstaking hours of all those craftsmen – they are all part of this ship. Part of them will go down with her.[90]

Perhaps the best summary of Belfast's current relationship with the *Titanic* can be seen in an educational radio programme broadcast as part of the BBC Northern Ireland's 'History and Literacy' series in May 2000. According to the BBC website, the programme attempted to 'redress' the frequent omission of Belfast from the *Titanic* story by 'focusing on those who built the vessel, and on the place it was built'. It tells the story of a young boy named Tom, an apprentice riveter at Harland & Wolff who is following in the footsteps of his father and grandfather. As he works on the *Titanic* and *Olympic*, however, he becomes dissatisfied with his existence and begins to aspire to the world of wealth and luxury the great ships represent. In search of a better life, he decides to emigrate to New York on the *Titanic*. He survives the sinking but arrives in New York penniless and ends up washing dishes in a hotel in order to earn a living. Having lost the status of a skilled tradesman that he enjoyed in Belfast, he becomes disillusioned and decides to return home to his job in the shipyard. He finds it, however, a different place from the one he left: the workers are nervous about the American inquiry into the sinking and fear that they will somehow be blamed. But when the results are announced, there is no criticism of the ship's design or construction, and they quickly regain their old pride in their work. This is one of the few stories of the *Titanic* that manages to provide a happy ending; the emphasis here is less on the tragedy that befell the ship and more on the prosperous future of the shipyard.[91]

The *Titanic* has thus come full circle in Belfast and is now back to being regarded as what it was in 1912: a vehicle for the hopes and aspirations of the community. There is a key difference, however: this time, *Titanic* is being promoted as a symbol of the *entire* Belfast community, not only Protestants but Catholics as well. 'I think people today are united in their view of the tragedy, which claimed the lives of Protestants and Catholics', says Douglas Carson, president of the Ulster *Titanic* Trust.[92] For the first time, the *Titanic* is being celebrated in Belfast as an *Irish* ship. In 1912, as we have previously seen, only Irish nationalists emphasized the ship's Irish heritage, while its builders and Belfast's Protestant, Unionist majority preferred to see it as a British vessel. In recent years, however, the *Titanic*'s Irishness has begun to be reclaimed. In an early scene of the 1997 blockbuster film, the character Tommy Ryan, whom director James Cameron claims he created to be 'a voice for the Irish emigrants', states, 'This is an Irish ship. She was built in Belfast by 15,000 Irishmen'.[93] In a recent BBC Northern Ireland documentary, entitled *Titanic: Made in Belfast*, journalist Kevin Myers observed, 'Everyone thinks of [*Titanic*] as a British ship, but everything about it was Irish. The people who made it were Irish men and women'. Partition, Myers continued, had not yet occurred in 1912; there was no formal division in Irish identity at that time.[94]

To be sure, the old, sectarian *Titanic* has not completely disappeared, just as the old, sectarian Belfast has not entirely disappeared. As recently as 1996, the Orange Order carried 'lush ornate banners portraying scenes of Ulster's darkest days – the sinking of the *Titanic* in 1912, the battle of the Somme in 1916' in their Twelfth of July parades commemorating the anniversary of the battle of the Boyne.[95] And just off the Newtonards Road in Ballymacerrett, still an intensely Unionist part of Belfast, there is a *Titanic* mural, a commemoration of the area's contribution to the construction of the ship. Those on the other side of the political spectrum, meanwhile, can still see the *Titanic* as an emblem of British repression. Belfast's left-wing Glenravel Local History Project, whose objective of reclaiming history 'for ordinary people' clearly has nationalist implications, has devoted considerable time and energy to putting forth a view of the *Titanic* as a 'symbol of mass murder' due to the large numbers of third-class passengers who perished in the sinking. Using the experience of third-class Irish emigrants as its primary evidence, the project's report interprets the actions of the *Titanic*'s British crew as 'nothing less than cold-blooded murder' and the subsequent

British inquiry into the disaster as a 'cover-up'.[96] The project's Joe Baker declares, 'The *Titanic* is remembered for all the wrong reasons. It was not a great ship, as it was constructed in a cost-cutting way using cheaper metals. Also, more importantly, it did not do what great ships are meant to do – get people from one place to another without killing them'.[97]

Such views of the *Titanic* doubtless send shivers down the spines of Belfast's current civic leaders, most of whom clearly hope that such sectarian interpretations of the disaster – Unionist and Nationalist alike – are archaic remnants of a past that will soon fade away entirely. For the prospects of the new, prosperous Belfast depend upon cooperation; what threatens Belfast most of all now is a return to the sectarian strife of old. If Belfast were to collide with that iceberg, all hopes of an economic recovery would surely founder.

In the spring of 2002, the Ulster *Titanic* Society, in conjunction with Belfast City Council and with sponsorship from Belfast Citybus, held a nine-day event entitled *Titanic: Made in Belfast* that represented the first substantial attempt to generate both local and tourist interest in Belfast's central role in the *Titanic* story. Belfast, claimed the publicity brochure for the event, is 'the city most clearly connected with the *Titanic*'s genesis and launch. For three years, Belfast and the *Titanic* shared the same space and time, and those times have been forged by memory and story into indissoluble links'.

But if *Titanic: Made in Belfast* was clearly meant to announce Belfast's intention of reclaiming the *Titanic*'s legacy, it was also intended to accomplish a more ambitious objective. 'We hope that events like this will bring people to Belfast who will act as ambassadors for the city', explained Gerry Copeland, the Events Manager for Belfast City Council's Development Department. Copeland quickly dismissed any suggestion that the *Titanic*'s old sectarian associations might hinder its elevation as a symbol of a new, tourist-friendly Belfast. 'I wouldn't worry too much about the politics', he said, hastening to point out that both his father and grandfather worked at Harland & Wolff, even though they were Catholic.[98] Copeland's objectives for *Titanic: Made in Belfast* were typical. Una Reilly, too, stressed her Catholic ancestry, again attempting to prove that *Titanic* now belonged to all of Belfast, not just to Unionists.[99] Clearly, there was more at stake here than merely gaining greater recognition that the *Titanic* had been built in Belfast. In the eyes of Copeland and Reilly, the economic future of the city was also hanging in the balance.

Not surprisingly, the tone of *Titanic: Made in Belfast* was overwhelmingly positive. 'The *Titanic* was the greatest thing on the face of the earth in terms of man-made engineering and luxury', said city council spokesperson Mark Ashby. 'The city was very proud of her, and we're trying to recapture that pride'.[100] The exhibition at City Hall focused on four fictional men and women from Belfast, none of whom died in the disaster. The description of Tommy Tierney, a twelve-year-old boy who saw *Titanic* depart from Belfast in April 1912, displays the positive nature of the exhibition:

> Looking back Tommy could not help remembering how sad he had been when the great ship had left Belfast, its home, never to return. He also remembered the sadness in Belfast when news had arrived that the *Titanic* had come to rest at the bottom of the Atlantic. But it was the splendour of the great ship that Tommy remembered mostly, the mighty funnels, the gigantic propeller that was the size of a big house, the gleaming white decks and the excitement in Belfast when she gracefully and powerfully slipped down the Lough. It was a truly magnificent ship, something for Belfast people to be proud of, and Tommy had seen her in all her glory.

Also trying to minimize the tragic side of *Titanic* were the 'memories' of Daniel Clyde, a naval architect at Harland & Wolff: 'He always reminded himself that although the events of 14–15 April 1912 were a terrible tragedy, the *Titanic* herself, and the day that she was launched, were glorious and wonderful and something for everyone at Harland & Wolff to be proud of. He certainly was'.[101]

The organizers of *Titanic: Made in Belfast* were clearly happy with the results, which saw thousands of people visit City Hall during the nine-day event. 'It was a resounding success, one of the best things we have done', declared Lord Mayor Jim Rodgers.[102] For me, two moments during *Titanic: Made in Belfast* best represented contemporary Belfast and the *Titanic*'s place in it. The first occurred on Easter Monday, when the event was in full swing as people took advantage of the holiday. I was participating in a walking tour entitled 'Thomas Andrews' Belfast: An Edwardian Walk About *Titanic* City', when we were interrupted by the noisy spectacle of an Apprentice Boys parade.[103] A series of uniformed fife-and-drum bands, some wearing the purple-and-orange Apprentice Boys colours, others in the red, white and blue of the Union Jack or in khaki as if they had just stepped off of a First World War battlefield, marched down Donegall Place towards City Hall. These bands are often referred to as 'blood and thunder' bands because of the sheer din they create with their huge drums, often carried by one person and pounded on by two more, one on each side, for the maximum generation of volume. After each band came a contingent of Apprentice Boys from that particular lodge, dressed in the traditional Unionist costume of a black suit and a bowler hat.

Our tour guide tried valiantly to persevere over the pounding drums, while the participants, all of whom were local save a Canadian post-graduate student and myself, attempted to ignore the parade. Eventually, however, we gave up: the parade blocked our route and in any event the noise was preventing us from hearing the guide's descriptions. As I walked back towards City Hall, I watched the bands march under the *Titanic: Made in Belfast* banner that hung across Donegall Place, wondering which version of Belfast's present I should accept: the one that Gerry Copeland, Una Reilly and so many others had tried to show me all week, a present in which such aggressive displays of sectarian pride were becoming archaic, or the one that the parade represented, a present in which the divisions of the past were still alive and well. And did the future lie with the vast majority of people who, like our tour guide, simply went about their business and tried to ignore the parade, or with the minority who lined the street and enthusiastically cheered the marchers on?

The second moment occurred while I was taking a tour of the Harland & Wolff shipyard. This was the first time that Harland & Wolff had allowed large-scale public access to the yard. Stephen Cameron of the Ulster *Titanic* Society showed us around, pointing out the ramp from which the *Titanic* was launched, the fitting-out basin where it was completed and the immense Thompson dry dock built especially for the *Olympic*-class liners. The most compelling part of the tour, however, was a visit to the drawing office where the detailed plans that had enabled the *Titanic* to be transformed from Lord Pirrie's dream to buildable reality had been created. There is a famous photograph of the drawing

office from the *Titanic* era in which ship designers wearing tweed suits
are hunched over long tables, while sunlight streams in from the huge
windows in the barrel-vaulted roof. Here is where the creative engineering genius that was necessary to build cutting-edge ships like the
Titanic expressed itself.

Today the drawing office is a sad and desolate place. The paint is
peeling, the floor is crumbling, and the glass in the windows is cracked.
There are holes in the walls where the plaster has fallen away, exposing
wires and wood beams. But here, it is hoped, Belfast's future will be
determined. There are plans to transform the almost derelict shipyard
into the *Titanic* Quarter, 'a major economic engine contributing to the
future of Belfast and Northern Ireland, attracting inward investment
from numerous companies from a diversity of high technology areas,
supporting the continued development of existing industries and under-
pinning social development'. The idea behind the *Titanic* Quarter is to
create an area that will contain facilities for high-tech industry; housing,
shopping and dining opportunities, primarily for the employees (a
so-called 'work-live zone') but for other city residents and visitors as
well; and a visitor attraction that will 'celebrate the legacy of Harland
& Wolff and *Titanic*'.[104]

Although the current plans for the *Titanic* Quarter contain space for
Harland & Wolff to continue building ships, this aspect of the scheme
is little emphasized in the publicity materials. Over the last decade or
so, the company has been forced to come to grips with the fact that it
can no longer compete on a global scale and that it must begin to look
elsewhere if it is to survive.[105] At the same time, Harland & Wolff's
managers have come to recognize that the firm's associations with the
Titanic, long regarded as an embarrassment, may hold the key to its
economic future. In March 2001, Harland & Wolff opened a new
information technology division called *Titanic* Information Services,
intended to provide communication solutions to Northern Irish companies. Chairman Fred Olsen sought to remind the press of Harland &
Wolff's distinguished past as a promoter of cutting-edge technology,
embodied by the *Titanic*. 'Within Northern Ireland, Harland & Wolff
played a leading role in [the] change process', said Olsen, 'pioneering
the development of new methodology and processes within engineering
and manufacturing, as epitomised by the *Titanic*.'[106] To further

strengthen the link between past and present, the headquarters of *Titanic* Information Services was located in a building called Thomas Andrews House.

The glitz and prosperity of the projected *Titanic* Quarter, however, seemed a long way off as I stood in the derelict drawing office. Ten years from now, perhaps it will have been transformed, as the plans call for, into what the plans refer to as a '*Titanic* Icon', a heritage centre celebrating Harland & Wolff's shipbuilding accomplishments:

> Various historical buildings on Queen's Island remain as magnificent remnants of the spirit of the *Titanic* era. Their conservation could provide a home to a range of public spaces which recognise this heritage and support the development of a visitor attraction of global proportions, evoking the scale, experience and engineering achievement of the past. Whereas the Belfast skyline was once dominated by the huge gantries which were the birthplace of the great liners such as *Titanic,* the future could see a suitable icon forming the centrepiece of a *Titanic* 'envelope'.[107]

Whatever commemorations of the *Titanic* occur on the site, however, Harland & Wolff will have no involvement, for in June 2003, the company's Norwegian owners sold their interest in the land on which the shipyard sits to a property development firm for £47 million. Plans are to develop it for high-tech industry and private housing. But if Belfast's political and economic future is still far from secure, the *Titanic* seems certain be at the centre of it.

10

Southampton

Southampton's docks are located near the end of the eight-mile inlet, known as Southampton Water, which extends in a north-westerly direction from Calshot Spit in the Solent, the stretch of water that separates the Isle of Wight from the Hampshire coast. The Solent is shaped like a chevron, with the entrance to Southampton Water at its point. Larger ships usually enter it along the eastern channel, while smaller or less heavily laden vessels enter from the west. At their peak, Southampton docks handled almost half of the ocean passenger traffic of the United Kingdom, with as many as seventeen passenger liners arriving or departing each day. In the mid 1930s, ten of the twelve largest ships in the world regularly called at Southampton.[1]

In contrast to Liverpool, whose development was closely connected to the industrial growth of the midlands and the expansion of the canal system, Southampton grew as a port primarily because of its ideal geographical location. Situated halfway along the south coast on the routes leading to the English Channel and North Sea, Southampton was a convenient port of call for journeys to and from the Continent. Moreover, the short distance between Southampton and London enhanced the port's attractiveness to passenger traffic. Above all, however, Southampton owed its success to its position adjacent to the Isle of Wight, which protects it from the open sea and creates a commodious and sheltered deep-water harbour with wide approach channels. 'A seaport without the sea's terrors, an ocean approach within the threshold of the land', proclaimed one nineteenth-century commentator.[2]

Southampton's location offered the shipping trade more than just a sheltered harbour. It also resulted in a unique double tide caused by the port's position at the midway point of the Channel, combined with the Atlantic Pulse and the relative positions of the sun and moon. As the tide ebbs down the Channel towards the Atlantic, enough water is diverted by the projecting spur of the Ryde peninsula to reflood the entire estuary. This phenomenon produces a greatly extended period of high tide, giving large ships a much longer window in which to dock, and making lock entrances unnecessary unlike at London, Liverpool and Bristol.[3]

Southampton's history as a port is long and rich. As Philip Hoare has written:

> Centuries have passed through this inseminal conduit. From Roman barges to ocean liners; from plague ships to Pilgrim Fathers; from French marauders to Hollywood film stars; from Francis Drake's *Golden Hind*, laden with Spanish gold for the Virgin Queen, to Goering's bombers, heavy with a deadlier cargo. Enemies or tourists, missionaries or immigrants, they all entered or left the land here, and in some other age their phantoms are still processing along Southampton Water.[4]

In 1415 Henry V's army embarked from Southampton on its way to France and the battle of Agincourt. In 1620, the Pilgrims departed from Southampton on their famous journey to New England in the North American colonies, though they put in briefly at Plymouth when the *Speedwell* started leaking so badly that it had to be abandoned and continued their journey on the *Mayflower*. But the most famous historical association of the Southampton docks is one that occurred much more recently: on 10 April 1912, the *Titanic* set sail from there on its ill-fated maiden voyage, a voyage which ended abruptly five days later in the middle of the North Atlantic.

For Southampton, the sinking of *Titanic* was devastating. The vast majority of *Titanic*'s nine hundred crew members lived in the city, and almost seven hundred of them died. The impact was immense, as hundreds of families were left bereft of their primary breadwinners, hundreds of wives were left widows, and hundreds of children were left fatherless. Nothing of this magnitude had happened to Southampton since the French sacked the town in the early stages of the Hundred Years War in 1338, and nothing was to have such a major impact again until the German bombing raids of 1940. At a single school, Northam Council School, 125 children suffered the loss of a parent or other close relative.[5] The nature of *Titanic*'s relationship with Southampton means that there the story is not the romanticized tale featured in Hollywood films or even the heroic myth that prevailed in Britain immediately following the sinking. In Southampton, 'women and children first' had a less noble ring to the local citizenry, because that order condemned their husbands, fathers, sons and brothers to an icy death. There, perhaps more than anywhere else in the world, the sinking of *Titanic* was a very real and immediate tragedy. In Southampton, there was no myth of *Titanic*, only cold reality, and this continues to shape the city's relationship with the disaster to this day.

On 9 June 1815, nine days before the defeat of Napoleon at Waterloo, the yacht *Thames* travelled up the Solent into Portsmouth. Its arrival was scarcely noticed, but the little ship was a harbinger of a revolution that was to change the face of the Solent ports, and Southampton in particular. For the *Thames* was a steamship, and it was steam power – on both the land and the sea – that would transform Southampton into the most important commercial port in the British Empire. At the time, however, the impact of the *Thames*'s arrival would have been impossible to predict. In the early nineteenth century, Southampton was notable primarily as a spa town, and would remain so for another twenty years. To be sure, there had been docks in the town since at least the middle ages, and trade had gone on with London, the Continent and the Channel Islands, but its development as a port was limited by the long haul for sailing vessels up the English Channel and Southampton Water.

   Steam was required to make that extended voyage practicable. Initially, it was the entrepreneurs of Cowes on the Isle of Wight who saw Southampton's potential on the packet service linking the island with the mainland. In 1820 the small paddle-steamer *Prince of Coburg* began making the crossing three times a day, irrespective of the state of wind and tide, a considerable improvement on the service offered by sailing ships. The public, however, was nervous about the possibility that the new propulsion system might explode, and the service's operators were forced to issue a statement explaining that 'this steam vessel is fitted with the lower-pressure engine and safety valve as enacted by Act of Parliament, and that from such fitting and construction the danger that existed in steam vessels without this improvement and security is entirely removed'.[6] The *Prince of Coburg* was joined by two more steam packets on the Isle of Wight run in 1821, and two years later paddle-steamers began making journeys to the Channel Islands and across the

Channel to Le Havre. By the early 1830s, competition amongst the
various steamship companies operating from Southampton was fierce.
Occasionally, these rivalries would spill over into brawls as touts employed by the companies attempted to persuade passengers to use their
services.

Despite promises of greater reliability than sailing vessels could provide, the early steamers were extremely fragile and suffered from
frequent breakdowns. In addition, they were unable to cross in heavy
winter weather, a weakness much exploited by the operators of sailing
ships. But the advantages of steam were rapidly becoming apparent. In
1827 2000 passengers entered or left Southampton by steamship every
week during the summer months; by 1830 that number had increased
to an annual total of over 100,000.[7] The town quay, however, had not
been expanded to accommodate this massive increase in traffic, and
passengers had to clamber through barrows, ropes and piles of merc-
handise – and past rowdy sailors – to get on and off the steamers. A
new pier was completed in 1831, the first in a series of improvements
to Southampton's docks.

The success of steam navigation on the Solent was certainly impressive,
but Southampton's future as a port would not be secure without a better
land connection to London. In February 1831 the Southampton and
London Railway and Dock Company was formed. The name reflected
the reality that the profitability of the railway would depend upon the
traffic generated by the docks, and that traffic in turn depended on the
existence of a rapid connection with the capital.[8] The portions of the
line from Nine Elms to Basingstoke and from Winchester to Southampton opened in 1839; until the link between Basingstoke and Winchester
was completed the following year a stage-coach was carried on a truck
to allow passengers and cargo to complete the middle section of the
journey.

Once the railway was finished further expansion of the docks could
take place. In 1835 a group of investors from London formed the
Southampton Docks Company. Initially, the company faced opposition
from those who felt that the development of the docks should be
undertaken by the harbour commission and the corporation rather than
by outsiders, and its application to purchase part of the mudflats on
the banks of the River Itchen was refused. But in January 1837 the

company was permitted to purchase 216 acres for £5000, and they opened their first dock five years later. Its development did not quite proceed as anticipated. The docks company hoped to transform South-ampton into a port from which a wide variety of goods would come into and go out of Britain. The geographical situation of the port, however, meant that its future lay in steamships, and steamships in the mid nineteenth century were only profitable when they were used to carry passengers or high-value cargo such as specie and government-subsidized mail. Recognizing this, the company quickly reoriented its marketing campaign, and it was rewarded in 1843 when the government chose Southampton to replace Falmouth as its principal packet station. The departure of emigrants from Southampton to North America began the following year, when the port was chosen as the emigrant station for Canada; soon, ships were carrying emigrants to South Africa and Australia as well. Still, the growth of trade failed to meet the expectations of the docks company's investors. In 1856 Southampton ranked only fifth in the country in terms of tonnage imported and exported.[9]

The company continued to put money into the docks, but lacked sufficient capital to keep up with the expansion necessitated by the increasing size of steamships. By the 1870s, the docks were in danger of obsolescence, and there were rumours that several of the bigger lines, including P & O and Union Castle, might pull out of Southampton. Southampton's location and natural advantages made it a desirable terminus for the transatlantic trade, but the lack of suitable facilities was endangering its future. In 1890, however, Southampton's fortunes were revived when the London and South-Western Railway agreed to provide a loan of £250,000 to finance the construction of the huge new Empress Dock. Two years later, the railway purchased the Southampton Dock Company outright for £1,360,000, an event that led to the city's meteoric rise as Britain's main passenger centre. The railway's chairman proclaimed his intention to transform Southampton into the 'Liverpool of the South', a promise that would be fulfilled in 1912 when South-ampton became Britain's main passenger port.[10] The railway's capital permitted expansion projects that would have crippled the previous owners. By 1895 the London and South-Western had already spent more than £2,200,000, and passenger traffic through the port had increased by 71 per cent. This massive expansion continued as the railway invested an average of £350,000 a year in the docks, over a quarter of all dock investment in England and Wales. In 1905, a huge tidal dock and drydock was opened that could accommodate the very largest passenger vessels; it is a measure of the rapid increase in the size of ships in this period that only six years after the new drydock was complete it could barely hold the world's largest ship, the German liner *Imperator*.

Over the next decade one North Atlantic line after another moved its operations to Southampton.[11] In 1907 the White Star Line transferred its North Atlantic Express Service from Liverpool, opening offices in Canute Road.[12] On 30 May of that year, White Star's *Adriatic*, the largest ship in the world, created great excitement when it arrived in the port. The main street was illuminated and bells were rung; the *Southampton Echo*'s correspondent noted that 'the vast importance of the move South of the White Star cannot yet be estimated at its true proportions'.[13] Within five years, Southampton had overtaken Liverpool as Britain's busiest passenger port.

In order to comprehend the significance of Southampton's status as a port in the early twentieth century, it is necessary to trace the evolution of the passenger shipping trade, particularly on the North Atlantic, always the busiest route. The sea lanes connecting Europe and North America carry more people and goods than all the other oceans of the world combined.[14] This does not mean, however, that the North Atlantic has been tamed, for, if it is the most heavily travelled ocean in the world, it is also the most dangerous. In summer and autumn, there are hurricanes. In winter, there are near-constant storms. In spring, there are icebergs. And, all year round, there is fog. Until relatively recently, the hazards of North Atlantic travel were still very real: in the early nineteenth century, one in six ships failed to reach its destination. In her guide *Ocean Notes for Ladies* (1877), the American author Katie Ledoux advised female passengers always to dress properly, because a body washed ashore wearing good clothes would be treated with greater respect than one wearing rags.[15]

For most of human history, however, the only way to get across the North Atlantic has been by boat, and thus human beings have been forced to brave its dangers. The Vikings were the first to make the crossing: four centuries before Columbus they reached Newfoundland, navigating with a remarkably accurate sun compass. It was not until the nineteenth century, however, that regular passenger service began, as a growing number of European emigrants sought passage to the New World. At first, the service was dominated by American sailing vessels, which originated the term 'liner' to describe a ship that left port on a specific date and made directly for its destination, rather than waiting an indefinite period for its holds to fill with passengers and cargo. Sailing ships, however, were extremely vulnerable to the vicissitudes of wind and weather, and considerable deviations from scheduled arrival times were common. Not until steam power was employed on ocean-going vessels did the passenger liner truly come into being.

The first ship to cross the Atlantic using steam was the American vessel *Savannah* in 1819. Along the way, the *Savannah* turned down repeated offers to help put out the fire that was causing smoke to pour from amidships, and the ship confounded Her Majesty's Revenue Cutter *Kite* when it sped away despite having its sails furled. The *Savannah*, however, used its steam engines only as an auxiliary power source. It was not until 1833 that a ship, the Canadian vessel *Royal William*, crossed the Atlantic using steam primarily. There were still difficulties: the salt from the seawater used to fill the ship's boilers clogged the engines, and the *Royal William* had to be stopped for several hours every day so that it could be scraped off. Samuel Hall solved this problem with his invention of the marine condenser the following year, and in 1838 the British vessel *Sirius* became the first ship to cross the Atlantic under continuous steam power.

All of these developments were closely observed by a young Canadian entrepreneur named Samuel Cunard, who was part-owner of the *Royal William* and the operator of a small fleet of sailing vessels. Cunard was convinced that steam was the way forward, and the British government concurred. Recognizing that they could never overcome the superiority of the transatlantic sailing service offered by the Americans, the British government decided to try steam. In 1838 the government invited offers to carry mail between Liverpool and North America by steamship. Cunard quickly seized the opportunity: he proposed a fleet of three steamers to carry mail to America and back twice monthly. For this service he demanded £55,000 a month.

Cunard got the contract; now all that remained was to build the ships.

He commissioned John Napier's yard on the Clyde in Glasgow to build
three paddle-steamers of around 1150 tons each and capable of a steady
nine knots. Cunard told Napier that he wanted 'plain and comfortable
boats' with 'not the least unnecessary expense for show'.[16] The first ship,
the *Britannia*, sailed for Boston on 4 July 1840, making the journey in
fourteen days. (In a sailing ship the westward passage took anywhere
from twenty-two to thirty-eight days, though the eastward journey could
be as short as seventeen due to the prevailing winds.) Upon arrival, the
passengers presented the captain with a silver cup that can be seen today
in the dining room of Cunard's flagship, the *Queen Elizabeth 2*. The
Cunard Line enjoyed immediate success, establishing a solid reputation
for reliability and safety. To this day, Cunard has never lost a passenger
by shipwreck in peacetime.[17] 'Speed is nothing', Cunard instructed his
masters. 'Follow your own road, deliver her safe, bring her back safe –
safety is all that is required.'[18]

Cunard's passengers, however, might not have agreed with the notion
that safety was all that mattered. Charles Dickens crossed on the *Britannia* in 1842 and was appalled by the standard of accommodation.
The decks were impassable, piled high with luggage and provisions. A
cow penned amidships bellowed constantly, and fresh vegetables were
stored beneath overturned lifeboats. A series of winter gales kept the
passengers confined below as the ship pitched and rolled. The violently
ill Dickens remained in his cabin – which he described as 'an utterly
impractical, thoroughly hopeless and profoundly preposterous box' –
until the waves at last died down. Venturing up on deck, he found that
a lifeboat had been battered to matchwood in its davits and that part
of the starboard paddle box had been carried away. He spent the
remainder of the voyage playing whist with the ship's doctor, collecting
his tricks in his pocket so that they would not be thrown onto the floor
by the movement of the ship. Even if he had felt like eating, the food
was scarcely enticing. The 'dining saloon' was 'a hearse with windows',
and meals consisted of 'more potatoes and meat' followed by a 'rather
mouldy dessert'. The crossing ended with the *Britannia* temporarily
aground outside Halifax harbour.[19] When he returned to Britain,
Dickens went by sailing packet.

Dickens may have been exaggerating, but only slightly. Cunard's
passengers certainly had to endure cramped conditions. The ships were

so small that stewards were customarily summoned by shouting, to which the standard reply was, 'What cabin number, sir?' Cabins were tiny, and the cheapest tickets provided merely a rudimentary berth in the saloon, where the benches that lined the walls were converted to bunks at night. The steam engines and paddle-wheels took up all of the space amidships, and so passenger accommodation had be located fore and aft, where passengers suffered the worst of the ship's movement. There was no hot water or proper plumbing. Nor were Cunard ships noted for the quality of the food they provided. After being prepared in the galley, meals were carried across the open deck to the saloon, which meant that they usually arrived cold and soggy with seawater. A staple was sea-pie, a mysterious concoction of salted fish topped by mashed potatoes.

One entrepreneur thought that he could do better. In 1850 Edward Knight Collins, the owner of one of the biggest American sailing packet lines, proposed a steamship service that would challenge Cunard in the two areas where his service was weakest: speed and comfort. In return, he asked for a subsidy from the American government in the form of a lucrative contract to carry mail, which was readily granted – Congressman Thomas Bayard from Delaware declared to the House of Representatives that the American shipping lines should 'proceed with the absolute conquest of this man Cunard'.[20] Collins's ships – the *Atlantic*, *Pacific*, *Arctic* and *Baltic* – were faster, larger and more comfortable than Cunard's, with palatial interiors based on those of American riverboats. At 2800 tons each, they could devote greater space to passenger cabins, and they provided additional amenities such as steam heating and improved ventilation. Some of their apparent luxuries were, however, deceptive. When passengers boarded the ships, they were greeted by rich carpets and brocade fabrics, but once the ships left port such finery was packed away and replaced by coconut matting and canvas, which were better able to withstand salt water and seasickness.

Initially, the Collins Line's strategy seemed to be working: after twenty-eight voyages his ships had carried over 4300 passengers and Cunard's fewer than 3000. But Collins had lost $1,700,000, even with the government subsidy of almost $900,000. And in the end, Cunard's commitment to safety won out. In his effort to win the battle for speed, Collins urged his captains to steam full-speed ahead at all times. In 1854 the *Arctic* was steaming through fog off Cape Race when it was rammed by a small French ship and quickly sank. Three-quarters of the ship's 365 passengers and crew died, including Collins's wife and two children. Two years later, when the *Pacific* disappeared without a trace, the public's confidence in the Collins Line evaporated. Collins lost his subsidy, and shortly thereafter what was left of his fleet had to be sold to pay his creditors. In its brief history, however, the Collins Line dramatically affected the future of the transatlantic passenger trade in two ways. First, it had become clear that iron rather than wooden hulls could better withstand the pounding and hazards of the North Atlantic. Secondly, Collins had created the notion that passenger liners were not only a means of transport but floating luxury hotels. Cunard could never again afford to be complacent about the standard of accommodation on board its vessels.

The failure of the Collins Line was soon followed by the outbreak of the Civil War in the United States, and the Americans lost interest for the time being in the competition for the North Atlantic passenger trade. This did not mean, however, that the field was left entirely to Cunard. The number of emigrants seeking passage from Europe to North America was growing with each passing year, and new steamship lines eager to carry them were springing up in a number of countries. The six years from 1856 to 1862 saw the establishment of three new companies on the European continent: Germany's Hamburg-Amerika and Norddeutscher Lloyd Lines and France's Compagnie Générale Transatlantique. Cunard also faced increasing competition from other British lines, including, from the early 1870s, the White Star Line.

In 1867 a thirty-one-year-old entrepreneur named Thomas Henry Ismay had paid £1000 for the name, flag and reputation, such as it was, of the bankrupt White Star Line, a sailing service that had plied the route from Britain to Australia. Ismay had his eye on the potentially more lucrative North Atlantic trade, but he needed financial backing so that he could build the requisite steamships. His friend Gustav Schwabe offered to loan him the necessary funds, as long as Ismay would order his new ships from the Belfast shipbuilding firm of Harland & Wolff, where Schwabe's nephew Gustav Wolff was a partner. Ismay readily agreed, and in 1869 signed a contract for Harland & Wolff to build three steamships of around 4000 tons each. Launched the following year, the first of these vessels, the *Oceanic*, is often regarded as the first modern ocean liner. The first-class cabins and dining saloon were amidships instead of fore and aft. Skylights and deckhouses were joined together, with the roofed-over perimeter serving as the first Promenade Deck. Wooden bulkheads were replaced with iron railings, allowing the swifter drainage of decks in rough weather. The cabins were much larger than on any previous ship, with running water and electric bells for summoning stewards. The dining room featured individual chairs rather than the customary benches. Gentlemen were provided with a room to which they could retire after dinner and smoke, while ladies could pass the time in a carpeted lounge complete with piano.

The *Oceanic* and White Star's other new ships were justifiably lauded. Sir Bertram Hayes, later captain of *Titanic*'s sister ship *Olympic*, said of Thomas Ismay that 'he was the most far seeing man of steamers, and I am not sure that the travelling public have ever realised the debt they owe to his foresight. He was the pioneer in including most of the comforts, not to say luxuries, which they now take as a matter of course'.[21] Soon White Star was attracting some of the world's wealthiest and most prestigious passengers. Two of the richest men in the world, the American plutocrats William Henry Vanderbilt and J. P. Morgan, nearly came to blows over a cabin on White Star's *Britannic*. After the incident, Morgan reserved cabins on several ships on several dates for years in advance, so that he could be assured of getting the one he wanted.[22]

By the end of the nineteenth century, there were around a half-dozen major competitors for the North Atlantic passenger trade. Each vessel built by one company was in essence a response to a vessel built by another, as they sought to trump their rivals in three areas: size, comfort and speed. Ships got bigger, faster and more luxurious with each passing year. By the late 1880s the top-of-the-line ships were around 10,000 tons and were capable of twenty knots; within five years size had increased by a third and speed by two knots. Technological improvements followed rapidly one after another: screws replaced paddle-wheels, and masts and sails finally disappeared for good. And always lurking in the background, though sometimes in opposition to the other areas, was the issue of safety. As the hazards of transatlantic travel diminished, however, it came increasingly to be taken for granted. In the forty years

prior to the sinking of the *Titanic*, not a single passenger life was lost
on the North Atlantic. Ships were now powerful and fast enough to sail
through even severe gales quickly, and storms were transformed from
life-threatening terrors to highlights of the passage; passengers were now
disappointed if they did not get to pass through at least one on their
crossing.

In the twenty-year period between 1890 and 1910, three dynamics
shaped the transatlantic passenger shipping trade. First, a fierce competition arose between the British and the Germans, mirroring the
economic, political and military rivalry that would ultimately be a major
factor in the outbreak of the First World War. Secondly, other British
companies, in particular White Star, continued to challenge Cunard's
dominance. And thirdly, the Americans re-entered the field. In 1893, the
formerly British Inman Line changed the registry of its ships to the
United States and became part of the American Line. This was significant, for only Cunard shipped more passengers on an annual basis. That
same year, however, there was an event that was to have an even greater
long-term impact on the future of the transatlantic trade. On a transatlantic crossing, a fellow passenger asked J. P. Morgan whether it was
possible to bring together the North Atlantic shipping lines into a single
consortium so that they could focus on making greater profits rather
than cutting each other's throats. After a pause, Morgan grunted, 'Ought
to be'.[23] A decade later, when Morgan had completed his efforts to
monopolize the railroad and steel industries, this conversation would
bear fruit; it would also lead directly to the construction of the *Titanic*.

In 1889 the new German Emperor, Wilhelm II, was invited by his uncle
Edward, Prince of Wales, to see a naval review at Spithead. Wilhelm
was impressed by the torpedo boats and dreadnoughts, but he was most
struck by Her Majesty's Armed Cruiser *Teutonic*, which was in reality
a new White Star liner with armour plating and a few small guns added
for the occasion, the idea being that in wartime the ship would double
as a merchant cruiser. Wilhelm spent almost two hours looking around
at the *Teutonic*'s fine woodwork, leather armchairs and electric lights,
and as he disembarked he said, 'We must have some of these'.[24]

It was a promise that he kept. Prior to 1890, the German Hamburg-
Amerika and Norddeutscher Lloyd Lines had focused on the emigrant

trade and had not competed with Cunard and White Star for first-class passengers. Their ships were fast enough, but not the fastest, and they were scattered over a variety of routes worldwide rather than being concentrated on the North Atlantic. After Wilhelm's tour of the *Teutonic*, however, all this changed and changed rapidly. The German Fleet Law of 1897 stated that German trade had to be protected by a naval fleet of sufficient strength that even the most powerful adversary – which could only mean Britain – would think its supremacy uncertain. This meant that not only a strong battle fleet was needed but a strong merchant marine as well. Suddenly Germany, which had previously built most of its ships in Britain, began building its own vessels. And what vessels they were! The 14,350-ton *Kaiser Wilhelm der Grosse* was launched in 1897 with a top speed of 22½ knots; it had been built by the Vulkan yard at Stettin on the understanding that if it failed to break the speed record Norddeutscher Lloyd would not pay for it. There was no danger of such a failure: the *Kaiser Wilhelm* easily took the Blue Riband from Cunard's aging *Lucania*, and no British ship held the record for the next ten years.[25] Instead, ships such as Norddeutscher Lloyd's *Kaiser Wilhelm II*, *Kronprinz Wilhelm* and *Kronprinzessin Cecilie* and Hamburg-Amerika's *Deutschland* dominated the field. Their overtly patriotic names indicate that more was at stake than mere profits; this was a battle for national pride, and for the moment the Germans were winning. In the late 1890s Norddeutscher Lloyd had almost a quarter of the North Atlantic passenger trade and sold more first-class tickets than Cunard. By 1903 the German lines were the proud possessors of the four fastest ships in the world.

The British competed as best they could. In 1899 White Star launched its second *Oceanic*, the largest vessel in the world and the most luxurious. White Star did not, however, attempt to challenge the speed of the German liners. They could have built a ship that could steam at 25 knots, they insouciantly – and almost certainly fallaciously – declared, but their passengers preferred a seven-day to a five-day voyage. This was a philosophy that White Star was to maintain over the next decade, culminating in the building of the *Olympic* and *Titanic*. They would not compete for speed; the last White Star liner to hold the Blue Riband was the *Teutonic* in 1891. Instead, White Star would make its mark in size and in luxury, which they felt were more important to its passengers.

Building bigger and more luxurious ships was expensive, and White Star did not have the capital to compete with its German rivals. An infusion of cash was desperately needed, and it came from across the Atlantic. In 1902 J. P. Morgan formed International Mercantile Marine, a consortium with which he intended to take over the North Atlantic shipping trade, currently suffering grievously from a ruinous rate war that had brought the price of a one-way steerage ticket down to less than £8. IMM quickly snapped up the Red Star, Atlantic Transport, National, Shaw Savill and Albion, Dominion and Leyland Lines. Morgan then went after a bigger fish: White Star. At first, his efforts were resisted by Thomas Ismay's son Bruce, who had taken over the firm in 1892. Ismay described Morgan's scheme as 'a swindle and a humbug'.[26] A majority of White Star's stockholders felt, however, that only the massive financial backing that Morgan could provide would enable the line to remain competitive. Ismay reluctantly submitted, and White Star was sold to IMM in 1902 for £10,000,000. Two years later, Ismay became the consortium's president and managing director, with full control over all operations.

Already carrying a third of all passengers, IMM was now in a position to dominate the transatlantic passenger trade as thoroughly as Morgan's US Steel corporation dominated the steel industry. Flexing its muscles, it reached an agreement to stagger sailing dates with Hamburg-Amerika and Norddeutscher Lloyd, ensuring that its ships would face no direct competition from the German lines.[27] Suddenly, Cunard found itself in the unenviable position of being the only significant rival to the American behemoth.[28] After purchasing White Star, Morgan had approached Cunard and offered 80 per cent above the market value of its shares. Cunard rejected the deal, but let it be known that a higher offer might be received favourably. They knew that the British government was extremely nervous about having its two major shipping lines pass into American control.[29] An empire with no means of moving its troops around the globe would be extremely vulnerable. Cunard also knew that it could not possibly compete with either the German lines or IMM without a major subsidy from the British government. The government had a choice: subsidize Cunard, or watch the largest British transatlantic shipping line follow the second largest into American hands.

In the end, the British government chose the lesser, but more expensive, evil: Cunard received a loan of £2,600,000 to build two new ships that would beat anything the Germans or IMM could put in the water for size and speed, and it would get an additional subsidy of £150,000 a year. In return, Cunard agreed not to sell out to the Americans or anyone else for the next twenty years. Additionally, the ships would be designed to the Royal Navy's specifications, with double hulls, watertight compartments, stronger decks to allow the installation of guns, and coal bunkers positioned to protect the engines from enemy fire. Launched in 1907, the two new Cunarders, the *Lusitania* and the *Mauretania*, were, at almost 32,000 tons each, 50 per cent larger than any ship yet built and eighty feet longer. Their revolutionary steam turbine engines, the first ever fitted on large passenger liners, were designed to produce 24½ knots but in practice well exceeded that, making them easily the fastest ships in the world.[30]

The *Lusitania* and *Mauretania* were not, however, the most luxurious ships afloat, for the British government's interest in the ships required an economy of frills. Their public rooms and staterooms were extremely handsome, to be sure, but the desired effect was one of refinement, rather than the riotous luxury that the German liners preferred. Moreover, with the narrow beams that speed demanded, the *Lusitania* and *Mauretania* were not the most comfortable ships in which to sail. They became famous for the dive and swoop of their pitch; steaming hard into a rough sea they were known to lift their bows sixty feet in the air and then dip and bury them. Entries such as 'labouring, pitching, lurching, spraying all over' were commonplace in their logs. During his crossing on the *Mauretania*, the future American President Franklin Delano Roosevelt did not enjoy the excessive movement, although he did allow that if ever a ship had a soul, this one did.[31]

Recognizing the futility of continuing the competition for speed, Cunard's competitors conceded the race for the Blue Riband; it would be more than two decades before a rival took the record from the *Mauretania*, which proved the slightly faster of the two sisters. Instead, they opted to build slower but larger and more luxurious ships, with White Star's entry into the field three new ships – the *Olympic*, the *Titanic* and a yet-unnamed sister – so large that no berth in the world could accommodate them. This posed a challenge for Southampton, where yet another expansion of the docks was now clearly required. The new White Star Dock, which was still incomplete at the time of the

Olympic's maiden voyage in June 1911, cost slightly under £500,000, covering sixteen acres and providing 3840 feet of quay.

The vast new liners also needed deeper channels in Southampton Water. White Star's Southampton manager Philip Curry wrote to the harbour commission in December 1908 to warn them that ships would draw around thirty-five feet of water. 'The steamers may be expected to take their places in the service in the spring of 1912', he declared, 'and we confidently hope to receive an assurance from your Board that whatever dredging may be necessary to enable them to sail promptly, and to land their passengers without detention will be undertaken and completed before they are delivered.' [32] The harbour commission, however, was not anxious to spend a further £100,000 pounds on dredging work, and they asked White Star to foot the bill. White Star's director, Harold Sanderson, was astonished:

> I really think that is a question which surprises me very much indeed, that we should be asked to provide improvements at the ports the ships will frequent. I really think that such a novel proposal would not have been made by any other port in Great Britain ... In bringing two ships' trade to Southampton we feel we are doing all that might be asked ... Years before we came to Southampton it was the boast of Southampton that ships could arrive and sail without having to wait for water, as in other ports. If you, gentlemen, come to the conclusion that this boast is one which you do not agree to maintain, the value of our argument vanishes.

Sanderson concluded with a threat to move White Star's transatlantic operations to Plymouth if the harbour commission refused to carry out the dredging, and pointed out that White Star was not the only line to be in the process of building such large ships: 'I do not think it is fair that we should be looked harshly at for being the first people to bring large ships to Southampton. We were not the first to produce large ships, and we shall be followed in a short time by others'.[33] Ultimately, the London and South-Western Railway intervened and paid for the necessary dredging, but the episode reveals Southampton's growing frustration with the rapid expansion in the size of passenger liners.

The White Star Dock, later renamed the Ocean Dock, became the symbol of Southampton's supremacy in the transatlantic passenger trade. In the period prior to the Second World War all of the world's great passenger liners – the *Aquitania*, the *Queen Mary*, the *Queen*

Elizabeth, the *Normandie* – could be seen berthed there. Its most famous tenant, however, remained the ship that only docked there on a single occasion in April 1912.

The *Titanic* arrived in Southampton after its overnight journey from Belfast at midday on 4 April 1912. After some initial confusion following the replacement of the *Titanic*'s original Chief Officer, William Murdoch, by Henry Wilde at the request of Captain Smith, the officers settled into their usual routine.[34] When not on watch, they were accustomed to being permitted to go ashore, but there was so much to do on board the *Titanic* that trips into town were infrequent. The *Titanic* had arrived not quite ready for its maiden voyage: staterooms and public rooms still lacked carpets, paint and furniture; mattresses and bedding had to be distributed and mirrors and draperies put into place.

The situation was further complicated by a massive national coal strike that had been going on since January. Although the strike was finally settled on 6 April, it was not possible to get newly-mined coal to Southampton in time for the *Titanic*'s departure. The *Titanic*'s coal therefore had to be cannibalized from the other IMM liners in the port. This made the coaler's job much dirtier and even more difficult than it ordinarily was, for every spare pound of coal had to be removed from the holds of the other ships and transferred to the *Titanic*. With little else going in and out of the port due to the lingering effects of the strike, however, the coaling firm of R. & J. H. Rea was happy to have the work.

Equally pleased were the numerous Southampton firms involved in provisioning the *Titanic*. Miller's Naval Tailors were in charge of providing uniforms for the crew. Due to the unusually large number, they had to perform the job in a hurry, and one exhausted tailor told a crewman when he came to pick up his uniform, 'I hope I shall never see this again'.[35] Sadly, many of the bills for these uniforms were not issued until long after their purchasers had ceased to require them. The *Titanic* exhibition in the Southampton Maritime Museum displays a bill for £4 4s. from Miller's dated June 1912 for the uniform of Steward Sidney Sedunary, who did not survive.

The *Titanic*'s 57,000 pieces of crockery and 29,000 pieces of glassware were supplied by Stonier and Company, which was based in Liverpool

but had a store at Southampton docks. The ship's 15,000 bottles of beer
came from Charles George Hibbert and Company, which issued special
posters declaring that they provided 'bottled beer for the White Star
liner *Titanic*, the largest vessel in the world'. Decorative plants, some
three to four hundred of them, were supplied by F. G. Bealing and Son;
eleven-year-old Eileen Lenox Conyingham later remembered the *Titanic*
as a 'ship full of flowers'. Paper goods came from W. H. Smith, and
tablecloths from Edwin Jones (now Debenham's). Most of the food was
provided by Grey and Company: the *Titanic* required 75,000 pounds of
meat, 40,000 eggs, 40 tons of potatoes, 7000 heads of lettuce, 10,000
pounds of sugar, 36,000 oranges, 1500 gallons of milk and 6000 pounds
of butter.[36]

Alongside the provisioning of the *Titanic* came the recruitment of the
ship's crew. Only the senior officers had accompanied the ship from
Belfast; the remainder of the crew was recruited locally. In 1912 passenger
liners did not have permanent crews. Instead, they were hired for one
voyage at a time and paid off when it was complete. They therefore
could not depend on steady employment, though they might remain
with the same ship year after year if they performed good work and the
signing-on officer knew them. Waiters and stewards in particular could
become favourites of passengers, who would alter their bookings in
order to be on their ships. Most of the time, though, crew members
served on a variety of ships and with a number of different lines.

Despite the steady growth of the passenger shipping trade in Southampton, there always seemed to be more men seeking places on the big
liners than there were jobs. The city's population had expanded rapidly,
from 25,000 in 1836 to 120,000 in 1912, as a steady flow of people arrived
looking for employment, which they did not always find. The situation
in the winter of 1903–4 was particularly grim, as the *Southampton Times*
reported:

> In almost every street numbers of working men were aimlessly about idle.
> Men went out in the early morning to look for work, pulling their belts tighter
> to make up for their lack of breakfast, while their children went to school
> cold and with their hunger only partly satisfied and their weary eyed wives
> perhaps pawned something more in order to find some sort of an apology
> for dinner in the family. Large numbers of men wandered about near the
> docks and haunted Canute Road like ghosts, those nearest the dock gates

hoping to be among the fortunate ones when workers were called for; all with a hungry look in their eyes that turned to one of hopeless misery if the work was supplied without them, and they were condemned to go home as they came out, with empty pockets as well as stomachs.[37]

The situation had improved somewhat by 1912, thanks in part to the formation of a number of trade unions, including the National Sailors' and Firemens' Union of Great Britain and Ireland, the National Union of Ships' Stewards, Cooks, Butchers and Bakers, the British Seafarers' Union, the National Union of Stewards and the Dock Wharf and Riverside Workers Union. The previous year, a labour dispute had arisen when porters had received orders to begin coaling the *Olympic* at 6 a.m., but then had to wait until 11 before they could begin. They were refused 'standing by' money and went on strike. The *Olympic*'s firemen, seamen and stewards also struck, citing the 'special difficulties' of working on such a large vessel. The port was at a standstill for several days until Southampton Corporation was able to arrange a settlement with the shipping companies. In June 1911, White Star and the other lines grudgingly agreed to recognize the unions.

In April 1912, however, Southampton's dockworkers and seamen were in no position to demand further concessions. The coal strike had made many ships idle, and idle ships meant idle men. More than 17,000 men were out of work, forcing many families to rely on municipal and private charity. The logbooks of Northam Girls School reveal the extent of the problem. On 14 March the headmistress Annie Hopkins recorded, 'twenty-two free meals given today. The distress is daily becoming more acute owing to stagnation caused by the coal strike'. Eight days later, she added, 'Distress is great amongst [the] children'. Northam was one of several suburbs that sprang up in the late nineteenth century to accommodate Southampton's growing population of people who worked on the large liners. In a city where the neighbourhood in which one lived reflected one's shipboard status, Northam ranked near the bottom of the hierarchy: its inhabitants were lowly firemen, greasers and trimmers. In the spring of 1912, Northam was emerging from a difficult winter, in which unusually cold weather and flooding in early March had forced many families to rely upon the charity of the parish. The coal strike added to the distress, both by putting breadwinners out of work down at the docks and by causing a shortage of fuel for home heating.[38]

The *Titanic*'s arrival in Southampton therefore came as a welcome relief at least for those men – and a few women – who would find employment either on its maiden voyage or in helping to prepare the ship for it. White Star had promised the ship would sail despite the strike, although its speed would be limited to twenty knots in order to conserve coal. This meant that, from the beginning, Southampton's relationship to the *Titanic* was thoroughly pragmatic rather than romantic: the ship was a source of jobs, not of celebration. When *Titanic* docked on 4 April, there was relatively little fanfare; the *Hampshire Independent* reported that 'quietly and unostentatiously without any blare of trumpets, the *Titanic*, the world's latest and biggest ship steamed up the silent waters of the Solent and docked at Southampton'. And as *Titanic* lay moored in its berth for a week, the local populace was fairly blasé. John Wright, who saw the ship from Southampton Common, recalled that 'the *Titanic* was just another ship to us at the time ... We thought not an awful lot about her until the terrible happening'.[39]

But if there were no cheering and flag-waving crowds as there had been when the ship had sailed from Belfast, there were thousands of local citizens eager to apply for positions as crew members in the tight labour market of April 1912. In signing-on for the *Titanic*, 699 of the 898 crew members gave Southampton as their current address, though some listed temporary lodgings in hotels and boarding houses.[40] Of these, the majority were not originally from Southampton and its environs; only about 40 per cent of the crew can be identified as Hampshire-born. The rest were from all over Britain and Ireland, with a substantial number from Lancashire who had followed White Star from Liverpool to Southampton in 1907.[41]

In making its selection from the large number of eager applicants, White Star looked for experience on large liners, and there was a clear preference shown towards men who had served on *Titanic*'s sister ship. 'It was practically a crew from the *Olympic*', recalled Chief Baker Charles Joughlin.[42] Only after they were among the lucky ones who were selected could the *Titanic*'s crew members appreciate the finer qualities of the ship. 'Like the *Olympic*, yes, but so much more elaborate', said Baker Reginald Burgess:

> Take the dining saloon – *Olympic* didn't even have a carpet, but the *Titanic* – ah, you sank up to your knees. Then there's the furniture. So heavy you

could hardly lift it. And that panelling ... They can make them bigger and faster but it was the care and effort that went into her. She was a beautiful wonderful ship.[43]

The families of the crew members, meanwhile, felt themselves fortunate that their husbands, brothers, sons and, in a few cases, daughters had been chosen.[44] The *Daily Graphic*, which sent a reporter from London to cover the *Titanic*'s departure, reported that 'all these Southampton women were proud that their men had entered into service on the greatest vessel ever built by man. They prattled of the *Titanic* with a sort of suggestion of proprietorship'.[45]

That pride, of course, rapidly changed to despair and grief when the news that the *Titanic* had sunk reached Southampton. The shock was made even more cruel by the fact that the first press accounts reported that all passengers and crew had been saved and that the ship was being towed to Halifax. Soon, however, more accurate reports confirmed that there had been a grievous loss of life. Stephen Townsend, a young boy at the time, recalled the pandemonium that prevailed in the city:

> There was no radio or television or anything like that, naturally. People were running round the street 'the *Titanic* sunk' panic, panic stations everywhere. Women running out and going down to the Shipping Office, you know, down near the dock gates there and the *Titanic*, they can't sink the *Titanic* because everybody talked about the *Titanic*, it was the unsinkable ship ... And even as young as I was it impressed me because there wasn't a family in the whole of the area that never had anybody associated with that ship. Fathers and sons on board, grandsons and all this sort of thing, to be on the great *Titanic*, you see. And well there were all shipping community, shipping and dock working community and, as I say, everybody down there, all of us. It was real panic, I can see it now, I can visualise them. The women running out, you know, in their aprons they were busy doing their household chores and forget everything and all run down to the Shipping Office.[46]

Soon, the initial shock turned to despair. The *Southern Daily Echo* reported that 'the pathetic scenes in Southampton ... after the dread news of the *Titanic*'s foundering had been confirmed would have moved the hardest heart to compassion'.[47] Virtually every major London paper sent a reporter to the port, and their stories were almost identical. The *Daily Chronicle* described the city as being in 'the depth of gloom' on

17 April and the next day asserted that 'the same cloud of grief covers all alike'.[48] Its reporter compared the scene in Southampton to 'the semi-darkness of the pit's mouth while the kindred of ghastly, distorted remains were seeking to recognize, yet fearing to know'.[49] The *Daily Mirror* stated that 'hopeless misery has cast its wing over the town' and that 'nothing approaching this appalling blow has ever fallen upon the port'.[50] Flags flew at half-mast all over the city, and numerous public functions were cancelled.

Specific information about who had survived and who had perished was frustratingly slow to trickle in. After the first notice of the disaster was posted outside of the White Star offices on Monday, hundreds of people gathered frantically seeking further details about the fate of their loved ones. The Salvation Army sent in special 'slum officers' to watch the children so that mothers could go down to White Star and try to get information regarding their husbands, fathers and brothers. The correspondent from the *War Cry*, the organization's newspaper, wrote:

> None but a heart of stone would be unmoved in the presence of such anguish. Night and day that crowd of pale, anxious faces had been waiting patiently for the news which did not come. Nearly every one in the crowd had lost a relative. Some of the poor little women in black, who were bearing their overwhelming sorrow with wonderful courage, notwithstanding their tears, stood with little children in their arms and toddlers at their skirts.[51]

Tuesday passed with no additional news other than the fact that five of the *Titanic's* officers had survived. Captain Smith's wife Eleanor, a Southampton resident, posted a message to her 'poor fellow sufferers' offering her sympathy: 'My heart overflows with grief for you all, and is laden with sorrow that you are weighed down with this terrible burden that has been thrust upon us'.[52] On Wednesday afternoon, a workman appeared and nailed a large blackboard to the railings outside the offices, in obvious preparation for posting the names of the survivors. The board, however, remained stubbornly blank, and every time a White Star clerk came outside, the crowd would plead for information. 'We haven't any', they were told. 'As soon as we hear anything it will be posted up.'[53] Other messages of sympathy appeared, including ones from King George and Queen Mary and from the Queen Mother, but they had little effect. The people of Southampton were not interested in public expressions of grief and grandiose commemorations; what they wanted was the news that their loved ones were safe.

By Thursday, tensions were nearing breaking point. 'Is there any hope? They must know something inside', a woman in the crowd pleaded with one of the policemen guarding the door. 'They know nothing yet', he told her. 'The moment they do the names will be posted.' An itinerant preacher attempted to offer religious consolation, but his efforts only further strained already frayed nerves, and the crowd's discontentment convinced him to desist. Finally, early on Friday morning, the first lists of survivors' names were received. A clerk came out of the office holding a long strip of paper, which he pinned to the black board. The crowd pressed forward, trying desperately to read the names. A few people burst forth with exclamations of gratitude when they saw their loved one's name, but for most the search was in vain. Of *Titanic*'s 898 crew members, only 212 survived.

Many parts of the city were utterly devastated. In the summer of 2001, I drove through Southampton with Brian Ticehurst, the President of the British *Titanic* Society, as he rattled off the list of victims from each street that we passed. Few were omitted, and on some streets as many as one in four houses suffered the loss of a family member. In the *Daily Mirror* on 18 April, the wife of a crew member on the *Olympic* described the situation in her neighborhood:

> Mrs May across the way lost her husband and oldest son ... The son was married a year ago and his wife had a baby six weeks ago. Mrs Allen around the corner lost her husband, George ... And the young girl there in black ... is Mrs Barnes. She lost her brother ... The woman going into the shop is Mrs Gosling. She lost a son ... And Mrs Preston of Princes Street, a widow, she lost her son too.[54]

The press featured a plethora of heartrending stories, including those of a family of seven children left fatherless and a house where five lodgers were among the missing.

Nowhere, however, was more devastated than the district of Northam, which provides a microcosm of the impact of the sinking of *Titanic* on Southampton. 'Old Northam, where I lived, was plunged into mourning', recalled one local resident. 'Nearly every house in Northam had lost a son or husband ... every blind was drawn.'⁵⁵ On 16 April, Annie Hopkins wrote in the logbook of Northam Girls' School, 'A great many girls are absent this afternoon owing to the sad news regarding the *Titanic*. Fathers and brothers are on the vessel and some of the little ones in the school have been in tears all afternoon'. Two days later, when many families' worst fears had been realized, she continued, 'I feel I must record the sad aspect in school today owing to the *Titanic* disaster. So many of the crew belonged to Northam. It is pathetic to witness the children's grief and in some cases faith and hope of better news'. The school did the best it could to help the pupils cope with the trauma. On 7 May, clothes were distributed to the victims' children, and on 23 May the Mayoress visited 'the orphans of the *Titanic*'.⁵⁶

Many of the bereaved had more to contend with than their grief, for the loss of income meant serious economic deprivation for families that had already been suffering for months from the effects of the coal strike. 'The distress in the stricken quarters of Southampton is incredible', reported the *Daily Mail*:

> During the coal strike many breadwinners were out of work, furniture was sold or pawned, and numerous families received notice to quit. Then came the *Titanic*, and firemen, greasers and trimmers, who had known no work for many weeks, eagerly joined the big ship to save their homes. Today hundreds of women are clamouring for food for themselves and milk for their babies.⁵⁷

Mayor George Bowyer declared that the corporation was caring for 600 families, with an average size of five members each. 'I wonder if your readers quite appreciate the position here', he told the *Daily Chronicle*. 'For more than a month most of these families ... had been kept alive by the mayor's fund raised in connection with the coal strike, and many of them have sold or pawned everything that could raise money. Now, even where husbands are safe, they have lost all their clothes and not infrequently the money they possessed.'⁵⁸ Bowyer immediately travelled to London to discuss the possibility of funds being diverted from the national relief effort to Southampton. Several trade unions and the Seaman's Friendly Society also set up relief depots in order to distribute food and other necessities. Some people wanted more than material aid; one woman threw the tickets entitling her to relief back in the face of the union representative who gave them to her: 'I want news of my son, I don't want tickets!' [59] Most people, however, were glad to get whatever they could. In St Mary's parish, there were sixty-one 'cases' that arose from the disaster, the majority of which involved the loss of young men who had been wholly or partially supporting their parents. Tom James recalled that his father, the new vicar of St Luke's church, had as one of his first tasks 'to visit the bereaved families, and in some cases to carry the news for the first time'.[60]

The tragedy that struck Southampton when the *Titanic* sank was thus of a very different type from that which the rest of the world experienced. Elsewhere, on both sides of the Atlantic, a '*Titanic* myth' very quickly took shape that sought to extract meaning from the disaster by emphasizing the heroic conduct of the first-class male passengers. Account after account depicted these elite men as chivalrously stepping aside so that women and children, including those travelling third class, could board the lifeboats first. The evidence to support this view was flimsy at best, but that was of little consequence, for it supported contemporary British conceptions of patriotism and of class and gender hierarchies.

To the bereaved families of Southampton, however, this mythic interpretation of the disaster offered little solace. What comfort could they derive from the notion that first-class men had saved third-class women and children, even if it had been true? This view not only ignored their loved ones but displaced and diminished them, for missing from it was any effort to commemorate the heroism of the crew. There was no way, therefore, for Southampton to participate in the kind of myth-making that quickly subsumed the real story of what had happened. In Southampton, the tragedy was, quite simply, a tragedy; there is no 'myth of the *Titanic*' there, but only the story of a very real, very painful and, for many residents, very personal disaster.

This helps to explain why Southampton is not eager to exploit the *Titanic*'s potential to attract tourism. On visiting the city, one might expect to find numerous attempts to capitalize on the tourist interest created by the discovery of the wreck in 1984 and the success of the 1997 James Cameron film. There is, however, very little. A flip through the relevant section of the Southampton phone directory reveals that there is not a single business – no pub, no restaurant, no souvenir shop – named after the *Titanic*.

This is despite the fact that Southampton offers few other obvious enticements to tourists. Physically, it is an odd and incongruous mix of new and old, often side by side. Portions of the old city wall snake through modern tower block developments; sagging, half-timbered Tudor buildings stand next to brand new shopping malls. On most residential streets, Victorian houses are interspersed with modern dwell-ings in haphazard fashion. There is a simple explanation for Southampton's chaotic appearance. During the Second World War, the Luftwaffe did its best to level the city, and it is still easy to pick out where the bombs fell by identifying the buildings constructed since 1945. Couple this with some poor decisions by city planners in the 1960s and 1970s to pull down many of the older neighbourhoods and replace them with modern blocks of flats, and the result is a place lacking obvious aesthetic charm.

The *Titanic* seems a surefire magnet to lure visitors who might not otherwise be interested in Southampton, but the city seems unwilling to take advantage of the association. To be sure, there is a display in the Maritime Museum, though it pales in comparison to the *Titanic* exhibitions found in other cities, Belfast and Liverpool in particular, with close connections to the disaster. Southampton City Council's web site features a '*Titanic* Trail' for visitors to walk and see various sites associated with the ship, including some of the numerous public memo-rials that are scattered around the city. But there is little else. In a world in which everything having to do with the *Titanic* is ruthlessly exploited for every penny of profit that can be squeezed out of it, this is surprising, perhaps even astonishing.

Certainly, there are some practical problems. The site that would be most attractive to *Titanic* tourists is Berth 4, the spot from which the ship departed on its maiden voyage. Berth 4, however, is still an im-portant part of the working docks and is all but inaccessible to the public, with entry to see the small memorial plaque strictly controlled by Associated British Ports. There are, however, plenty of other sites. Why not promote them? The obvious explanation is that the story of the *Titanic* in Southampton was not the romantic, heroic tale told in the British press and elsewhere, but a story of death and destitution that directly affected hundreds of local families. Given the intense devastation, both emotional and financial, that the sinking of the *Titanic* inflicted on Southampton, it is scarcely surprisingly that the city is not eager to turn the disaster into a theme park. Southampton's memories of the disaster are clearly not suitable material for a Disney-style animatronic ride.

It would be inaccurate to assume, however, that Southampton's reluctance to exploit its link to the *Titanic* stems entirely from the lingering impact of the disaster. As time has passed, demographic change has removed most of the immediate connection. Only a single *Titanic* survivor, Millvina Dean, still resides in the city. When the James Cameron film premiered in Southampton in early 1998, the British press predicted that it would meet with an 'icy welcome' because the story would be 'a little too close to home'. Instead, the film received the same enthusiastic reception as in other British cities and broke attendance records at several local cinemas. This was primarily because the young people who made up the film's primary audience felt little personal connection to the tragedy. A nine-year-old girl told an interviewer that she went to see it 'because Leonardo DiCaprio is in it and it's a really good film', an answer not substantially different from what one of her peers in New York or London might have given. If Southampton audiences acknowledged the link between the tragedy and the city at all, they merely remarked that it was 'cool' to be in the place from which the *Titanic* had departed.[61]

There is, however, another, more compelling reason why Southampton is uninterested in reminding itself of its role in the most famous maritime disaster in history. Commercial shipping has been the city's economic lifeblood for centuries. Why, of all the great ships that have come and gone from Southampton docks, should the city choose to remember the one with the least successful career? It might be appropriate for other places to wax romantic about what happened on the night of 14–15 April 1912, but Southampton prefers to get on with its business. In Sotonian eyes, the *Titanic* is hardly a good advertisement for the industry upon which it still depends. Why not focus on the *Olympic* instead, a ship that was equally as beautiful as its sister and far more successful as a passenger liner?

In a more general sense, Southampton's commercial focus means that it has not traditionally been inclined to focus on the past. This helps to explain why not only does the city downplay the *Titanic*, but also its role as Henry V's staging area for his army bound for France and as the true point of departure for the *Mayflower*. All these things seem ripe for the attraction of tourists, yet none of them are exploited. Lindsay Ford, Assistant Curator of the Southampton Maritime Museum, speculates that this attitude may be the product of the transience of the local population, who for centuries have tended to pass through without putting down roots, in keeping with the city's status as Britain's most important passenger port.[63] Moreover, unlike Portsmouth or Plymouth, Southampton has always viewed its orientation as a port city as private and mercantile rather than naval, which breeds a pragmatic attitude towards the sea rather than a romantic one. In Southampton, the sea is for making money, not history. T. P. Henry, a member of the Totton and Eling Historical Society, sees Southampton as a 'working city', a place that's more about 'ships and football' than about heritage. Southampton, Henry says, 'doesn't sell itself' on the basis of its history or culture, but rather on its status as a 'frontline port'.[64]

For some, this attitude can be frustrating. Nigel Wood, the curator of the city's West End Local History Museum, complains of a 'complacency' about Southampton's history, which he says is 'taken for granted'. The *Titanic*, in particular, is 'underexploited' by the local government, which has missed excellent opportunities to purchase prime sites for a museum devoted to the tragedy and to the golden age of passenger liners. The Ocean Terminal, where passengers waited to board the *Queen Elizabeth*, *Queen Mary* and other famous liners, was torn down in 1982; the White Star building on Canute Road was turned into offices; and the South Western Hotel, where J. Bruce Ismay and some of the *Titanic*'s wealthiest passengers stayed the night before the ship departed, has recently been converted into luxury flats. As proof of what *Titanic* could do for the city, Wood points to its impact even on his small museum, which generated considerable publicity from its dedication of a memorial to Captain Arthur Rostron of the *Carpathia* in 1999. 'We've got a lot of mileage on the back of *Titanic*', he says. 'You've got to exploit what you've got.'[65] Others, however, argue that Southampton's failure to take advantage of its connection to the *Titanic* is the product not of a lack of will but of wherewithal. Kevin White, Conservation Manager for Southampton City Council, told me that the council is exploring the possibility of building a *Titanic* museum, but that a lack of funding has to date kept plans from proceeding beyond the drawing board. 'We'd love to do more', he declares, 'but it's a question of funding and priorities.' He adds that the city budget suffered a £3,500,000 cut in 2000.[66]

For various reasons, then, the use of the *Titanic* for commercial tourism purposes is a problematic endeavour in Southampton, and the city's relationship with the *Titanic* is likely to remain an understated one. Even Southampton's public commemorations of the sinking are, in keeping with the nature of the tragedy that struck the city, intensely personal, emphasizing individuals rather than groups, unlike *Titanic* commemorations elsewhere in Britain. While the exhibitions in the Ulster Folk and Transport Museum and the Liverpool Maritime Museum focus on the ship, and refer only to a few of the most prominent passengers and highest-ranking ship's officers, the Southampton Maritime Museum devotes much of its display to Sidney Sedunary, a third-class steward. Sedunary became body 178 in the Halifax mortuary, and the items found in his pockets form part of the display. Included are his pocket-watch with the hands stopped at 1.50 a.m. Also found in the display is a telegram dated 19 April from White Star to Madge that simply states, 'Much regret Sedunary not saved'. Similarly, the West End Museum and Heritage Centre focuses its *Titanic* display on James Jukes, a greaser whose body was never found. In addition, numerous local churches features plaques and memorials to crew members from that parish, and the gravestones of *Titanic* victims and survivors have through the years been carefully tended by the British *Titanic* Society and other groups.

Even in those cases in which a local memorial is not devoted to a single person, there is still an effort to remember individual victims in Southampton. Dedicated in April 1913, the musician's memorial on the public library lists the names of all eight members of the *Titanic*'s band above the inscription 'They Died at Their Posts Like Men.'.[67] Unveiled the following year before a crowd of 10,000, the huge bronze and granite engineer's memorial in East Park includes eighteen names; its inscription, from John 15:13, reads 'Greater love hath no man than this, than

a man lay down his life for a friend'. These memorials serve as precursors
to the kinds of public memorials that would become all too common
in Britain during and immediately after the First World War, when the
listing of the names of the dead functioned as a way to recognize ordinary
people who had performed their duty in extraordinary circumstances.
Rather than heroic deeds, these types of memorials commemorated
those who 'stayed at their post' in the face of grave danger, much as
many members of the *Titanic*'s crew had done. They do not celebrate
'service beyond the call of duty, but rather ... faithful performance of
an allotted role'. These memorials are inherently democratic, for they
do not commemorate those who achieved special distinction and thereby
stood out from the masses. Instead naming the dead served as a recognition that they had 'all been equally valuable members of [the]
community, because they had performed their allotted tasks to the
extremity of death'. This style of commemoration began on war memorials in the mid nineteenth century, but it was not until the Great War
that all those who had fallen were listed together, alphabetically and
irrespective of rank. This concept of the 'equality of sacrifice' was crucial
to postwar commemorative efforts. It reached its peak of influence in
1920, when the Imperial War Graves Commission decreed that all British
war graves in military cemeteries abroad would be marked by a single,
unadorned cross. The idea, according to the commission, was to assert
that all were equally worthy of honour, 'great and lowly, peer and
peasant, rich and poor, learned and ignorant, raised to one supreme
level in death by common sacrifice for a common cause'.[68]

Southampton's memorial to the *Titanic*'s engineers thus represents
an early manifestation of the type of memorial that would appear in
many places in Britain during and after the First World War. This
suggests the extent of the impact of the tragedy upon Southampton, an
impact not unlike that of a major war, at least among certain social
and occupational groups. To gauge this impact further, contrast Southampton's memorial to the engineers to its counterpart in Liverpool, on
which none of the dead are named. This testifies to Liverpool's very
different relationship to the disaster, for it was merely White Star's
corporate home, and only a handful of people from the city died. Or
contrast Southampton's engineer's memorial to Belfast's, which includes
the names of the dead but lists them in order of rank rather than

alphabetically. This greater concern with hierarchy stems from the smaller number of victims from the city. Belfast lost twenty-two citizens to Southampton's seven hundred.

There is, however, one memorial in Southampton that does not list any names. On 27 July 1915 a Portland stone fountain commemorating all of the *Titanic*'s crew members was unveiled on Southampton Common. Paid for by public subscription, the fountain remained on the Common until 1972, when vandalism caused it to be moved to the ruins of Holyrood church, which had been destroyed by German bombs in the Second World War. In its current state and location, it functions as the most insular of all the city's *Titanic* memorials. The fountain offers little in the way of obvious aesthetic appeal. Exposed to the elements for almost sixty years, the bas-relief of the *Titanic* has almost entirely worn away, and the badly eroded inscription can barely be discerned:

> This memorial was erected in memory of the crew,
> stewards, sailors and firemen, who lost their lives in the
> SS *Titanic* disaster April 15th 1912.
> It was subscribed for by the widows, mothers and friends
> of the crew.

To the casual observer, this is merely a decrepit memorial in a ruined church. Knowledge of Southampton's history, however, allows the viewer to 'read' the memorial as a poignant statement about two devastating civic events: the sinking of the *Titanic* and the bombing by the Luftwaffe. Tourists familiar only with the romantic myth of *Titanic* or the James Cameron film would doubtless be unimpressed, but there could be no more appropriate commemoration of the city's two worst twentieth-century tragedies.

It will be interesting to see if Southampton's reluctance to turn tragedy into tourism persists. With computerization and the rise of container shipping, the docks employ far fewer people than they once did, creating a need for greater economic diversification. As we have seen, Belfast, which has a very different but equally intimate relationship with the *Titanic*, has begun to set aside its traditional reluctance to exploit the tragedy and make a big pitch for *Titanic* tourism. Will Southampton do the same? For now, the answer is no. Southampton is focusing on technology as the key to its future prosperity. In other words, as it has done for the last century, the city is getting on with its business. Looking forward, not back – that's the Southampton way.

11

Queenstown

Queenstown, or Cobh (pronounced 'Cove') as it was renamed in 1920, is located on the Great Island, the largest interior island of Ireland. Approximately seven miles long and three miles in breadth at its widest point, the island is about fifteen miles from Cork off Ireland's southwestern coast. Queenstown Harbour lies at the point where the River Lee meets the Atlantic Ocean; it is created by Spike Island, which provides a breakwater from the ocean, producing one of the finest natural harbours in the world.

Despite Queenstown's geographic advantages, it took some time for a substantial settlement to grow up there. Although the first human beings set foot on the Great Island as early as 5000 BC, it was not until the late eighteenth century that anything resembling a town began to develop. In the 1760s, as tensions with the American colonies mounted, the British Admiralty began expanding its naval operations in preparation for taking measures to subdue the unruly colonists. In 1765, an Admiralty House was constructed in the small village of Ballyvaloon, which occupied a strategic position overlooking the harbour; it followed shortly thereafter by a fort, which the Admiralty named Cove Fort. Shortly thereafter, the Admiralty changed the name of the village to Cove. After formal hostilities broke out with America in 1775, Cove played a major role as a staging area for naval convoys carrying troops, supplies and armaments, and the town prospered as a result.

After the Napoleonic Wars ended in 1815, the naval presence in Cove diminished sharply, along with the town's economy. The local landlord, Viscount Midleton, recognized that Cove would have to find an alternative source of wealth, and he began to develop the town as a health spa and resort. The humble cottages in which many residents lived were steadily demolished and replaced by attractive villas overlooking the harbour, and a walkway was constructed along the water's edge to allow convalescents to take beneficial strolls.

It was as a port of emigration, however, that Cove gained its greatest fame and prosperity. As early as the 1820s, passenger ships began calling to pick up Irish emigrants bound for America, Australia, Canada and New Zealand; by 1825 more than two thousand people a month were sailing from Cove, most of them never to return to Ireland. During the Irish Potato Famine, this emigrant traffic increased dramatically, and in the same period the port also handled much of the corn and maize that was being imported into Ireland in an effort to relieve the famine's effects. (Cove was one of the very few places in Ireland where the population *increased* during the Famine, because some of those who had intended to emigrate changed their minds at the last minute and settled in the town.)

In 1849 Queen Victoria visited Ireland and made Cove her first stop. She recorded her first impressions in her journal:

> Arrived here after a quick, but not very pleasant passage ... When we went to dock after eight in the evening we were close to the Cove of Cork, and we could see many bonfires on the hills and the lights and rockets that were set off from the different steamers. The harbour is immense, though the land is not very high and entering by twilight had a very fine effect.

The Queen's visit had a significant impact on the town, for it led to a change of name from Cove to Queenstown, in honour of its being, as Victoria wrote, 'the first spot on which I set foot upon Irish ground'. (Her stay in the town was brief: after stepping on shore 'amidst the roar of the cannon' and 'the enthusiastic shouts of the people', she imme-diately re-embarked and proceeded up the River Lee to Cork.) [1]

Eight years after the Queen's visit, the Inman steamship line made Queenstown a regular port of call, which put it on the map as a major transatlantic port. Other passenger shipping lines soon followed suit, including Cunard, whose *Britannia* first called at Queenstown in 1867. (Cunard ships continued to call regularly until the 1960s, and the Cunard flagship *Queen Elizabeth II* stopped there as recently as 1993.) The first White Star Line ship to call at Queenstown was the *Oceanic* in 1871, and thereafter the port became a stopping point for all of the company's transatlantic liners. Between the 1848 and 1950, over six million people emigrated from Ireland, almost half of them from Queenstown. At times up to five liners waited in the harbour for the arrival of the tenders carrying passengers from the quayside. The emigrant trade became the town's economic bread and butter: in 1912, there were twenty establishments calling themselves emigrant lodging houses, as well as fourteen boarding houses and two hotels. A week before the *Titanic* sailed, the Queenstown correspondent of the *Cork Examiner* wrote about Irish emigration: 'A stranger would think it a remarkable spectacle to see thousands of country people pouring into the town carrying their belongings. But to us in Queenstown, the spectacle is no new one as it has been repeated year after year for decades'.[2]

The *Titanic* stopped at Queenstown, its final port of call, on the morning of 11 April 1912. With the grey hills of Cork slowly appearing out of the morning mist, the ship travelled up St George's Channel towards Queenstown Harbour, its course tracing a gentle arc as it executed a long turn to port. The south coast of Ireland, with its granite cliffs towering over sandy beaches, looked beautiful, but few passengers felt the urge to brave the brisk wind on the open deck to go out and see it.

After stopping at the Daunt Light Vessel to pick up the pilot, the *Titanic* continued to the opening of Queenstown Harbour at Roche's Point. At 11.30 a.m., the engine-room telegraph signalled full stop and the huge anchor splashed into the water. Crowds of people lined the shore; they were accustomed to seeing big liners, but this was the largest ship in the world, half again as large as its nearest rivals. People had started gathering hours before, some from as far away as Cork city, a journey that required a twenty-mile trek around the coast. They had to be content with viewing the *Titanic* from a distance, for the ship was too big to dock at Queenstown's small pier, so it anchored about two miles offshore. The tenders *America* and *Ireland* ferried out 1385 sacks of mail, along with three first-class, seven second-class and 113 third-class passengers. Most of the latter were young Irish men and women who had never been more than a day or two's journey from their homes, but had now booked a one-way passage to America, where they hoped to improve their fortunes.[3] They were part of the nearly 30,000 Irishmen and women who would emigrate in 1912, with more than two-thirds going to the United States and most of the rest to

Canada. They were overwhelmingly young – in their late teens and twenties – single, Roman Catholic and from agricultural or labouring backgrounds. They brought little with them by way of monetary wealth or possessions; many were only able to afford the trip because a relative who was already in the United States had sent back the necessary funds or purchased a prepaid ticket for them. Very few of them would return home.[4]

Also at Queenstown, the handful of passengers who were not travelling across the Atlantic disembarked. Among them was Francis M. Browne, a thirty-two-year-old teacher who was studying for the priesthood. An enthusiastic amateur photographer, Browne carried his camera and a packet of exposed plates, little knowing that his pictures of the *Titanic*'s decks and public rooms would become the only visual record of the ship's maiden voyage. As Browne rode back to shore on one of the tenders, he was joined by stoker John Coffey, who had taken the opportunity to sneak off the *Titanic* by hiding under some mail bags. He was a resident of the town, and most likely had planned from the time he had signed on as a crew member to use the ship for a free passage home, although he later claimed that he had departed because he had been seized by a strong sense of foreboding. If Coffey did feel something odd, he was not alone. As the *Titanic* stood in Queenstown Harbour, an incident occurred that disturbed several passengers. As the tenders were unloading their cargo, one of the *Titanic*'s firemen climbed up a ladder inside the aftermost funnel.[5] When he reached the top, he stuck his head out of the funnel and peered down at the few passengers who had braved the cold to stand on deck and watch the proceedings. The sudden appearance of his soot-covered face caused considerable consternation, and several people interpreted it as a bad omen.

Most of the *Titanic*'s passengers, however, were simply impatient to be on their way to New York. The new arrivals were conducted to their quarters, which took less time than at Southampton or Cherbourg, since the stewards were now more familiar with the ship. This latest group was a little easier to handle, as well: 'at least this lot spoke English', recalled one steward.[6] As soon as the last passengers and sacks of mail had been transferred from the tenders, the *Titanic*'s whistles gave a long blast, signalling that the huge ship was ready to depart. At 1.30 p.m., the mooring lines were cast off and the gangways dropped as the tenders and other small craft in the harbour scrambled to get clear. Following a final stop at the lightship to drop off the pilot, the *Titanic* headed out into the Atlantic, though Captain Smith maintained a course that kept the ship close to the Irish coast. The Old Head of Kinsale was soon left behind, followed by other landmarks such as the Seven Heads and the Fastnet Light. As nightfall approached and Ireland disappeared over the horizon, many of the Irish emigrants gathered on the stern to catch a final glimpse of their homeland. One of them, Eugene Daly from Athlone, played 'Erin's Lament' on his uileann pipes, a traditional Irish instrument, as the *Titanic* sailed west into the setting sun.[7]

Since the overwhelming majority of the *Titanic*'s Irish passengers were travelling third class, they faced long odds in getting to a lifeboat after the collision with the iceberg. Some resorted to desperate measures. Edward Ryan from Ballinaveen in County Tipperary later admitted impersonating a woman. In a letter to his parents printed in the *Cork Examiner* on 6 May 1912, Ryan wrote, 'I had a towel around my neck. I just threw this over my head and let it hang at the back. I wore my waterproof raincoat. I then walked very stiff past the officers ... They didn't notice me. They thought I was a woman'. Another Irishman, Daniel Buckley of Kingwilliamstown in County Cork, managed to crawl into a boat but was nearly evicted when an officer ordered all male passengers to get out. As he cowered in fear and sobbed, a woman, whom he later claimed was Madeleine Astor, threw her shawl over him, which either concealed him or fooled the officer into thinking he was a woman.[8]

Most of the *Titanic*'s Irish passengers were not so fortunate. They, along with their fellow emigrants in steerage, were confined below decks until it was too late by a combination of racism, snobbery, deference and physical barriers. Of these factors, the last has been the greatest source of controversy. It is clear that at least some of the gates that separated the *Titanic*'s third-class areas from the remainder of the ship were locked. Seventeen-year-old Katie Gilnagh reported that a barrier guarded by a seaman held her back, along with her friends Katie Mullen and Katie Murphy. Another Irish steerage passenger, James Farrell, roared at the seaman, 'Great God, man! Open the gate and let the girls through!' Intimidated, the seaman meekly complied; Gilnagh, Mullen and Murphy survived, although Farrell did not. Another Irish third-class passenger, Annie Kelly, also reported that the staircase leading out of third class was blocked, for fear of 'the excitement [the steerage passengers] would cause to the people up there who were getting away in the lifeboats'. They were held back 'to the last moment'; Kelly survived only because a steward with whom she had become friendly escorted her up to the Boat Deck and put her in a lifeboat.[9] In an interview printed in the *Irish Independent* on 9 May 1912, Margaret Murphy of Fostragh, County Longford, stated that

> Before all the steerage passengers had even a chance of their lives, the *Titanic*'s sailors fastened the doors and companionways leading up from the third-class section ... A crowd of men was trying to get up to a higher deck and were fighting the sailors; all striking and scuffling and swearing. Women and some children were there praying and crying. Then the sailors fastened down the hatchways leading to the third-class section. They said they wanted to keep the air down there so the vessel could stay up longer. It meant all hope was gone for those still down there.[10]

From the other side of the barriers, others also saw third-class passengers being prevented from getting to the boats. As he returned to his cabin for a pair of boots, Seaman John Poingdexter saw a hundred third-class men waiting with their baggage beside a ladder to second class, which was being blocked by several stewards. First-class passenger Charlotte Collyer reported seeing First Officer William Murdoch 'place guards by the gangways to prevent others ... from coming on deck'.[11] Even if the barriers had not been in place, the difficulty of making one's way through the *Titanic*'s numerous decks, corridors and stairwells without guidance was a near-impossible task, particularly given that as the night wore on more and more of them would have been filled or half-filled with freezing seawater.

What may have been a more significant factor, however, were the social and racial attitudes that caused the *Titanic*'s officers and first- and second-class passengers to view their third-class counterparts as expendable, attitudes which were in many cases not challenged by the third-class passengers themselves. Steward John Hart, who claimed he made the only organized effort to lead third-class women and children to safety, admitted that the steerage passengers were falsely reassured and kept below decks until 1.15 a.m., when most of the lifeboats were already gone. Discipline and proper procedure, it was assumed, required that first- and second-class be loaded first; no thought was given to the fact that this policy was in effect a death sentence for most of third class, since there was an insufficient number of lifeboats.

For all of these reasons, most third-class passengers did not reach the Boat Deck until very late, if they made it there at all. Only minutes before the *Titanic* sank, Colonel Archibald Gracie saw 'a mass of humanity several lines deep', including 'women as well as men', emerge on the Boat Deck from the entrance to the Grand Staircase; he assumed they were 'steerage passengers who had just come up from the decks below'. Most of the Irish emigrants who survived escaped in some of the last lifeboats to depart: 13 and 15 on the starboard side and 14 and 16 on the port, none of which left before 1.27 a.m., nearly an hour and a half after Captain Smith had first given the order to begin loading and launching the boats.[12] Of the 113 third-class Irish passengers who boarded at Queenstown, forty survived (35 per cent). This suggests that they were a resourceful lot, since the survival rate for third class as a whole was only 25 per cent.

Attached to some of the *Titanic*'s Irish victims were heartbreaking stories. Of fifteen kinfolk from County Mayo who were travelling to Chicago together, only two survived. As the ship was sinking, Jeremiah Burke of County Cork, who perished, scrawled a note reading 'From *Titanic*. Good Bye all' and stuck it in a holy water bottle given to him by his mother on the day he had departed from Ireland. Over a year later, it washed up on shore not far from his home and was found by a coachman, who delivered it to the family. Catherine Buckley from Springmount, County Cork, had given in to the urgings of her sister Margaret to join her in America, against the wishes of her parents, who very much wanted her to remain in Ireland with them. When Catherine was lost, Mr and Mrs Buckley never forgave Margaret; when she returned home later in 1912, they called her a 'murderer' and slammed the door in her face. Against the wishes of both their families, Denis Lennon and Mary Mullin were eloping to America. Vowing to kill his sister's defiler, Mary's brother Joe set off in hot pursuit, missing them by mere minutes at the quayside in Queenstown, where he stood pounding the barrier in frustration, little knowing that in four days Lennon – and Mary – would perish at sea. Kate Connolly's mother received an erroneous report that her daughter had been saved, only to find out a week later that she had in fact perished. The tragic distinction of the biggest loss by a single Irish family went to the Rices of Athlone: thirty-nine-year-old Margaret Rice died, along with all five of her sons: Albert (aged ten), George (aged eight), Eric (aged six), Arthur (aged five) and Eugene Francis (aged two). When her body was found, Margaret was wearing a religious object around her neck dedicated to the Virgin Mary. Almost every Irish emigrant had purchased some type of talisman to protect them on their journey, and many of the Irish bodies retrieved from the sea by the *Mackay-Bennett* were still clutching rosary beads or wearing protective scapulars.

Upon my arrival in Cobh in the summer of 2002, I found what my American sensibility had been expecting in other places in the British Isles with close connections to the *Titanic* like Belfast and Southampton: a serious effort to capitalize on the commercial potential of the tragedy. Most obviously, Cobh was the home of '*Titanic* Queenstown', a bright yellow bar and restaurant that occupied the former offices of James Scott and Company, the shipping agents who arranged for the *Titanic*'s passengers to be ferried out to the ship. *Titanic* Queenstown was the product of an eccentric impulse on the part of a local entrepreneur. In 1994 an unemployed Cobh resident named Vincent Keaney won a million pounds in the Irish lottery. With his winnings, he purchased the building, which was at the time being used as a post office and unemployment office. He transformed the upper floor into a restaurant, which, according to *Titanic* Queenstown's promotional brochure, was intended to be 'a recreation of the Verandah Cafe aboard *Titanic* ... Relax amidst trellised ivy, oval topped mirrors, Villeroy & Boch tiling, exquisite service and an extensive wine selection'. The blatant boosterism of this tone is typical: *Titanic* Queenstown was an overtly commercial enterprise intended to attract tourists and not a museum for serious *Titanic* aficionados. In addition to the restaurant and downstairs bar, it featured a gift shop, 'the perfect place to find that special memento of your visit to Cobh and to our historic buildings'. Nothing that I saw in any of the places with *Titanic* connections in Britain remotely approached *Titanic* Queenstown in its aggressive effort to attract tourism. (The effort was a failure, as *Titanic* Queenstown closed in December 2002.)

To be sure, there are less overtly commercial *Titanic* activities available in Cobh. A local journalist and historian named Michael Martin leads a daily walk entitled the '*Titanic* Trail', in which he provides an extremely informative and detailed narrative about the town's maritime history. But even this has its commercial side: the walk concludes with a visit to a local pub, in which the punters are lubricated by a free half-pint of Guinness and encouraged to purchase a copy of his book for seven euros, with an autograph and official '*Titanic* Trail' stamp at no extra charge.

In some ways Cobh's more cavalier attitude about the *Titanic* is easily explained. As we have already seen, the *Titanic* was only one of dozens of emigrant ships that called at Queenstown. Moreover, if Cobh has a sentimental attachment to any one of those ships, it is to the *Lusitania*, the Cunard liner that sank off the Old Head of Kinsale after being torpedoed by a German U-boat in 1915. When the First World War broke out in August 1914, the Admiralty originally intended to use the *Lusitania* and its sister *Mauretania* as armed merchant cruisers to supplement the naval fleet by performing a variety of tasks. During their construction, which had been subsidized by the British government with the understanding that they could be requisitioned in wartime, the two ships had been fitted with reinforced emplacements for guns and large storage spaces that could easily be converted to magazines. The Royal Navy's first attempt to use a passenger liner as an armed merchant cruiser, however, ended unsatisfactorily. In August 1914 the converted Cunard liner *Campania* attacked the German vessel *Kaiser Wilhelm der Grosse*, which had also been converted to an auxiliary cruiser. The *Campania* managed to sink the *Kaiser Wilhelm*, but it was so badly damaged in the process that repairs took over a year to complete. The Admiralty was forced to recognize the unsuitability of passenger liners for military use, and the idea of using them as armed merchant cruisers was quickly abandoned.

The opening months of the conflict therefore saw the *Mauretania* stripped of its luxurious appointments while it sat idle, waiting for the Admiralty to decide what should be done with it. The *Lusitania*, meanwhile, continued to make its normal transatlantic run between Liverpool and New York, completing one round trip a month. Although the Germans had declared that all British vessels were fair game as U-boat targets, few military or political leaders believed that they would sink an armed passenger vessel. They also assumed that the *Lusitania*'s famed speed, which, even with six boilers shut down to conserve fuel, was still a healthy twenty-one knots, would protect it from German torpedoes.

On 1 May 1915 the *Lusitania* left New York as scheduled, carrying hundreds of American passengers despite the fact that several newspapers that very morning had carried a warning from the German government stating that vessels flying the British flag were subject to attack and that persons travelling on such vessels did so at their own risk. (A number of passengers also personally received telegrams informing them that the *Lusitania* was to be sunk, all signed 'Morte'.) The ship's captain, William Turner, also received repeated warnings from British naval intelligence that U-boats were active along his intended course off the coast of Ireland; in fact three British merchant ships were sunk in those very waters as the *Lusitania* neared the end of its voyage. Nevertheless, as the *Lusitania* entered the most dangerous part of its journey, Captain Turner slowed down to a leisurely eighteen knots, apparently concerned about patchy fog. He posted extra lookouts, but ignored the Admiralty's other directives for avoiding German submarines. He steamed close to shore, where U-boats commonly lurked, rather than sticking to the safer open water. He also failed to zig-zag to make it more difficult for U-boats to fix on their target. None of this was particularly unusual: the *Lusitania*'s previous captain had been even more cavalier and had sailed even closer to shore. And the Admiralty, too, must be criticized for complacency, as it was deemed unnecessary to provide the *Lusitania* with a destroyer escort.

Whoever was to blame, the result was catastrophic. At 1.20 p.m. on 7 May, U–20, under the command of Kapitänleutnant Walther Schweiger, sighted a large steamer about thirteen miles away. 'Starboard ahead four funnels and two masts of a steamer with course at right angles to us', Schweiger wrote in his log. Submerging, U–20 set forth full-speed ahead to intercept the ship, a task that was made easier when the unsuspecting *Lusitania* turned towards it. Without providing any warning, the submarine fired its bow torpedo at around 2.10 p.m. It struck the *Lusitania* forward on the starboard side. The detonation of the torpedo inside the hull was quickly followed by a second, even more massive explosion, apparently in the boiler rooms. Almost immediately, the *Lusitania* began listing sharply to starboard and settling by the head. Water poured through the gaping hole in the ship's side and into the numerous open portholes on the lower decks. The electricity quickly failed, trapping many passengers in elevators between decks. Most of the lifeboats on the port side could not be launched because of the severe list to starboard, while many on the starboard side were improperly lowered, injuring their occupants or dumping them into the sea.

It took only eighteen minutes for the *Lusitania*'s stern to disappear beneath the waves. 1198 passengers and crew members went with it, leaving 761 survivors. The entire sequence of events was visible from shore, and word of the disaster spread quickly along the Irish coast. In Queenstown, dozens of boats of all descriptions and sizes set sail to try and rescue the survivors. A chaotic scene greeted the rescuers when they reached the wreck site: the huge ship was gone, leaving behind a floating mass of debris and the few lifeboats that had been launched before the *Lusitania* sank. The rescue operation lasted for almost ten hours, as boat after boat returned to Queenstown carrying the living and the dead. The town became a virtual morgue as the bodies of many of the victims were laid out in various public buildings. On the following Monday, the sound of hearses rolling through the town could be heard all day long as those bodies that were unclaimed or unidentified were buried in three mass graves in Queenstown's Old Church cemetery. A few months later, a monument was erected in the town square (now Roger Casement Square), commemorating the victims and the heroic efforts to save as many people as possible; it features an angel surmounting a plinth against which lean two exhausted rescuers.

In contrast, a *Titanic* memorial, featuring a bas-relief of Margaret Rice and her five sons, was not put up in Cobh until 1998, in another effort to capitalize on the ship's ability to lure tourists following the recent surge of interest sparked by the discovery of the wreck and the Cameron film. But Ireland, apart from Ulster where the ship was built, has always been more cynical about the *Titanic*. There the connection to the tragedy is far less immediate; even the tragic deaths of numerous Irish emigrants represents only a drop in the bucket of the Irish demographic disaster of the last century and a half. And in darker, more overtly political interpretations, those selfsame deaths represent only one of the many ways in which Ireland has suffered at British hands.

Who Escaped in Which Boat?

It is impossible to determine in which lifeboat every *Titanic* survivor escaped, because the evidence is often contradictory. The most reliable sources of information on this subject are the transcripts of the British and American inquiries. Interviews with survivors can also be helpful, but they often contain inaccuracies and inconsistencies. Afterwards, as questions were asked about the courage of virtually every man who survived, it became expedient for male passengers and crewmen to claim that they had been picked up from the water rather than admitting that they had boarded a lifeboat before it was launched from the *Titanic*. A number of men claimed that they had swum around in the water for some time (in some cases several hours) before being picked up by a lifeboat. The two inquiries, however, established that only thirteen people were rescued from the water. Lifeboat 4 picked up eight people, two of whom died, and Lifeboat 14 picked up four, one of whom died. Numerous other men claimed that they had survived by clinging to overturned Collapsible B, which was swept off the Titanic's deck by onrushing water in the ship's final moments. (Only thirty men at most were on Collapsible B.)

In reality, most of the boats launched from the starboard side, which First Officer Murdoch permitted men to enter if there were no more women and children nearby, contained a significant number of men. In fact, of the boats launched from that side, only Lifeboat 11 and Collapsible C contained a majority of women and children. Another complicating factor is that a large number of survivors claimed that they left in the 'last boat', far more than actually could have done so. The last boat lowered was Collapsible D, which according to Second Officer Lightoller, who loaded it, contained 'fifteen or twenty people'.

The list below is therefore an educated guess based on a comparison of survivor recollections, the official inquiries, other written sources and

some basic arithmetic. See the website *Encyclopedia Titanica* (www.
encyclopedia-titanica.org).

Lifeboat 1

Emergency Lifeboat 1 (capacity forty persons) was launched from the starboard
side at 1.10 a.m. under the command of Lookout George Symons. It contained
twelve people.

First-Class Passengers

Duff Gordon, Sir Cosmo Edmund
Duff Gordon, Lady (Lucy Christiana Sutherland)
Salomon, Mr Abraham L.
Stengel, Mr Charles Emil Henry

First-Class Servants

Francatelli, Miss Laura Mabel, maid to Lady Duff Gordon

Deck Crew

Able-Bodied Seaman: Horswell, Mr Albert Edward James
Lookout: Symons, Mr George Thomas Macdonald (in charge)

Engineering Crew

Leading Fireman: Hendrickson, Mr Charles George
Fireman: Collins, Mr Samuel
Fireman: Pusey, Mr Robert William
Fireman: Taylor, Mr James
Trimmer: Sheath, Mr Frederick

Lifeboat 2

Emergency Lifeboat 2 (capacity forty persons) was launched from the port side
at 1.45 a.m. under the command of Fourth Officer Joseph Boxhall. It contained
eighteen people.

First-Class Passengers

Allen, Miss Elisabeth Walton
Appleton, Mrs Edward Dale (Charlotte Lamson)
Cornell, Mrs Robert Clifford (Malvina Helen Lamson)

Douglas, Mrs Walter Donald (Mahala Dutton)
Madill, Miss Georgette Alexandra
Robert, Mrs Edward Scott (Elisabeth Walton McMillan)

First-Class Servants

Kreuchen, Miss Emilie, maid to Mrs Edward Scott Robert
LeRoy, Miss Berthe maid to Mrs Walter Donald Douglas

Third-Class Passengers

Coutts, Mrs William (Winnie 'Minnie' Trainer)
Coutts, Master William Loch 'Willie'
Coutts, Master Neville Leslie ('Eden')
Kink, Mr Anton
Kink, Mrs Anton (Louise Heilmann)
Kink, Miss Louise Gretchen

Deck Crew

Able-Bodied Seaman: Osman, Mr Frank
Fourth Officer: Boxhall, Mr Joseph Grove (in charge)

Victualling Crew

Assistant Vegetable Cook: Ellis, Mr John Bertram (possibly)
Saloon Steward: Johnson, Mr James

Lifeboat 3

Lifeboat 3 (capacity sixty-five persons) was launched from the starboard side at 1.00 a.m. under the command of Able-Bodied Seaman George Moore. It contained thirty-eight or forty people.

First-Class Passengers

Anderson, Mr Harry
Cardeza, Mrs James Warburton Martinez (Charlotte Wardle Drake)
Cardeza, Mr Thomas Drake Martinez
Daniel, Mr Robert Williams (probably)
Davidson, Mrs Thornton (Orian Hays)
Dick, Mr Albert Adrian
Dick, Mrs Albert Adrian (Vera Gillespie)
Graham, Miss Margaret Edith
Graham, Mrs William Thompson (Edith Junkins)

Harper, Mr Henry Sleeper (and Sun Yat Sen, his pekinese)
Harper, Mrs Henry Sleeper (Myna Haxtun)
Hawksford, Mr Walter James
Hays, Mrs Charles Melville (Clara Jennings Gregg)
Saalfeld, Mr Adolphe
Simonius-Blumer, Colonel Alfons
Spedden, Mr Frederic Oakley
Spedden, Mrs Frederic Oakley (Margaretta Corning Stone)
Spedden, Master Robert Douglas
Stähelin, Dr Max

First-Class Servants

Burns, Miss Elizabeth Margaret, nurse to Master Robert Douglas Spedden
Hassah, Mr Hamad, dragoman to Mr Henry Sleeper Harper
Lesurer, Mr Gustave, manservant to Mr Thomas Drake Martinez Cardeza
Perreault, Miss Mary Anne, maid to Mrs Charles Melville Hays
Shute, Miss Elizabeth Weed, governess to Margaret Edith Graham
Ward, Miss Anna, maid to Mrs James Warburton Martinez Cardeza
Wilson, Miss Helen, maid to Mrs Frederic Oakley Spedden

Deck Crew

Able-Bodied Seaman: Anderson, Mr J.
Able-Bodied Seaman: Moore, Mr George Alfred (in charge)

Engineering Crew

Fireman: Combes, Mr G. (possibly)
Fireman: Couper, Mr Robert (possibly)
Fireman: Haggan, Mr John (possibly)
Fireman: Mason, Mr Frank Archibald Robert (possibly)
Fireman: Mayzes, Mr Thomas (possibly)
Fireman: Moore, Mr John J. (possibly)
Fireman: Nutbean, Mr William (possibly)
Fireman: Podesta, Mr John (possibly)
Fireman: Triggs, Mr Robert (possibly)
Trimmer: Binstead, Mr Walter (possibly)

Victualling Crew

Second-Class Chief Pantryman: Seward, Mr Wilfred Deable

Lifeboat 4

At around 12.30 a.m. a small group of passengers loitered by the windows of the enclosed promenade on the port side of A Deck. They were waiting for Lifeboat 4 (capacity sixty-five persons) to be lowered to A Deck so that it could be loaded. (Captain Smith and Second Officer Lightoller thought it would be easier to load from there.) The boat was lowered to A Deck, but both Smith an Lightoller had forgotten that, unlike on the *Olympic*, on the *Titanic* the A Deck promenade was enclosed by glass windows. After about half an hour Chief Second Steward George Dodd directed the passengers up to the Boat Deck via the crew-only forward stairway, Again they waited while the other boats were launched. Finally, Lightoller remembered them and, since the windows on A Deck were now open, directed them downstairs again. The ship's list to port meant the boat had swung away from the ship, and it had to be hauled in with boat hooks. Then, using deck chairs as steps, the passengers finally boarded Lifeboat 4. It was lowered at around 1.55 a.m. with twenty-nine or thirty people in it. Lightoller lowered the boat with only a single crewman, Storekeeper Foley, aboard. Quartermaster Perkis and Able-Bodied Seaman McCarthy were sent down the falls to join the boat. Perkis assumed command and had the boat rowed to the aft gangway doors, where Lightoller told him to go to pick up more passengers. The doors never opened, however. While waiting at the gangway Greasers Ranger and Scott Slid down the falls of Lifeboat 16, which hung near Lifeboat 4 in the water. Ranger dropped into Lifeboat 4 safely, but Scott lost his grip and fell into the water and had to be pulled into the boat. Perkis then gave up on the gangways and ordered the boat to be pulled away from the ship.

First-Class Passengers

Astor, Mrs John Jacob (Madeleine Talmadge Force)
Carter, Mrs William Ernest (Lucile Polk)
Carter, Miss Lucile Polk
Carter, Master William T. the Second
Chaffee, Mrs Herbert Fuller (Carrie Constance Toogood)
Clark, Mrs Walter Miller (Virginia Estelle McDowell)
Cumings, Mrs John Bradley (Florence Briggs Thayer)
Eustis, Miss Elizabeth Mussey
Hippach, Miss Jean Gertrude
Hippach, Mrs Louis Albert (Ida Sophia Fischer)
Ryerson, Mrs Arthur Larned (Emily Maria Borie)
Ryerson, Miss Emily Borie

Ryerson, Master John Borie
Ryerson, Miss Suzette Parker
Stephenson, Mrs Walter Bertram (Martha Eustis)
Thayer, Mrs John Borland (Marian Longstreth Morris)
Widener, Mrs George Dunton (Eleanor Elkins)

First-Class Servants

Bidois, Miss Rosalie, maid to Mrs John Jacob Astor
Bowen, Miss Grace Scott, governess to Master John Borie Ryerson
Chaudanson, Miss Victorine, maid to Mrs Arthur Larned Ryerson
Endres, Miss Caroline Louise, nurse to Mrs John Jacob Astor
Fleming, Miss Margaret, maid to Mrs John Borland Thayer
Gieger, Miss Amalie Henriette ('Emily'), maid to Mrs George Dunton Widener
Serreplan, Miss Auguste, maid to Mrs William Ernest Carter

Second-Class Passengers

Hämäläinen Mrs William (Anna)
Hämäläinen Master Wiljo
Hocking, Mrs Elizabeth (Eliza Needs) (possibly)
Hocking, Miss Ellen ('Nellie') (possibly)
Richards, Master George (possibly)
Richards, Mrs Sidney (Emily Hocking) (possibly)
Richards, Master William Rowe (possibly)

Deck Crew

Lamp Trimmer: Hemming, Mr Samuel Ernest (pulled from water)
Able-Bodied Seaman: Lyons, Mr William Henry (pulled from water – died
  on the *Carpathia*)
Able-Bodied Seaman: McCarthy, Mr William
Quartermaster: Perkis, Mr Walter John (in charge)
Storekeeper: Foley, Mr John 'Jack'

Engineering Crew

Trimmer: Dillon, Mr Thomas Patrick (pulled from water)
Greaser: Ranger, Mr Thomas (slid down falls)
Greaser: Scott, Mr Frederick (pulled from water)
Greaser: White, Mr Alfred (pulled from water)

Victualling Crew

Bedroom Steward: Cunningham, Mr Andrew (pulled from water)

Bedroom Steward: Siebert, Mr Sidney Conrad (pulled from water – died in boat)

Assistant Storekeeper: Prentice, Mr Frank (pulled from water)

Lifeboat 5

Lifeboat 5 (capacity sixty-five persons) was launched from the starboard side at 12.55 a.m. under the command of Third Officer Herbert Pitman. It contained thirty-five or thirty-six people.

First-Class Passengers

Beckwith, Mr Richard Leonard
Beckwith, Mrs Richard Leonard (Sallie Monypeny)
Behr, Mr Karl Howell
Calderhead, Mr Edward Pennington
Cassebeer, Mrs Henry Arthur Jr (Genevieve Fosdick)
Chambers, Mr Norman Campbell
Chambers, Mrs Norman Campbell (Bertha Griggs)
Daly, Mr Peter Denis (possibly 9)
Dodge, Mrs Washington (Ruth Vidaver)
Dodge, Master Washington
Flynn, Mr John Irwin (?Irving)
Frauenthal, Dr Henry William (jumped to boat)
Frauenthal, Mrs Henry William (Clara Heinsheimer)
Frauenthal, Mr Isaac Gerald (jumped to boat)
Frölicher-Stehli, Mr Maximilian Josef
Frölicher-Stehli, Mrs Maximilian Josef (Margaretha Emerentia Stehli)
Frölicher, Miss Hedwig Margaritha
Goldenberg, Mr Samuel L.
Goldenberg, Mrs Samuel L. (Nella Wiggins or Wiggens)
Harder, Mr George Achilles
Harder, Mrs George Achilles (Dorothy Annan)
Kimball, Mr Edwin Nelson Jr
Kimball, Mrs Edwin Nelson Jr (Gertrude Parsons)
Newsom, Miss Helen Monypeny
Østby, Miss Helene Ragnhild
Silverthorne, Mr Spencer Victor
Stengel, Mrs Charles Emil Henry (Annie May Morris)
Warren, Mrs Frank Manley (Anna Sophia Atkinson)

Deck Crew

Quartermaster: Olliver, Mr Alfred
Third Officer: Pitman, Mr Herbert John (In Charge)

Engineering Crew

Fireman: Shiers, Mr Alfred
Fireman: Unidentified

Victualling Crew

Stewardess: Bennett, Mrs Mabel
Bedroom Steward: Etches, Mr Henry Samuel
Assistant Boots: Guy, Mr Edward John
Stewardess: McLaren, Mrs H.

Lifeboat 6

Lifeboat 6 (capacity sixty-five persons) was launched from the port side at 12.55 a.m. under the command of Quartermaster Robert Hichens. It contained twenty-four people.

First-Class Passengers

Baxter, Mrs James (Hélène de Laudenière Chaput)
Bowerman, Miss Elsie Edith
Brown, Mrs James Joseph (Margaret Tobin)
Candee, Mrs Edward (Helen Churchill Hungerford)
Cavendish, Mrs Tyrell William (Julia Florence Siegel)
Chibnall, Mrs Alfred (Edith Martha Bowerman)
De Villiers, Madame Berthe (Mayne)
Douglas, Mrs Frederick Charles (Suzette Baxter)
Lindström, Mrs Carl Johan (Sigrid Posse)
Meyer, Mrs Edgar Joseph (Leila Saks)
Newell, Miss Madeleine
Newell, Miss Marjorie
Peuchen, Major Arthur Godfrey
Rothschild, Mrs Martin (Elizabeth Jane Barrett)
Smith, Mrs Lucien Philip (Mary Eloise Hughes)
Spencer, Mrs William Augustus (Marie Eugenie)
Stone, Mrs George Nelson (Martha Evelyn)

First-Class Servants

Barber, Miss Eleanor ('Nellie'), maid to Mrs Tyrell William Cavendish
Icard, Miss Amelie, maid to Mrs George Nelson Stone
Lurette, Miss Elise, maid to Mrs Spencer (probably)

Third-Class Passengers

Zenni, Mr Philip (Fahim Leeni) (possibly)

Deck Crew

Lookout: Fleet, Mr Frederick
Quartermaster: Hichens, Mr Robert (in charge)

Victualling Crew

Cashier: Bowker, Miss Ruth
Second Cashier: Martin, Miss Margaret E. ('Mabel')

Lifeboat 7

Lifeboat 7 (capacity sixty-five persons) was loaded by by First Officer Murdoch, assisted by Fifth Officer Lowe. The first boat to be lowered, it was launched from the starboard side at 12.45 a.m. under the command of Lookout George Hogg and contained twenty-eight people.

First-Class Passengers

Bishop, Mr Dickinson H.
Bishop, Mrs Dickinson H. (Helen Walton)
Blank, Mr Henry
Chevré, Mr Paul Romaine
Crosby, Mrs Edward Gifford (Catherine Elizabeth Halstead)
Crosby, Miss Harriet R.
Earnshaw, Mrs Boulton (Olive Potter)
Flegenheimer, Mrs Alfred (Antoinette Liche)
Gibson, Miss Dorothy Winifred
Gibson, Mrs Leonard (Pauline C. Boeson)
Greenfield, Mrs Leo David (Blanche Strouse)
Greenfield, Mr William Bertram
Hays, Miss Margaret Bechstein and her pomeranian
Maréchal, Mr Pierre
McGough, Mr James Robert

Omont, Mr Alfred Fernand
Potter, Mrs Thomas Jr (Lily Alexenia Wilson)
Seward, Mr Frederic Kimber
Sloper, Mr William Thompson
Snyder, Mr John Pillsbury
Snyder, Mrs John Pillsbury (Nellie Stevenson)
Taylor, Mr Elmer Zebley
Taylor, Mrs Elmer Zebley (Juliet Cummins Wright)
Tucker, Mr Gilbert Milligan Jr

Second-Class Passengers

Nourney, Mr Alfred ('Baron von Drachstedt')

Deck Crew

Lookout: Hogg, Mr George Alfred (in charge)
Lookout: Jewell, Mr Archie
Able-Bodied Seaman: Weller, Mr William

Lifeboat 8

Lifeboat 8 (capacity sixty-five persons) was launched from the port side at 1.10 a.m. under the command of Able-Bodied Seaman Thomas Jones. It contained twenty-eight people.

First-Class Passengers

Bonnell, Miss Elizabeth
Bonnell, Miss Caroline
Bucknell, Mrs William Robert (Emma Eliza Ward)
Cherry, Miss Gladys
Holverson, Mrs Alexander Oskar (Mary Aline Towner)
Kenyon, Mrs Frederick R. (Marion Stauffer)
Leader, Dr Alice (Farnham)
Pears, Mrs Thomas (Edith)
Peñasco y Castellana, Mrs Victor de Satode (Maria Josefa Perez de Soto y Vallejo)
Rothes, the Countess of (Noëlle Lucy Martha Dyer-Edwardes)
Swift, Mrs Frederick Joel (Margaret Welles Barron)
Taussig, Mrs Emil (Tillie Mandelbaum)
Taussig, Miss Ruth
White, Mrs J. Stuart (Ella Holmes)
Wick, Miss Mary Natalie

Wick, Mrs George Dennick (Martha Hitchcock)
Young, Miss Marie Grice

First-Class Servants

Bazzani, Miss Albina, maid to Mrs William Robert Bucknell
Bird, Miss Ellen, maid to Mrs Isidor Straus
Bissetti, Miss Amelia, maid to Mrs J. Stuart White
Daniels, Miss Sarah, maid to Mrs Hudson J. C. Allison
Maioni, Miss Roberta, maid to the Countess of Rothes
Oliva y Ocana, Doña Fermina, maid to Mrs Victor de Satode Peñasco y Castellana

Deck Crew

Able-Bodied Seaman: Jones, Mr Thomas William (in charge)
Able-Bodied Seaman: Pascoe, Mr Charles H. (possibly)

Victualling Crew

Bedroom Steward: Crawford, Mr Alfred
Scullion: Simmons, Mr Alfred (possibly)

Lifeboat 9

Lifeboat 9 (capacity sixty-five persons) was launched from the starboard side at 1.30 a.m. under the command of Boatswain's Mate Albert Haines. It contained between forty-five and forty-eight people.

First-Class Passengers

Aubart, Mme Leontine Pauline
Bradley (aka Brayton), Mr George (possibly)
Lines, Mrs Ernest H. (Elizabeth Lindsey James)
Lines, Miss Mary Conover
Romaine, Mr Charles Hallace (possibly)

First-Class Servants

Sägesser, Mlle Emma, maid to Mme Leontine Pauline Aubart

Second-Class Passengers

Buss, Miss Kate
Collett, Mr Sidney C. Stuart
Herman, Miss Alice
Herman, Miss Kate

Herman, Mrs Samuel (Jane Laver)
Kelly, Mrs Florence 'Fannie' (possibly)
Padro y Manent, Mr Julian
Pallas y Castello, Mr Emilio
Pinsky, Miss Rosa
Reynaldo, Mrs Encarnacion
Smith, Miss Marion Elsie (possibly)
Toomey, Miss Ellen
Trout, Mrs William H.
Watt, Mrs James (Bessie Inglis Milne)
Watt, Miss Bertha J.
Wilhelms, Mr Charles
Wright, Miss Marion

Third-Class Passengers

Niskänen, Mr Juha
Pickard (Trembisky), Mr Berk
Strandén, Mr Juho

Deck Crew

Boatswain's Mate: Haines, Mr Albert M. (in charge)
Quartermaster: Wynn, Mr Walter
Able-Bodied Seaman: McGough, Mr George M.
Able-Bodied Seaman: Peters, Mr William Chapman

Engineering Crew

Fireman: Kaspar, Mr Franz Vilhelm (possibly)
Fireman: Kemish, Mr George
Fireman: Street, Mr Thomas Albert

Victualling Crew

Saloon Steward: Baggott, Mr Allen Marden
Saloon Steward: Pfropper, Mr Richard
Saloon Steward: Harrison, Mr Aragon D.
Saloon Steward: Ryerson, Mr William Edwy
Saloon Steward: Ward, Mr William
Saloon Steward: Yearsley, Mr Harry
Boots: Chapman, Mr Joseph Charles
Bath Steward: Widgery, Mr James George

Lifeboat 10

Lifeboat 10 (capacity sixty-five persons) was launched from the port side at 1.20 a.m. under the command of Able Seaman Edward Buley. It contained thirty to thirty-two people.

First-Class Passengers

Andrews, Miss Kornelia Theodosia
Fortune, Miss Alice Elizabeth (possibly)
Fortune, Miss Ethel Flora (possibly)
Fortune, Miss Mabel Helen (possibly)
Fortune, Mrs Mark (Mary McDougald) (possibly)
Hogeboom, Mrs John C. (Anna Andrews)
Longley, Miss Gretchen Fiske
Marvin, Mrs Daniel Warner (Mary Graham Carmichael Farquarson)
Willard, Miss Constance (possibly)

Second-Class Passengers

Abelson, Mrs Samuel (Hannah Wizosky)
Ball, Mrs Ada E. Hall
Drew, Mrs James Vivian (Lulu Thorne Christian) (possibly)
Drew, Master Marshall Brines (possibly)
Hold, Mrs Stephen (Annie Margaret Hill) (possibly)
Hosono, Mr Masabumi
Keane, Miss Nora A.
Mallet, Mrs Albert (Antoinette Magnin) (possibly)
Mallet, Master André (possibly)
Siukkonen, Miss Anna
Ware, Mrs John James (Florence Louise Long) (possibly)
Weisz, Mrs Leopold (Mathilde) (possibly)
West, Miss Barbara Joyce
West, Miss Constance Mirium
West, Mrs Edwy Arthur (Ada Mary Worth)

Third-Class Passengers

Dean, Mrs Bertram Frank (Eva Georgetta Light) (possibly)
Dean, Master Bertram Vere (possibly)
Dean, Miss Elizabeth Gladys 'Millvina' (possibly)
Lundin, Miss Olga Elida
Krekorian, Mr Neshan (possibly)

Thorneycroft, Mrs Percival (Florence Kate Stears)

Deck Crew

Able-Bodied Seaman: Buley, Mr Edward John (in charge)
Able-Bodied Seaman: Evans, Mr Frank Olliver

Engineering Crew

Fireman: Rice, Mr Charles

Victualling Crew

Second Saloon Steward: Burke, Mr William

Lifeboat 11

Lifeboat 11 (capacity sixty-five persons) was launched from the starboard side at 1.35 a.m. under the command of Quartermaster James Humphreys. It contained between fifty-five and sixty people.

First-Class Passengers

Allison, Master Hudson Trevor
Mock, Mr Philipp Edmund
Rosenbaum (Russell), Miss Edith Louise
Schabert, Mrs Paul (Emma Mock)
Silvey, Mrs William Baird (Alice Munger)

First-Class Servants

Cleaver, Miss Alice Catherine, nurse to Trevor Allison

Second-Class Passengers

Angle, Mrs William A. (Florence Agnes Hughes)
Becker, Mrs Allen Oliver (Nellie E. Baumgardner)
Becker, Miss Marion Louise
Becker, Master Richard F.
del Carlo, Mrs Sebastiano (Argene Genovesi) (possibly)
Harper, Miss Nina
Jerwan, Mrs Amin S. (Marie Marthe Thuillard)
Leitch, Miss Jessie Wills
Nye, Mrs Elizabeth Ramell
Phillips, Miss Kate Florence ('Mrs Kate Louise Phillips Marshall')
Quick, Mrs Frederick Charles (Jane Richards)

Quick, Miss Phyllis May
Quick, Miss Winifred Vera
Sincock, Miss Maude

Second-Class Servants

Brown, Miss Amelia (Mildred), cook to Mr Hudson Joshua Creighton Allison

Third-Class Passengers

Aks, Master Philip Frank
De Mulder, Mr Theodoor (possibly)
Hansen, Mrs Claus Peter (Jennie Louise Howard)
Sap, Mr Julius (possibly)
Scheerlinckx, Mr Jean (possibly)

Deck Crew

Quartermaster: Humphreys, Mr Sidney James (in charge)
Able-Bodied Seaman: Brice, Mr Walter T.

Engineering Crew

Fireman: Unidentified

Victualling Crew

Assistant Second Steward: Wheat, Mr Joseph Thomas
Saloon Steward: Gibbons, Mr Jacob William
Saloon Steward: Hartnell, Mr Frederick
Saloon Steward: MacKay, Mr Charles Donald
Saloon Steward: McMicken, Mr Arthur ('Alfred')
Saloon Steward: Wheelton, Mr Ernest Edward
Assistant Steward: Terrell, Mr Frank
Bedroom Steward: Cullen, Mr Charles
Bedroom Steward: Faulkner, Mr William Stephen
Bedroom Steward: Theissinger, Mr Alfred
Third-Class Steward: Hyland, Mr James Leo
Third-Class Steward: Prior, Mr Harold John (possibly)
Third-Class Steward: Savage, Mr Charles J.
Stewardess: Gold, Mrs Katherine 'Kate'
Stewardess: Lavington, Miss Bessie
Stewardess: Martin, Mrs Annie
Stewardess: Pritchard, Mrs A.
Stewardess: Robinson, Mrs Annie

Stewardess: Smith, Miss Katherine E.
Stewardess: Stap, Miss Sarah Agnes
Turkish Bath Attendant: Caton, Miss Annie
Turkish Bath Attendant: Slocombe, Mrs Maud
Second-Class Smoking Room Steward: Witter, Mr James William Chatham

Lifeboat 12

Lifeboat 12 (capacity sixty-five persons) was launched at 1.30 a.m. under the command of Able-Bodied Seaman John Poingdestre. It contained twenty-eight people.

Second-Class Passengers

Bentham, Miss Lilian W.
Bryhl, Miss Dagmar Jenny Ingeborg
Christy, Mrs Alice Frances
Christy, Miss Julie R.
Duran y More, Miss Asuncion
Duran y More, Miss Florentina
Garside, Miss Ethel
Jacobsohn, Mrs Sidney Samuel (Amy Frances)
Kantor, Mrs Sinai (Miriam Sternim)
Lehmann, Miss Bertha (probably)
Parrish, Mrs Lutie (Davis)
Phillips, Miss Alice Frances Louisa
Renouf, Mrs Peter Henry (Lillian Jefferys)
Rugg, Miss Emily
Shelley, Mrs William (Imanita Hall)
Webber, Miss Susan

Third-Class Passengers

Cohen, Mr Gurshon 'Gus'
Cribb, Miss Laura Mae

Deck Crew

Able-Bodied Seaman: Poingdestre, Mr John Thomas (in charge)
Able-Bodied Seaman: Clench, Mr Fredrick

Lifeboat 13

Lifeboat 13 (capacity sixty-five persons) was launched from the starboard side at 1.40 a.m. under the command of Leading Fireman Frederick Barrett. It contained sixty or sixty-two people.

First-Class Passengers

Dodge, Dr Washington

Second-Class Passengers

Beane, Mr Edward
Beane, Mrs Edward (Ethel Clarke)
Becker, Miss Ruth Elizabeth
Beesley, Mr Lawrence
Caldwell, Mr Albert Francis
Caldwell, Mrs Albert Francis (Sylvia Mae Harbaugh)
Caldwell, Master Alden Gates
Davis, Miss Mary
Hewlett, Mrs Mary D.
Oxenham, Mr Percy Thomas
Ridsdale, Miss Lucy
Slayter, Miss Hilda Mary

Third-Class Passengers

Aks, Mrs Sam (Leah Rosen)
Asplund, Mr Johan Charles
Bradley, Miss Bridget Delia
Buckley, Mr Daniel
Connolly, Miss Kate
DeMessemaeker, Mrs Guillaume Joseph (Anna)
Dowdell, Miss Elizabeth
Emanuel, Miss Virginia Ethel
Glynn, Miss Mary Agatha
Johannessen, Mr Bernt Johannes
Karlsson, Mr Einar Gervasius
Landergren, Miss Aurora Adelia
Madsen, Mr Fridtjof
McDermott, Miss Bridget Delia
McGovern, Ms Mary
Nilsson, Miss Helmina Josefina

Nysten, Miss Anna Sofia
O'Leary, Miss Hanora 'Norah'
Olsen, Master Arthur Karl
Riordan, Miss Johanna 'Hannah'
Sandström, Mrs Hjalmar (Sandström, Agnes Charlotta)
Sandström, Miss Beatrice Irene
Sandström, Miss Marguerite Rut
Smyth, Miss Julia
Svensson, Mr Johan Cervin
Tenglin, Mr Gunnar Isidor (possibly)
Vartunian, Mr David (possibly)
One of the Chinese Sailors (possibly Foo, Mr Choong)

Deck Crew

Lookout: Lee, Mr Reginald Robinson
Able-Bodied Seaman: Hopkins, Mr Robert John
Able-Bodied Seaman: Vigott, Mr Philip Francis

Engineering Crew

Leading Fireman: Barrett, Mr Fredrick William (In Charge)
Fireman: Beauchamp, Mr George William
Fireman: Crimmins, Mr James (Possibly)
Fireman: Major, Mr William
Trimmer: Fryer, Mr A. E.

Victualling Crew

Saloon Steward: Knight, Mr George
Saloon Steward: Littlejohn, Mr Alexander James
Saloon Steward: Ray, Mr Frederick Dent
Assistant Steward: Williams, Mr Walter John (jumped from deck)
Third-Class Steward: Foley, Mr William C.
Third-Class Steward: Port, Mr Frank
Glory Hole Steward: Wright, Mr William
Sauce Cook: Windebank, Mr Alfred Edgar
Assistant Baker: Neale, Mr Henry
Scullion: Colgan, Mr Joseph (possibly)
Scullion: Martin, Mr F. (possibly)
Scullion: Ross, Mr Horace Leopold (possibly)
Kitchen Porter: Hardwick, Mr Reginald (possibly)
Plate Washer: Ball, Mr Percy (possibly)

Plate Washer: Burrage, Mr Alfred
Restaurant Clerk: Maugé, Mr Paul (jumped from deck)

Lifeboat 14

Lifeboat 14 (capacity sixty-five persons) was launched from the port side at 1.25 a.m. under the command of Fifth Officer Harold Lowe. It contained between forty-two and forty-five people. After the sinking the boat went back and picked up four from the water, one of whom died.

First-Class Passengers

Compton, Mrs Alexander Taylor (Mary Eliza Ingersoll)
Compton, Miss Sara Rebecca
Hoyt, Mr William Fisher (pulled from water – died in boat)
Minahan, Mrs William Edward (Lillian E. Thorpe)
Minahan, Miss Daisy E.

Second-Class Passengers

Brown, Mrs Thomas William Solomon (Elizabeth Catherine Ford)
Brown, Miss Edith Eileen
Cameron, Miss Clear Annie
Clarke, Mrs Charles V. (Ada Maria Winfield)
Collyer, Mrs Harvey (Charlotte Annie Tate)
Collyer, Miss Marjorie
Cook, Mrs Selena (Rogers)
Davies, Mrs John Morgan (Elizabeth Agnes Mary White)
Davies, Master John Morgan Jr
Hart, Mrs Benjamin (Esther Ada Bloomfield)
Hart, Miss Eva Miriam
LaRoche, Mrs Joseph (Juliette Marie Louise) (possibly)
LaRoche, Miss Louise (possibly)
LaRoche, Miss Simone Anne Marie (possibly)
Lemore, Mrs Amelia
Louch, Mrs Charles Alexander (Alice Adelaide)
Mellinger, Mrs Elizabeth Anne
Mellinger, Miss Madeleine Violet
Portaluppi, Mr Emilio (pulled from water – possibly)
Walcroft, Miss Nellie
Wells, Mrs Arthur Henry ('Addie' Dart Trevaskis)
Wells, Miss Joan

Wells, Master Ralph Lester
Williams, Mr Charles Eugene

Third-Class Passengers

Heikkinen, Miss Laina ('Laila') (possibly)
Moor, Mrs Beila
Moor, Master Meier
Ryan, Mr Edward
Thomas, Mrs Alexander (Thamine or 'Thelma') (possibly)
One of the Chinese Sailors (possibly Lang, Mr Fang – pulled from the water)

Deck Crew

Fifth Officer: Lowe, Mr Harold Godfrey (in charge)
Able-Bodied Seaman: Scarrott, Mr Joseph
Window Cleaner: Harder, Mr William

Engineering Crew

Leading Fireman: Threlfall, Mr Thomas
Fireman: Harris, Mr Frederick

Victualling Crew

Saloon Steward: Crowe, Mr George Frederick
Saloon Steward: Phillimore, Mr Harold Charles William (pulled from water)
Bath Steward: Morris, Mr Frank Herbert
Third-Class Steward: Pugh, Mr Alfred

Lifeboat 15

Lifeboat 15 (capacity sixty-five persons) was loaded by First Officer Murdoch assisted by Sixth Officer Moody and launched from the starboard side at 1.40 a.m. under the command of Fireman Frank Dymond. It contained about sixty-five people.

First-Class Passengers

Homer, Mr Harry ('Mr E. Haven')

Second-Class Passengers

Harris, Mr George

Third-Class Passengers

Abrahamsson, Mr August
Albimona, Mr Nassef Cassem
Asplund, Mrs Carl (Selma Augusta Emilia Johansson)
Aspland, Master Edvin Rojj Felix
Asplund, Miss Lillian Gertrud
Barah, Mr Hanna Assi
Dahl, Mr Charles Edward ('Karl Edwart')
Daly, Miss Margaret Marcella ('Maggie')
De Messemaeker, Mr Guillaume Joseph
Finoli, Mr Luigi (Possibly)
Hakkarainen, Mrs Pekka Pietari (Elin Matilda Dolk)
Hedman, Mr Oscar
Hirvonen, Mrs Alexander (Helga E. Lindqvist)
Hirvonen, Miss Hildur E.
Jals(evac, Mr Ivan
Jonsson, Mr Carl
Johansson, Mr Oskar Leander (Palmquist)
Johnson, Mrs Oscar W. (Elisabeth Vilhelmina Berg) (possibly)
Johnson, Miss Eleanor Ileen (possibly)
Johnson, Master Harold Theodor (possibly)
Jussila, Mr Erik
Karun, Miss Anna (Manca)
Karun, Mr Franz
Kennedy, Mr John (possibly)
Lindqvist, Mr Eino William
Lulic, Mr Nikola
Lundström, Mr Thure Edvin
Madigan, Miss Margaret ('Maggie')
Mamee, Mr Hanna
McCarthy, Miss Catherine ('Katie') (possibly)
Midtsjø, Mr Karl Albert
Mulvihill, Miss Bertha E.
Persson, Mr Ernst Ulrik (possibly)
Sundman, Mr Johan Julian
Törnquist, Mr William Henry
Turja, Miss Anna Sofia
Turkula, Mrs Hedwig
Vartunian, Mr David (possibly)

Deck Crew

Lookout: Evans, Mr Alfred Frank

Engineering Crew

Fireman: Dymond, Mr Frank (in charge)
Fireman: Clark, Mr William
Fireman: Noss, Mr Henry
Fireman: Pearse, Mr J.
Fireman: Priest, Mr Arthur John
Fireman: Taylor, Mr William Henry
Trimmer: Avery, Mr James Frank
Trimmer: Blake, Mr Percival Albert
Trimmer: Cavell, Mr George Henry
Trimmer: Fredricks, Mr W.
Trimmer: White, Mr William George

Victualling Crew

Verandah Steward: Stewart, Mr John ('Jack')
Saloon Steward: Crafter, Mr Frederick
Saloon Steward: Keene, Mr Percy Edward
Saloon Steward: Thomas, Mr Albert Charles
Saloon Steward: Thomas, Mr Benjamin James
Saloon Steward: Toms, Mr F.
Assistant Steward: Nichols, Mr Walter Henry ('Nicholas')
Bath Steward: Rule, Mr Samuel James
Third-Class Steward: Lewis, Mr Arthur Ernest Read
Third-Class Steward: Halford, Mr Richard
Third-Class Steward: Hart, Mr John Edward
Stewardess: Bliss, Mrs Ernest John (Emma Junod)
Extra Third Baker: Burgess, Mr Charles Reginald

Lifeboat 16

Lifeboat 16 (capacity sixty-five persons) was loaded by Second Officer Lightoller and Sixth Officer Moody and launched from the port side at 1.35 a.m. under the command of Master-at-Arms Bailey. It contained about forty people.

Second-Class Passengers

Wilkinson, Mrs Elizabeth Anne

Silvén, Miss Lyyli Karoliina
Troutt, Miss Edwina Celia 'Winnie' (probably)

Third-Class Passengers

Abelseth, Miss Karen Marie
Corr, Miss Helen ('Ellen') (possibly)
Davison, Mrs Thomas Henry (Mary Finck)
Dyker, Mrs Adolf Fredrik (Anna Elisabeth Judith Andersson)
Gilnagh, Miss Katherine ('Katie')
Healy, Miss Hanora
Jensen, Miss Carla Christine
Kelly, Miss Anna Katherine
Mannion, Miss Margaret
McCormack, Mr Thomas Joseph (probably)
McCoy, Miss Agnes (possibly)
McCoy, Miss Alicia (possibly)
McCoy, Mr Bernard (possibly)
Mockler, Miss Ellen Mary
Moran, Miss Bertha Bridget
Mullen, Miss Katherine ('Katie')
Murphy, Miss Catherine ('Kate') (possibly)
Murphy, Miss Margaret Jane ('Mary', 'Maggie') (possibly)
Murphy, Miss Nora (possibly)
Sjöblom, Miss Anna Sofia
Thomas, Master Assad Alexander
Wilkes, Mrs James (Ellen Needs)

Deck Crew

Master-at-Arms: Bailey, Mr Joseph Henry (slid down falls – in charge)
Able-Bodied Seaman: Forward, Mr James
Able-Bodied Seaman: Archer, Mr Ernest Edward

Engineering Crew

Fireman: Unidentified
Trimmer: Pelham, Mr George

Victualling Crew

Assistant Steward: Andrews, Mr Charles E.
Stewardess: Gregson, Miss Mary
Stewardess: Jessop, Miss Violet Constance

Stewardess: Leather, Mrs Elizabeth M.
Stewardess: Marsden, Miss Evelyn
Stewardess: Roberts, Mrs Mary Keziah
Stewardess: Sloan, Miss Mary (probably)

Collapsible Lifeboat A

Collapsible Lifeboat A (capacity forty-nine persons) was stowed on the starboard side of the officers' quarters roof. It was dropped down to the boat deck and attached to the falls that Lifeboat 1 and Collapsible C had been launched from. Before it could be loaded, however, the forward end of the boat deck went under and the boat began to float away while still attached to the davits. Saloon Steward Edward Brown and another man jumped into the boat and cut the falls; shortly after a wave crashed over the boat, washing the handful of people who climbed aboard out and swamping it. The sides of the boat were still down, and water poured over the sides, flooding it even more as survivors climbed aboard, some of whom died during the night. In the morning they were transferred to Lifeboat 14. Three dead bodies were left in the collapsible as it was cast adrift. A month later, the White Star liner *Oceanic* encountered Collapsible A two hundred miles south west of the position where the *Titanic* had sunk. The three bodies were still inside; they were sewn into canvas bags, draped with the Union Jack and buried at sea.

First-Class Passengers

Beattie, Mr Thomson (died in boat)
Daly, Mr Peter Dennis (possibly)
Rheims, Mr George Alexander Lucien
Williams, Mr Richard Norris II

Third-Class Passengers

Andersson, Mr August ('Mr August Edvard Wennerström')
Abbott, Mrs Stanton (Rosa)
Abelseth, Mr Olaus Jørgensen
Jansson, Mr Carl Olof
Keefe, Mr Arthur (died in boat)
Lindell, Mr Edvard Bengtsson (died in boat)
Lindell, Mrs Edvard Bengtsson (Elin Gerda) (died in boat)
Olsson, Mr Oscar Wilhelm (Johansson)

Engineering Crew

Trimmer: McIntyre, Mr William
Fireman: Thompson, Mr John

Victualling Crew

Saloon Steward: Brown, Mr Edward
Saloon Steward: Lucas, Mr William
Barber: Weikman, Mr Augustus H.

Collapsible Lifeboat B

Collapsible Lifeboat B (capacity forty-nine persons) was stowed on the port side officers' quarters roof. It was dropped down to the boat deck but landed upside down. Several men tried to right it and push it over to the davits, but when the bridge went under the wave it produced washed the boat and most of the men working to launch it overboard. Capsized in the water, the boat was washed clear of the ship by another wave that swept up after the forward funnel collapsed. Throughout the night as many as thirty men managed to climb aboard the upturned craft, which sank deeper with their weight, forcing the men already aboard to turn away many swimmers. In the morning the men were rescued, with four or five transferred to Lifeboat 4 and the remainder going to Lifeboat 12. Collapsible B was then abandoned.

First-Class Passengers

Barkworth, Mr Algernon H. Wilson
Gracie, Colonel Archibald IV
Thayer, Mr John Borland Jr

Second-Class Passengers

Mellors, Mr William John

Third-Class Passengers

Daly, Mr Eugene Patrick (possibly)
Dorking, Mr Edward Arthur
Harmer, Mr Abraham (David Livshin) (died in boat)
Moss, Mr Albert Johan
O'Keefe, Mr Patrick
Persson, Mr Ernst Ulrik (possibly)
Sunderland, Mr Victor Francis

Deck Crew

Second Officer: Lightoller, Mr Charles Herbert

Engineering Crew

Trimmer: Allen, Mr Ernest F.
Trimmer: Hebb, Mr A.
Fireman: Hurst, Mr Walter
Mess Steward: Fitzpatrick, Mr Charles William N.
Fireman: Judd, Mr Charles E.
Fireman: Lindsay, Mr William Charles
Trimmer: McGann, Mr James
Fireman: Mason, Mr Frank Archibald Robert (possibly)
Trimmer: O'Connor, Mr John
Greaser: Pragnell, Mr George
Fireman: Senior, Mr Henry ('Harry')
Trimmer: Snow, Mr Eustace Philip

Victualling Crew

Wireless Operator: Bride, Mr Harold Sydney
Scullion: Collins, Mr John
Third-Class Steward: Daniels, Mr Sidney Edward
Chief Baker: Joughin, Mr Charles John
Entrée Cook: Maynard, Mr Isaac ('John', 'Joseph')
Wireless Operator: Phillips, Mr John George (possibly died on board)
Saloon Steward: Whiteley, Mr Thomas

Collapsible Lifeboat C

Collapsible Lifeboat C (capacity forty-nine persons) was launched from the starboard side at 1.40 a.m. under the command of Quartermaster George Rowe. It contained about forty people.

First-Class Passengers

Carter, Mr William Ernest
Ismay, Mr Joseph Bruce

Third-Class Passengers

Abraham, Mrs Joseph (Sophie Halaut Easu)
Assaf, Mrs Mariana

Baclini, Miss Eugenie
Baclini, Miss Helene Barbara
Baclini, Miss Maria Catherine
Baclini, Mrs Solomon (Latifa)
Badman, Miss Emily Louise
Bing, Mr Lee (probably)
Chip, Mr Chang (probably)
Banoura, Miss Ayoub
Devaney, Miss Margaret
Foo, Mr Choong (possibly)
Goldsmith, Mrs Frank John (Emily Alice Brown) (possibly)
Goldsmith, Master Frank John William (Frankie) (possibly)
Hee, Mr Ling (probably)
Hellström, Miss Hilda Maria
Howard, Miss May Elizabeth
Hyman, Mr Abraham
Lam, Mr Ali (probably)
Lang, Mr Fang (possibly)
Moubarek, Mrs George (Amenia)
Moubarek, Master George
Moubarek, Master Halim Genios (William George)
Musselmani, Mrs Fatima Musselmani
Nackid, Mr Said
Nackid, Mrs Said (Mary Mowad)
Nackid, Miss Mary
Najib, Miss Adele Jane Kiamie
Nicola-Yarred, Miss Jamila (possibly)
Nicola-Yarred, Master Elias (possibly)
Öhman, Miss Velin
Joseph Peter, Master Michael J. ('Michael Joseph') (possibly)
Roth, Miss Sarah A.
Salkjelsvik, Miss Anna Kristine
Stanley, Miss Amy Zillah Elsie
Touma, Mrs Darwis (Hanna Youssef Razi) ('Thomas')
Touma, Miss Maria Youssef ('Mary Thomas')
Touma, Master Georges Youssef ('George Thomas')
Whabee, Mrs George Joseph (Shawneene Abi-Saab) (possibly)
Yazbeck, Mrs Antoni (Selini Alexander)

Deck Crew

Quartermaster: Rowe, Mr George Thomas (in charge)

Engineering Crew

Fireman: Doel, Mr Frederick
Trimmer: Hunt, Mr Albert
Fireman's Messman: Knowles, Mr Thomas

Victualling Crew

Third-Class Pantryman: Pearcey, Mr Albert Victor
Assistant Butcher: Mills, Mr Charles

Collapsible Lifeboat D

Collapsible Lifeboat D (capacity forty-nine persons) was launched from the
port side at approximately 2.05 a.m. under the command of Quartermaster
Arthur John Bright. It was the last boat to be successfully lowered from the
Titanic and contained twenty-four people.

First-Class Passengers

Björnström-Steffansson, Mr Mauritz Håkan (jumped to boat)
Brown, Mrs John Murray (Caroline Lane Lamson)
Futrelle, Mrs Jacques (Lily May Peel)
Harris, Mrs Henry Birkhardt (Irene Wallach)
Hoyt, Mr Frederick Maxfield (picked up)
Hoyt, Mrs Frederick Maxfield (Jane Anne Forby)
Thorne, Mrs Gertrude Maybelle
Woolner, Mr Hugh (jumped to boat)

Second-Class Passengers

Navratil, Master Edmond Roger
Navratil, Master Michel M.

Third-Class Passengers

Andersson, Miss Erna Alexandra
Backström, Mrs Karl Alfred (Maria Mathilda Gustafsson)
Duquemin, Mr Joseph
Jermyn, Miss Annie
Kelly, Miss Mary

Nilsson, Miss Berta Olivia
O'Driscoll, Miss Bridget
Joseph Peter, Mrs (Catherine Rizk) (possibly)
Joseph Peter, Miss Anna ('Mary Joseph') (possibly)

Deck Crew

Quartermaster: Bright, Mr Arthur John (in charge)
Able-Bodied Seaman: Lucas, Mr William (transferred to 12)

Engineering Crew

Fireman: Unidentified
Fireman: Unidentified (possibly Murdoch, Mr William John)

Victualling Crew

Chief Second-Class Steward: Hardy, Mr John T.

APPENDIX 2

Joseph Conrad and George Bernard Shaw on the Titanic

1

Joseph Conrad
'Some Reflections on the Loss of the *Titanic*'
English Review, May 1912

It is with a certain bitterness that one must admit to oneself that the late SS *Titanic* had a 'good press'. It is perhaps because I have no great practice of daily newspapers (I have never seen so many of them together lying about my room) that the white spaces and the big lettering of the headlines have an incongruously festive air to my eyes, a disagreeable effect of a feverish exploitation of a sensational God-send. And if ever a loss at sea fell under the definition, in the terms of a bill of lading, of Act of God, this one does, in its magnitude, suddenness and severity; and in the chastening influence it should have on the self-confidence of mankind.

I say this with all the seriousness the occasion demands, though I have neither the competence nor the wish to take a theological view of this great misfortune, sending so many souls to their last account. It is but a natural REFLECTION. Another one flowing also from the phrase-ology of bills of lading (a bill of lading is a shipping document limiting in certain of its clauses the liability of the carrier) is that the 'King's Enemies' of a more or less overt sort are not altogether sorry that this fatal mishap should strike the prestige of the greatest Merchant Service of the world. I believe that not a thousand miles from these shores certain public prints have betrayed in gothic letters their satisfaction – to speak plainly – by rather ill-natured comments.

In what light one is to look at the action of the American Senate is
more difficult to say. From a certain point of view the sight of the august
senators of a great Power rushing to New York and beginning to bully
and badger the luckless 'Yamsi' – on the very quayside so to speak –
seems to furnish the Shakespearian touch of the comic to the real tragedy
of the fatuous drowning of all these people who to the last moment put
their trust in mere bigness, in the reckless affirmations of commercial
men and mere technicians and in the irresponsible paragraphs of the
newspapers booming these ships! Yes, a grim touch of comedy. One
asks oneself what these men are after, with this very provincial display
of authority. I beg my friends in the United States pardon for calling
these zealous senators men. I don't wish to be disrespectful. They may
be of the stature of demi-gods for all I know, but at that great distance
from the shores of effete Europe and in the presence of so many guileless
dead, their size seems diminished from this side. What are they after?
What is there for them to find out? We know what had happened. The
ship scraped her side against a piece of ice, and sank after floating for
two hours and a half, taking a lot of people down with her. What more
can they find out from the unfair badgering of the unhappy 'Yamsi', or
the ruffianly abuse of the same?

'Yamsi', I should explain, is a mere code address, and I use it here
symbolically. I have seen commerce pretty close. I know what it is worth,
and I have no particular regard for commercial magnates, but one must
protest against these Bumble-like proceedings. Is it indignation at the
loss of so many lives which is at work here? Well, the American railroads
kill very many people during one single year, I dare say. Then why don't
these dignitaries come down on the presidents of their own railroads,
of which one can't say whether they are mere means of transportation
or a sort of gambling game for the use of American plutocrats. Is it
only an ardent and, upon the whole, praiseworthy desire for information? But the reports of the inquiry tell us that the august senators,
though raising a lot of questions testifying to the complete innocence
and even blankness of their minds, are unable to understand what the
second officer is saying to them. We are so informed by the press from
the other side. Even such a simple expression as that one of the look-out
men was stationed in the 'eyes of the ship' was too much for the senators
of the land of graphic expression. What it must have been in the more

recondite matters I won't even try to think, because I have no mind for smiles just now. They were greatly exercised about the sound of explosions heard when half the ship was under water already. Was there one? Were there two? They seemed to be smelling a rat there! Has not some charitable soul told them (what even schoolboys who read sea stories know) that when a ship sinks from a leak like this, a deck or two is always blown up; and that when a steamship goes down by the head, the boilers may, and often do break adrift with a sound which resembles the sound of an explosion? And they may, indeed, explode, for all I know. In the only case I have seen of a steamship sinking there was such a sound, but I didn't dive down after her to investigate. She was not of 45,000 tons and declared unsinkable, but the sight was impressive enough. I shall never forget the muffled, mysterious detonation, the sudden agitation of the sea round the slowly raised stern, and to this day I have in my eye the propeller, seen perfectly still in its frame against a clear evening sky.

But perhaps the second officer has explained to them by this time this and a few other little facts. Though why an officer of the British merchant service should answer the questions of any king, emperor, autocrat, or senator of any foreign power (as to an event in which a British ship alone was concerned, and which did not even take place in the territorial waters of that power) passes my understanding. The only authority he is bound to answer is the Board of Trade. But with what face the Board of Trade, which, having made the regulations for 10,000 ton ships, put its dear old bald head under its wing for ten years, took it out only to shelve an important report, and with a dreary murmur, 'Unsinkable', put it back again, in the hope of not being disturbed for another ten years, with what face it will be putting questions to that man who has done his duty, as to the facts of this disaster and as to his professional conduct in it – well, I don't know! I have the greatest respect for our established authorities. I am a disciplined man, and I have a natural indulgence for the weaknesses of human institutions; but I will own that at times I have regretted their – how shall I say it? – their imponderability. A Board of Trade – what is it? A Board of ... I believe the Speaker of the Irish Parliament is one of the members of it. A ghost. Less than that; as yet a mere memory. An office with adequate and no doubt comfortable furniture and a lot of perfectly irresponsible gentlemen who exist packed in its equable atmosphere softly, as if in a lot of cotton-wool, and with no care in the world; for there can be no care without personal responsibility – such, for instance, as the seamen have – those seamen from whose mouths this irresponsible institution can take away the bread – as a disciplinary measure. Yes – it's all that. And what more? The name of a politician – a party man! Less than nothing; a mere void without as much as a shadow of responsibility cast into it from that light in which move the masses of men who work, who deal in things and face the realities – not the words – of this life.

Years ago I remember overhearing two genuine shellbacks of the old type commenting on a ship's officer, who, if not exactly incompetent, did not commend himself to their severe judgment of accomplished sailor-men. Said one, resuming and concluding the discussion in a funnily judicial tone: 'The Board of Trade must have been drunk when they gave him his certificate'. I confess that this notion of the Board of Trade as an entity having a brain which could be overcome by the fumes of strong liquor charmed me exceedingly. For then it would have been unlike the limited companies of which some exasperated wit has once said that they had no souls to be saved and no bodies to be kicked, and thus were free in this world and the next from all the effective sanctions of conscientious conduct. But, unfortunately, the picturesque pronouncement overheard by me was only a characteristic sally of an annoyed sailor. The Board of Trade is composed of bloodless departments. It has no limbs and no physiognomy, or else at the forthcoming inquiry it might have paid to the victims of the *Titanic* disaster the small tribute of a blush. I ask myself whether the Marine Department of the Board of Trade did really believe, when they decided to shelve the report on equipment for a time, that a ship of 45,000 tons, that ANY ship, could be made practically indestructible by means of watertight bulkheads? It seems incredible to anybody who had ever reflected upon the properties of material, such as wood or steel. You can't, let builders say what they like, make a ship of such dimensions as strong proportionately as a much smaller one. The shocks our old whalers had to stand amongst the heavy floes in Baffin's Bay were perfectly staggering, notwithstanding the most skilful handling, and yet they lasted for years. The *Titanic*, if one may believe the last reports, has only scraped against a piece of ice which, I suspect, was not an enormously bulky and comparatively easily seen berg, but the low edge of a floe – and sank. Leisurely enough, God knows – and here the advantage of bulkheads comes in – for time is a great friend, a good helper – though in this lamentable case these bulkheads served only to prolong the agony of the passengers who could not be saved. But she sank, causing, apart from the sorrow and the pity of the loss of so many lives, a sort of surprised consternation that such a thing should have happened at all. Why? You build a 45,000 tons hotel of thin steel plates to secure the patronage of, say, a couple of thousand rich people (for if it had been for the emigrant trade alone, there would have been no such exaggeration of mere size), you decorate it in the style of the Pharaohs or in the Louis Quinze style – I don't know which – and to please the aforesaid fatuous handful of individuals, who have more money than they know what to do with, and to the applause of two continents, you launch that mass with two thousand people on board at twenty-one knots across the sea – a perfect exhibition of the modern blind trust in mere material and appliances. And then this happens. General uproar. The blind trust in material and appliances has received a terrible shock. I will say nothing of the credulity which accepts any statement which specialists, technicians and office-people are pleased to make, whether for purposes of gain or glory. You stand there astonished and hurt in your profoundest sensibilities. But what else under the circumstances could you expect?

For my part I could much sooner believe in an unsinkable ship of 3000 tons than in one of 40,000 tons. It is one of those things that stand to reason. You can't increase the thickness of scantling and plates indefinitely. And the mere weight of this bigness is an added disadvantage. In reading the reports, the first reflection which occurs to one is that, if that luckless ship had been a couple of hundred feet shorter, she would have probably gone clear of the danger. But then, perhaps, she could not have had a swimming bath and a French café. That, of course, is a serious consideration. I am well aware that those responsible for her short and fatal existence ask us in desolate accents to believe that if she had hit end on she would have survived. Which, by a sort of coy implication, seems to mean that it was all the fault of the officer of the watch (he is dead now) for trying to avoid the obstacle. We shall have presently, in deference to commercial and industrial interests, a new kind of seamanship. A very new and 'progressive' kind. If you see anything in the way, by no means try to avoid it; smash at it full tilt. And then – and then only you shall see the triumph of material, of clever contrivances, of the whole box of engineering tricks in fact, and cover with glory a commercial concern of the most unmitigated sort, a great Trust, and a great ship-building yard, justly famed for the super-excellence of its material and workmanship. Unsinkable! See? I told you she was unsinkable, if only handled in accordance with the new seamanship. Everything's in that. And, doubtless, the Board of Trade, if properly approached, would consent to give the needed instructions to its examiners of Masters and Mates. Behold the examination-room of the future. Enter to the grizzled examiner a young man of modest aspect: 'Are you well up in modern seamanship?' 'I hope so, sir'. 'H'm, let's see. You are at night on the bridge in charge of a 150,000 tons ship, with a motor track, organ-loft, etc., etc., with a full cargo of passengers, a full crew of 1500 café waiters, two sailors and a boy, three collapsible boats as per Board of Trade regulations, and going at your three-quarter speed of, say, about forty knots. You perceive suddenly right ahead, and close to, something that looks like a large ice-floe. What would you do?' 'Put the helm amidships'. 'Very well. Why?' 'In order to hit end on.' 'On what grounds should you endeavour to hit end on?' 'Because we are taught by our builders and masters that the heavier the smash, the smaller the damage, and because the requirements of material should be attended to.'

And so on and so on. The new seamanship: when in doubt try to ram fairly – whatever's before you. Very simple. If only the *Titanic* had rammed that piece of ice (which was not a monstrous berg) fairly, every puffing paragraph would have been vindicated in the eyes of the credulous public which pays. But would it have been? Well, I doubt it. I am well aware that in the eighties the steamship *Arizona*, one of the 'greyhounds of the ocean' in the jargon of that day, did run bows on against a very unmistakable iceberg, and managed to get into port on her collision bulkhead. But the *Arizona* was not, if I remember rightly, 5000 tons register, let alone 45,000, and she was not going at twenty knots per hour. I can't be perfectly certain at this distance of time, but her sea-speed could not have been more than fourteen at the outside. Both these facts made for safety. And, even if she had been engined to go twenty knots, there would not have been behind that speed the enormous mass, so difficult to check in its impetus, the terrific weight of which is bound to do damage to itself or others at the slightest contact.

I assure you it is not for the vain pleasure of talking about my own poor experiences, but only to illustrate my point, that I will relate here a very unsensational little incident I witnessed now rather more than twenty years ago in Sydney, NSW. Ships were beginning then to grow bigger year after year, though, of course, the present dimensions were not even dreamt of. I was standing on the Circular Quay with a Sydney pilot watching a big mail steamship of one of our best-known companies being brought alongside. We admired her lines, her noble appearance, and were impressed by her size as well, though her length, I imagine, was hardly half that of the *Titanic*.

She came into the Cove (as that part of the harbour is called), of course very slowly, and at some hundred feet or so short of the quay she lost her way. That quay was then a wooden one, a fine structure of mighty piles and stringers bearing a roadway – a thing of great strength. The ship, as I have said before, stopped moving when some hundred feet from it. Then her engines were rung on slow ahead, and immediately rung off again. The propeller made just about five turns, I should say. She began to move, stealing on, so to speak, without a ripple; coming alongside with the utmost gentleness. I went on looking her over, very much interested, but the man with me, the pilot, muttered under his breath: 'Too much, too much'. His exercised judgment had warned him of what I did not even suspect. But I believe that neither of us was exactly prepared for what happened. There was a faint concussion of the ground under our feet, a groaning of piles, a snapping of great iron bolts, and with a sound of ripping and splintering, as when a tree is blown down by the wind, a great strong piece of wood, a baulk of squared timber, was displaced several feet as if by enchantment. I looked at my companion in amazement. 'I could not have believed it', I declared. 'No', he said. 'You would not have thought she would have cracked an egg – eh?'

I certainly wouldn't have thought that. He shook his head, and added: 'Ah! These great, big things, they want some handling'.

Some months afterwards I was back in Sydney. The same pilot brought me in from sea. And I found the same steamship, or else another as like her as two peas, lying at anchor not far from us. The pilot told me

she had arrived the day before, and that he was to take her alongside
to-morrow. I reminded him jocularly of the damage to the quay. 'Oh!'
he said, 'we are not allowed now to bring them in under their own
steam. We are using tugs.'

A very wise regulation. And this is my point – that size is to a certain
extent an element of weakness. The bigger the ship, the more delicately
she must be handled. Here is a contact which, in the pilot's own words,
you wouldn't think could have cracked an egg; with the astonishing
result of something like eighty feet of good strong wooden quay shaken
loose, iron bolts snapped, a baulk of stout timber splintered. Now,
suppose that quay had been of granite (as surely it is now) – or, instead
of the quay, if there had been, say, a North Atlantic fog there, with a
full-grown iceberg in it awaiting the gentle contact of a ship groping its
way along blindfold? Something would have been hurt, but it would
not have been the iceberg.

Apparently, there is a point in development when it ceases to be a
true progress – in trade, in games, in the marvellous handiwork of men,
and even in their demands and desires and aspirations of the moral and
mental kind. There is a point when progress, to remain a real advance,
must change slightly the direction of its line. But this is a wide question.
What I wanted to point out here is – that the old *Arizona*, the marvel
of her day, was proportionately stronger, handier, better equipped, than
this triumph of modern naval architecture, the loss of which, in common
parlance, will remain the sensation of this year. The clatter of the presses
has been worthy of the tonnage, of the preliminary paeans of triumph
round that vanished hull, of the reckless statements, and elaborate
descriptions of its ornate splendour. A great babble of news (and what
sort of news too, good heavens!) and eager comment has arisen around
this catastrophe, though it seems to me that a less strident note would
have been more becoming in the presence of so many victims left
struggling on the sea, of lives miserably thrown away for nothing, or
worse than nothing: for false standards of achievement, to satisfy a vulgar
demand of a few moneyed people for a banal hotel luxury – the only
one they can understand – and because the big ship pays, in one way
or another: in money or in advertising value.

It is in more ways than one a very ugly business, and a mere scrape
along the ship's side, so slight that, if reports are to be believed, it did

not interrupt a card party in the gorgeously fitted (but in chaste style) smoking-room – or was it in the delightful French cafe? – is enough to bring on the exposure. All the people on board existed under a sense of false security. How false, it has been sufficiently demonstrated. And the fact which seems undoubted, that some of them actually were reluctant to enter the boats when told to do so, shows the strength of that falsehood. Incidentally, it shows also the sort of discipline on board these ships, the sort of hold kept on the passengers in the face of the unforgiving sea. These people seemed to imagine it an optional matter: whereas the order to leave the ship should be an order of the sternest character, to be obeyed unquestioningly and promptly by every one on board, with men to enforce it at once, and to carry it out methodically and swiftly. And it is no use to say it cannot be done, for it can. It has been done. The only requisite is manageableness of the ship herself and of the numbers she carries on board. That is the great thing which makes for safety. A commander should be able to hold his ship and everything on board of her in the hollow of his hand, as it were. But with the modern foolish trust in material, and with those floating hotels, this has become impossible. A man may do his best, but he cannot succeed in a task which from greed, or more likely from sheer stupidity, has been made too great for anybody's strength.

The readers of the *English Review*, who cast a friendly eye nearly six years ago on my Reminiscences, and know how much the merchant service, ships and men, has been to me, will understand my indignation that those men of whom (speaking in no sentimental phrase, but in the very truth of feeling) I can't even now think otherwise than as brothers, have been put by their commercial employers in the impossibility to perform efficiently their plain duty; and this from motives which I shall not enumerate here, but whose intrinsic unworthiness is plainly revealed by the greatness, the miserable greatness, of that disaster. Some of them have perished. To die for commerce is hard enough, but to go under that sea we have been trained to combat, with a sense of failure in the supreme duty of one's calling is indeed a bitter fate. Thus they are gone, and the responsibility remains with the living who will have no difficulty in replacing them by others, just as good, at the same wages. It was their bitter fate. But I, who can look at some arduous years when their duty was my duty too, and their feelings were my feelings, can remember some of us who once upon a time were more fortunate.

It is of them that I would talk a little, for my own comfort partly, and also because I am sticking all the time to my subject to illustrate my point, the point of manageableness which I have raised just now. Since the memory of the lucky *Arizona* has been evoked by others than myself, and made use of by me for my own purpose, let me call up the ghost of another ship of that distant day whose less lucky destiny inculcates another lesson making for my argument. The *Douro*, a ship belonging to the Royal Mail Steam Packet Company, was rather less than one-tenth the measurement of the *Titanic*. Yet, strange as it may appear to the ineffable hotel exquisites who form the bulk of the first-class Cross-Atlantic Passengers, people of position and wealth and refinement did not consider it an intolerable hardship to travel in her, even all the way from South America; this being the service she was engaged upon. Of her speed I know nothing, but it must have been the average of the period, and the decorations of her saloons were, I dare say, quite up to the mark; but I doubt if her birth had been boastfully paragraphed all round the Press, because that was not the fashion of the time. She was not a mass of material gorgeously furnished and upholstered. She was a ship. And she was not, in the apt words of an article by Commander C. Crutchley, RNR, which I have just read, 'run by a sort of hotel syndicate composed of the Chief Engineer, the Purser, and the Captain', as these monstrous Atlantic ferries are. She was really commanded, manned, and equipped as a ship meant to keep the sea: a ship first and last in the fullest meaning of the term, as the fact I am going to relate will show.

She was off the Spanish coast, homeward bound, and fairly full, just like the *Titanic*; and further, the proportion of her crew to her passengers, I remember quite well, was very much the same. The exact number of souls on board I have forgotten. It might have been nearly three hundred, certainly not more. The night was moonlit, but hazy, the weather fine with a heavy swell running from the westward, which means that she must have been rolling a great deal, and in that respect the conditions for her were worse than in the case of the *Titanic*. Some time either just before or just after midnight, to the best of my recollection, she was run into amidships and at right angles by a large steamer which after the blow backed out, and, herself apparently damaged, remained motionless at some distance.

My recollection is that the *Douro* remained afloat after the collision for fifteen minutes or thereabouts. It might have been twenty, but certainly something under the half-hour. In that time the boats were lowered, all the passengers put into them, and the lot shoved off. There was no time to do anything more. All the crew of the *Douro* went down with her, literally without a murmur. When she went she plunged bodily down like a stone. The only members of the ship's company who survived were the third officer, who was from the first ordered to take charge of the boats, and the seamen told off to man them, two in each. Nobody else was picked up. A quartermaster, one of the saved in the way of duty, with whom I talked a month or so afterwards, told me that they pulled up to the spot, but could neither see a head nor hear the faintest cry.

But I have forgotten. A passenger was drowned. She was a lady's maid who, frenzied with terror, refused to leave the ship. One of the boats waited near by till the chief officer, finding himself absolutely unable to tear the girl away from the rail to which she clung with a frantic grasp, ordered the boat away out of danger. My quartermaster told me that he spoke over to them in his ordinary voice, and this was the last sound heard before the ship sank.

The rest is silence. I daresay there was the usual official inquiry, but who cared for it? That sort of thing speaks for itself with no uncertain voice; though the papers, I remember, gave the event no space to speak of: no large headlines – no headlines at all. You see it was not the fashion at the time. A seaman-like piece of work, of which one cherishes the old memory at this juncture more than ever before. She was a ship commanded, manned, equipped – not a sort of marine Ritz, proclaimed unsinkable and sent adrift with its casual population upon the sea, without enough boats, without enough seamen (but with a Parisian cafe and four hundred of poor devils of waiters) to meet dangers which, let the engineers say what they like, lurk always amongst the waves; sent with a blind trust in mere material, light-heartedly, to a most miserable, most fatuous disaster.

And there are, too, many ugly developments about this tragedy. The rush of the senatorial inquiry before the poor wretches escaped from the jaws of death had time to draw breath, the vituperative abuse of a man no more guilty than others in this matter, and the suspicion of this aimless fuss being a political move to get home on the MT Company, into which, in common parlance, the United States Government has got its knife, I don't pretend to understand why, though with the rest of the world I am aware of the fact. Perhaps there may be an excellent and worthy reason for it; but I venture to suggest that to take advantage of so many pitiful corpses, is not pretty. And the exploiting of the mere sensation on the other side is not pretty in its wealth of heartless inventions. Neither is the welter of Marconi lies which has not been sent vibrating without some reason, for which it would be nauseous to inquire too closely. And the calumnious, baseless, gratuitous, circumstantial lie charging poor Captain Smith with desertion of his post by means of suicide is the vilest and most ugly thing of all in this outburst of journalistic enterprise, without feeling, without honour, without decency.

But all this has its moral. And that other sinking which I have related here and to the memory of which a seaman turns with relief and thankfulness has its moral too. Yes, material may fail, and men, too, may fail sometimes; but more often men, when they are given the chance, will prove themselves truer than steel, that wonderful thin steel from which the sides and the bulkheads of our modern sea-leviathans are made.

2

George Bernard Shaw
'The *Titanic*: Some Unmentioned Morals'
Daily News, 14 May 1912

Why is it that the effect of a sensational catastrophe on a modern nation is to cast it into transports, not of weeping, not of prayer, not of sympathy with the bereaved nor congratulations of the rescued, not of poetic expression of the soul purified by pity and terror, but of a wild defiance of inexorable Fate and undeniable Fact by an explosion of outrageous romantic lying?

What is the first demand of romance in a shipwreck? It is the cry of Women and Children First. No male creature is to step into a boat as long as there is a woman or child on the doomed ship. How the boat is to be navigated and rowed by babies and women occupied in holding the babies is not mentioned. The likelihood that no sensible woman would trust either herself or her child in a boat unless there was a considerable percentage of men on board is not considered. Women and children first; that is the romantic formula. And never did the chorus of solemn delight at the strict observance of this formula by the British heroes on board the *Titanic* rise to sublimer strains than in the papers containing the first account of the wreck by a surviving eye witness, Lady Duff Gordon. She described how she escaped in the captain's boat. There was one other woman in it, and ten men: twelve all told. One woman for every five men. Chorus: 'Not once or twice in our rough island story', etc., etc.

Second romantic demand. Though all men (except the foreigners, who must all be shot by stern British officers in attempting to rush the boats over the bodies of the women and children) must be heroes, the captain must be a super-hero, a magnificent seaman, cool, brave, delighting in death and danger, and a living guarantee that the wreck was nobody's fault, but, on the contrary, a triumph of British navigation. Such a man Captain Smith was enthusiastically proclaimed on the day when it was reported (and actually believed, apparently) that he had shot himself on the bridge, or shot the first officer, or been shot by the first officer, or shot anyhow to bring the curtain down effectively. Writers who had never heard of Captain Smith to that hour wrote of him as they would hardly write of Nelson. The one thing positively known was that Captain Smith had lost his ship by deliberately and knowingly steaming into an ice field at the highest speed he had coal for. He paid the penalty; so did most of those for whose lives he was responsible. Had he brought them and the ship safely to land, nobody would have taken the smallest notice of him.

Third romantic demand. The officers must be calm, proud, steady, unmoved in the intervals of shooting the terrified foreigners. The verdict that they had surpassed all expectations was unanimous. The actual evidence was that Mr Ismay was told by the officer of his boat to go to hell, and that boats which were not full refused to go to the rescue of those who were struggling in the water in cork jackets. Reason frankly given: they were afraid. The fear was as natural as the officer's language to Mr Ismay: who of us at home dare blame them or feel sure that we should have been any cooler or braver? But is it necessary to assure the world that only Englishmen could have behaved so heroically, and to compare their conduct with the hypothetic dastardliness which lascars or Italians or foreigners generally – say Nansen or Amundsen or the Duke of Abruzzi – would have shown in the same circumstances?

Fourth romantic demand. Everybody must face death without a tremor; and the band, according to the *Birkenhead* precedent, must play 'Nearer My God to Thee', as an accompaniment to the invitation to Mr Ismay to go to hell. It was duly proclaimed that thus exactly it fell out. Actual evidence: the captain and officers were so afraid of a panic that, though they knew the ship was sinking, they did not dare to tell the passengers so – especially the third-class passengers – and the band played Rag Times to reassure the passengers, who, therefore, did not get into the boats, and did not realize their situation until the boats were gone and the ship was standing on her head before plunging to the bottom. What happened then Lady Duff Gordon has related, and the witnesses of the American inquiry could hardly bear to relate.

I ask, What is the use of all this ghastly, blasphemous, inhuman, braggartly lying? Here is a calamity which might well make the proudest man humble, and the wildest joker serious. It makes us vainglorious, insolent, and mendacious. At all events, that is what our journalists assumed. Were they right or wrong? Did the Press really represent the public? I am afraid it did. Churchmen and statesmen took much the same tone. The effect on me was one of profound disgust, almost of national dishonour. Am I mad? Possibly. At all events, that is how I felt and how I feel about it. It seems to me that when deeply moved men should speak the truth. The English nation appears to take precisely the contrary view. Again I am in the minority. What will be the end of it? – for England, I mean. Suppose we came into conflict with a race that had the courage to look facts in the face and the wisdom to know itself for what it was. Fortunately for us, no such race is in sight. Our wretched consolation must be that any other nation would have behaved just as absurdly.

Notes

Notes to Introduction

1 *Titanic: James Cameron's Illustrated Screenplay*, annotated by Randall Frakes (New York: Harper Collins, 1997), p. 59.
2. Christopher Tookey, 'A Fright to Remember', *Daily Mail*, 23 January 1998.
3. *Titanic: James Cameron's Illustrated Screenplay*, p. 128.
4. See Anne Massey and Mike Hammond, '"It Was True! How Can You Laugh?": History and Memory in the Reception of *Titanic* in Britain and Southampton', in *Titanic: Anatomy of a Blockbuster*, ed. Kevin S. Sandler and Gaylyn Studlar (New Brunswick: Rutgers University Press, 1999), pp. 244–47.

Notes to Chapter 1: What Have We Struck?

1. Wyn Craig Wade, *Titanic: End of a Dream* (revised edn, New York: Penguin, 1986), p. 20.
2. Daniel Allen Butler, *'Unsinkable': The Full Story of RMS Titanic* (Mechanicsburg, Pennsylvania: Stackpole Books, 1998), p. 11.
3. The Board of Trade's regulations required ships of over 10,000 tons to carry a minimum of sixteen lifeboats, which the *Titanic* exceeded with its complement of twenty. The regulations had not been altered since the 1890s, when the largest ships were only a quarter of the *Titanic*'s size.
4. Butler, *'Unsinkable'*, p. 94.
5. White Star cannibalized remnants of coal from its other ships to make the *Titanic*'s maiden voyage possible.
6. John P. Eaton and Charles A. Haas, *Titanic: Triumph and Tragedy* (2nd edn, Sparkford, Somerset: Patrick Stephens, 1994), p. 76.
7. Harris never saw the man again, and assumed that he must have carried out his promise. Butler, *'Unsinkable'*, p. 42.
8. Wade, *Titanic: End of a Dream*, p. 28.
9. Donald Hyslop, Alastair Forsyth and Sheila Jemima, *Titanic Voices: Memories from the Fateful Voyage* (Thrupp, Stroud: Sutton, 1997), p. 81.

10. Butler, 'Unsinkable', p. 32.
11. Subsequent to the disaster, one of Stead's friends wrote, 'A pity his spirits didn't warn him not to risk that crossing – he should have travelled by Cunard'. Geoffrey Marcus, *The Maiden Voyage: A Complete and Documented Account of the Titanic Disaster* (London: Unwin, 1969), p. 208.
12. Butler, 'Unsinkable', p. 19.
13. Many of them had in fact been scheduled to travel first class on White Star ships unable to sail due to the coal strike, but could not afford the price of a first-class ticket when they were transferred to the *Titanic*.
14. Marcus, *Maiden Voyage*, p. 109.
15. Marcus, *Maiden Voyage*, pp. 66–67.
16. Eaton and Haas, *Titanic: Triumph and Tragedy*, p. 114.
17. The *Titanic* had also received a warning about ice on Friday, 12 April, from the French liner *La Touraine*. Complete transcripts of all the ice warnings that the *Titanic* received may be found in John Booth and Sean Coughlin, *Titanic: Signals of Disaster* (Westbury, Wiltshire: White Star, 1993).
18. Butler, 'Unsinkable', pp. 58–59.
19. Eaton and Haas, *Titanic: Triumph and Tragedy*, p. 113.
20. Booth and Cooghlan, *Titanic: Signals of Disaster*, p. 17.
21. At 3.50 p.m. they did find time to deliver an ice warning from the *Noordam* to the bridge, which Smith acknowledged.
22. Eaton and Haas, *Titanic: Triumph and Tragedy*, p. 115.
23. Paul Heyer, *Titanic Legacy: Disaster as Media Event and Myth* (Westport, Connecticut: Praeger, 1995), p. 41.
24. Marcus, *The Maiden Voyage*, p. 254.
25. Prior to the invention of wireless communication, a number of ships had disappeared without a trace, and icebergs may have been to blame. The most famous such occurrence was the disappearance of the Collins Line's *Arctic* in 1856.
26. Butler, 'Unsinkable', p. 48.
27. Eaton and Haas, *Titanic: Triumph and Tragedy*, p. 115.
28. Eaton and Haas, *Titanic: Triumph and Tragedy*, p. 115.
29. Marcus, *Maiden Voyage*, pp. 86, 176.
30. Unlike the *Titanic*, the *Californian* had only a single wireless operator. When he was off duty, no messages could be received or transmitted. Required safety precautions, such as the posting of a twenty-four hour watch, did not include wireless operations. Heyer, *Titanic Legacy*, p. 42.
31. Eaton and Haas, *Titanic: Triumph and Tragedy*, p. 137.
32. Although starboard was the right side of a ship, sailors continued to use

terminology left over from the days of sail, when they turned the tiller one way to get the rudder to turn the other.

33. Eaton and Haas, *Titanic: Triumph and Tragedy*, p. 138.
34. Eaton and Haas, *Titanic: Triumph and Tragedy*, p. 138.
35. Butler, *'Unsinkable'*, p. 70.
36. Butler, *'Unsinkable'*, p. 71.
37. Wade, *Titanic: End of a Dream*, p. 180.
38. Although the damage extended along a 300-foot section of the ship, it was not continuous. Instead, there were intermittent ruptures in the hull, with a total area of about twelve square feet, approximately the size of a doorframe. In most places the damage was no wider than a human finger.
39. Eaton and Haas, *Titanic: Triumph and Tragedy*, p. 143.
40. Wade, *Titanic: End of a Dream*, p. 173.
41. Butler, *'Unsinkable'*, pp. 67–69.
42. Wade, *Titanic End of a Dream*, p. 174.
43. Wade, *Titanic: End of a Dream*, p. 175.
44. Wade, *Titanic: End of a Dream*, p. 176.
45. Butler, *'Unsinkable'*, pp. 79–80.
46. Wade, *Titanic: End of a Dream*, pp. 177–78.
47. Butler, *'Unsinkable'*, pp. 76–77.
48. Butler, *'Unsinkable'*, p. 79.
49. Butler, *'Unsinkable'*, p. 84.
50. Butler, *'Unsinkable'*, p. 90.
51. Butler, *'Unsinkable'*, p. 82.
52. Marcus, *Maiden Voyage*, p. 132.
53. Butler, *'Unsinkable'*, p. 111.
54. Marcus, *Maiden Voyage*, p. 55.
55. Butler, *'Unsinkable'*, pp. 121–22.
56. Butler, *'Unsinkable'*, p. 123.
57. Butler, *'Unsinkable'*, p. 125.
58. Butler, *'Unsinkable'*, p. 127.
59. Butler, *'Unsinkable'*, pp. 129–30.
60. Butler, *'Unsinkable'*, p. 130.
61. 'Nearer My God to Thee' seems a more likely prospect, as it was the hymn traditionally played at the funeral of a member of the Musicians' Union. Moreover, not long before the *Titanic*'s sailing, Hartley had told a friend that he would select it for his own funeral. Eaton and Haas, *Titanic: Triumph and Tragedy*, p. 159.
62. Butler, *'Unsinkable'*, p. 131.
63. Butler, *'Unsinkable'*, p. 134.

64. Wade, *Titanic: End of a Dream*, p. 227.
65. Wade, *Titanic: End of a Dream*, pp. 135–36, 225.
66. Wade, *Titanic: End of a Dream*, pp. 228–30.
67. Wade, *Titanic: End of a Dream*, p. 229.
68. Wade, *Titanic: End of a Dream*, p. 231.
69. Butler, 'Unsinkable', pp. 140–42.
70. Butler, 'Unsinkable', pp. 142–43.
71. Butler, 'Unsinkable', pp. 144–45.
72. Butler, 'Unsinkable', pp. 149–50.
73. CQD was an older distress call standing for 'Come Quick, Danger'.
74. Eaton and Haas, *Titanic: Triumph and Tragedy*, p. 177.
75. Eaton and Haas, *Titanic: Triumph and Tragedy*, p. 177.
76. Eaton and Haas, *Titanic: Triumph and Tragedy*, p. 178.
77. Marcus, *Maiden Voyage*, pp. 185–86.
78. Marcus, *Maiden Voyage*, p. 194.
79. Butler, 'Unsinkable', p. 160.
80. Butler, 'Unsinkable', pp. 161–62.
81. Marcus, *Maiden Voyage*, p. 212.
82. Butler, 'Unsinkable', p. 162.
83. The *Titanic* fired eight rockets that night.
84. Eaton and Haas, *Titanic: Triumph and Tragedy*, p. 165.
85. Butler, 'Unsinkable', pp. 163–64.
86. When the *Californian* arrived in Boston on 19 April, rumours quickly began to circulate that some members of the crew had seen rockets and a distant ship at the exact time when and place where the *Titanic* was sinking. Captain Lord denied the rumours, but Ernest Gill sold his story to the *Boston American* for $500. He and Lord were immediately summoned to testify at the inquiry into the disaster being held by Senator William Alden Smith. Lord's conduct was criticized by both the American and British inquiries, though he was not officially punished in any way. The press and public were less charitable, and Lord became, along with Ismay, a scapegoat for the disaster. He always denied that the other ship had been the *Titanic* and pressed for a reopening of the case against him until his death in 1962. In 1992 a new inquiry by the British Department of Transport's Marine Accident Investigation Branch was inconclusive. With estimates ranging from five to twenty miles, the investigators disagreed as to precisely how close the *Californian* was to the sinking *Titanic*. They concurred, however, that the *Californian* had indeed observed *Titanic*'s distress rockets and that Lord should have gone to its aid, or at least awakened Evans and ordered him to try and find out further

information by wireless. But even if Lord had started for the wreck site immediately upon seeing the first rocket, the investigators concluded that it was unlikely the *Californian* would have arrived in time to save a substantial number of the *Titanic*'s passengers. Heyer, *Titanic Legacy*, pp. 43, 98, 148–49.

87. Marcus, *Maiden Voyage*, p. 287.

88. Butler, *'Unsinkable'*, p. 200.

89. Alan Hustak, *Titanic: The Canadian Story* (Montreal: Véhicule Press, 1998), p. 127.

90. Hustak, *Titanic: The Canadian Story*, p. 128.

91. Eaton and Haas, *Titanic: Triumph and Tragedy*, p. 229.

92. Hustak, *Titanic: The Canadian Story*, p. 128.

93. Eaton and Haas, *Titanic: Triumph and Tragedy*, p. 229.

94. Hustak, *Titanic: The Canadian Story*, pp. 131–32.

95. Eaton and Haas, *Titanic: Triumph and Tragedy*, p. 234.

96. A private funeral for J. Bruce Ismay's private secretary, William Harrison, took place on 1 May.

97. Hustak, *Titanic: The Canadian Story*, pp. 140–41.

Notes to Chapter 2: The Best Traditions of the Sea

1. Sarnoff claimed that he intercepted a direct transmission from the *Titanic*'s sister ship, the *Olympic*, but this would have been impossible. Almost certainly, what he heard was other ships relaying information that had originally come from the *Olympic*. Paul Heyer, *Titanic Legacy: Disaster as Media Event and Myth* (Westport, Connecticut: Praeger, 1995), p. 52.

2. Heyer, *Titanic Legacy*, pp. 68–69.

3. Wyn Craig Wade, *Titanic: End of a Dream* (revised edn, New York: Penguin, 1986), p. 33.

4. The *New York Times* first received word of an accident to the *Titanic* at 1.20 a. m. on Monday 15 April via a wireless bulletin from the Associated Press. The paper had just been put to bed, and there was barely sufficient time to change the morning edition. In the chaos no one noticed that an advertisement for the *Titanic*'s return voyage appeared on page 11. Heyer, *Titanic Legacy*, pp. 67–68, 83.

5. 'Titanic Sinking', *Evening Standard*, 15 April 1912; 'The Largest Shipwreck in the World', *Evening News*, 15 April 1912.

6. John P. Eaton and Charles A. Haas, *Titanic: Triumph and Tragedy* (2nd edn, Sparkford, Somerset: Patrick Stephens, 1994), p. 180.

7. This may have simply been a case of a delayed transmission; the *Carpathia*'s

wireless set was too weak to reach the shore from the ship's current position and its messages had to be relayed by other ships. Or perhaps *Carpathia*'s wireless operator, Harold Cottam, was overwhelmed by the amount of incoming and outgoing traffic he had to deal with as the world clamoured for news of the *Titanic* and as the survivors sent messages to friends and relatives. Or it may have been because Cottam and *Titanic*'s junior wireless officer, Harold Bride, who had survived and was assisting him, decided that it might be more profitable to limit the amount of information about the sinking of *Titanic* so that they could sell their story to the highest bidder once they reached New York. On 18 April Frederick Sammis, the Marconi Company's chief engineer in New York, sent a message telling Bride: 'Marconi Company taking care of you. Keep your mouth shut and hold your story. It is fixed so you will get big money'. Bride received $1000 for his story from the *New York Times*; Cottam received $750.

8. The *Olympic* was on its way east on the return journey from New York and was approximately four hundred miles from the *Titanic*'s position at the time of the collision. Eaton and Haas, *Titanic: Triumph and Tragedy*, p. 205.

9. Daniel Allen Butler, *'Unsinkable': The Full Story of RMS Titanic* (Mechanicsburg, Pennsylvania: Stackpole Books, 1998), p. 169; Wade, *Titanic: End of a Dream*, p. 35.

10. Wade, *Titanic: End of a Dream*, p. 39.

11. 'Appalling Disaster of the Sea', *Daily Chronicle*, 16 April 1912.

12. 'Disaster to the *Titanic*' and 'Many Lives Lost in Disaster to *Titanic*', *Daily Mirror*, 16 April 1912.

13. '*Titanic* Wrecked by an Iceberg' and 'Stop-Press News', *Daily Express*, 16 April 1912.

14. Wade, *Titanic: End of a Dream*, p. 37.

15. The Board of Trade's regulations required ships of over 10,000 tons to carry a minimum of sixteen lifeboats, which *Titanic* exceeded with its complement of twenty.

16. Heyer, *Titanic Legacy*, pp. 69–72.

17. 'The Tragedy of the *Titanic*', *Daily Graphic*, 17 April 1912.

18. 'The Wreck of the *Titanic*', *Evening News*, 16 April 1912.

19. See Richard Howells, *The Myth of the Titanic* (New York: St Martin's, 1999), chapter 3.

20. '*Titanic* Catastrophe', *Daily Chronicle*, 17 April 1912.

21. 335 men were saved from the *Titanic*, along with 314 women and 54 children.

22. 'Only 868 Alive of 2200 on Stricken Liner *Titanic*', *Daily Mirror*, 17 April 1912.

23. 'The Victory over Death', *Daily Mail*, 17 April 1912.

24. '*Titanic* Catastrophe', *Daily Chronicle*, 17 April 1912.

25. See Howells, *Myth of the Titanic*, chapter 4.

26. 'The Heroes of the *Titanic*', *Daily Chronicle*, 20 April 1912.

27. 'What Millions Could Not Buy', *Daily Mirror*, 19 April 1912.

28. 'White Man's Law', *Daily Miirror*, 17 April 1912.

29. 'Full Story of the *Titanic* Disaster', *Daily Express*, 20 April 1912.

30. 'The Victory Over Death', *Daily Mail*, 17 April 1912.

31. 'The *Titanic*'s End', *Daily Express*, 20 April 1912.

32. See Howells, *Myth of the Titanic*, chapter 5. Troublesome passengers were so frequently referred to by *Titanic* crew members as 'Italians' that the Italian ambassador to the United States made a formal complaint. Several crewmen were forced to apologize. Donald Hyslop, Alastair Forsyth and Sheila Jemima, *Titanic Voices: Memories from the Fateful Voyage* (Phoenix Mill, Stroud: Sutton, 1997), p. 79.

33. George Bernard Shaw, 'The *Titanic*: Some Unmentioned Morals', *Daily News*, 14 May 1912.

34. Steven Biel, *Down with the Old Canoe: A Cultural History of the Titanic Disaster* (New York and London: Norton, 1996), p. 23.

35. Geoffrey Marcus, *The Maiden Voyage: A Complete and Documented Account of the Titanic Disaster* (London: Unwin, 1969), p. 18.

36. Butler, *'Unsinkable'*, p. 28.

37. Gary Cooper, *The Man Who Sank the Titanic? The Life and Times of Captain Edward J. Smith* (2nd edn, Cotes Heath, Stafford: Witan, 1998), p. 104.

38. Butler, *'Unsinkable'*, p. 127.

39. John Jacob Astor V was the son of William Astor, John Jacob IV's cousin.

40. Butler, *'Unsinkable'*, p. 27.

41. Butler, *'Unsinkable'*, p. 135.

42. Biel, *Down with the Old Canoe*, pp. 41–42.

43. Biel, *Down with the Old Canoe*, pp. 68, 80.

44. 'Go Down Like Gentlemen', *New York Times*, 20 April 1912.

45. Butler, *'Unsinkable'*, p. 123.

46. Biel, *Down with the Old Canoe*, pp. 39–48.

47. Biel, *Down with the Old Canoe*, pp. 106–7.

48. Biel, *Down with the Old Canoe*, pp. 122–23.

49. Biel, *Down with the Old Canoe*, p. 113.

50. Biel, *Down with the Old Canoe*, pp. 114–15.

51. 'Women First!', *Daily Mail*, 20 April 1912.

52. Lady Laura Aberconway, 'Women First', *Daily Mail*, 23 April 1912; 'Women First', *Daily Mail*, 25 April 1912.

53. Charles F. Forshaw, ed., *Poetical Tributes on the Loss of the RMS Titanic* (London, 1912), p. 12.

54. Forshaw, *Poetical Tributes*, p. 300.

55. The American Navy had intercepted wireless transmissions from Ismay to the White Star offices declaring his intention to get himself and the *Titanic*'s crew back to Britain as soon as possible; he had asked Franklin to hold the *Cedric* until Friday morning for that purpose. These messages were passed along to Smith, whose quick arrival at the pier reflected his determination to prevent Ismay from escaping before he could testify.

56. On 21 April the inquiry moved to Washington DC.

57. Butler, '*Unsinkable*', p. 181.

58. Marcus, *Maiden Voyage*, p. 217.

59. Some of the British hostility towards Senator Smith stemmed from his opposition to the General Arbitration Treaty a month before the *Titanic* disaster. The treaty had originally been planned as an agreement between the United States and Great Britain that issues 'justiceable in their nature' would be arbitrated by the Permanent Court of Arbitration at the Hague. But when France and Germany got wind of the treaty, they asked to be included. Despite the objections of the British Ambassador, James Bryce, President William Howard Taft agreed to include the French but excluded the Germans. In March 1912 the treaty was referred to the Senate Foreign Relations Committee. There Smith led the opposition, arguing that if the treaty was truly for the purpose of promoting international peace, it should be extended to all the major European powers, including Germany. Thanks largely to Smith's efforts, the treaty was not ratified by the Senate. Shortly thereafter, Bryce made a trip to Michigan to explore the chance for defeating Smith in the election of 1912. Smith was furious when he found out about the trip, and his relationship with Bryce remained icy. Wade, *Titanic: End of a Dream*, pp. 156–57.

60. Smith claimed that he had asked the question only to put to rest the false hopes of relatives of the *Titanic*'s victims.

61. Wade, *Titanic: End of a Dream*, pp. 190–91.

62. 'Government Inquiry Announced', *Daily Mirror*, 23 April 1912.

63. 'Senator Smith's Inquiry', *Daily Mail*, 26 April 1912.

64. 'Two Records Broken', *Evening Standard*, 23 April 1912.

65. Wade, *Titanic: End of a Dream*, p. 189.

66. 'Wrong Ways and Right,' *Daily Express*, 23 April 1912.

67. 'The *Titanic* Inquiry', *Daily Chronicle*, 22 April 1912.

68. In 1915 Mersey headed the investigation into the sinking of the *Lusitania*, which many observers also viewed as something of whitewash intended to disavow any culpability on the part of the Cunard Line.

69. Butler, *'Unsinkable'*, p. 193.

70. Marcus, *Maiden Voyage*, p. 263.

71. Eaton and Haas, *Titanic: Triumph and Tragedy*, p. 265.

72. Marcus, *Maiden Voyage*, p. 264; Eaton and Haas, *Titanic: Triumph and Tragedy*, p. 266.

73. Smith's statement was never confirmed by any reliable survivor account and is almost certainly fictitious.

74. Forshaw, *Poetical Tributes*, p. 41.

75. Forshaw, *Poetical Tributes*, p. 62.

76. Forshaw, *Poetical Tributes*, p. 159.

77. Forshaw, *Poetical Tributes*, p. 245.

78. Forshaw, *Poetical Tributes*, p. 103

79. 'Final Scenes of Tragic Heroism on the Sinking *Titanic*', *Daily Mirror*, 20 April 1912.

80. Forshaw, *Poetical Tributes*, p. 67.

81. Forshaw, *Poetical Tributes*, p. 246.

82. 'How the *Titanic* Heroes Went to Their Doom', *Daily Sketch*, 20 April 1912.

83. 'The Duty of the Nation', *Daily Chronicle*, 17 April 1912.

84. Forshaw, *Poetical Tributes*, pp. 253–54.

85. Forshaw, *Poetical Tributes*, p. 208.

86. John Peck, *Maritime Fiction: Sailors and the Sea in British and American Novels, 1719–1917* (Houndmills, Basingstoke, Hampshire: Palgrave, 2001), p. 27.

87. Cynthia Fansler Behrman, *Victorian Myths of the Sea* (Athens, Ohio: Ohio University Press, 1977), p. 26.

88. Paul Kennedy, *The Rise and Fall of the Great Powers: Economic Change and Military Conflict from 1500 to 2000* (London: Unwin, 1988), pp. 151–52.

89. Kennedy, *Rise and Fall of the Great Powers*, pp. 226–27.

90. Aaron L. Friedberg, *The Weary Titan: Britain and the Experience of Relative Decline, 1895–1905* (Princeton: Princeton University Press, 1988), p. 138.

91. Marcus, *Maiden Voyage*, p. 219.

92. Wade, *Titanic: End of a Dream*, pp. 41–42.

93. Forshaw, *Poetical Tributes*, p. 81.

94. Forshaw, *Poetical Tributes*, p. 268.

95. 'Heroes Indeed', *Daily Chronicle*, 18 April 1912.

96. 'The Heroes of the *Titanic*', *Daily Chronicle*, 20 April 1912.
97. Marcus, *Maiden Voyage*, p. 217.
98. Marcus, *Maiden Voyage*, p. 210.
99. Letter from George V. Briscoe, *Daily Graphic*, 24 April 1912.
100. Roger Casement Collection, National Library of Ireland, MS 31, p. 725.
101. Forshaw, *Poetical Tributes*, pp. 13–15.
102. There are a handful of exceptions, such as F. T. Read's verses:

> 'Should anything happen!' Tut! it won't!
> But the boats are the 'first-class' right;
> Twould be something to laugh at when we meet
> In our mansion saloons at night.
> We have nothing to do with the lower crowds,
> Who as copper to gold compare;
> And the company looks to the safety first
> Of the 'eminent' millionaire!

Forshaw, *Poetical Tributes*, p. 216. The suffragette Sylvia Pankhurst was reported to have said that men deserved no credit for giving up their seats in the boats to women because that was the rule of the sea. In response, G. K. Chesterton wrote, 'Whether this was a graceful thing for a gay spinster to say to 800 widows in the very hour of doom is not worth inquiry. Like cannibalism, it is a matter of taste'. Terry Coleman, *The Liners: A History of the North Atlantic Crossing* (London: Allen Lane, 1976), p. 85.
103. Marcus, *Maiden Voyage*, p. 287.
104. The film *A Night to Remember* (1958) was made in Britain and did pay considerable attention to third class, but as it was a faithful depiction of Lord's book it cannot be counted as an independent British response to the disaster.

Notes to Chapter 3: Heroes and Villains

1. Steven Biel, *Down with the Old Canoe: A Cultural History of the Titanic Disaster* (New York and London: W. W. Norton, 1996), p. 33.
2. During her lifetime Brown was known as 'Margaret' or 'Maggie'. The nickname 'Molly' was given to Brown by Richard Morris, the author of the book *The Unsinkable Molly Brown* (the basis for the musical and film of the same name), because he felt that it was easier to sing.
3. Kristen Iversen, *Molly Brown: Unravelling the Myth* (Boulder, Colorado: Johnson Books, 1999), p. 90.
4. Iversen, *Molly Brown*, p. 3.

5. Iversen, *Molly Brown*, p. 10.

6. Iversen, *Molly Brown*, pp. 14–24.

7. Iversen, *Molly Brown*, p. 34.

8. Iversen, *Molly Brown*, p. 35.

9. Iversen, *Molly Brown*, p. 229.

10. There is no public memorial to Margaret Tobin Brown, but both the house in which she was born in Hannibal, Missouri, and the House of Lions in Denver are open to the public.

11. Brown never actually said this. In reality, the sobriquet 'unsinkable' was given to her by Denver society columnist Polly Pry, who was the first to refer to her as 'the unsinkable Mrs Brown'. Iversen, *Molly Brown*, p. 177.

12. Biel, *Down with the Old Canoe*, p. 169.

13. Daniel Allen Butler, *'Unsinkable': The Full Story of RMS Titanic* (Mechanicsburg, PA: Stackpole, 1998), p. 151.

14. Richard Howells, *The Myth of the Titanic* (Houndmills, Basingstoke: Macmillan, 1999), p. 67.

15. Charles F. Forshaw, ed., *Poetical Tributes on the Loss of the RMS Titanic* (London, 1912), pp. 63, 136, 244.

16. J. A. Mangan, 'Social Darwinism and Upper-Class Education in Late Victorian and Edwardian England', in J. A. Mangan and James Walvin, eds, *Manliness and Morality: Middle-Class Masculinity in Britain and America, 1800–1940* (Manchester: Manchester University Press, 1987), p. 137.

17. Mangan, 'Social Darwinism', pp. 146–47.

18. See John Tosh, *A Man's Place: Masculinity and the Middle-Class Home in Victorian England* (New Haven and London: Yale University Press, 1999), pp. 169–82. The emergence of male preserves in Victorian country houses is traced in Mark Girouard, *Life in the Victorian Country House* (Harmondsworth: Penguin, 1980), pp. 292–98.

19. Allen Warren, 'Popular Manliness: Baden-Powell, Scouting and the Development of Manly Character', in Mangan and Walvin, p. 203.

20. Forshaw, *Poetical Tributes*, pp. 66, 124.

21. Forshaw, *Poetical Tributes*, p. 62.

22. Tosh, *A Man's Place*, p. 184.

23. Forshaw, *Poetical Tributes*, pp. 128, 221.

24. Warren, 'Popular Manliness', p. 200.

25. Mangan, 'Social Darwinism', p. 143.

26. Butler, *'Unsinkable'*, pp. 93, 97.

27. Butler, *'Unsinkable'*, p. 126.

28. Geoffrey Marcus, *The Maiden Voyage: A Complete and Documented Account of the Titanic Disaster* (London: Unwin, 1969), pp. 205–6.

29. Marcus, *Maiden Voyage*, p. 207.
30. Marcus, *Maiden Voyage*, p. 205.
31. Butler, *'Unsinkable'*, p. 182.
32. In the end, both towns kept their names. Biel, *Down with the Old Canoe*, pp. 72–73.
33. Biel, *Down with the Old Canoe*, p. 72.
34. Marcus, *Maiden Voyage*, p. 206.
35. Howells, *Myth of the Titanic*, pp. 72–73.
36. Howells, *Myth of the Titanic*, p. 72.
37. 'Wrong Ways and Right', *Daily Express*, 23 April 1912.
38. Butler, *'Unsinkable'*, p. 233.
39. Meredith Etherington-Smith and Jeremy Pilcher, *The 'It' Girls: Lucy, Lady Duff Gordon, the Couturière 'Lucile', and Elinor Glyn, Romantic Novelist* (London: Hamish Hamilton, 1986), pp. 85–87.
40. Etherington-Smith, *The 'It' Girls*, pp. 150–51.
41. Etherington-Smith, *The 'It' Girls*, p. 151.
42. Etherington-Smith, *The 'It' Girls*, p. 152.
43. Etherington-Smith, *The 'It' Girls*, p. 152.
44. Etherington-Smith, *The 'It' Girls*, p. 153.
45. Etherington-Smith, *The 'It' Girls*, pp. 154–55.
46. Etherington-Smith, *The 'It' Girls*, pp. 154–55.
47. John P. Eaton and Charles A. Haas, *Titanic: Triumph and Tragedy* (2nd edn, Sparkford, Somerset: Patrick Stephens, 1994), p. 192.
48. Etherington-Smith, *The 'It' Girls*, pp. 157–58.
49. Etherington-Smith, *The 'It' Girls*, p. 158.
50. Marcus, *Maiden Voyage*, p. 244.
51. Etherington-Smith, *The 'It' Girls*, p. 159.
52. Marcus, *Maiden Voyage*, p. 250–52.
53. Etherington-Smith, *The 'It' Girls*, p. 160.

Notes to Chapter 4: Jack Phillips

1. John Janaway, *Yesterday's Town: Godalming* (Buckingham: Barracuda, 1987), p. 98.
2. John Janaway, *Godalming: A Short History* (Godalming: Ammonite Books, 1993), p. 63.
3. *Godhelmian*, July 1949. This magazine can be found in the Godalming Museum.
4. John Booth and Sean Coughlan, *Titanic: Signals of Disaster* (Westbury, Wiltshire: White Star, 1993), p. 23.

5. Booth and Coughlan, *Titanic: Signals of Disaster*, p. 24.
6. Paul Heyer, *Titanic Legacy: Disaster as Media Event and Myth* (Westport, Connecticut: Praeger, 1995), p. 38.
7. John P. Eaton and Charles A. Haas, *Titanic: Triumph and Tragedy* (2nd edn, Sparkford, Somerset: Patrick Stephens, 1994), pp. 44–46.
8. As the *Titanic* departed from Southampton, Guglielmo Marconi's wife and daughter saw the ship steam past their country cottage on the Isle of Wight. Marconi had been supposed to be on board, but was in a hurry to get to New York and had crossed three days earlier on the *Lusitania*.
9. Booth and Coughlan, *Titanic: Signals of Disaster*, pp. 20, 22.
10. Booth and Coughlan, *Titanic: Signals of Disaster*, p. 35.
11. Harold Bride, 'Thrilling Tale by *Titanic*'s Surviving Wireless Man', in Jack Wincour, ed., *The Story of the Titanic as Told by its Survivors* (New York: Dover, 1960), pp. 314–15.
12. Bride, 'Thrilling Tale', pp. 316–20.
13. Richard Howells, *The Myth of the Titanic* (Houndmills, Basingstoke: Macmillan, 1999), p. 105.
14. 'How the End Came', *Daily News*, 20 April 1912.
15. Operator's Coolness', *Daily Mirror*, 17 April 1912.
16. Forshaw, *Poetical Tributes*, pp. 43, 120, 226.
17. 'Full Story of the *Titanic* Tragedy', *Daily Chronicle*, 20 April 1912.
18. Oglethorpe's reputation was somewhat dubious, however, on account of his suspected Jacobite sympathies. He was cashiered from the British Army in 1746 following a charge of misconduct levelled against him by the Duke of Cumberland as a result of his actions at the Battle of Culloden.
19. 'Post-Office Memorial', *Surrey Advertiser and County Times*, 27 April 1912.
20. Report of the Phillips Memorial Committee of the Town Council of the Borough of Godalming to Such Council at its Meeting Held on the 6th Day of May, 1913. The records of Godalming Town Council are held by the Godalming Museum.
21. Report of the Phillips Memorial Committee to a Meeting of the Town Council to be Held on the 9th Day of November, 1912.
22. Report of the Phillips Memorial Committee ... on the 9th Day of November, 1912.
23. Report of the Phillips Memorial Committee ... on the 6th Day of May, 1913.
24. Minutes of the Quarterly Meeting of the Council of the Borough of Godalming, 10 November 1913.
25. Minutes of the Quarterly Meeting of the Council of the Borough of Godalming, 3 February 1914.

26. The church debated the design and location of the plaque for months before allowing Phillips's parents to make the decisions.
27. *Farncombe Parish Magazine*, July 1913. This magazine can be found in the Godalming Museum.
28. This reference comes from an undated issue of the *Godhelmian* that is held by the Godalming Museum. George Young dated the magazine to the early 1930s.
29. 'Survivor Visits Museum's Tribute to *Titanic* Tragedy', *Surrey Advertiser*, 4 April 1997.
30. 'Survivor Visits Museum's Tribute to *Titanic* Tragedy', *Surrey Advertiser*, 4 April 1997.

Notes to Chapter 5: Wallace Hartley

1. Chris Aspin, *The First Industrial Society: Lancashire, 1750–1850* (revised edn, Preston: Carnegie, 1995), p. 72.
2. Aspin, *First Industrial Society*, p. 83.
3. 'A Colne Hero', *Colne and Nelson Times*, 26 April 1912.
4. Walter Lord, *The Night Lives On* (New York: William Morrow, 1986), p. 138.
5. Lord, *The Night Lives On*, p. 137.
6. Stephen J. Spignesi, *The Complete Titanic* (Seacaucus, New Jersey: Carol, 1998), p. 248.
7. Lord, *Night Lives On*, p. 139.
8. Harold Bride, 'Thrilling Tale by *Titanic*'s Surviving Wireless Man', in Jack Wincour, ed., *The Story of the Titanic as Told by its Survivors* (New York: Dover, 1960), p. 317.
9. Richard Howells, *The Myth of the Titanic* (Houndmills, Basingstoke: Macmillan, 1999), p. 129.
10. 'The Musician Heroes of the *Titanic*', *Daily Chronicle*, 20 April 1912.
11. 'Band Goes Down Playing', *Daily Mirror*, 20 April 1912.
12. 'Nearer My God to Thee', *Daily Sketch*, 20 April 1912.
13. Wallace Hartley Collection, Colne Public Library, Colne, Lancashire.
14. Howells, *Myth of the Titanic*, pp. 121–23.
15. Wallace Hartley Collection, Colne Public Library.
16. 'Colne Musician Lost in the *Titanic*', *Colne and Nelson Times*, 19 April 1912.
17. 'The Lost *Titanic*', *Colne and Nelson Times*, 26 April 1912.
18. 'Civis', *Colne and Nelson Times*, 26 April 1912.
19. 'Colne's *Titanic* Hero', *Colne and Nelson Times*, 3 May 1912.

20. 'Titanic Hero's Funeral', Liverpool Daily Post and Mercury, 18 May 1912.
21. 'Mr Wallace Hartley's Funeral', Colne and Nelson Times, 17 May 1912.
22. Wallace Hartley Collection, Colne Public Library.
23. 'The Wallace Hartley Memorial', Colne and Nelson Times, 24 May 1912.

Notes to Chapter 6: Thomas Andrews

1. Shan Bullock, *Thomas Andrews: Shipbuilder* (new edn, Belfast: Blackstaff, 1999), pp. 3–5.
2. Bullock, *Thomas Andrews*, p. 20.
3. Bullock, *Thomas Andrews*, p. 50.
4. Bullock, *Thomas Andrews*, p. 50.
5. Bullock, *Thomas Andrews*, p. 31.
6. Bullock, *Thomas Andrews*, pp. 59–60.
7. Bullock, *Thomas Andrews*, pp. 62–64.
8. Bullock, *Thomas Andrews*, p. 70.
9. Daniel Allen Butler, *'Unsinkable': The Full Story of RMS Titanic* (Mechanicsburg, Pennsylvania: Stackpole Books, 1998), p. 95.
10. Butler, *'Unsinkable'*, p. 102.
11. 'Belfast and the Disaster', *Belfast News-Letter*, 17 April 1912.
12. 'The *Titanic* Disaster', *Belfast Evening Telegraph*, 22 April 1912.
13. Bullock, *Thomas Andrews*, p. 77.
14. 'Mr Andrews's Heroism', *Belfast News-Letter*, 22 April 1912.
15. 'The Late Mr Thomas Andrews', *Belfast Evening Telegraph*, 22 April 1912.
16. 'Belfast and the Disaster', *Northern Whig*, 22 April 1912.
17. 'Belfast Victims', *Irish Weekly*, 27 April 1912.
18. 'The Late Mr Thomas Andrews', *Herald and County Down Independent*, 11 October 1912.
19. Bullock, *Thomas Andrews*, p. xiii.
20. Peter Stone and Maury Yeston, *Titanic: The Complete Book of the Musical* (New York: Applause Books, 1997), pp. 16, 20.
21. Stone, *Titanic: The Complete Book of the Musical*, p. 146.
22. Stone, *Titanic: The Complete Book of the Musical*, pp. 161–65.
23. *Titanic: James Cameron's Illustrated Screenplay*, annotated by Jonathan Frakes (New York: Harper Collins, 1998), pp. 92–93.
24. *Titanic: James Cameron's Illustrated Screenplay*, p. 112.
25. *Titanic: James Cameron's Illustrated Screenplay*, pp. 129–30.
26. William Barnes, *Thomas Andrews: Voyage into History. Titanic Secrets Revealed Through the Eyes of her Builder* (Gillette, New Jersey: Edin Books, 2000).

Notes to Chapter 7: Edward Smith

1. In 1910 the six pottery towns of Hanley, Tunstall, Burselm, Stoke, Fenton and Longton were federated into the single city of Stoke-on-Trent.

2. Almost 50 per cent of the labour force was comprised of women and children under fifteen. Marguerite W. Dupree, *Family Structure in the Staffordshire Potteries, 1840–1880* (Oxford: Clarendon, 1995), pp. 50, 57.

3. Dupree, *Family Structure*, p. 73.

4. Dupree, *Family Structure*, p. 81.

5. Dupree, *Family Structure*, p. 84.

6. Dupree, *Family Structure*, p. 59.

7. Gary Cooper, *The Man Who Sank the Titanic? The Life and Times of Captain Edward J. Smith* (2nd edn, Cotes Heath, Stafford: Witan, 1998), p. 9.

8. Cooper, *The Man Who Sank the Titanic?*, p. 22.

9. Cooper, *The Man Who Sank the Titanic?*, p. 26.

10. Cooper, *The Man Who Sank the Titanic?*, p. 33.

11. Smith's daughter experienced much tragedy in her life. In addition to the death of her father, her mother was killed by a bus, one son died of polio and the other in the Second World War, and her husband committed suicide.

12. Cooper, *The Man Who Sank the Titanic?*, p. 38.

13. Cooper, *The Man Who Sank the Titanic?*, p. 39.

14. *Captain Edward John Smith Memorial: A Souvenir of July 29th, 1914* (Lichfield: Johnson's Head, 1914), p. 30. This booklet can be found in the Local History Collection of the Lichfield Public Library.

15. Daniel Allen Butler, *'Unsinkable': The Full Story of RMS Titanic* (Mechanicsburg, Pennsylvania: Stackpole, 1998), p. 48.

16. Cooper, *The Man Who Sank the Titanic?*, p. 59.

17. John P. Eaton and Charles A. Haas, *Titanic: Triumph and Tragedy* (2nd edn, Sparkford, Somerset: Patrick Stephens, 1994), p. 72.

18. It could be argued that the episode played a pivotal role in the *Titanic* disaster, as it forced the *Olympic* to return to Belfast for repairs. The *Titanic*'s propeller shaft had to be transferred to the *Olympic*, which caused the *Titanic*'s maiden voyage to be delayed by three weeks, from 20 March to 10 April.

19. Cooper, *The Man Who Sank the Titanic?*, p. 77.

20. One passenger did claim to have seen Smith drinking, but this was disputed by both the Wideners and the Thayers, who were at his table.

21. Cooper, *The Man Who Sank the Titanic?*, p. 96.

22. Butler, *'Unsinkable'*, p. 91.

23. Cooper, *The Man Who Sank the Titanic?*, p. 106.

24. Cooper, *The Man Who Sank the Titanic?*, p. 109.

25. Cooper, *The Man Who Sank the Titanic?*, p. 111.

26. Cooper, *The Man Who Sank the Titanic?*, p. 121.

27. 'The End of the *Titanic*', *Daily Mail*, 20 April 1912; 'How the *Titanic* Heroes Went to Their Doom', *Daily Sketch*, 20 April 1912.

28. Cooper, *The Man Who Sank the Titanic?*, p. 135.

29. 'Captain's Last Act', *Daily Express*, 20 April 1912.

30. '"Be British!" Brave Captain's Last Call to the Crew', *Daily Chronicle*, 20 April 1912.

31. 'Final Scenes of Tragic Heroism on the Sinking *Titanic*', *Daily Mirror*, 20 April 1912.

32. Cooper, *The Man Who Sank the Titanic?*, p. 136.

33. '"Be British!" Brave Captain's Last Call to the Crew', *Daily Chronicle*, 20 April 1912.

34. 'Captain's Last Act', *Daily Express*, 20 April 1912.

35. Richard Howells, *The Myth of the Titanic* (Houndmills, Basingstoke: Macmillan, 1999), p. 68.

36. Charles F. Forshaw, ed., *Poetical Tributes on the Loss of the RMS Titanic* (London, 1912), p. 125.

37. *Captain Edward John Smith Memorial*, p. 5.

38. *Captain Edward John Smith Memorial*, pp. 5–7.

39. 'The Late Captain Smith', *Stoke Sentinel*, 16 April 1913.

40. Cooper, *The Man Who Sank the Titanic?*, p. 141.

41. Cooper, *The Man Who Sank the Titanic?*, p. 142.

42. 'The Late Captain Smith', *Stoke Sentinel*, 16 April 1913.

43. 'The Late Captain E. J. Smith', *Stoke Sentinel*, 24 April 1913.

44. *Captain Edward John Smith Memorial*, pp. 5–6.

45. Letter to the Editor, *Lichfield Mercury*, 5 June 1914.

46. Letter to the Editor, *Lichfield Mercury*, 8 June 1914.

47. 'The Late Captain E. J. Smith', *Lichfield Mercury*, 19 June 1914.

48. *Captain Edward John Smith Memorial*, p. 14.

49. David J. Woodall, 'A Lichfield Memorial to the *Titanic* Captain', *Lichfield Mercury*, 7 November 1958.

50. The *Titanic* Brewery's '*Titanic* Stout' won the award for Best Bottle-Conditioned Beer in a special tasting commissioned by the *Guardian* in 1994. The company also produced a beer called 'Captain Smith's Strong Ale and Wreckage'. Roger Protz, 'Beer: Raising the *Titanic*', *Guardian*, 27 August 1994.

51. 'Statue Seekers Told "No Deal" as Debate Rolls On', *Lichfield Mercury*, 15 November 1985.
52. 'Schoolchildren Lead Bid for Statue', *Stoke Sentinel*, 15 January 1994.
53. Steve Sharma, 'Bid to Move Statue', *Lichfield Mercury*, 6 February 1997.
54. '*Titanic* Success Could Breathe New Life into Home Town Hero', *Birmingham Post*, 27 February 1998.
55. '*Titanic* Success Could Breathe New Life into Home Town Hero', *Birmingham Post*, 27 February 1998.

Notes to Chapter 8: William Murdoch

1. Andrew McCulloch, *Galloway: A Land Apart* (Edinburgh: Birlinn, 2000), pp. 453–57.
2. Matthew Gallagher, 'Murdoch of the *Titanic*', *Scots Magazine*, April 1992, p. 57.
3. Susanne Störmer, *Good-Bye, Good Luck: The Biography of William Murdoch* (Kosel, Germany: the author, n.d.), p. 50.
4. Jack Wincour, ed., *The Story of the Titanic as Told by its Survivors* (New York: Dover, 1960), p. 277.
5. Störmer, *Good-Bye, Good Luck*, p. 85.
6. Störmer, *Good-Bye, Good Luck*, p. 88.
7. Wincour, *Story of the Titanic*, p. 282. In his testimony before the American inquiry, Lightoller gave a different version of this conversation in which he claimed that he and Murdoch did not discuss 'the iceberg situation': 'We remarked on the weather, about its being calm, clear. We remarked the distance we could see. We seemed to be able to see a long distance. Everything was very clear. We could see the stars setting down to the horizon'. Tom Kuntz, ed., *The Titanic Disaster Hearings: The Official Transcripts of the 1912 Senate Investigation* (New York: Pocket, 1998), p. 48.
8. In 1912 helm orders were still given as if ships were sailing vessels with tillers that were pushed one way in order to make the rudder move in the opposite direction. Hichens thus spun the wheel to the right in order to make the rudder, and the ship, turn left. Helm orders on British ships were not rationalized until the 1930s, when it was finally decided to set up the helm controls so that the wheel and the rudder moved in the same direction. Standby Quartermaster Alfred Olliver later claimed that he heard Murdoch give the order to 'hard-a-port' in order to complete the manoeuvre, but no other survivor seems to have heard him.
9. There are many versions of this conversation, but they all agree on its

general parameters. This one is a composite of that reported by Daniel Allen Butler in *'Unsinkable': The Full Story of the RMS Titanic* (Mechanicsburg, Pennsylvania: Stackpole Books, 1998), p. 70, and the testimony of Quartermaster Hichens at the American inquiry, as found in Kuntz, *Titanic Disaster Hearings*, p. 234.

10. Butler, *'Unsinkable'*, p. 93.
11. Butler, *'Unsinkable'*, p. 110–11.
12. Wyn Craig Wade, *The Titanic: End of a Dream* (revised edn, New York: Penguin, 1986), p. 222.
13. Wade, *Titanic: End of a Dream*, p. 58.
14. Butler, *'Unsinkable'*, p. 136.
15. Kuntz, *Titanic Disaster Hearings*, p. 21.
16. Wade, *Titanic: End of a Dream*, pp. 182–83.
17. In his account of the sinking, Daniel Allen Butler claims that the officer who committed suicide was most likely Chief Officer Wilde, who is curiously absent from most survivors' accounts describing the events of that night. Butler interprets this as an indication that Wilde 'lost his nerve'. Of the eyewitnesses, Carl Jansen did state that it was 'the Chief Officer' who had placed his revolver in his mouth and shot himself. Butler, *'Unsinkable'*, p. 136.
18. 'Disaster to Great Liner', *Dumfries and Galloway Standard and Advertiser*, 17 April 1912.
19. 'The *Titanic* Disaster', *Dumfries and Galloway Standard and Advertiser*, 24 April 1912.
20. Wilson H. Armistead, 'The Loss of the *Titanic*', *Kirkcudbrightshire Advertiser*, 26 April 1912.
21. 'The *Titanic* Disaster', *Dumfries and Galloway Standard and Advertiser*, 11 May 1912.
22. 'Proposed Memorial to Lieutenant Murdoch', *Dumfries and Galloway Standard and Advertiser*, 21 August 1912.
23. Italics Cameron's. *Titanic: James Cameron's Illustrated Screenplay*, annotated by Randall Frakes (New York: Harper Collins, 1998), p. 86.
24. *Titanic: James Cameron's Illustrated Screenplay*, pp. 119–20.
25. This line may have been ad-libbed by Ewan Stewart, as it is not in the published screenplay.
26. *Titanic: James Cameron's Illustrated Screenplay*, p. 128.
27. Kevin Jackson, 'The *Titanic* Hero They Could Not Sink', *Mail on Sunday*, 17 May 1998.
28. Audrey Gillan, 'Small Town Gangs up on Hollywood', *Scotland on Sunday*, 8 March 1998.

29. Gavin Madeley, 'Suicide Scene Angers *Titanic*'s Officer's Nephew', *Glasgow Herald*, 19 January 1998.

30. Audrey Gillan, 'Small Town Gangs up on Hollywood', *Scotland on Sunday*, 8 March 1998.

31. Dorothy-Grace Elder, 'Rattling the Cages: Charges Against Yesterday's Heroes that Just Won't Stick', *Scotland on Sunday*, 22 February 1998.

32. Frank Ryan, 'MPs Protest at Blockbuster's Slur on Scottish Seaman', *Scotsman*, 27 February 1998.

33. 'It's a Titanic Liberty with the Truth', *Mirror*, 16 April 1998.

34. Trevor Phillips, 'Does Any Movie Have the Right to Call This Brave Man a Coward?', *Independent*, 18 April 1998.

35. Audrey Gillan, 'Small Town Gangs up on Hollywood', *Scotland on Sunday*, 8 March 1998; Dorothy Grace-Elder, 'Rattling the Cages: The Babe in the Bath Water Exposes the Naked Truth', *Scotland on Sunday*, 15 March 1998.

36. Jim McBeth, 'Hollywood Offers *Titanic* Apology to a Small Town', *Scotsman*, 8 April 1998.

37. James Murray and Dorothy-Grace Elder, 'Film-Makers Decline to Apologise to Town', *Scotland on Sunday*, 12 April 1998.

Notes to Chapter 9: Belfast

1. Michael McCaughan, 'Reclaiming a Part of Our Past', *Belfast Telegraph 90th Anniversary Souvenir*, 23 February 2002, p. 25.

2. C. E. B. Brett, *The Buildings of Belfast, 1700–1914* (London: Weidenfeld and Nicolson, 1967), p. 54.

3. In spite of all the links between City Hall and the *Titanic*, there is no model or painting of the ship inside. In April 2002, Lord Mayor Jim Rodgers proposed changing this by renaming the Councillors' Robing Room after the ship and placing a permanent exhibition there. 'City Hall to Name Room after Vessel', *Belfast Telegraph*, 12 April 2002.

4. I was told by several people in Belfast that Lord Pirrie had admired the woodwork during his term as Lord Mayor and had therefore decided to duplicate it on the *Olympic*-class liners. This would have been impossible, however, as Pirrie was Lord Mayor from 1896–97, ten years before City Hall opened.

5. Jeremy Hawthorn writes, 'In Ireland, then, and more especially in Belfast, the ship symbolized something more than just British achievement when it was launched; by symbolizing British achievement it also registered and underwrote Ireland's position as a part of Britain'. Jeremy Hawthorn, *Cunning Passages: New Historicism, Cultural Materialism and*

Marxism in the Contemporary Literary Debate (London: Arnold, 1996), p. 152.

6. A. T. Q. Stewart, *The Ulster Crisis: Resistance to Home Rule, 1912–1914* (Aldershot: Gregg Revivals, 1993), p. 48.

7. Michael Moss and John R. Hume, *Shipbuilders to the World: 125 Years of Harland & Wolff, Belfast* (Belfast: Blackstaff, 1986), p. 15.

8. Moss and Hume, *Shipbuilders to the World*, p. 28.

9. Michael McCaughan, *The Birth of the Titanic* (Belfast: Blackstaff, 1998), p. 14.

10. *Olympic* came in at 45,324 gross tons, and *Titanic* at 46,328.

11. McCaughan, *Birth of the Titanic*, p. 125.

12. In his study of the labour movement in Belfast, Henry Patterson writes that at the shipyards the 'predominance of skilled men and apprentices made it relatively easy to maintain a virtually Protestant labour force'. Henry Patterson, *Class Conflict and Sectarianism: The Protestant Working Class and the Belfast Labour Movement, 1868–1920* (Belfast: Blackstaff, 1980), p. xvii.

13. David Hammond writes, 'At the shipyard, there was the craftsman's pride, a Protestant and unionist pride. [However] that craftsman's pride was assumed into a wider community, the local pride of East Belfast. In Ballymacarrett, there was a deep sense of family and kinship; the shipyard was a way of life, a subculture that was more important than institutions ... of education and religion'. David Hammond, 'The Making of a Twentieth- Century Myth', *Causeway: Cultural Traditions Journal*, winter 1996, p. 19.

14. A. C. Hepburn and B. Collins, 'Industrial Society: The Structure of Belfast, 1901', in Peter Roebuck, ed., *Plantation to Partition: Essays in Ulster History in Honour of J. L. McCracken* (Belfast: Blackstaff, 1981), p. 225.

15. Moss and Hume, *Shipbuilders to the World*, p. 26.

16. Moss and Hume, *Shipbuilders to the World*, p. 31.

17. Moss and Hume, *Shipbuilders to the World*, p. 55.

18. Stewart, *Ulster Crisis*, p. 50.

19. Patterson, *Class Conflict and Sectarianism*, p. 88.

20. Patterson, *Class Conflict and Sectarianism*, p. 89.

21. Patterson, *Class Conflict and Sectarianism*, p. 90.

22. John Wilson Foster writes, 'Designed and built in Belfast, fitted out there and bade farewell from there, it was impossible that *Titanic* should escape embroilment in the heated politics of the island. *Titanic* was built by an overwhelmingly (but not exclusively) Protestant workforce intent like their coreligionists on retaining an unqualified British citizenship in defiance

of the strenuous wishes of Irish nationalists, most of them Catholic. That the ship should founder during the crucial stages of the third Home Rule Bill's passage ... is a coincidence to warm the heart of any cultural historian'. John Wilson Foster, *The Age of Titanic: Cross-Currents of Anglo-American Culture* (Dublin: Merlin, 2002), pp. 195–96.

23. John Wilson Foster, *The Titanic Reader* (New York: Penguin, 1999), p. 18.

24. Foster, *Titanic Reader*, p. 19.

25. Foster, *Titanic Reader*, p. 22.

26. '*Titanic* Launched', Belfast *Telegraph*, 1 June 1911. See also Foster, *Age of Titanic*, pp. 132–33.

27. 'Launch of the Titanic', *Ulster Echo*, 31 May 1911.

28. McCaughan, *Birth of the Titanic*, p. 96.

29. John Parkinson's memories are taken from a personal interview conducted on 1 August 2001 and from John Parkinson, *A Belfastman's Tale* (Belfast, n.d.). He has on at least one occasion recalled that the song sung by the crowd was 'Land of Hope and Glory', another patriotic *British* anthem.

30. Roger Casement Collection, National Library of Ireland, MS 31, p. 725.

31. Parkinson, *A Belfastman's Tale*, p. 6.

32. David Hammond, ed., *Steelchest, Nail in the Boot and the Barking Dog: The Belfast Shipyard. A Story of the People Told by the People* (Belfast: Flying Fox Films, 1986), p. 104.

33. *Titanic: Born in Belfast*, documentary film, British Broadcasting Company Northern Ireland, broadcast 4 April 2002.

34. 'Idea to Preserve Historic Home', *Belfast News-Letter*, 2 February 2001.

35. 'Belfast and the Disaster', *Belfast News-Letter*, 17 April 1912.

36. 'Mr Andrews's Heroism', *Belfast News-Letter*, 22 April 1912.

37. 'Belfast and the Disaster', *Belfast News-Letter*, 17 April 1912.

38. Michael McCaughan writes, 'Inevitably, the creation and destruction of *Titanic* became a popular text which reflected the political, religious and sectarian tensions fissuring Ireland in the Home Rule crisis of that time'. McCaughan, *Birth of the Titanic*, p. 32.

39. John Wilson Foster, *The Titanic Complex: A Cultural Manifest* (Vancouver: Belcouver Press, 1997), p. 77.

40. Hammond, 'The Making of a Twentieth-Century Myth', p. 19.

41. John Wilson Foster writes, '*Titanic* was the product of a long intertwined culture of industrialism, entrepreneurship, the Calvinist work ethic, meritocratic ideas, Ulster-Scots application and Victorian English progressivism'. Foster, *Titanic Reader*, p. 337.

42. Michael McCaughan, '*Titanic*: Out of the Depths and into the Culture', *Symbols in Northern Ireland*, ed. Anthony D. Buckley (Belfast: Institute of

Irish Studies, 1998), pp. 141–42. The myth that anti-Catholic slogans were painted on *Titanic*'s hull as it was being constructed survives into the present. The CD ROM *James Cameron's Titanic Explorer* claims, 'The Protestants took advantage of the fact that they were building ships taller than anything else in town. Without permission, they painted anti-Catholic slogans on the ships' hulls, visible from much of Belfast. Catholics believed that *Titanic* was doomed because of such blaspheming, although the slogans were eventually painted over'. *James Cameron's Titanic Explorer* (Twentieth Century Fox, 1997), disc 1. No evidence that *Titanic* was ever assigned number 390904 in any shipyard listing has ever been found; the ship was assigned number 401 by Harland & Wolff. This story, however, recurs in many contexts. Second-class passenger and *Titanic* survivor Edwina Troutt shared a cabin with Nora Keane. Troutt later claimed that Keane told her that she saw the words 'No Pope', a reflection of the numbers 3606 04 on the water from *Titanic*'s hull, as she boarded the ship at Queenstown. Keane was so startled that she nearly dropped her rosary and prayer book. Troutt, however, doubted her tale, as the water was much too choppy that afternoon for such a detailed reflection to be visible. *James Cameron's Titanic Explorer*, disc 1.

43. Catholics in Ulster and throughout Ireland joined in the expressions of grief that were commonplace in the British Isles in April 1912; there is no evidence that they celebrated the disaster as a Unionist failure. Instead, they too mourned the victims, Catholic and Protestant. For example, in the Catholic church of Ardoyne, a Catholic and nationalist area of Belfast, remembrance was offered for Thomas Andrews, despite the fact that he was a Protestant from a prominent Unionist family. And the Irish Nationalist Convention, which was meeting in Dublin at the time of the sinking, issued a resolution declaring its 'feelings of deep sorrow and heartfelt sympathy at that terrible disaster which had touched Ireland as much as any other country … This Convention, representing all creeds and classes of the Irish people, hereby places upon record the expression of its profound sorrow at the loss of the *Titanic*'. Foster, *Age of Titanic*, p. 215; 'Belfast and the Disaster', *Belfast News-Letter*, 24 April 1912.

44. Foster, *Titanic Complex*, p. 77.

45. Hawthorn, *Cunning Passages*, p. 153.

46. Hammond, 'The Making of a Twentieth-Century Myth', p. 19.

47. Stephen Cameron, *Titanic: Belfast's Own* (Dublin: Wolfhound, 1998), p. 76.

48. Foster, *Titanic Complex*, p. 78.

49. County Borough of Belfast Minutes, January-June 1912, City Council Meeting, 1 May 1912, p. 1. The Minute Books of Belfast City Council from the

early twentieth century are held by the Belfast Central Library. The following month at the 3 June meeting, the town clerk reported receipt of acknowledgements of the council's resolution.

50. Cameron, *Titanic: Belfast's Own*, p. 83.
51. County Borough of Belfast Minutes, July-September 1912, Improvement Committee Meeting, 30 July 1912, p. 37.
52. County Borough of Belfast Minutes, July-September 1912, Improvement Committee Meeting, 6 August 1912, p. 1.
53. The significance of this is discussed in Chapter 10 below.
54. No survivor account shows any of the Belfast men clearly saving anyone's life, though Thomas Andrews's efforts to get as many passengers as possible into the lifeboats were repeatedly mentioned.
55. Cameron, *Titanic: Belfast's Own*, p. 88.
56. Foster, *Titanic Complex*, p. 75.
57. Foster, *Titanic Complex*, p. 75.
58. Samuel K. Cowan, *From Ulster's Hills: A Book of Verse* (Belfast, 1912), pp. 43–46.
59. *Titanic: Born in Belfast*, produced and directed by Liam Creagh, Paul McAuley, Patricia Wilkinson and Dave McClean, one hour, Red Box Media Productions, n.d., videocassette.
60. Gillian McIntosh, *The Force of Culture: Unionist Identities in Twentieth-Century Ireland* (Cork: Cork University Press, 1999), p. 79.
61. Hammond, 'The Making of a Twentieth-Century Myth', p. 18.
62. Cameron, *Titanic: Belfast's Own*, pp. 87–88.
63. Fran Breaton has linked the sinking of the *Titanic* to the Battle of the Somme as totemic events in Ulster Unionist history. The Somme, however, had a fundamentally different – and much more positive – outcome than the *Titanic* disaster, when evaluated from an Ulster point of view, for it was the sacrifice that led to the creation of the Northern Irish state in 1922. Certainly, the massive casualties suffered by the 36th Ulster Regiment at the Somme, as well as Ulster's fierce loyalty throughout the entire First World War, made it far more difficult for the British government to abandon the Unionists to their fate after the war ended. Fran Brearton, 'Dancing unto Death: Perceptions of the Somme, the *Titanic* and Ulster Protestantism', *Irish Review* 20 (1997), pp. 89–103.
64. As John Wilson Foster puts it, 'The fact and fate of *Titanic* could hardly be contemplated with equanimity: the Ulster perspectives on them were too radically different'. Foster, *Titanic Complex*, p. 76.
65. Foster, *Titanic Complex*, pp. 70–74.
66. Foster has termed this the 'New Realism', which he defines as a willingness

'in cultural and academic circles to discuss openly and make arguments publicly, uninhibited by a muzzling politeness'. Foster, *Titanic Complex*, p. 78.

67. Stewart Parker, 'The Iceberg', in *The Honest Ulsterman* (Belfast: Regency Press, 1975), p. 33.

68. Parker, 'The Iceberg', p. 45.

69. Parker, 'The Iceberg', pp. 47–48.

70. Parker, 'The Iceberg', p. 60.

71. Frank McGuiness, *Observe the Sons of Ulster Marching towards the Somme* (London: Faber and Faber, 1986), pp. 49–51.

72. Robert Johnstone, *Eden to Edenderry* (Belfast: Blackstaff, 1989), pp. 12–13.

73. Mary Costello, *Titanic Town: Memoirs of a Belfast Girlhood* (London: Mandarin, 1993), pp. 25–26.

74. Anne Devlin, *Titanic Town* (London: Faber and Faber, 1998), p. 48.

75. McCaughan, 'Reclaiming', p. 25.

76. McCaughan, 'Reclaiming', p. 25.

77. Vincent Kearney, 'Belfast Told to Stop Feeling Guilty and Hold *Titanic* Day', *Times*, 18 January 1998.

78. www.ulstertitanic.com

79. Una Reilly, 'Special Convention Appraisal', *Titanic at Home International Convention Report*, 14–16 April 1997, p. 4.

80. www.gilbertlogan.com

81. www.titanicirishlinenplussales.com

82. www.laganboatcompany.com/tours_titanic.htm

83. 'Tycoon Presents *Titanic* II Proposal', BBC News, 9 June 2000. There have been a series of proposals for a '*Titanic* II' over the past decade or so. The most recent came from the RMS *Titanic* Shipping Holding Company, which is floating shares on the London Stock Exchange in an effort to raise the first £12 million of the £575 million required for the project. Harland & Wolff drew up an initial design for a 1200-foot replica of *Titanic*, complete with recreations of the grand staircase and several of the most luxurious staterooms. The firm, though, remains guarded about the possibility of these plans becoming a reality. 'We've had numerous approaches from people with proposals to build replicas of *Titanic*, and to various degrees of authenticity', said Harland & Wolff's Director of Corporate Communications Peter Harbinson. 'Obviously none of these has ever come to fruition.' 'A Ticket on the New *Titanic*', *Belfast Telegraph*, 17 February 2001.

84. 'Council Sees Titanic Tourist Potential', *Belfast Telegraph*, 28 July 1999.

85. 'Call for Liner Monument', *Belfast News-Letter*, 15 April 2001.

86. *Titanic: Made in Belfast*, videocassette.

87. Claire Regan, 'City Pays Homage to Pioneering Spirits', *Belfast Telegraph*, 2 April 2002.

88. Foster, *Titanic Complex*, p. 84.

89. Stewart Love, '*Titanic*' (unpublished, 1997). My thanks to the Ulster Hall for providing me with a copy of this play.

90. Michael Fieldhouse, *The Song of the Hammers* (unpublished, 2002). My thanks to Mr Fieldhouse for providing me with a copy of his play, which was performed during the *Titanic Made in Belfast* festival in April 2002.

91. www.bbc.co.uk/northernireland/education/summer2000/today/pro3.shtml

92. Vincent Kearney, 'Belfast Told to Stop Feeling Guilty and Hold *Titanic* Day', *Times*, 18 January 1998.

93. *Titanic: James Cameron's Illustrated Screenplay*, annotated by Russell Frakes (New York: HarperCollins, 1997), p. 54.

94. *Titanic: Born in Belfast*, documentary film, British Broadcasting Company Northern Ireland, broadcast 4 April 2002.

95. Michael McCaughan, 'The Ultimate Disaster Symbol', *Causeway: Cultural Traditions Journal*, winter 1996, p. 28.

96. 'Mass Murder on the *Titanic*', *Belfast Magazine*, pp. 15, 22–26.

97. Joe Baker, 'Fiction and Facts', *Belfast Magazine*, pp. 11, 14.

98. Interview with Gerry Copeland, 30 March 2002.

99. Interview with Una Reilly, 4 April 2002.

100. 'Celebration of the *Titanic*', BBC News, 30 March 2002.

101. *Titanic: Made in Belfast*, exhibition in Belfast City Hall.

102. 'City Hall to Name Room after Vessel', *Belfast Telegraph*, 12 April 2002.

103. The Apprentice Boys derive their name from the siege of Derry in 1689, or Londonderry, when a group of young apprentices supposedly barred the gates of the city in order to prevent a Catholic force loyal to James II from entering the city. Their action resulted in a 105-day siege in which an estimated 15,000 of the besieged died of starvation and disease. Finally, William of Orange's ships were able break the siege. This lives on in Unionist folk memory as a key event that proved that endurance, intransigence and faith would persevere in the end. Today they have a rougher reputation than the more mainstream Unionist Orange Order. See Ruth Dudley Edwards, *The Faithful Tribe: An Intimate Portrait of Loyalist Institutions* (London: Harper Collins, 2000), pp. 193–99.

104. The quotes in this paragraph come from a brochure produced by Harland & Wolff entitled '*Titanic* Quarter: The Voyage Begins towards the Vision of Northern Ireland as a Knowledge-Based Society'. At one point, plans

for *Titanic* Quarter included the possibility of bringing a theme park style attraction called 'James Cameron's *Titanic* Experience' to Belfast from Sydney, Australia. The attraction, which recreates sets from the block-buster film and allows visitors 'to experience the horror of the sinking of the famous ship', was a commercial flop in Sydney, causing its owners to look for a buyer. The £28 million cost of purchasing the attraction and transporting it to Belfast ultimately scuttled the idea. Ciaran McGuigan, '*Titanic* to Ulster Plan is Scuttled', *Belfast Telegraph*, 17 November 2001.

105. Impeding Harland & Wolff's efforts to move away from shipbuilding are the terms of the lease that the firm was given for the Queen's Island shipyard in the mid nineteenth century. This allowed them the use of the land for 900 years, but only on the condition that they use it to build ships. In March 2002 Harland & Wolff presented a plan to the Northern Irish Enterprise Ministry that proposes to sell off seventy-eight acres of land in order to raise £15 million. The legal implications of this proposal are still being determined. 'Yard's Fate Rests with Stormont', *Belfast Telegraph*, 12 April 2002.

106. John Manley, 'H & W Launches New *Titanic*', *Irish News*, 21 March 2001.

107. '*Titanic* Quarter' brochure.

Notes to Chapter 10: Southampton

1. David L. Williams, *Southampton* (Shepperton, Surrey: Ian Allan, 1984), p. 4.

2. Philip Hoare, *Spike Island: The Memory of a Military Hospital* (London: Fourth Estate, 2001), p. 35.

3. Williams, *Southampton*, p. 6.

4. Hoare, *Spike Island*, p. 35.

5. Adrian Rance, *Southampton: An Illustrated History* (Portsmouth: Milestone, 1986), p. 133.

6. Rance, *Southampton: An Illustrated History*, p. 99.

7. Rance, *Southampton: An Illustrated History*, p. 101.

8. In 1839 the name was changed to the London and South-Western Railway.

9. Rance, *Southampton: An Illustrated History*, p. 116.

10. Rance, *Southampton: An Illustrated History*, p. 132.

11. The American Line had previously moved to Southampton in 1893.

12. White Star's head office remained in Liverpool. Therefore that city's name was emblazoned on the *Titanic*'s stern.

13. Donald Hyslop, Alastair Forsyth and Sheila Jemima, *Titanic Voices:*

Memories from the Fateful Voyage (Phoenix Mill, Stroud: Sutton, 1997), p. 19.

14. John Maxtone-Graham, *The Only Way to Cross* (Cambridge: Patrick Stephens, 1983), p. 1.

15. Maxtone-Graham, *The Only Way to Cross*, p. 2.

16. Maxtone-Graham, *The Only Way to Cross*, p. 5.

17. More than 1200 of Cunard's passengers perished on the *Lusitania* when it was torpedoed by a German U-boat during the First World War in 1915.

18. Maxtone-Graham, *The Only Way to Cross*, p. 5.

19. Maxtone-Graham, *The Only Way to Cross*, pp. 5–6.

20. Terry Coleman, *The Liners: A History of the North Atlantic Crossing* (London: Allen Lane, 1976), p. 24.

21. Hyslop, *Titanic Voices*, p. 10.

22. Coleman, *The Liners*, pp. 28–29.

23. Coleman, *The Liners*, p. 48.

24. Coleman, *The Liners*, p. 41.

25. A second Norddeutscher Lloyd liner was ordered from a Danzig shipyard at the same time. When it failed to be faster than the *Kaiser Wilhelm*, it was handed back without payment. The ship sat in the yard for ten years until it was sold to a French company at a third of its cost. Coleman, *The Liners*, p. 42.

26. Hyslop, *Titanic Voices*, p. 14.

27. Harland & Wolff also purchased a 51 per cent interest in Holland-Amerika on Morgan's behalf.

28. The smaller French Line also remained independent.

29. White Star's ships continued to be British registered, which meant that they were ostensibly still available for wartime service. However, both the British public and the Admiralty feared that, should a war break out, the Americans would simply ignore this fact and keep the ships in American ports.

30. Two Allan liners, the *Victorian* and the *Virginian*, were the first turbine-driven merchant ships on the North Atlantic. Cunard had previously experimented with the new technology on the *Carmania*.

31. Coleman, *The Liners*, pp. 59–60.

32. Hyslop, *Titanic Voices*, p. 29.

33. Hyslop, *Titanic Voices*, pp. 30–31.

34. The move bumped Murdoch to First Officer and Charles Lightoller, who had been First Officer, to Second Officer. The original Second Officer, David Blair, was forced to relinquish his berth. Blair wrote to his sister

that he was 'very disappointed' not to make *Titanic*'s maiden voyage. Hyslop, *Titanic Voices*, p. 36.

35. Hyslop, *Titanic Voices*, p. 46.
36. Hyslop, *Titanic Voices*, pp. 44–54.
37. Hyslop, *Titanic Voices*, p. 18.
38. I am grateful to T. P. Henry of the Totton and Eling Historical Society for the information from the Northam School log books.
39. Hyslop, *Titanic Voices*, pp. 36, 84.
40. Hyslop, *Titanic Voices*, pp. 67–68.
41. Hyslop, *Titanic Voices*, p. 64.
42. Hyslop, *Titanic Voices*, p. 70.
43. Hyslop, *Titanic Voices*, p. 82.
44. Twenty-three of *Titanic*'s 898 crew members were female.
45. Hyslop, *Titanic Voices*, p. 82.
46. Hyslop, *Titanic Voices*, p. 169.
47. 'Stricken Southampton', *Southern Daily Echo*, 17 April 1912.
48. '1000 Bereaved at Southampton', *Daily Chronicle*, 17 April 1912; 'A City of Sorrow', *Daily Chronicle*, 18 April 1912.
49. 'Grief-Stricken Southampton', *Daily Chronicle*, 19 April 1912.
50. 'Widowed Southampton', *Daily Mirror*, 18 April 1912.
51. An undated copy of this article was shown to me by Brian Ticehurst, the President of the British *Titanic* Society.
52. '*Titanic* Disaster', *Southern Daily Echo*, 17 April 1912.
53. 'Pathetic Scenes at Southampton', *Southern Daily Echo*, 17 April 1912.
54. Hyslop, *Titanic Voices*, p. 171.
55. Hyslop, *Titanic Voices*, p. 172.
56. See note 36 above.
57. 'Homes of Despair', *Daily Mail*, 19 April 1912.
58. 'Southampton's Cry for Help', *Daily Chronicle*, 20 April 1912.
59. 'Southampton's Cry for Help', *Daily Chronicle*, 20 April 1912.
60. Hyslop, *Titanic Voices*, pp. 168–69.
61. Anne Massey and Mike Hammond, '"It Was True! How Can You Laugh?": History and Memory in the Reception of *Titanic* in Britain and Southampton', in *Titanic: Anatomy of a Blockbuster*, ed. Kevin S. Sandler and Gaylyn Studlar (New Brunswick: Rutgers University Press, 1999), pp. 250, 260.
62. Personal interview with Lindsay Ford, 22 June 2001.
63. Personal interview with T. P. Henry, 23 June 2001.
64. Personal interview with Nigel Wood, 23 June 2001.
65. Personal interview with Kevin White, 23 June 2001.

66. The musician's memorial was destroyed in the Second World War. A replica was placed on the same site in 1990.
67. Alex King, *Memorials of the Great War in Britain: The Symbolism and Politics of Remembrance* (Oxford: Berg, 1998), pp. 184–87.

Notes to Chapter 11: Queenstown

1. Mary Broderick, *History of Cobh (Queenstown) Ireland* (2nd edn, Cobh: Carraig, 1994), pp. 89–90.
2. Senan Moloney, *The Irish Aboard Titanic* (Dublin: Wolfhound, 2000), p. 18.
3. The three first-class passengers who boarded at Queenstown were all American, as was one of the second-class passengers. Another second-class passenger was Canadian. All of the third-class passengers who boarded at Queenstown were Irish.
4. Moloney, *The Irish Aboard Titanic*, p. 18.
5. The *Titanic*'s fourth funnel was a dummy that was used only for ventilating the galleys and engine rooms. The builders included it because many passengers thought that ships with four funnels were superior to and safer than ships with a smaller number.
6. John P. Eaton and Charles A. Hass, *Titanic: Triumph and Tragedy* (2nd edn, Sparkford, Somerset: Patrick Stephens, 1994), p. 101.
7. Daly survived the sinking, but his pipes did not. He later filed a $50 insurance claim for their loss.
8. Buckley's luck ran out in 1918. He was killed a month before the end of the First World War while serving in the United States Army.
9. Moloney, *The Irish Aboard Titanic*, pp. 73, 101.
10. Moloney, *The Irish Aboard Titanic*, p. 162.
11. Moloney, *The Irish Aboard Titanic*, pp. 14–15.
12. Moloney, *The Irish Aboard Titanic*, p. 16.

Bibliography

Much of the material used in this book is not contained in traditional historical archives; it comes instead from the collections, recollections and opinions of *Titanic* experts, local historians and others who have a connection to the most famous maritime disaster in history in Great Britain and the United States. I hope that all of these persons have been mentioned and appropriately thanked in the acknowledgements.

In preparing this book, I have relied heavily on the work of previous authors who have written about the construction, maiden voyage and sinking of the *Titanic*. The best general histories of the *Titanic* are John P. Eaton and Charles A. Haas's *Titanic: Triumph and Tragedy* (new edition, 1994) and Daniel Allen Butler's '*Unsinkable*': *The Full Story of RMS Titanic* (1998). Geoffrey Marcus's *Maiden Voyage: A Complete and Documented Account of the Titanic Disaster* (1966) is also useful as well as beautifully written, though any history of the *Titanic* that was published prior to the discovery of the wreck in 1984 inevitably contains some speculations that have proved erroneous. Walter Lord's *A Night to Remember* (1955) remains a classic account, despite that fact that it is now almost fifty years old.

The context for and history of the construction of the *Titanic* is detailed in Michael McCaughan's *The Birth of the Titanic* (1998). The American perspective on the aftermath of the disaster can be found in Wyn Craig Wade's *The Titanic: End of a Dream* (new edition, 1986) and Stephen Biel's *Down with the Old Canoe: A Cultural History of the Titanic Disaster* (1996). For the British response, see Richard Howells, *The Myth of the Titanic* (1999) and John Wilson Foster, *The Titanic Complex: A Cultural Manifest* (1997). Foster traces the general cultural context in Britain and America both before and after the disaster in *The Age of Titanic: Cross-Currents of Anglo-American Culture* (2002).

Most of what is known about the sinking of the *Titanic* comes from the transcripts of the British and American inquiries, numerous copies of which were printed and circulated and are easily obtainable. The transcript of the British inquiry can be found in the Public Record Office, along with other official material related to the disaster. The transcript of the American inquiry was published, edited by Tom Kuntz, in 1998 and is still in print. Other first-hand information comes from survivor accounts. The most frequently cited are those by Lawrence Beesley, Harold Bride, Archibald Gracie, Charles Lightoller and Jack Thayer, but there are dozens of others.

NEWSPAPERS AND PERIODICALS

Belfast Evening Telegraph
Belfast Magazine
Belfast News-Letter
Belfast Telegraph
Birmingham Post
Colne and Nelson Times
Daily Chronicle
Daily Express
Daily Graphic
Daily Mail
Daily Mirror
Daily News
Daily Sketch
Dumfries and Galloway Standard
　and Advertiser
Evening News
Evening Standard

Farncombe Parish Magazine
Glasgow Herald
Godhelmian
Guardian
Herald and County Down Independent
Irish Weekly
Kirkcudbrightshire Advertiser
Lichfield Mercury
Liverpool Daily Post and Mercury
Mail on Sunday
Northern Whig
Scotland on Sunday
Scotsman
Southern Daily Echo
Stoke Sentinel
Surrey Advertiser
Ulster Echo

SECONDARY SOURCES

Aspin, C., The First Industrial Society: Lancashire, 1750–1850 (revised edn, Preston, 1995).

Behrman, C. F., Victorian Myths of the Sea (Athens, Ohio, 1977).

Biel, S., Down with the Old Canoe: A Cultural History of the Titanic Disaster (New York and London, 1996).

Booth, J., and Coughlin, S., Titanic: Signals of Disaster (Westbury, Wiltshire, 1993).

Brearton, F., 'Dancing unto Death: Perceptions of the Somme, the Titanic and Ulster Protestantism', Irish Review, 20 (1997), pp. 89–103.

Brett, C. E. B., The Buildings of Belfast, 1700–1914 (London, 1967).

Buckley, A. D., Symbols in Northern Ireland (Belfast, 1998).

Bullock, S., *Thomas Andrews: Shipbuilder* (new edn, Belfast, 1999).

Butler, D. A., *'Unsinkable': The Full Story of RMS Titanic* (Mechanicsburg, Pennsylvania, 1998).

Cameron, J., *Titanic: James Cameron's Illustrated Screenplay*, annotated by Randall Frakes (New York, 1997).

Cameron, S., *Titanic: Belfast's Own* (Dublin, 1998).

Coleman, T., *The Liners: A History of the North Atlantic Crossing* (London, 1976).

Cooper, G., *The Man Who Sank the Titanic? The Life and Times of Captain Edward J. Smith* (2nd edn, Cotes Heath, Stafford, 1998).

Dupree, M., *Family Structure in the Staffordshire Potteries, 1840–1880* (Oxford, 1995).

Eaton, J. P., and Haas, C. A., *Titanic: Triumph and Tragedy* (2nd edn, Sparkford, Somerset, 1994).

Edwards, R. D., *The Faithful Tribe: An Intimate Portrait of Loyalist Institutions* (London, 2000).

Etherington-Smith, M., and Pilcher, J., *The 'It' Girls: Lucy, Lady Duff Gordon, the Couturière 'Lucile', and Elinor Glyn, Romantic Novelist* (London, 1986).

Forshaw, C., *Poetical Tributes on the Loss of the RMS Titanic* (London, 1912).

Foster, J. W., *The Age of Titanic: Cross-Currents in Anglo-American Culture* (Dublin, 2002).

Foster, J. W., *The Titanic Complex: A Cultural Manifest* (Vancouver, 1997).

Foster, J. W., ed., *The Titanic Reader* (New York, 1999).

Friedberg, A. L., *The Weary Titan: Britain and the Experience of Relative Decline, 1895–1905* (Princeton, 1988).

Girouard, M., *Life in the Victorian Country House* (Harmondsworth, 1980).

Hammond, D., ed., *Steelchest, Nail in the Boot and the Barking Dog: The Belfast Shipyard. A Story of the People Told by the People* (Belfast, 1986).

Hawthorn, J., *Cunning Passages: New Historicism, Cultural Materialism and Marxism in the Contemporary Literary Debate* (London, 1996).

Heyer, P., *Titanic Legacy: Disaster as Media Event and Myth* (Westport, Connecticut, 1995).

Hoare, Philip, *Spike Island: The Memory of a Military Hospital* (London, 2001).

Howells, R., *The Myth of the Titanic* (New York, 1999).

Hyslop, D., Forsyth, A., and Jemima, S., *Titanic Voices: Memories from the Fateful Voyage* (Thrupp, Stroud, 1997).

Janaway, J., *Godalming: A Short History* (Godalming, 1993).

Janaway, J., *Yesterday's Town: Godalming* (Buckingham, 1987).

Kennedy, P., *The Rise and Fall of the Great Powers: Economic Change and Military Conflict from 1500 to 2000* (London, 1988).

King, A., *Memorials of the Great War in Britain: The Symbolism and Politics of Remembrance* (Oxford, 1998).

Kuntz, T., ed., *The Titanic Disaster Hearings: The Official Transcripts of the 1912 Senate Investigation* (New York, 1998).

Lord, W., *The Night Lives On* (New York, 1986).

Mangan, J. A., and Walvin, J., *Manliness and Morality: Middle-Class Masculinity in Britain and America, 1800–1940* (Manchester, 1987).

Marcus, G., *The Maiden Voyage: A Complete and Documented Account of the Titanic Disaster* (London, 1969).

Maxtone-Graham, J., *The Only Way to Cross* (Cambridge, 1983).

McCaughan, M., *The Birth of the Titanic* (Belfast, 1998).

McCulloch, A., *Galloway: A Land Apart* (Edinburgh, 2000).

McIntosh, G., *The Force of Culture: Unionist Identities in Twentieth-Century Ireland* (Cork, 1999).

Moss, M., and Hume, J. R., *Shipbuilders to the World: 125 Years of Harland & Wolff, Belfast* (Belfast, 1986).

Patterson, H., *Class Conflict and Sectarianism: The Protestant Working Class and the Belfast Labour Movement, 1868–1920* (Belfast, 1980).

Peck, J., *Maritime Fiction: Sailors and the Sea in British and American Novels, 1719–1917* (Houndmills, Basingstoke, Hampshire, 2001).

Rance, A., *Southampton: An Illustrated History* (Portsmouth, 1986).

Roebuck, P., ed., *Plantation to Partition: Essays in Ulster History in Honour of J. L. McCracken* (Belfast, 1981).

Sandler, K. S., and Studlar, G., *Titanic: Anatomy of a Blockbuster* (New Brunswick, New Jersey, 1999).

Stewart, A. T. Q., *The Ulster Crisis: Resistance to Home Rule, 1912–1914* (Aldershot, 1993).

Stone, P., and Yeston, M., *Titanic: The Complete Book of the Musical* (New York, 1997).

Störmer, S., *Goodbye, Good Luck: The Biography of William Murdoch* (Kosel, Germany, n.d.).

Tosh, J., *A Man's Place: Masculinity and the Middle-Class Home in Victorian England* (New Haven and London, 1999).

Wade, W. C., *Titanic: End of a Dream* (revised edn, New York, 1986).

Williams, D. L., *Southampton* (Shepperton, Surrey, 1984).

Wincour, J., ed., *The Story of the Titanic as Told by its Survivors* (New York, 1960).

Index

Hoare, Philip 248
Hodder Williams, J. E. 164
Hogg, G. A. 170, 299
Holdsworth, Edwin 96
Hopkins, Annie 265, 270
Hopkins, Robert 106
Horner, Willie 93
Hubbard, Elbert 63
Hume, Jock 131
Humphreys, James 304
Hurst, Walter 19, 21, 170
Hutchinson, Jim 16

icebergs 10, 12, 13–14
Imperator 77, 252
Imperial War Graves Commission
    276
Inman Line 258, 280
Independent 202
inquiries 67–71
    American 67–69, 344 n. 56
    British 69–71, 101
International Mercantile Marine 48,
    80, 97, 102, 218, 260
Iquique 187
Ireland 281
Ismay, J. Bruce 10, 11, 16, 25, 34, 45,
    49, 67, 69, 84, 131, 193–94, 213,
    260, 274
    accusations of villainy 97–102,
        108–109, 159, 340 n. 86, 344 n.
        55
    American views of 99–100, 101
    British views of 100–101
Ismay, Thomas Henry 213, 256, 257
Ismay, Montana 100, 346 n. 32
Ismay, Texas 100, 346 n. 32

James, Tom 271
Jameson Raid 69

Jansen, Carl 28, 193, 355 n. 17
Jekyll, Gertrude 120–21
John Bull 99
Johnson, Carl 18
Johnson, Jack 64
Johnson, James 17
Johnstone, Robert 234
Jones, A. G. and Company 38
Jones, Edwin 264
Jones, John Paul 186
Jones, Mother 64
Jones, Thomas 30, 93, 168, 300
Joughlin, Charles 266
Joyce, Archibald 134
Jukes, James 275

Kaiser Wilhelm II 259
Kaiser Wilhem der Grosse 259, 287
Keane, Nora 359 n. 42
Keaney, Vincent 286
Kelly, Annie 284
Kipling, Rudyard 211
Kirkwood, Linda 200, 202
Kite 253
Knight, E. A. Lempiere 72
Krins, George 131
Kronprinz Wilhelm 13, 259
Kronprinzessen Cecile 259

La Touraine 114, 338 n. 17
Lagan Boat Company 237
Lapland 69
Lardner, F. H. 38, 41, 45
Larkin, James 216
Ledbetter, Hudie 'Leadbelly' 64
Ledoux, Katie 252
Lee, Baker P. 100
Lee, Reginald 15
Lennon, Dennis 285
Leslie, Shane 46

McGuiness, Frank 232–33
McLaughlin, Sam 224
McMordie, Julie 225–26
Medic 188
Melling, Fred 140
merchant shipping, British 76–77
Mersey, Lord 69, 70–71, 101, 107,
    108, 344–45 n. 68
Mesaba 13, 115
Meyer, Leila 31
Miller, Laura xvi
Miller's Naval Tailors 263
Millet, Frank 6, 27
Minia 41
Mitchell, Reginald 181
Mitford, Nancy 108
Moffat, Lyndsay 200
Montgomery, James 150
Montmagny 42
Moody, Ellwand 133
Moody, James 15, 164, 168, 191, 310,
    312
Moore, George 293
Morgan, Alasdair 201, 202
Morgan, J. P. 97, 218, 257, 258, 260
Morning Post 79
Mount Olivet Cemetery 44–45
Mount Temple 38
Mullen, Katie 283
Mullin, Mary 285
Murdoch, Ada 189, 193, 196–97
Murdoch, Andrew 186
Murdoch, John 186
Murdoch, Samuel 186
Murdoch, Scott 200, 202
Murdoch, William 12, 14, 15, 20, 21,
    23, 24, 25, 84, 98, 104, 167, 168,
    263, 284, 291, 299, 310, 354 n. 7,
    354 n. 8, 364 n. 34
  alleged suicide 193, 195, 196

attempts to avoid collision with
    iceberg 191
commemoration 185, 197–98
culpability 193–95
early life and career 185–89
heroism 195–96
in *Titanic* (1997) xv, 199–202
loading of lifeboats 192–93
on *Titanic* 189–93
Murphy, Katie 283–84
Murphy, Margaret 284
Myers, Kevin 240

Napier, John 254
national identity, British 77–81
National Line 260
National Sailors' and Firemens'
    Union 265
National Union of Ships' Stewards,
    Cooks, Butchers and Bakers 265
National Union of Stewards 265
Neeson, Scott 202–3
New York 3–4, 166, 167
New York Journal 47
New York Times 47–48, 52, 77, 116,
    134, 165, 341 n. 4, 342 n. 7
Newell, Arthur W. 43
Newell, Frank 43
Newlands, Francis 100
Newton, Robert 237
Niagara 10
Niobe 41
Noordam 338 n. 21
Norddeutscher-Lloyd Line 77, 256,
    258–59, 260, 364 n. 25
Normandie 263

Oceanic 45–46, 188, 257, 259, 280,
    314
O'Connell, Daniel 215